"Symphonic in form, euphoric in heart, this [volume is] a great, sometimes-desperate chorus that ought [to resound] wherever there is oil and gas-rich shale below [the surface.] The politics and economics of fossil fuels has never been a pretty thing, but the ingenious barbarity of fracking against a vulnerable and increasingly debauched planet, may be the ugliest of all extractive methods. From memory to musings, in facts and fictions, in reason and rhyme, these assembled pieces offer acutely aware and knowledgeable perspectives on a disastrously flawed practice. Listen before it's too late."

> —Lynn Stegner, author of five works including, *Because a Fire Was in My Head*

"This stunning collection of essays, poems, and fiction is gripping and illuminating. The implications of fracking on our land, air, water, and human communities are powerfully evoked. Indeed, no where else has such a gifted group of writers been assembled for a clarion call to awakening for our future generations."

> —Mary Evelyn Tucker, co-director of the Forum on Religion and Ecology at Yale, co-author, *Journey of the Universe*

"Most environmental calamities come to us packaged in dense scientific reports. *Fracture* breaks the mold, forging a path to awareness through superb poetry and prose. The collection leads the reader on a haunting and unforgettable journey through mutilated landscapes and torn-apart communities across America that bear witness to the ravages of fracking. In the end, *Fracture* is not just an indictment of an industry's ruthless ambition, but a call to all of us to confront our own complicity in this ongoing violence—and to find a path back to our own humanity before it is simply too late. Profound and poignant, *Fracture* manifests nothing less than a cultural awakening."

> —Mary Christina Wood, author, *Nature's Trust: Environmental Law for a New Ecological Age*

"If you are looking for information on fracking, you will find it here—but that is only the beginning. These brilliant voices remind us that our responsibility to the Earth runs beneath the surface-place we normally occupy, leading us on an Orphic journey that extends the depths of our knowledge, our compassion, and our capacity for meaningful action. This is not just another literary anthology—it is an urgent act of witness."

> —John T. Price, editor, *The Tallgrass Prairie Reader*

"One imagined that the energy industry would find ways to dig deep enough and find forms of pressure strong enough to force the last crushed history of the earth's vegetation up out of the earth, into refineries, and then into combustion engines, and then into the atmosphere, but most of us had not imagined they would do so by risking the pollution of the world's deep aquifers, finding a way to foul air and water in a single technology. It requires a seismic response from the human imagination: this anthology is doing that work."

> —Robert Hass, Poet Laureate of the United States, 1995 to 1997

"As you read these words, a shudder of the earth in Oklahoma might be knocking a book off a shelf in a family's home; and if it's night, the Bakken oil field is burning waste fuel in such quantities, it shows up in satellite photos bright as a major city. Between earthquake and nightfall, all our lives take place, at home within the world our being-at-home threatens. Fracture—this collection of essays, poems, stories—enters into the profound dilemma of our appetite for energy—not to argue the obvious points, not to rant or rave, but witness and speak about the daily-ness of our life, to call us all back to keener attention, a focus which reminds us that underneath the political fray human lives go about their deepest work: living, loving, tending carefully to the world that tends also to them. Taylor Brorby and Stefanie Brook Trout have gathered together voices that burn brighter than the refinery flame. It's a light we must learn to see by. In it is that age old encouragement to live a good life, one connected to land and to people, one that cares past immediate needs, out to the longer ethic that envelopes those lives still to come in its generous light."

> —Dan Beachy-Quick, author of five books of poetry,
> including *Circle's Apprentice*

"Fracking is the latest curse imposed upon the Earth by industrial civilization. Fracking permits the energy industry to tap formerly inaccessible sources of oil and gas, which, when burned, accelerates CO_2 emissions contributing to global warming, not to mention the very act of fracking fragments wildlife habitat, pollutes air and water, and by degrading the land diminishes our natural heritage. It is another nail in the coffin of Mother Earth. This anthology helps us acknowledge the perils of fracking so that we might build a world of hope for future generations."

> —Douglas R. Tompkins, President, Foundation for Deep
> Ecology, Founder, Tompkins Conservation

"If you called the roll of those you wanted to hear from on fracking, the writers gathered here would be it. Their varied angles of vision and genre yield a rich treatment."
> —Larry Rasmussen, Reinhold Niebuhr Professor Emeritus of Social Ethics, Union Theological Seminary, New York City

"Frack. Fracking. Fracked. How should we think about fracking? What should we feel? How can we imagine fracking and its aftermath, its alternatives? The courageous voices in this landmark collection confront this foolhardy technology and fortify our will to fight it."
> —Cheryll Glotfelty, Professor of English, University of Nevada-Reno

"*Fracture* is a remarkable and remarkably important collection that addresses one of North America's most critical environmental issues: hydraulic fracturing. From the beautiful but urgent essays by writers such as Barbara Hurd and Kathleen Dean Moore to the searing poetry of Wayne Mennecke and Linda Hogan, this deep collection is essential reading for those passionate about place. And it should be required reading for policymakers across the land."
> —Simmons Buntin, Editor-in-Chief, *Terrain.org: A Journal of the Built + Natural Environments*

"A high law of morality requires us to protect that miraculous skin featuring our soils, our waters, our forests, our prairies, our oceans, our agricultural fields and our atmosphere. Unfortunately, it is legal to rip the tops off mountains for coal, legal to drill for oil and natural gas—from the Gulf to the Arctic. And now, fracking. Here are fifty authors eloquently addressing this latest insanity, knowing that it is philosophically embedded in the larger destructive legal. This IS a clarion call for action."
> —Wes Jackson, President, The Land Institute

"*Fracture* is a collective cry of the heart by writers of all sorts from throughout the USA that achieves its extraordinary cumulative power through a combination of cogent on-the-ground narratives, poems, and short stories that ultimately tell the same tale in different ways: the poisoning of our bodies and the brutal rape of Mother Earth."
> —Bruce Joshua Miller, editor, *Curiosity's Cats: Writers on Research*

FRACTURE

essays, poems, and stories on fracking in america

Taylor Brorby &
Stefanie Brook Trout, editors

Ice Cube Press, LLC
North Liberty, Iowa

Fracture: Essays, Poems, and Stories on Fracking in America

Copyright © 2016 Taylor Brorby and Stefanie Brook Trout, editors

Isbn 9781888160901

Library of Congress Control Number: 2015944412

Ice Cube Press, LLC (Est. 1993)
205 N. Front Street North Liberty, Iowa 52317
319-594-6022 www.icecubepress.com
steve@icecubepress.com twitter: @icecubepress

No portion of this book may be reproduced in any way without permission, except for brief quotations for review, or educational work, in which case the publisher shall be provided copies. The views expressed in *Fracture: Essays, Poems, and Stories on Fracking in America* are solely those of the authors not the Ice Cube Press, LLC.

The paper used in this publication meets the minimum requirements of the American National Standard for Information Sciences—Permanence of Paper for Printed Library Materials, ANSI Z39.48-1992.

Made with recycled paper.

Manufactured in Canada.

FRACTURE

Fracking:
A Fable

Barbara Hurd

for our grandchildren, with apologies

In the past, everything took forever.

Rain fell for centuries, and millions of years after that, the ancient Appalachian Basin just west of what is now the East Coast spent even more millennia becoming a sprawling, shallow bowl. And then nothing much happened. Another million years passed. Mountain ranges slowly rose and receded, and continents wandered into each other and eventually the basin began to fill with seawater and for another million years, the surrounding mountains slid wetly down the slopes of themselves and settled into the bottom sludge of the basin.

More tens of thousands of centuries passed while the water sloshed and the undersea mud thickened, and in all that time, no human ever stood on its shores, no blue crab ever scurried in the ooze. There were no witnesses. And even if there had been, who could have stood the boredom of watching that slow, barely breathing world? The only testimony ever made to that languid time was locked in the mud.

For yet another several million years, it piled up—thick, black, and putrid. Over the next millennia, minuscule creatures evolved: phytoplankton, blue-green algae. They floated in the shallow seas until they died and drifted down to be entombed in the ooze that lay fifty, one hundred, two hundred feet deep.

Then came more mountains moving. A few continents collided, some peaks rose, some valleys sank. Meanwhile, down in the black ooze, remnants of those tiny creatures that had been held in the mud were shoved more tightly together, packed side by side with sludged-in sediment, cemented together, cooked by the heat deep in the earth, and converted into hydrocarbons. Layer after layer of crammed-together particles and silt began to sink under the accumulating weight of the mountains that grew above. Wrung of its moisture, its pliability, its flow, the mud slowly, slowly, over millions of years, turned into gas-rich rock.

And there it lay, miles under the surface, as the old basin above it emptied and rose and more continents meandered into each other and finally the sun dried the Appalachians, which eroded and softened, and three hundred million years after the first mud settled on the bottom of that basin, humans appeared. We developed with lightning speed—geologically speaking—our brains and vision and hands, our fast and furious tools, our drills and ingenuity, and all the while that ooze-become-rock lay locked and impenetrable, deep in the earth, farther than anything, including anyone's imagination, reached, until in the split second that is humankind's history on this planet we pushed a drill with a downhole mud-motor a mile deep and made it turn sideways and snaked it into that ancient rock speckled with evidence of another eon, and a few minutes later we detonated small explosives and blasted millions of gallons of slick water—sand and water and a bit of biocide in case anything was alive down there—into what hadn't seen water or light for four hundred million years.

The shale shattered, the black rock spider-webbed with skinny fissures as the above world inserted its tendrils, and into those tiny rifts we rammed more sand to keep them wedged open wider.

And then—remember the blue-green algae?—the gas that had been locked in that stony underworld for almost four hundred million years suddenly had an exit. It flowed through the intricate shudderings of brand new fissures and up the borehole through the limestone that had been laid down millions of years after the mud, and up through the bedrock just below someone's pasture and out into a world with air and fresh water where we humans, fur-less and in need of fuel to stay warm, exercised our resourceful minds.

And then in another split-second's time—geologically speaking—we drilled another thousand wells, fracked another million tons of stony earth a mile beneath our feet.

And when the slick water was withdrawn from the fissures and small slither-spaces and that prehistoric bedrock was lickety-split forever changed, no one could predict the impact, not even we inventive humans whose arrival on this planet is so recent, whose footprints, so conspicuous and large, often obliterate cautionary tales.

And soon the unpredictable, as always, occurred.

And now, in no time at all, not everything takes forever any longer.

Contents:

i | Barbara Hurd   Fracking: A Fable

1 | Pam Houston   Introduction: Still Enough of the Earth

8 | Mary Heather Noble   Seduction

10 | Patricia Nelson Limerick   Hydraulic Fracturing: A Guide to the Terrain of Public Conversation

14 | Michelle Donahue   Digging

26 | Bill Roorbach   Huckster

38 | Amy Weldon   A Miniature Handbook for New Women Activists

49 | Susan Truxell Sauter   Academy Awards of Expendable

52 | Kathryn Miles   Slick: The (Mis)fortunes of an Oklahoma Oil Town Faithfully Presented in Nine Parts and with Special Attention Paid to Geographic Features Therein.

63 | Debra Marquart   Small Buried Things

68 | Kathleen Dean Moore   The View From 31,000 Feet: A Philosopher Looks at Fracking

77 | Wayne Mennecke   Ag Land

79 | Paul Bogard   The Occupation

92 | Stephanie Schultz   Earth Elegy

94 | Louise A. Blum   Faith on the Front Lines

103 | John Kenyon   The Way of Sorrows

118 | Wayne Mennecke   Vacation Land

120 | Tyler Priest   Frackenstein's Monster: A History of Unconventional Oil and Gas Technology

136 | Claire Krüesel   Surfacing

141 | STEPHEN TRIMBLE   One Well: Drilling the Bears Ears

149 | MORT MALKIN   Energy,

150 | RICK BASS   The World Below

163 | TAYLOR BRORBY   White Butte

173 | BETH LOFFREDA   Towards

180 | RACHEL MORGAN   An orbital tour of cities at night

181 | STEPHANIE LeMENAGER   Oil Town Palimpsest, or A Brief Material History of Frackland

194 | SARAH LYN EATON   Fire on the Mountain

207 | SCOTT SLOVIC   What We Take for Granted

211 | FREDERICK L. KIRSCHENMANN   Fracking and Its Two-Pronged Problem

217 | ROBERT JENSEN   Epic Fail

226 | AHNA KRUZIC AND ANGIE CARTER   A Feminist's Guide to Fighting Pipelines

231 | JAN BINDAS-TENNEY   The Story of Staying

246 | MARK TRECHOCK   Prophecy

247 | JEREMY MILLER   The Shining: A Night in the Heart of Energy Independence

261 | ANTONIA FELIX   The Extravagance of Vice

281 | WAYNE MENNECKE   Peace Garden State

283 | STEPHANIE MILLS   Last Call: Frack Wells, Wood Frogs, and Leopold's Ethic

291 | JACQUELINE ROBB   Double Run

297 | MICHELE JOHNSON   Empires

303 | VIVIAN WAGNER   Strata

309 | KARLA LINN MERRIFIELD   Tercet for Kitty

310 | CAROLYN RAFFENSPERGER   The Tree of Life Holds the Scales of Justice

320 | MARK TRECHOCK   Yucatán

322 | DAVID GESSNER   The Town That ♥s Drilling

336 | WAYNE MENNECKE   Shift

338 | JON JENSEN   Sand in My Backyard

349 | MICHELLE DONAHUE   A Stranger in a Bar

351 | MARYANN LESERT   The Ultimate Out of Balance

360 | MARK TRECHOCK   Down the Road

362 | ANDREA PEACOCK   Three Rivers Quartet

388 | LINDA HOGAN   Greed

390 | STEFANIE BROOK TROUT   Hear No Evil

394 | BILL MCKIBBEN   Why Not Frack

404 | RICHARD MANNING   Now We're Talking Price

429 | DERRICK JENSEN   Insanity

440 | ALISON HAWTHORNE DEMING   Homeland Security

444 | NOTES

451 | CREDITS

452 | ABOUT THE EDITORS

454 | ABOUT THE CONTRIBUTORS

469 | PARTNERS

Still Enough of the Earth

Introduction by Pam Houston

I live at nine thousand feet on a one hundred twenty-acre ranch in Southwestern, Colorado, and am a fan of major league baseball. My team is the Colorado Rockies, which, if you know anything about baseball, will tell you that I pray to Saint Jude Thaddeus, the Saint of Lost Causes. One of the greatest, simple pleasures of my summers is coming inside after a day of fence fixing or tree planting or cleaning out the horse trough that was starting to go green with algae and equine slobber, fixing some supper, turning on the game, curling up with the dogs on the couch, and watching the Rockies find some new way to lose.

This pleasure has been diminished significantly in the last few years because between nearly every inning, before nearly every pitching change, one or another in a series of Big Brother-style commercials sponsored by "Coloradoans for Responsible Energy Development" comes on TV. Any one of them elevates my blood pressure, but the one that makes me want to take my largest cast iron skillet and hurl it through the center of my aging, first generation flat-screened television is the one where an ostensible ranch woman—a bit calf-like in her aspect—sits on a fence with her hair blowing in the wind and says, "Jason's grandparents built this ranch and we've worked hard to keep it in the family, so we do our best to protect what's ours." The camera pans through a montage of schmaltz: a cowboy herding cattle under a bluebird sky, ranch hands unloading sacks of grain in the slanting sun of a late afternoon, the same woman pushing her blonde, blue eyed daughter in a tire swing hanging from a hundred year old oak tree. "With all the stories out there some people were surprised that we allowed fracking on our land"—she continues, and here the camera returns to her on the fence—"but we talked with the experts and learned the facts about drilling for oil and natural gas, and guess what?"

Here she pauses, her last two words ringing in the air, in the precise tone of a middle school girl's bathroom bully—"It's safe!" she continues, smug and more than a little irritated with any of us who are going to tell her it isn't. "Safe for our land, our water, and the air."

I have seen that commercial maybe three hundred times in the last two years, and I still can't decide if the woman is a real rancher or an actress, don't know if the Wrangler shirts with mother of pearl buttons her "husband" and his "friends" wear as they toss horseshoes into a pit backlit by a golden sunset came from "wardrobe" or somebody's actual closet, don't even know if it is more cynical, more dastardly if the whole commercial was shot in some studio in Culver City with a painted backdrop or not. (There is another commercial in the series where a similarly homespun farm woman, one who calls herself an organic goat farmer and who snipes, in a similarly directed manner, "Those who would ban fracking ignore our rights and that just gets my goat!" She was revealed shortly after the commercial aired to be a thirty-year employee of the oil and gas industry—a higher up—managing land acquisition, divestitures and coordinating successful drilling joint ventures.)

"Oh! It's safe!" I find myself almost spitting back at the television way too often to the calf-faced woman, alarming the dogs. "How great to know! What a lot of time that will save all those scientists recording the deaths of livestock exposed to stream water poisoned by fracking chemicals, the activists investigating the sudden spike in infant mortality in heavily fracked areas like Vernal, Utah, the geologists studying the relationships between fracking and earthquakes in Oklahoma and Kansas. They should have just asked *you*!"

But it is easy to be cynical at the edge of the apocalypse, and easier still to let ourselves be brainwashed, which is what the corporations who are paying for these 24/7 ads are counting on. It is much harder to wake up in the morning and face the fact that inside more than eighty-two thousand oil and gas wells nationwide, poison is being pumped into the ground and released into the air, and that number is increasing, in some areas exponentially. And while cynicism and denial might protect us momentarily, superficially, it is not going to stop the air from filling with dangerous levels of ozone and particulate matter, or stop benzene and formaldehyde from finding its way into our tap water, into our food sources, and onto our grocery's shelves.

The thing that gives me the most hope about the environment these days is when some individual spends the time and energy, risks the blow back and the heartbreak, and risks—in some cases—being run out of town on a rail to reveal the fallacies in the logic handed to us by the billionaires, the oil companies, and the policy makers who are on their payroll. The book you hold in your hands contains essays, poems, and stories written by fifty of those people. They are environmental scientists, novelists, ranchers, activists, students, journalists, public servants, sociologists, historians, high school teachers, editors, philosophers, parents, geographers, geologists, archaeologists, lawyers, and organic farmers, and what they all have in common is a need to express themselves on the subject of fracking. Their essays, poems, and stories do what art has been doing since the beginning of time: take the unbearable and approach it with compassion, give it a face and a form, give it a way to enter our hearts and to change our lives.

I will admit up front that for me reading this book wasn't easy. Not because its contents surprised me, but because it confirmed so many of the things I already feared. Like how deeply in their pockets the oil industry holds the United States government, like how low public health is on their list of priorities, like how much people are willing to destroy because it puts more money in their hands. It's not easy to read about the loss of millions of acres of wildlife rich land in northwest Colorado, Wyoming, or North Dakota (to name only a few places), to think about the deer and elk, the coyotes and bears who are drinking the same water that is making the cows stop giving milk, stop giving birth, stop drawing breath. It's not easy to pull up the map of fraccidents: spills and accident sites (many of them with multiple fatalities) published by Earth Justice, a pox of skull and cross bones spreading from sea to sea.

Harder than all of these things, maybe, is to try to reckon with the insidious timing of the fracking boom, that in this absolutely critical moment in the progression of climate change, a moment when we have affordable solar and wind technology at our disposal, we are going to squander the few years and a few billion gallons of drinkable water we have left between us and full-on environmental disaster. We are going to let a roomful of corporate executives hold our foot to the throttle as we send the earth, the only home we have, careening over a precipice of no way back, just to put a few more dollars in the same pockets that are already stuffed so full of dollars there isn't room for any more. If I didn't know better I would think fracking was something invented by the Joker or the Riddler, a plan concocted by some cartoonishly evil mind, designed to render the citizens of Gotham City utterly unable to help themselves.

This magnificent, miraculous, life giving, and life sustaining planet wasn't even mapped properly a couple of hundred years ago, and now we are on the eve of its destruction at our hands. For me that is the most terrible, the most painful in my entire repertoire of self-torturing thoughts. But I grew up in hard circumstances and it was the beauty and the bounty of the earth that saved me from despair. I will not turn away from her now, out of sorrow or frustration or helplessness or out of some misguided notion that if I abandon all hope it will protect me from some bigger pain later. The earth isn't dead yet and neither are we, and self-torture—even grief—is its own brand of narcissism.

The authors in this anthology stared down their sorrow and their fears, faced the difficult facts and made art out of them. Collectively, they have created a kind of love song to the earth. Like all the best music it is fiery, mournful, wistful, heartbroken, hopeful, and full of a complicated and hard won love.

A little over a year ago I started making it a priority to walk five miles a day, wherever I found myself, whatever else the day had in store. I bought a Fitbit, to keep myself honest in this pursuit and have walked, it tells me, 3,113 miles since I first put it in my pocket. One of the many things my walking practice has revealed to me is that right now, in 2015, there is, on the earth, a heck of a lot of magnificence left. Beauty worth seeing, worth saving, worth fighting for with everything we've got.

In the past several weeks alone, I have walked in the high meadows near my home in Creede, Colorado, and seen, because of this weirdly rainy summer, the most glorious display of Indian paintbrush, blue phlox, silvery lupine, and scarlet gilia that I have seen in twenty-five years of living here. I have walked in the desert south of Santa Fe, with thunderstorms in three directions, lightning writing what looked for all the world like sentences across the sky. I have walked across the breakwater in Provincetown, Massachusetts, under a full moon, and seen the bioluminescence rushing under the rocks, lighting the sea like some kind of disco for crustaceans. On these walks I have had personal (I would go so far as to say *meaningful*) encounters with many animals: an elk calf, some spotty mule deer twins, a bald eagle, a great blue heron, several coyotes, and about a million cottontails. I have stood on a cliff in Big Sur and counted twenty whales and hundreds of dolphins beyond the kelp beds, seals and cormorants a thousand feet below me. I have kayaked off Lopez Island in Washington state and spent an hour in some sort of communication with a curious harbor seal, and I have paddle boarded in Puget Sound over a jellyfish whose body was more massive than my torso, and whose tentacles—if fully extended—would reach beyond two lengths of me. Last September I had the once in one hundred lifetimes good fortune of crossing paths with six to eight hundred narwhal as they made their way south along the coast of Bylot Island to their winter waters far off shore in Baffin Bay.

I know I am beyond lucky that my occupation takes me to all of these places, and that my actual job (and by that I mean, the thing I get paid for) begins with bearing witness to them. But when I am in those places I can't help wishing that the CEO of Royal Dutch Shell was standing beside me, can't help wondering how long it has been since he took a walk in the wilderness, how long it has been since he slept on the ground. Surely, I think, if he were here, he would understand the intrinsic value of those narwhal, or the elk calf, or the Indian paintbrush. Surely he would want his children and grandchildren to be able to see them, to have air to breathe and water to drink and a stable planet to put their feet on. I don't imagine the CEO of Royal Dutch Shell will read this book, but if he did, I would like to believe that he is still enough of this earth that it might give him pause for thought. For the rest of us, these essays, poems, and stories will help us to be smarter and more compassionate than the lies that are designed to pacify us, to keep us silent. The words of these writers will help us act with hope and resolve.

Pam Houston's most recent book is *Contents May Have Shifted*, published in 2012. She is also the author of two collections of linked short stories, *Cowboys Are My Weakness* and *Waltzing the Cat*, the novel, *Sight Hound*, and a collection of essays, *A Little More About Me*, all published by W.W. Norton. She is Professor of English at UC-Davis, directs the literary nonprofit Writing By Writers and teaches in The Pacific University low residency MFA program and at writer's conferences around the country and the world. She lives on a ranch at 9,000 feet in Colorado near the headwaters of the Rio Grande.

Seduction

Mary Heather Noble

It's a bit like adolescence, all this newfound attention that you think you understand, and the young man sitting on your mother's flowered couch is polite and respectful in a way that she'd sworn had gone extinct, talking about your future and security and the wealth of opportunities to come; and though you barely even know him, you can't help but feel a little taken with his outsider accent, his pressed polo shirt with the company logo over his heart, the way he folds his long fingers around your mother's chipped coffee mug, as the steam from the brew rises and dances around his lips—which keep moving and assuring you that it will be safe, and think of the potential of this place. He uses noble words like *exploration* and *independence* and speaks of *recovery* in a way that means returning to normal or a healthy state of being, as if the way that you've been living here is neither of these things. He speaks of recovery, as in returning something to its rightful owner, which is you and your family—of course you want what's yours. You'll remember those moving lips when the trucks come rumbling in hour after hour, again and again, and the midnight light from the drill pad trespasses through your drawn bedroom curtains, the clanging and pounding invading the silence of your room. You'll remember those promises as you try to ignore the chemical veil and swallow the anxiety of what could be seeping into your well. Of course you want what's yours. But you won't know what they are taking when you unlock the gate and let them in, forcing and drilling, injecting God-knows-what into God-knows-where, and you'll think you're doing this for your future, think you're doing this out of love, but what do you know of love except for your mother's Palmolive hands and the dance of the willows before a storm? A clean glass of water. The crescendo of cicada in the afternoon, the smell of wildflower dew. You'll be fooled by the softness of what they promise in the beginning—the *FFF-finesse*—but shocked by the unexpected violence of a fraCK. There's a persistent sting to innocence lost, a trace of diesel in the air.

Hydraulic Fracturing:
A Guide to the Terrain of Public Conversation

Patricia Nelson Limerick

A new cartography for us to master,
In whose legend we read where we are bound:
Terra infirma, a stranger land, and vaster.
Or have we always stood on shaky ground?
—A. E. Stallings, "Aftershocks"

Time spent on digging in
May prove expensive.
—Aristophanes, *The Frogs*

Imagine two people with opposite views on hydraulic fracturing who are taking part in a calm, open, respectful, and productive discussion. If sketching this congenial scenario has not already stretched imagination beyond its snapping point, then imagine a conclusion of the conversation in which both of these participants say to each other, "I am not entirely in agreement with you, but what I have heard you say has caused me to question some of the assumptions and convictions

I held." If a reporter came upon this scene, the rarity of this event should earn featured headline:

ENTRENCHED HYDRAULIC FRACTURING
OPPONENTS CONVERSE WITHOUT DISTRUST,
ARRIVING AT A BETTER UNDERSTANDING OF
THE ISSUE AND EACH OTHER!

Back in the world as we know it, the public discussion of hydraulic fracturing continues to founder in an atmosphere thick with resentment, defensiveness, and cynicism. For several years, that fog has been my ambience. Working at an interdisciplinary, university-based center where we apply historical perspective to contemporary dilemmas, I have tried many experiments to clear the air, hosting a series of public programs called FrackingSENSE. I have participated in more panels, forums, and conversations on the subject than I can count. Sometimes distrusted by people who have mobilized to fight hydraulic fracturing projects in proximity to their homes, and sometimes distrusted by people in the oil and gas industry, I have become a resident, in the words of poet A. E. Stallings, of "shaky ground."

In very recent times, the combination of two forms of technology brought a vast resource of energy into reach: the oil and gas trapped in impermeable shale. The practice known as hydraulic fracturing has mobilized a process to release gas and oil from impermeable ("tight") underground formations. The technique known as horizontal drilling makes it possible to drill a well vertically and to branch off horizontally and thereby to reach a much greater area of the subsurface for fracturing. Bringing a vast resource of shale gas and shale oil into reach, the convergence of hydraulic fracturing and horizontal drilling have called into question once-confident prophecies of the looming scarcity of US-produced oil and natural gas.

The recent boom of activity in the planet's underworld has brought to the surface an abundance of natural gas and oil, and, equally, an abundance of once-buried political and social tension. So closely entwined are the rearrangements of the geological and psychological subsurfaces that there are, indeed, good reasons to see the controversy over hydraulic fracturing as a "proxy debate." In truth, a full inventory—what we are fighting about when we fight about fracking—would require a text of great length, featuring, for instance, an enormous chapter on capitalism, property, and profit. But just as worthy of our attention is a surprisingly neglected question: Which people are fighting with intensity when we fight about fracking, and what lines of division structure their fight? Conventional observations and commentary has come to rest on the notion that the American people are divided into two clearly defined and rigidly opposed cohorts, one in support of hydraulic fracturing ("pro-industry") and another in opposition to hydraulic fracturing ("anti-industry"). Just beneath the surface of that notion lie layers and layers of complexity.

First and often pushed to the side of attention, there is a very sizable sector of opinion that is barely visible and nearly inaudible. Citizens in this sector have not made up their minds, though many of them may hover in the vicinity of the mild-mannered view that hydraulic fracturing is a technique that offers great promise but needs to be regulated carefully. They may, for instance, find more cheer than gloom in the news that our American nation turns out to have enormous holdings in oil and gas that were barely noticed until recent years. Even as they acknowledge that the responsible handling of this unexpected fortune comes with a crucial challenge in responsible stewardship, people in this sector do not organize themselves into associations, convene rallies, gather signatures for ballot initiatives, buy advertisements, put out position papers, or hire attorneys to file lawsuits in support of their interests. This population, which may well be the vast majority, is itself divided into several subcategories. Some are indifferent; some are bored; some are intimidated by an issue that seems so "technical"; and many are preoccupied with more urgent and immediate life challenges. Still, in a conviction arising from many conversations, US citizens struggling to find intelligible meaning in the collision of contradictory assertions in the public sphere are the largest group of all.

And, second, the categories of social class and of race receive very sparse recognition in the conventional casting of the participants in the controversy over hydraulic fracturing and natural gas development. To put this clumsily, most of the people who are taking clearly defined stances of opposition on hydraulic fracturing are white and middle- or upper-class. Figuring out the positions of working class and/or poor people is, at this point, an enterprise close to guesswork.

Third, the individuals and groups who have taken firm positions are aligned in a lot more ways than "two sides." Both the "pro" and "con" sides are honeycombed with their own internal divisions and fractures. A closer look at the differences and divisions concealed within these categories charts a direct route to greater realism.

INDUSTRY

When you encounter the phrase "fossil fuel industry," you're given an important opportunity to ask for further information. While coal, oil, and natural gas are all fossil fuels, the people who work in the production of those resources are far from unified and homogeneous in their positions and attitudes. Representatives from the natural gas industry are eager and willing to point out the unfortunate emissions produced by the combustion of coal. Coal industry representatives are equally eager to point out that coal holds various advantages over natural gas: coal remains abundant and matched to the operations of many existing electrical generation plants.

Hydraulic fracturing, meanwhile, is used to produce both the natural gas and the oil embedded in shale rock. Inevitably teamed up in the phrase "oil and gas"—it is almost as difficult to say "oil" without "and gas," as it is to say "Lewis" without "and Clark"—oil does not deliver the significant climate advantage of cleaner-burning natural gas. The difference in outcomes of combustion is so important that separating the discussion of hydraulic-fracturing-to-produce-oil from the discussion of hydraulic-fracturing-to-produce-natural-gas would contribute a degree of clarity currently under-supplied in the public sphere.

If we shift our focus to the natural gas industry itself, evidence of a coordinated and homogeneous enterprise remains elusive. Companies developing natural gas come in all sizes, from vast multi-nationals to small family businesses. While there is a lot of room for variation in the choices made by individual company leaders, there is an unmistakable pattern by which large companies have more financial resources to invest in precautions and protections against leaks (of both fluids and airborne substances), as well as in investments in or compensations to affected communities.

Also worth attention is the difference between the operator (the natural gas company that is the principal player in a particular development) and a big range of subcontractors. The service companies are particularly important to note. While the operator holds primary responsibility for the site, service companies perform the actual work of hydraulic fracturing and production. This is particularly worth noting, since the leaders of companies like Halliburton and Schlumberger have seen the components of fracturing fluid as their key intellectual property or trade secret; thus, the exemption from disclosure of these components mattered much more to the service companies than it did to the exploration and development companies. Subcontractors also supply the trucking services that bring water to the site for fracturing—and take water away from the site for disposal or treatment. (Pipelines, of course, provide an alternative to trucks, but that, in turn, brings another subcontractor into the story.) As in any such chain of commissioned services, a clear line of responsibility and accountability becomes increasingly hard to track as more moving parts come into play.

Of all these distinctions and divisions, the toughest to address is the difference between good operators and not-so-good operators. As in every profession, variations in human character and judgment can make a big difference in performance. And, as in many other professions, a good player has no obvious mechanism or procedure for asking that his rivals meet his standards of good performance, even though the reputations of all companies will suffer from the careless or improvident behavior of one company.

NOT-INDUSTRY (A.K.A. GROUPS EXPRESSING CONCERN ABOUT OR DIRECT OPPOSITION TO HYDRAULIC FRACTURING AND NATURAL GAS DEVELOPMENT)

Here we are stuck with a wordy, clumsy sub-section title, because the terms "opposition" or "opponents" solidly fail at capturing a swirl of positions. Consider the spectrum of positions that would have to be blended to be fitted into a term like "anti-industry":

1) Residents who have learned that the locale of their homes is under consideration for gas development and whose concerns center on quality of life and health impacts. In a locale they chose for its quiet and tranquility, these people never had the slightest intention of living in proximity to the noise, bright lights, bustle, and smells of an industrial production site, as well as to prospective threats to their health from pollution and contamination of water and air. Many of the people in this category never saw themselves as activists, but the intrusion of natural gas rigs and wells into their neighborhood, possibly posing threats to their health from pollution and contamination of water and air, has mobilized them.

2) Residents who share the concerns of the people in the previous category but who were primed and ready, for reasons that preceded the arrival of hydraulic fracturing in their neighborhood, to denounce concentrations of power in corporations and to lament the failures of government to protect citizens.

3) People (maybe nearby residents and maybe not) who have had a long involvement in environmental causes, acting as advocates for clean air, pure water, and wildlife habitat. Having developed the habits of taking up these causes, these folks place natural gas development in a category of troubles (mines, dams, fossil-fuel-dependent transportation, suburban sprawl, etc.) they have been trying to correct or constrain for years. Often, the concerns of this cohort focus on oil and gas development on the public lands.

4) People who move to an area undergoing natural gas development in order to mobilize and channel local discontent, often on behalf of a national campaign to challenge the power of the fossil fuel industry (a term we just dissected) and to accelerate the shift to renewable energy.

While these various groups may converge and unite from time to time, industry groups often mix and mingle these varying agendas when they characterize their opponents—for instance, accusing an opponent of pushing a hidden agenda of bringing a halt to society's dependence on fossil fuel use, whether or not that goal ever figured in the motivations of that particular opponent. But it takes a fair amount of determination and heavy lifting to merge and conflate all these groups, since the differences among them are so sizable.

And we must recognize a further dimension in the diversity of opinion among residents living in proximity to drilling. The usual "two sides" configuration concedes no ground (literally!) to the group known as "royalty owners," people who own both the land on the surface and the mineral resources beneath the surface. Thus it is not at all uncommon to find one group of landowners, insisting on their right to the revenue from the development of their subsurface mineral rights, in direct conflict with another group of landowners who only own a portion of the surface and who resent the disruption and disturbance wrought by development from which they will not profit.

Both the owners of surface land and owners of the subsurface minerals celebrate the rights of private property, and yet the reality of the split estate has often meant that two forms of private property collide with each other. This collision can sometimes be negotiated in ways that both sets of owners find acceptable and even beneficial. But the split estate also presents plenty of circumstances in which different sub-cultures of ownership clash under tangled terms that are hard to manage and sometimes just very hard to understand.

Rarely of much use, the "two sides" model becomes a particular burden when we approach the uncomfortable issue of social class. Consider low-income households, where individuals and families struggle to pay their heating bills, facing difficult choices between paying for food or medications and keeping a house warm in winter. For those households, the boom in hydraulic fracturing set in motion a chain of production and dropping energy prices that, measurably, made life easier. In public discussions of hydraulic fracturing, the circumstances of this sector of society are rarely mentioned.

Protest against oil and natural gas development also stands in a puzzling relationship to the understanding of environmental justice. Traditionally, the environmental justice movement aims at correcting the pattern by which pollution and contamination disproportionately burden people who are disadvantaged by factors of race and class. Since the "anti-fracking" movement along the Front Range of Colorado is primarily populated by white, middle-class people, contests over hydraulic fracturing do not make a smooth fit to the conventional arrangements of environmental justice.

And then there are the workers. Jobs in natural gas development pay well. This is especially true for people without college degrees who, otherwise, face a dismal set of opportunities in "post-industrial" America. And yet the workers also face the highest risk of injury or, depending on the safety of operations at particular sites, of exposure to toxic substances as well as susceptibility to silicosis from inhaling the sand kept on site for use as the proppant in hydraulic fracturing fluid. Because the workers are often transitory newcomers, interactions between them and long-term residents concerned about natural gas development can be tense, or even hostile. While established residents in proximity to rigs and wells may express interest in workers because observations of their health could reveal risks that the nearby residents in proximity will face, the social distance between workers and established residents is itself an unsettling aspect of the industry's presence.

Near Mead, Colorado, in November of 2014, in a very cold spell, workers tried to thaw a water pipe at a well site. When the pipe broke at high pressure, it killed one worker and injured two others. Information about the worker who died was sketchy. Newspaper articles simply said that he had been identified as "Matthew Smith, 36." Had the person killed in this explosion been a nearby resident, or had he been an executive of an oil and gas company, it seems certain that we would have learned a lot more about him. Instead, the dimensions and dynamics of his life remain beneath the surface of our attention. If we were to try to return to the model of "two sides" to hydraulic fracturing, it would not be an easy matter to figure out where to place "Matthew Smith, 36."

Just beneath the surface of simple configurations of opinion and alignment lies an unsettled and unaddressed complexity. After all, oil and gas development allocates benefits and costs in a way that maximizes distrust and misunderstanding. The local communities in proximity to development experience the disturbance of an industrial site (the intrusion of very visible surface infrastructure, truck traffic, noise, bright lights, and anxiety about possible health troubles from water and air pollution) with immediacy and intensity. The principal benefits—national security, a cleaner-burning fossil fuel, heated homes, generated electricity, and, of course, of profits to company owners and stockholders—are received in distant locales.

Even with this inherent tension, moving beyond the tired, over-stretched categories of "pro-industry" and "anti-industry" could enhance the value of public conversation, at the very least giving some room for the participation of citizens who have not yet adopted a firm and settled position on the practice of hydraulic fracturing. Perhaps even more important, recognizing that there are many sides to this issue frees us from the fatalistic assumption that we are stuck with a repetitive, two-sided debate. Recognizing that many groups hold a variety of positions and including those groups as participants in the exchange, we are invited into something much closer to a conversation or a forum, with participants given an incentive to listen at least as much as they speak.

And here is one item of common ground among these participants: all the contestants engaged in disputes over hydraulic fracturing are, in one way or another, resting their weight on the thin veneer of the present, paying only selective and sporadic attention to the history concealed beneath that veneer. Current arguments will sometimes include appeals to history. But these appeals tend toward selectivity, picking the lessons that best support the case an advocate wants to make. History, however, is not choosing sides.

The oil and gas industry inherits the complicated history of Western extractive industry. The extraction of natural resources—gold, silver, coal, oil, timber, grass, water, soil nutrients—drove American expansion into the West. Extraction also left behind many messes: abandoned mines leaking acid drainage into water ways and open pit mines evolving into toxic lakes; clear-cut forest lands; eroded soil; ghost towns stranded when busts followed booms. Today, when an energy company puts forward a plan to drill for oil and gas, this legacy of disturbance—often uncorrected or even unnoticed by those who produced it—returns for a reckoning. In many people's minds, the natural gas industry gets easily cast as the latest villain in this long history of extractive companies racing to capture resources and making a quick departure without remedy, repair, or clean-up of what they left in their wake. Even though there has been a revolution in federal, state, and local regulatory power governing the conduct of extractive industries, the memory of the damage done by extraction is sharp and lasting. And so history has put a premium on the willingness of industry leaders to recognize that, fair or not, they inherit the legacy of Western extractive industry and that, accordingly, they must take every possible precaution to avoid replicating the injuries of the past.

Meanwhile, the residents of Colorado's Front Range towns and suburbs, for example, move through the present with an awkward historical legacy of their own. A number of these communities originated as coal-mining towns; occasionally, within their town limits, an abandoned mine undergoes subsidence and a road or structure slumps into the ground. More to the point, these towns were nodes of a burst of residential expansion after World War II. These communities would never have grown to anything close to their current size without a festival of combustion of fossil fuels, a festival that continues apace today. Commuting to and from the city of Denver became more and more viable with highways, abundant gasoline, and widespread automobile ownership. Just a few decades ago, sprawl—the rapid expansion of the population of these communities, a movement driven in part by white flight from urban desegregation—was a principal focus of alarm among conservationists and environmentalists, who were concerned about traffic congestion, smog, the disruption of wildlife habit by housing patterns that rejected density, and the celebration of consumerism that characterized suburbs nationwide. This history provides awkward footing for Front Range residents who would like to position themselves today on the environmental high ground.

And now, in 2015, bringing up this history in the context of protests against hydraulic fracturing is unlikely to be welcomed. The characterization of Front Range suburbs, before the arrival of rigs and wells, as places of pastoral calm, healthful living, aesthetically appealing landscapes, and environmental responsibility downplays the reality that the vigorous use of fossil fuels brought these communities into being and still transports their inhabitants, their food, and possessions, while also heating and lighting their homes. Just beneath the innocence and righteousness of these Front Range neighborhoods lies an infrastructure that steadily provides them with energy produced in other people's neighborhoods. History, in other words, requires us to face up to the cultural and psychological disconnection between energy production and energy consumption. But history does not require us to use the term "hypocrites" to characterize residents who resist fossil fuel production in proximity to their homes. By a long shot, it would be wiser to borrow the wonderful title of a book by historian Michael Kammen and refer to them as "people of paradox," after Justice Oliver Wendell Holmes's "There is nothing like a paradox to take the scum off your mind."

Open consideration of this complex and intertwined historical legacy—the environmental troubles left behind by extractive industry and by suburban sprawl—offers benefits as well as discomforts. At the least, the open acknowledgment of this legacy would level the playing field, and reduce the attraction—and rhetorical effectiveness—of the reciprocal condemnation that has come to pass for conversation.

In wilder moments of imagining routes out of our current stalemates, I dream of a custom in which public meetings on a controversial subject like hydraulic fracturing universally begin with a statement along these lines: *We cannot plan for our future until we face up to our history and directly acknowledge the complexity of our own moment in time.*

And, if that statement seems too prosaic and pedestrian, then here are two quotations to get conversations off to a promising start:

> There is no distinction, for all have sinned and fall short
> of the glory of God.
> —Romans 3:23

> Slowly you restore
> The fractured world and start
> To re-create the afternoon before
> It fell apart.
> —A. E. Stallings, "Jigsaw Puzzle"

Digging

Michelle Donahue

As a child I shoved my hands in dirt, unearthed
    worms, watched their writhing bodies.

I studied each segment, gave them names, genders,
    imbued life to such creatures.

I learned & uncovered what was beneath.
    Now our explorations have expanded:

old dinosaur bones, decayed, prehistoric
    plants turned thick black & settled deep.

We create horizontal veins, pump water,
    high pressure, to extract the black fuel,

that history & so the ground grows hollow.
    I look at this earth's horizon, the red of flesh,

splashed, bone yellow, the sun threatening
    to slip beneath that edge.

Now: a pumpjack, drilling rig
    oil moved from rock pores to wells.

Once, I held a worm in my palm, its head severed
    by my metal shovel, my inexpert hand.

It jerked & jerked.
    I kept waiting for it to stop.

Huckster

Fiction by Bill Roorbach

For reasons that will become obvious I must change the names of all but John Carson Dunne in this report. I met the great man back in college, and he was one of the smartest and most capable and least likely kids to succeed in our dorm, which was huge, at Our Great University, which was in a small city, a college town with a name the blind rhapsode Homer would have repeated thousands of times, singing his best tales. But let's just call the town Homer, as a town must have a name.

The usual hijinks, of course, but in Jack's case alcohol-free: rappelling down the twenty-story Benefactor's Tower at Homer University, tires rolled down Musk Oxen Street into a column of police marching to quell an anti-war demonstration, a van load of seafood liberated from the dining-service walk-ins with laser lock-picks after hours and distributed to the street people downtown, Carl the Hobo with two lobsters in his hands, shaking them at passersby for days. Pranks with a conscience, Jack called them. This was the late sixties, of course.

So I was shocked in 2015 when I saw the first of Jack's editorials in the *Homer Independent*, let's call it (editorials later to be reprinted nationwide, either vilified or championed, depending on the website, the paper, the payoffs—it's all graft, baby), editorials in fervid favor of the recovery via hydraulic fracturing of shale oils and gases in Iliad County, and in counties across the land, shocked and disgusted, especially as our fair (and former in my case) city was waging an ultimately successful campaign to institute a fracking ban, the first in the country, a model of legal maneuvering and public relations that, you see, had to be destroyed. Jack had sold out this beautiful environmental spirit and had become the enemy—so far as I was concerned. Jack, oh beautiful Jack, why? I asked. And why bother, sweet former friend, with editorials that undermined laws that had already been passed? Because the people who'd bought him didn't lose battles without securing the war, that's why.

Plainly, he'd gone mad, and not just been co-opted. The guy was even making puff films for and about deep-extractive industry, I learned, and these were to be shown at schools, two and three minutes long, very much designed to go viral on the internet, he crowed in his PR prospectus. Good luck, pal. He'd grown up middle class in suburban New Jersey, joined me in Homer for our undistinguished college careers, but then got very wealthy in one of the tech booms, as I discovered (continued obsessive investigation): he was the inventor of systems and apps and all sorts of background film tech I'll never understand, stuff that cruised the booms, that rode out all the busts. He'd stayed in Homer, still ran his huge company from there, Tarzan Films, named after the obscure fact that Homer had once been a movie capital and that some of the early Tarzan films had been made there. Famously, the owner of Tarzan fucking Films had been buying up farms. He'd been doing it for years. And now people knew why. It wasn't rural landscape preservation at all! It wasn't about heritage farming!

I'd gone a very different direction, was a reporter for *Newspeak* till it folded, then a freelancer for *The York New Times*, let's call it, among others, and because it was the *Times* that had run Jack's latest editorials, I thought a story about his apparent conversion was in order, and the editors of the *Sunday Magazine* agreed.

Jack wasn't hard to find. And when I called, he remembered me, a great booming laugh, and I was in love again, fell once again into his orbit, like a planet come home to its sun. I told him what I wanted, and he laughed even harder, and I laughed too. "Get ass up here," he said, a guy who talked like a telegram.

His home was modest by bazillionaire CEO standards, or really any standards, an old farmhouse at the edge of town—real acreage, however, and located on a fair trout stream, big barn in good repair, but really just a very simple house, not even a guest room. Though for the purposes of impartiality I wasn't going to stay with him in any case no matter what. He greeted me at the end of his driveway, hopping up and down with excitement. He was buff as ever (not I), dressed in running shorts and cowboy boots, huge Stetson hat in black. He had a Stetson for me, too, bright white, and there was no doubt: I was the good guy.

We had work to do. We stayed up half my first night there drinking hard and reminiscing, a lot of screaming laughter and great stories, though I remained wary, wary of Jack even as I woke with my cheek pasted to the kitchen floor next morning. But I hadn't misled the *Times*…Jack was my old friend and he'd gone wrong and that was exactly what the article was to be about.

At Jack's invitation, I broke my crapulous convalescence at my hotel and joined him two days later for a film shoot. And this shoot was nothing seat of the pants but full-on state-of-the-art everything, a crew of a dozen, at least, hardened, efficient pros, Babel of languages. The person of interest that day was a hot industry-of-the-moment lobbyist, famously gung-ho, famously effective, the man who was said to have coined the phrase that was the fighting song of the frackers: "Drill, Baby, Drill!" My own paper had called this man "the quintessential fracking dead ender" after he'd lost the Homer fracking wars, a bluff and handsome old marine in a sharkskin suit and purple shirt who insisted on leaning against his desk for the cameras so as to seem more approachable. Dr. Crude, let's call him, Dr. Dennis Crude.

And I admit it, much as I hated the dude, he was personable, articulate, gracious, should have been an actor. In thrillers. Not the bad guy, but the bad guy's monster, the one recently escaped, sharpened teeth, hands like steam-shovel buckets, unfocused eyes. I was introduced as crew, not my idea, and I was only to watch—no notes, no interviews of my own, Jack had warned me—just watch, maybe hold a light diffuser so as not to seem suspicious, plenty of story to come.

Anyway, there he was, the actual Dennis Crude, leaning on his desk, breathing methane. And my former bud John Carson Dunne, leaning on a bright windowsill in his subject's own beautiful office.

"We're talking to Dr. Dennis Crude," Jack began. "He's a geologist by training, a pragmatist by nature, and a great American businessman."

"Well, thanks, Jack," Dennis said smoothly.

"Perfect," Jack said, and two of the three cameras dropped, along with my heart. Jack said, "That's our set-up. Now, let's just talk a bit casually, get warmed up. The little camera there will roll continuously for color, facial expressions, appropriate laughter, that kind of thing, and we'll remember it's there—anything we can use we will—but when the interview is in progress, Mr. Crude, always talk into the big camera here—Jerry in the blue shirt."

Jerry waved distractedly from behind his downed rig.

"Got it," Dennis said easily.

"And just give us a minute here."

The techies arranged lights, moved booms, taped wires to fine furniture. Dennis Crude barely moved, not a twitch, like a Zen master in a twelve thousand dollar suit (I researched it later—signature blue piping: Ermenegildo Zegna bespoke).

"Just be a minute," Jack told him soothingly, taking his position in the window, a view miles across the face of the planet down to Lake Cayuga, views the other direction up into hills across vast pastures, gorgeous. Forget three-acre zoning—Dr. Dennis Crude was all alone up here, hundreds of acres. Far down the hill, more huge homes, but Crude looked over their roofs. The neighborhood was called Undermountain, right on the city line, next town Gullibleburg, let's call it, just over the barbed wire. There wasn't a mountain, though, only those hills, that elegant long slope, Dennis's perfectly mowed lawn giving over to pastures past that barbed-wire fence, that fictional line, a lone horse out there grazing, swishing its tail.

I tried to look like I wasn't just loitering, actually helped tape down the edges of the carpet so no one would trip and ruin the shot with cursing, seemingly the only one remembering that the unmanned third camera was running, a firm, fixed profile of Dennis.

"Man, this is one nice house!" Jack said after a while, puff of breath—fucking techies taking forever.

"Spoils of war," Dennis said.

"Great view," Jack said.

"You can't power the world on the view," Dennis said.

Jack laughed appreciatively. "I like the view. In fact, I think I might own some of that acreage back here behind you. One of the old farms. How would you like a fracking rig back here? I could position it probably no more than a hundred yards from your swimming pool!"

They both laughed hard. Dennis finally managed to sputter out his own joke: "Rare cancers, baby!"

"Half-life of forever!"

And they kept laughing, laughing like frat brothers who'd dropped a full keg into Homer Gorge just to see it blow. Dennis spouted: "I'm here because that ain't never going to happen." And calmed down some: "Little secret, Jackie, I bought this château just before the Bush crash, and my mortgage is so far underwater I have to send little men down in diving bells to do the fucking yard work. But give me a couple more years and we'll be able to pull the value back out, all the way out, defeat this ban business and move on. Truth? I hate this little burg. Homer, fuck me! How can you live here? Bunch of professors and burnwads. But I'm not done with my task yet. Have to keep pretending!"

Their laughter subsided some. The director was yelling at some techies in the glass-and-stainless-steel kitchen.

Confidential, all-kidding-aside tone, Jack said, "I'm surprised to hear you call it the Bush crash."

"Don't tell me you're fond of that little weasel!"

"I just thought."

"He was a great president? He was—because we wrote the legislation, baby. And his greatness was this: he knew it, and welcomed it. Guy didn't have to lift a fucking finger or twitch a single brain cell. Not that he had any."

At long last the camera people tilted the faces of the bigger cameras upwards, and all the sour moneygrubbing and treacherous glee fell out of Dr. Dennis Crude's face, replaced by the old avuncular charm, perfectly benign—relax, it was just a mistake in the X-ray room, no tumor here!

While the set manager counted down Jack composed himself, very smoothly started in on the script a professional two beats after his director pointed at him: "Explain hydraulic fracturing for us, would you, Doctor Crude? So many of us are worried it's been mischaracterized by the vegan professoriate, especially here in your lovely town."

"Isn't it lovely? I've made it my home, that's how lovely, and that's how much I care about Homer. Most beautiful real estate in the country. And of course, I want to keep it that way."

And so on, the usual propaganda. Not a word about the secret chemical mix that had poisoned water supplies, not a word about the filthy nature of the extraction and even the eventual product, not a word about how most of that product was destined for sale overseas, not a word about how few actual jobs were produced in the USA or anywhere except at banks, not a peep about the 400 percent increase in temblors in the area, not a word about any controversy at all, and only passing reference to the law the City of Homer had passed by a wide, beautiful, heartening margin, the famous and first county-sponsored fracking ban. Dennis referred to the law as a bump in the road, a wake-up call. He never said the word fracking, that's for sure. He called all that "clean extraction." And he called himself a concerned citizen. Freedom was at issue!

The cameras dropped.

"Little break?" Jack said.

"Fine by me," Dennis said.

The third camera still blinked, still kept its eye on Dennis.

Jack stretched, said, "Forward plan? I know you're never going to let this law stand."

"Well, you know, we hew to the chemical council's line. The plan is simple. Make it all sound benign. You just heard the basics. One, we want to make jobs. Two, the chemical mix is a small fraction of the total water used. Small, see. You emphasize the fraction, which is small indeed, tiny, wee, cute, even, when you're using millions upon millions of gallons of the local H_2O. But really it's like seventy thousand gallons of proprietary product per well, a lot! And three bucks a gallon, right back at the industry. But you don't say that. Three, you talk about how you recycle the water. Gotta say the word recycle at least twenty times per town meeting! But how you recycle is you dump the shit in their precious lake, or pump it back down in their stinking ground. And my favorite is this one, number four: you always, always mention local control. You always, always say that federal and state governments have no business telling localities what to do. As an industry, Jack, buddy, we used to fight for state control, because states are easier to fight than the feds. Now we fight for county control. But after this Homer County bullshit, we're going to start fighting for town control. The smaller the town, the better. Legal can overwhelm three idiots on a town board like nobody's business. Give 'em each a campaign contribution, for starters. These suckers have never seen that kind of money. Then write up your tailored ordinance. Go to the town meeting, get it passed by guys you basically just sucked off. We're doing it tonight in Gullibleburg. That's right fucking here. The line's my fence, Jackie my boy. Old nothing Gullibleburg. Barely even a fucking town anymore. They pass our ordinance on a voice vote with the old lady environmentalists still waiting in line to speak, and overnight we set up shop, just like that. Go down a mile, take a fucking left, drill horizontal right under fucking Homer University, right under the organic tampon and nut-cheese factory, blow all their fucking water and a bucket of those beautiful rare cancers into the hole, and slurp-blam-boom, suck the product right out from under them and their candy-ass laws."

Jack nodded through it all, egging him on, then said, "And then I, or anyone who owns land or mineral rights in the very next town, like right past your fucking fence, can drill."

"If we let 'em. Don't forget, those who own the equipment own the narrative. You drill if we let you lease our shit. But yes, then we can drill, drill, drill. It might not hold up long, fucking federal courts, so you get in there right away, get set up, get the jism flowing. It's harder for the weenies to shut down a running operation than a potential operation, almost impossible."

Jack nodded happily.

"Ready?" the famous film director said.

Ready. And the main cameras raised their noses to record more propaganda, Jack following Dennis's script precisely, heartbreakingly.

Near the end of the interview, after a long and warm and slightly condescending disquisition by Dennis on the safety of water supplies (We drill down a mile, well below water tables! Triple steel casing! Cement pipe jackets!), Jack asked, "So, Dr. Crude, you'd drink the water in a neighborhood where fracking is in progress?"

"Hell, I'd drink the fracking fluid, boy."

And so Jack's assistant, a huge young man, trundled briskly on set with a quart Mason jar, dropped it on Dennis's desk beside him.

For the cameras, Dennis looked at the bottle almost lovingly—life-blood!—but I saw the flinch: this wasn't in the script.

"Show us," Jack said. "It's fresh water recently recycled from a high-performing well down in Pennsylvania." And he gave Dennis a wink, nodded.

Which Dennis took to mean the fix was in. He lifted the big jar to his mouth and drank a hearty gulp. Instantly he spewed it out. "What the hell?" And then he coughed and spat, spat again, then vomited profusely, three cameras rolling.

That night, Gullibleburg town office. Not much to call an office, let alone a town. Jack owned a number of old farms there, everyone knew. I'd thought, we'd all thought, he'd bought them to preserve the farmscape, to promote traditional farming, subsidized land and equipment leases, grants of land and money to old-school farmers, the very ones who'd been pushed off the land, also their children, all of our children.

But this was a fracking referendum, and Dr. Dennis Crude had arranged it. He took the floor in the whitest sneakers I'd ever seen, brand new blue jeans, a flannel shirt (someone ought to tell him neither jeans nor flannels should be pressed), calmly addressed a previous proposal that would tie Gullibleburg policy to Homer's. There was a crowd, mostly college students from far away, but a nice knot of desperate farmers too, all of whom had been told how much they might make from a well. "Why should there be limits?" Dennis thundered. "Common sense will prevail! Do we want federal control?"

"No!" cried the farmers.

"Do we want state control?"

"No!" cried the farmers.

"We just want control," shouted a protester, piping voice, confused about where Crude's rhetoric was headed, about which side was which.

One of the board members very quietly said, "Move to introduce a bill to allow permits in our town." Then louder: "Our town! Our control!" All under Jack's cameras.

The farmers and their supporters cheered, quickly booed down by the protesters. But the board quietly voted unanimously in the interest of their benefactor, removed the limiting clause. And then added Dr. Crude's new one. Which allowed drilling all the way to within a single rod of boundary lines (but who knew what a rod was—few of us in that room!). The board had all been through a tough election, and they knew very well that their campaigns were funded by the calm men in suits, not by the loudmouths in flannel.

"Jobs, jobs, jobs," the lobbyists chanted, as if they too were protesters.

The next dawn, in the field where the horse had been, and right on the fence behind Dennis's house, beginning exactly at the now-legal sixteen-and-a-half-feet from his property line, Jack's fracking crew appeared, thirty good jobs that would last a week. And then—you gots to hurry—a line of tanker trucks, engines roaring, stacks belching diesel exhaust (You wouldn't believe how many and how fast they assembled behind the drilling rig!), a derrick on the back of an OVER-SIZE LOAD flatbed, hydraulics to tilt it upward, no more than an hour to arm the drillhead (This reporter timed everything, wrote every bit of jargon in his pad.). And then the noise began, a pounding, a whirling, a roaring, plumes of foul steam from the cooling jets. The excess fluids (which contained lubricants, of course, and stabilizers, and proprietary solvents, and who knew what all else—you no longer had to say in Gullibleburg) poured in a rippling, iridescent sheet down the hill and over the property line, shortly filled Dennis's pool.

Jack exhorted the crew: "Gotta get the well in, harder to stop you when it's in! Drill, babies, drill!"

Suddenly Dr. Dennis Crude came sputtering out onto his kitchen patio in boxer shorts and t-shirt, bald as a bubble without his toupee. "What the hell!" he shouted over the roaring.

"Morning, brother!" Jack shouted back.

Just then, the ground welled at Dr. Dennis Crude's bare feet, precious orange liquids having under-run his flagstones. In a flash like lightning he went from sleep-befuddled to purple with rage, began roaring epithets and poking angrily at his phone. Which if he'd used it to look at what was trending on Twitter might have pissed him off more: the closely edited interview footage from camera three had gone viral, and then had gone Emergency Room, as the kids say: Dr. Dennis Crude, smoothly leaning on his desk, telling it like it is. No, he wasn't going to get on Twitter. How was he supposed to do that while dancing in fake fracking fluid, boxer shorts askew? He was going to call… whom? Whom was he going to call? There was no one left to call. Dr. Crude was done.

Jack and his end-times games, my hero once again. The video pre-empted my article, in a way, but my article sealed the deal: Dr. Dennis Crude is deactivated, a bomb with the wires cut. Jack had used me, too, but I didn't mind. I was the fourth camera, you see. And whoever it was funding Dennis Crude didn't fail to notice my work—threats and lawsuits come in waves to this day. But Jack's got my back, bold Jack, lawyers to burn, bodyguards fit as Tarzan himself, and Jack and me, we're like this again, our sights set on bigger things.

A Miniature Handbook for New Women Activists

Amy Weldon

STEP ONE: LEARN TO SPEAK.

At the dinner table, your mother and your grandmother tell you, *Be quiet, your brother's talking. Be quiet, your father's talking. Be quiet, your husband's talking.* The men glance at you, then carry on with what they're saying, vindication in their eyes. You're pretty sure they mean it when they say *I love you.* But sometimes you wonder if they know exactly what love means.[*]

---

[*] The "you" is meant to be collective; some of these experiences are mine, some related or shared by other women.

Late at night in bed your husband weeps as he tells you how his father unbuckled his belt with that terrible look in his eye: *I'm gonna teach you, boy, not to talk back.*

Men so seldom say *love* to one another. They say, *Behave. Turn it down. Keep yourself quiet.* All in the name of *being safe.* And so your husband learned not to speak. He learned to keep the rest of his family from speaking, too, in any situation in which they weren't absolutely certain of their listener. He learned the story he—and perhaps all of you—still believe despite the evidence accelerating every day, with every citizen-voted ordinance ignored and every well poisoned and every seed-company executive appointed to the FDA: *Father knows best.*

Father knows best. Authorities can always be trusted to protect us. He learned that story early on, and in spite of everything he believes it. So, in spite of everything you know by now, do you. And fighting fracking or war or immigration raids or any other cause from your own communities on out still, if you are honest, so often means that first you fight that story in your own head. *Father knows best. He says be quiet.* First you fight the trap that story lays before you, a small shiny cage in which you are tempted to huddle, and hide, as the related stories wash over you: That bruise-blood filling the soft skin under your eye is a sign of your man's protective passion for you, too deep to restrain itself, spilling the boundaries of reason and flesh. The politician's noble televised profile matches an inner nobility you can surely trust, since you voted for him, and he would never disregard the wishes of those who put him in office. The fox guards the hen-house because he loves those plump sleeping ladies. Cherishes them, in fact. As dearly as a father. And to suggest otherwise is to be a bad, bad girl.

That fox still lives so deep in your own brain you may never dig him out, despite your most diligent efforts. He licks his lips slowly, savoring the feast to come, opening his mouth only to caution you in a silvery, scornful growl: *Be quiet, girl. Nobody wants to listen to you.*

STEP TWO: LEARN MORE.

Julia Crawford's voice shakes as she describes TransCanada's seizure of her farm near Paris, Texas. They've run lengths of gray-blue pipeline under her stream, under the grass where her puzzled horses stand watching. Off-duty welders sleep in their trucks. Armed guards keep everyone—including her—at a distance. Out-of-state license plates proliferate, belying company promises of local jobs. "I thought at first the worst was when they cut my fence," she says. "Then the worst was when they started digging, and the grass came up." Then she saw the pipeline itself, 36 inches in diameter, lying in wait to be buried, marked with her own name. The company promised her that in eighteen months, she wouldn't even know they'd been there. "I don't want to overuse this analogy," she says, "but would you ever say that to someone who had been…violated? 'Oh, in eighteen months, you'll forget all about it? Just go on about your life, go to your job, and everything will be normal?'"

Sandra Steingraber speaks up next. She's just spent six days in jail for blocking trucks that would dump fracking wastewater into an old salt mine, polluting a lake that supplies drinking water for ten thousand people. She's a biologist. She's a parent. She's a cancer survivor. She connects the dots: What uncontrolled corporate greed dumps into our air and water, with our government's collusion and consent, ends up in our bodies. We pay for it, even as we buy into the notion that our consumer-driven, energy-dependent way of life must continue on exactly as it is. "I thought it was important," she says, "not just to pay the fine and get off. The companies pay fines. I wanted to put my body on the line. These companies do not pay for their crimes."

Frozen on your couch, you can't stop listening to their voices on the radio. Out the window lies your own small yard in the early-June dusk, blooming with irises and wild columbine and young bean and tomato plants and a freshly planted grapevine, alive with finches and sparrows and red-winged blackbirds with their distinctive two-note song. You know how you would feel if bulldozers rampaged onto your land though you had done everything possible to forbid them, if they tore up the ground you had cared for and worked with your own hands. You know how you would feel if your ownership of your life and your land and your property were flatly denied, violated, as if what you wanted simply did not matter to anyone except yourself. Shoved down. Ripped open. Used. And then your attacker drives away, wiping his hands on his jeans.

"I'm trying to be reasonable," Julia Crawford says. "I'm trying to color inside the lines. But maybe the time is coming when I just won't be able to do that anymore."

You go to an anti-frac-sand mining conference in western Wisconsin, the hardest-hit of all the areas threatened by the frac-sand industry in your beautiful, wild corner of the upper Midwest. The opening prayer is offered by a member of the Ho-Chunk Nation. A retired geology professor teaches you that the suffix *-fer* means *bearer*, so *aquifer* means *bearer of water*. ("Once contaminated," he says, "an aquifer is poisoned for good.") A retired army colonel says, "I dread spring, now, because I can't open my windows without dust everywhere. We've all got a cough." Lawyers speak with a matter-of-factness that feels exciting yet terrifying: "We specialize in helping those arrested in direct-action, civil-disobedience protests. Here's our number."

STEP THREE: GET ANGRY.

Could you put your body on the line, like Sandra Steingraber?

Aren't you doing so already?

Ten years ago now, when you were in your late twenties, you read about a girl your age who'd discovered a cocktail of industrial chemicals in her breast milk, from PCBs to industrial flame retardants. This was a world of hurt that had literally never occurred to you. Like any woman, you knew about the dangers of just walking around in your body, and since adolescence you'd picked up traces of that different poison—self-consciousness walking down the street, the impulse to sit on your hands in class, the burning, helpless rage when bullying boys sniggered *cunt* into your ear on the school bus. And now, here was a new poison passed from your body into your baby's, without either of you knowing, or consenting, or having the power to stop it. You'll never forget your incredulity on reading that. Or the bone-deep recognition of a danger running like a dark familiar current under the ways of life you've always thought were *normal*.

You recognize that poison because we've all been living with it for a long, long time. A woman who's done nothing wrong gets her body taken from her, co-opted, polluted, in this way and many others. Sold liposuction and hair straightener and Botox to make her a little prettier, a little smoother, to help her take up just a little less space. Thrown in the trunk of a car by an online-dating "match." Slashed, raped, killed. Buried alive in cellars from Austria to Ohio, impregnated by strange men or fathers. Told in abstinence-only classes that her body, no longer virginal, will become like a lollipop sucked on, used up, thrown away, no longer wanted by anyone—a Mormon girl abducted, raped, and held by a crazed "prophet" will confirm, years after her escape, that rhetoric like that helped bind her to her captor, her head down in shame. But kidnapping gets people's attention: to advertise their product, a Texas company makes a decal that covers a truck tailgate with a picture of a bound, gagged woman huddled against a black bedliner. The company owner claims he was surprised by the angry reactions he got and was only trying to "see who noticed it." Over and over, a woman who's done nothing wrong suffers any-way. Her body is the holding pool for the runoff of centuries' worth of neuroses, rages, and toxins, figurative and literal.

Finally, she says it. Again and again, first softer, then louder. *Open the door. Let me out.* She gets louder and louder and bursts into the street. Finally she shouts. *Let me out. You don't have the right. This is simply not fair.*

STEP FOUR: KNOW YOUR HISTORY.
Last year, you stood beside your parents at the well on the family farm in rural Alabama. When you were a child, this place was Eden. All around this well were collards and tomatoes and gourds in a lush garden, a giant fig tree, and an orchard with peaches and plums and a scuppernong arbor that overflowed your scarred plastic buckets and baskets with fruit. Hearing, as a little girl in your Methodist Sunday School, about the hopes of those wandering desert Israelites for a lasting and bountiful home—and the Bible's many analogies of water, richness, gardens, trees, and fountains for the spiritual repleteness offered by the Jesus you pictured as vividly as a known person in your mind—it made perfect sense that they would dream of living water

as a metaphor for God, that God would speak to those who sought Him in terms of water, of thirst quenched and satisfied, of life that renews itself by mystery and grace as surely as our abused earth has struggled back to give, and give, and give again. You ran through the grass under those trees, batting away yellow jackets too full and happy to sting, tracking between your sister and your baby brother and your grandparents and your parents, soaking in the light flickering on your face through the leaves and the laden branches, convinced that this world as you knew it would never die.

The orchard and the fig tree and the garden are gone now. So is the silver-burnished tin dipper from which you drank that well water on every single trip to the orchard. Your mother lifts the well cover and your father drops a stone inside. From twenty feet away you hear the thunk—not a splash—where it hits. "Dry," your father says. You turn away. That lost orchard paints itself across your mind so vividly it threatens to eclipse the actual sight of the few remaining pecan trees in that spot.

The stream that ran across the back of that farm for years and years is also dry. Upstream is a new gravel quarry that has disrupted the flow of water to your farm and your neighbors'. Drought brought on by climate change is not a myth. It is not something happening somewhere else. It is here. And it is yours.

Because of this, when the threat of frac-sand mining and its land-poisoning and water-poisoning comes to your new home in the Midwest, and when fracking enters the boom stage of its inevitable boom-and-bust cycle all over the country, you can't look away. You can't be cowed by the oil-and-gas-industry, which promises *domestic energy independence* even as they sell Pennsylvania gas to China and Wisconsin-mined frac sand to Saudi Arabia, even as they obscure the vanishingly low rate of return on pipelined and fracked fuels and the massive amount of other fuel and water it takes to extract them. (Forty years ago, their PR firms were the ones hired by Big Tobacco to croon *smoking is good for you!*) Even if your elected officials won't, you know the people have to say, *'Energy independence' cannot mean the freedom to carry on exactly as we always have.* You cannot face the imagined children of the future, peering at you over the corpses of logged-out hills and sizzled-up grasslands, pleading, *You knew and you did nothing, why?*

Unbidden, when you need it, comes the image of your mother, taking care. You see her lifting an old lady from her bed in a county nursing home smelling of piss and boredom and rubbing her back to keep the flesh from mortifying and the sores from setting in. You see her hands over yours—you are six then, maybe seven—on a chain looped around a calf's feet sticking out of a blur of blood and fascia; in the headcatch, the cow bellows, and your mother calls, "I know, honey, we're going to get him out of there." She delights in the swallows that nest on her porch every spring and calls to tell you about the three baby killdeer, light as dandelion fluff, that skitter after their parents over the yard. When one of those little chicks dies, she holds it for your small niece to study in matter-of-fact reverence: "Feel how light he is, how small. But look, how wonderful."

The love of our world just is, in you. So is the wonder, everlastingly. You can't not write of it, you can't not love and therefore work for the protection of these creatures and this land. Of all your responsibility and guilt and forecasting and worry and excitement and hope you just know: there's no other way but to do this.

STEP FIVE: USE THE SYSTEM.

Your small town's Planning and Zoning Commission meets to debate a proposed moratorium on frac-sand mining in your county. More than two hundred people fill the courtroom and spill out into the hall. All the public comments but two—both from mining-company representatives—support the moratorium, for which you and your community activist group have been working since the previous fall. Yet several of the Planning and Zoning Commission members—particularly a couple of men in baseball caps—look doubtful, despite the documents in front of them. We're very close to a vote, which will ride on the ten minutes left in the meeting. "Here's a brief list of facts, pro and con," says one commission member, Wendy, smoothly handing everyone a sheet. "It might help." The men browse down the sheet and nod. The moratorium passes with only one dissenting vote and passes the county Board of Supervisors unanimously two weeks later.

You aren't surprised it's Wendy who did it. In her sixties, with a light step and a quick smile, she's a colleague of yours at the local college, where you've just helped celebrate her retirement from the biology department after forty-two years. She's famous for a pet boa constrictor named Sweetie (worn on her shoulders during the occasional lecture), her popularity with students, and her heroic efforts on behalf of advisees. Her first office was a janitor's closet. All her colleagues were men. She's been a mentor to you, and a role model.

And she shows you again, that night, that the rules are made by people who show up and work with what is here.

STEP SIX: DON'T BE NAÏVE.

Except when the rules are made by corporations. You are coming to believe that corporate money in politics and lawmaking may be the single greatest threat not just to lives in a democracy but to democracy itself. Corporations are powerful not just because they've bought politicians and ordinance-writers and permit-approvers but because they've bought us, too, inserting themselves into us as insidiously and completely as Big Brother inhabits Winston Smith by the end of George Orwell's *Nineteen Eighty-Four*. They create our desires and identities and sell them back to us: the appletini-sipping single woman, the stoic farmer for whom resisting Monsanto is un-American, the hip slingers of commercial catch-phrases that supplant our own words. They make questioning the will of any industry that wants something from us seem even more "un-American" than questioning the government itself.

But know a few things. You're not alone. You're not crazy. Honestly acknowledging any emotion—and the prisms of stress and prejudice and personal anxieties that bend it into and out of you—helps you deal with it. Particularly if you're female, being condemned as *liberal* or *radical* for objecting to losing your air, water, and rights to your own property and body really means being condemned for speaking up at all. It really means being condemned for arousing the Victorian lizard-brain twitch that objects to women anywhere but in the house, the shopping mall, or the car on the way to the shopping mall, smiling beatifically and answering, when asked, *Oh, I just vote with my husband on all those sorts of things.* As Rebecca Solnit writes, "Most women fight wars on two fronts, one for whatever the putative topic is and one simply for the right to speak, to have ideas, to be acknowledged to be in possession of facts and truths, to have value, to be a human being." You are in these two wars. Both are real. Read Terry Tempest Williams's beautiful book *When Women Were Birds* and be haunted by its opening image: shelves of her mother's journals, every page blank. Let yourself fill with grief for all the women who never did speak, and all the others who died without ever knowing what hit them.

You're a new woman activist. "New" is a relative term.

Remember that you are still alive. You still have a voice. Use it to speak what you know. And you do know this: it's the good woman, in the most difficult and necessary sense of the word, who forces conversations, who says, *Honey, the drinking has to stop. We are spending too much money. If this behavior does not change I will leave because I cannot raise our children here.*

Anti-fracking and anti-frac-sand-mining activism—to take just one, related set of examples—is forcing a conversation we need. If you do not stand up, no one will. If you do not force the conversation, no one will. *Our credit card's beyond maxed out. The party's over. We've got to wake up.*

STEP SEVEN: KEEP TALKING.

Wake up, honey. We can't afford to live like this anymore.

Academy Awards of Expendable

Susan Truxell Sauter

We took too much.
We licked the bowl,
licked the spoon,
ate the bowl,
the counter, the silverware
the drawer, the floor.

And now a Lifetime
Achievement Award,
featuring West Virginia in Her Starring Role.
       Soundtrack: The Beverly Hill
billies or Deliverance.
Pick one. Pick two. Pick
up your banjo, hill gypsy,
on tiptoe in your own land
clutching your humble
pie wrapped in a miner's kerchief

for the dark days underground.
        Profiled in Style: Carhartt
overalls-by-Blankenship,
        Gucci miner's lamp bag,
make-up by Massey,
(coal-creased skin)
        Special Effects: Three million
pounds of explosives per day.

Our time is limited.
Thanks must be abbreviated.
        A trailer: Oily
nails scrape the layered shale profile—defiled. (*We failed
you failed me.*) Baby drills
down, turns drill, releases
slick water, explode.

Applause now.
Raise your bedecked arms
bedazzled with Patek Phillipe
diamond time baubles, watch
over the collapsed ground,
throw back black
water toasts, etch the effluvia
onto your creamy, downy skin,
drip into your fluffed crevasses,
your Ralph-Laurened satined gowns.
Finish your Marcellus martinis.

I want to thank the titans of industry,
my producers, the consumers, the
stunning script, my stunned surface,
the neighbors who sold out,
the directors of apocalypse. I share
this award with all, including the vigilant
E. Gordon Gee-bow-tied, tongue-
tied board members who sat at the table
of the largest mining disaster
in recent history. And, for you,
the audience so adorned,
let me thank: fur-bearing animals
for dying, the canaries too,
as our oxygen thins worldwide.

Slick:

The (Mis)fortunes of an Oklahoma Oil Town Faithfully Presented in Nine Parts and with Special Attention Paid to Geographic Features Therein.

Kathryn Miles

Mad Tom Slick tripped into Cushing, Oklahoma, in the fall of 1911. Not yet in his third decade, the wildcatter wore his prematurely gray hair in a severe part and his tie in a stiff four-in-hand knot. His black touring car was the only automobile in town. When it rolled past the sandstone buildings on Broadway, the poorer residents of Payne County would sneer. They didn't need another oilman full of empty promises. But Tom Slick knew there were agreements to be had and deals to be struck. If he must, he'd let a landowner name his price or sign a contract in the middle of a busy street. Tom Slick collected leases by the dozens, and it didn't matter a bit that all his wells had thus far turned up dry.

Slick was dogged. Fearless, maybe. He told people he had a sixth sense—that he could smell oil sands like other men smelled perfume. He drove up and down those narrow country roads, blowing dust wherever he went. He pushed out farther and farther from town, collecting more drilling rights as he did. One evening, he forded three creeks, drove twelve miles down a wooded trail, and ran out of time to get back to his hotel. He found a small log house nearby and asked if he could stay the night. The cabin's owner, Frank Wheeler, wanted to say no: his place was already too crowded with nine kids; his wife didn't have enough to feed them that night. But she interceded, and Wheeler allowed the man inside. Slick hadn't intended to negotiate mineral rights from this struggling mason, but by supper's end he found himself offering Wheeler a dollar an acre and 12.5 percent of the profits if Slick's crews turned up any oil. Frank Wheeler would have sold his barren land outright for less than that. And so he gladly rode into town with Slick the next morning, then sat, still as stone, while a notary drew up the paperwork. Neither man knew it, but within a year they'd both be rich.

That the fortunes of Tom Slick and Frank Wheeler were built entirely on happenstance seems fitting for a community that, from its inception, lacked solidity. Twenty years earlier, applications to incorporate the town that would become Cushing were rejected on account of the inferior paper on which plans were drawn. Seventy years prior to that application, Washington Irving, whose tour of the region became the impetus for his 1832 book *A Tour of the Prairies,* wondered aloud how anyone could tolerate the undulating land that seemed more like ocean waves than bedrock. He bemoaned the "poor hungry soil," which he described as "loose and unsound; being little better at times than a mere quicksand." The Pawnee in his company told fantastical tales about thunder residing on that land, lying in wait for warriors foolish enough to try to grab it. Depending upon the story, those who tried to harness the storms were either blasted across the plains or driven down to the underworld, never to be seen again.

Pawnee tales are filled with capricious characters inhabiting the territory that became Cushing. In one, Coyote tries to reclaim a knife he left under a stone for Grandfather Spirit. The stone becomes angry at the selfishness of the wild dog and loosens itself from a hill, rolling after coyote. A colony of bull-bats try to break up the stone with their flatulence, but they are no match for the rolling rock. It chases down Coyote at the edge of a steep bank, where they both tumble over, the stone crushing Coyote as they land. In another tale, a white buffalo sends meteors to rip enormous, fiery holes in the earth, signaling the end of days. In a third, a poor Indian boy finds his fortune with a pony he fashioned out of mud. When the pony is certain the boy has secured his wealth, it returns to the ground, stripped of its spirit. The boy, who would gladly give up his riches to keep his only friend, grieves.

Did the Pawnee know what deep geologic time had left beneath their feet? Hundreds of millions of years ago, a warm salt sea swept across the region. It receded and reformed again and again, alternately leaving layers of marine life and rock sediment with each ebb and flow. Did early Indian explorers know? They would have found fossils, of course—aquatic invertebrates and ancient fish, later sharks and oysters. Probably they would have surmised that where they walked was once water. They would have seen those same undulations called "rolling" by Irving. If the nineteenth century Pawnee had words for such geologic features, they have been lost through assimilation. It would take another fifty years or so before white western geographers would apply their own nomenclature: faults and uplifts, folds and saddles, noses and domes. Each an attempt to explain what eons of flotsam created and, in turn, what the receding sea took away: debris rich in carbon, shale and limestone and sandstone, sometimes heaped into hummocks, more often leveled in an orderly geometry. "Think of tiramisu," offers Jim Scherrer, a contemporary advisor to energy companies. Dessert is not a metaphor that would have resonated with Irving's Pawnee. But they did know that some of those domes leached oil and gas. They saw the way it collected in streambeds; they smelled it emitting from springs. The neighboring Comanche deemed such sites medicinal and fed the oil to their children and animals. The Chickasaw brought fire to natural springs, burning the gas at its source in a continuous elaborate series of torches. In times, these illuminated places became known as places of healing— retreats where oil could make you whole again.

Mad Tom Slick studied the contours on the Wheeler farm for days. He liked the look of the dips and slopes—the way the land seemed to bulge like a blister. He was particularly interested in the western slope of Wheeler's field. That's where Slick located his first well: Wheeler No. 1, he called it.

On March 12, 1912, drillers there hit a gusher at 2,319 feet. That afternoon, over 200 barrels geysered out of the ground before workers could cap the hole with an old metal washtub. Tom Slick's first act was to cut Wheeler's phone line. Next, he covered the oily ground with clean soil, tamping it down to make it look like it had been there forever. Then he hired all the armed guards he could muster. They stood sentry over the Wheeler No. 1 Well, trying to keep secret what was happening behind a new string fence. But everyone knew it was too late: word had spread that Tom Slick finally hit paydirt. Within days, the farm became a tent city for hundreds and then thousands of men and their families looking for work on America's most productive rig. Hannah Wheeler's backwoods kitchen became an industrial cafeteria. Her eight girls worked from dawn until midnight serving meals. Tents became shanties then shotgun shacks—tiny boats on an oatmeal sea.

Those same contours and domes made railbeds and roads difficult to locate in Cushing, and that presented all kinds of problems for oilmen like Slick. The crude was coming out of the ground much faster than anyone could manage. By 1915, over seven hundred wells on Wheeler's field were producing 1.2 million barrels of oil. Each day, pipelines flushed forty thousand of those barrels to refineries in Texas and Kansas; two hundred rail cars carried the crude to additional markets every day. But that wasn't nearly enough. And so the oil spilled onto the land, pooling in low places and contaminating fields. Workers burned off natural gas, thinking it more an irritant than a commodity. Companies built refineries by the dozens in an attempt to keep up with production—in 1920, there were fifty of them. Thirty gasoline plants toiled nearby. But still it wasn't enough. So those same companies began building enormous steel tanks to hold the oil until it could be moved or processed. Workers poured in to help with construction. Towns with names likes Capper, Drumright, and Oilton began to pop up between the tank farms. They brought with them opera houses and creameries, brothels and taverns. The Ku

Klux Klan built its regional headquarters in Oilton. Over six thousand hooded men congregated there under the auspices of a rally to snuff out crime and vice. Later that year, some of those men took off their hoods and danced to Bob Wills and the Texas Playboys. In that moment, western swing was born to the beat of a steel guitar and a couple dozen pumpjacks.

The summer of 1930 was a scorcher. Tom Slick could barely breathe. His doctors said it was goiter and recommended surgery. Slick told them to spare no expense, and so they sent him to Johns Hopkins in Baltimore. The surgery went well, but just afterwards the pressure in Slick's skull became too much. Blood burst from arteries, pooled in his brain. He died on August 16th. The irony of his cause of death was lost on few.

Slick didn't live to see his oil field falter. Neither did Frank Wheeler, who died two years later. But production, which reached its peak in 1916, slowed every year afterward. First refineries shut down, then stores and theaters. Then the railroad stopped service to Cushing. Towns began to evaporate. Oilmen grew worried. They dug their wells wider, then deeper. When that didn't work, they attempted to crack the rock itself, hoping there was still oil to be leached. First they tried corrosives like sulfuric acid. Then they forced sand into the wells with enough velocity to crush the stone that acid couldn't eat away. On St. Patrick's Day, 1949, Erle Halliburton sent a team of his employees to a well in Duncan, Oklahoma, one hundred fifty miles southwest of Cushing. There, they pumped leased oil and one hundred fifty pounds of sand into the well hole—propping agents they called the slurry. Production increased seventy-five percent and the treatment cost Halliburton a mere nine hundred dollars. He decided to patent the process, which he dubbed "hydrafrac." By the end of that year, he had 332 fracking operations underway. Five years later, Halliburton had more than three thousand.

By 1983, Cushing, Oklahoma, didn't have much, but it did have pipelines—hundreds of them. And those big tank farms hadn't gone anywhere, either. Oil—light sweet crude, mostly—flowed freely in and out of Cushing, and it could rest there for however long anyone needed, too. In Cushing, you could buy and sell in real time or bank your oil for future prospects. It was an investor's dream. That year, the New York Mercantile Exchange made Cushing their clearing house. The town of 7,000 was still dirt poor, but now it was the epicenter of the oil world. More and more pipelines snaked into the region—the Pony Express from Wyoming, Spearhead from Illinois, Seaway from the Gulf Coast. The Keystone Pipeline arrived later, bringing with it over five hundred thousand barrels a day. The tank farms grew. And grew. And grew until they could hold more than eighty million barrels—more oil than you'll find in any other place on the planet.

Cushing, said investors, was steady. Except, of course, for the fact that it wasn't really.

The first tremors were barely noticeable—just a few hisses and pops. Cushing residents thought maybe some kids were lighting bottle rockets somewhere. They thought about how dry the fields were around town—about how easy it would be to set them ablaze even by accident. But there was no fire. And the pops got louder. "Like bombs," neighbors said to one another. The first big one happened on a Saturday night in 2011. The Sooners football team was playing Texas A&M. Fans there felt the stadium shake—wondered if the force of their cheering was enough to make all the concrete ripple and sway. Oklahoma didn't get earthquakes. Hell, the only living fault there hadn't seen activity in thirteen hundred years. Probability tables insisted that the chance the state would feel a major quake was less than one percent. Sure, there'd been one in 1952 strong enough to crack the capitol building, but that was supposed to have been an anomaly. Maybe it was. But the 2011 quake was not. Nor were the hundreds and hundreds that followed. Swarms, said seismologists. Faults that had lay dormant for thousands—even millions—of years had been awakened. Why? State geologists said they didn't know. The governor claimed it was an act of God. University scientists disagreed. They pointed to the millions of gallons of saltwater that were being pulled out of each fracking site, only to be injected into basement rock— part of the Arbuckle formation, a deep layer of sediment pocked by pores and cavities. Its "extensive fracture/cavity systems can extend laterally for tens of miles and result in extremely efficient reservoirs that can accept huge volumes of salt water at very low pressures," insisted Amerex Oil's webpage. "Accept," said university scientists, "is a very subjective word." "Shut up," said their chairs and deans. Turns out things like tenure and job security are subjective too.

By March 2014, Oklahoma was the most seismically active state in the lower forty-eight. "Three times as many quakes as California," marveled morning news anchors. They didn't mention the state had surpassed another milestone—3,200 active wastewater disposal wells, many of them in Payne County. The United States Geological Survey recorded eleven earthquakes in one day there, and vibrations were felt in Tulsa, seventy miles to the west.

That same month, the first definitive scholarly study linking Oklahoma's quakes and those 3,200 wastewater injection wells became public. It also marked the sixty-fifth birthday of fracking. The oil industry celebrated in grand style. The American Petroleum Institute sent out tens of thousands of birthday cards featuring stylized old photographs of Oklahoma fracking wells. Superimposed over the cards was whimsical bunting, along with little pink and green cupcakes with thick swirls of frosting and sprinkles. No one in Cushing received a card, despite the fact that they were surrounded by fracking sites, despite the fact that they had already experienced over one hundred earthquakes that year. They're still wondering about the cupcakes.

Oklahoma politics are as complicated as any you'll find. The same state that once relied upon the KKK for law enforcement and homespun entertainment is the state that now depends upon contradictory monetary crossovers: oil executives sit on university boards; elected officials sit on oil boards; state scientists are paid by both. It's a complicated place to take a stand, which is why many residents there don't. Sure, they'll sneer at oilmen the way Cushing residents looked at Mad Tom Slick a century earlier, but saying something outright is a much riskier venture. That's one reason why Oklahoma made international news in April 2015 when state seismologists publicly admitted the connection between wastewater injection wells and the thousands of earthquakes the state has experienced. "Injecting fluid into basement rock is considered a major risk factor for triggering earthquakes," wrote the Oklahoma Geologic Survey in 2015. It sent its seismologists out on the road to give public talks about earthquake preparedness. "Why won't you ban wastewater disposal," asked one Payne County resident at a meeting so packed that people poured out of a five thousand-seat Baptist church. "Because then we wouldn't have data for our studies," said the OGS head. Cushing residents didn't know what to do when they heard that. "We're not rats in a cage," they said, even though they knew they were. Industry insiders said publicly they thought these residents were being ridiculous. "A reaction of panic is not useful," Kim Hatfield, the regulatory chairman of the Oklahoma Independent Petroleum Association and president of Crawley Petroleum, told the *New York Times*.

A day later, the state passed legislation preventing towns and municipalities from banning or placing moratoriums on any activity related to drilling—including the use of wastewater sites. "What the fuck?" asked Jon Stewart on *The Daily Show* that night. "You finally admit fracking has turned your state into a giant Brookstone massage chair and your first response is to ensure that no one can ever stop it. Why?"

A lot of people in Cushing don't have cable. Even if they did, they probably wouldn't have watched the show. But they do know why history unfolds like this in small Oklahoma towns. They know that the only jobs to be had are at the prison or the tank farm—that you can get killed by an inmate an awful lot faster than you can by fumes and contaminated water. They're gamblers. They know the USGS drew a big red bullseye around their town; they know that the chance of a big quake—like a really big quake—has grown exponentially every year. They know that little quakes beget bigger quakes, that the ground is fluid and waves radiate out. There's a big faultline just to their west. It wouldn't take much to wake it up. So every morning, Cushing climbs out of bed and plays the odds. The tanks there were built to withstand tornadoes. No one really knows how they'd fare in a big shake. People there joke that they're like Coyote, always looking over their shoulder. They know what's coming isn't going to be anything as solid as a boulder. No, this one's going to be a tidal wave of oil. A real slick. They just hope they can ride it out.

How oil was first introduced and what affects it caused.

Small Buried Things

Debra Marquart

I. Quake

beyond the groundwater contamination
      now earthquakes in colorado, arkansas
            the swath of states between alabama and montana

a sixfold increase over twentieth century levels
      at least a dozen quakes last year in northern ohio
          one measuring up to 4.8 on the richter scale

speculation about the 30,000 disposal sites
      where fracking wastewater is deposited
          re-injected for final disposal
              into a deeper, unstable layer known
              as basement rock

and speculation about fracking itself
      the deep underground explosions to extract oil

the water causing shifting plates, lubricating faults

look for damage to homes
look for reports of contaminated drinking water
look for increases in breast cancer, miscarriages,
birth defects

we knew   we couldn't say   we didn't know   ground zero

and this just in: the air force reports
        150 minutemen silos still rest underground
        honeycombed deep below
        in northwestern north dakota
        embedded in the fracking zone

in news reports, the commander of the air base says,
      we certainly can co-exist with the oil industry
in news reports, the petroleum council vice president says,
      we're communicating about how we share our territory
in news reports, the air force commander says,
      the drilling frenzy has presented no ill-effects to the ICBMs

the public can be assured
      ultra-sensitive instruments possessed by the air force
          can detect seismic activity as far away as mexico
              capable of tracking even the slight vibrations
              caused by the simplest of thunderstorms

II. Lament

north dakota i'm worried about you
the companies you keep all these new friends north dakota
      beyond the boom, beyond the precious resources
           do you really think they care what becomes of you

north dakota you used to be the shy one
enchanted secret land loved by only a few north dakota

when i traveled away and told people i belonged to you north dakota
      your name rolled awkwardly from their tongues
           a mouth full of rocks, the name of a foreign country

north dakota you were the blushing wallflower
the natural beauty, nearly invisible, always on the periphery
north dakota *the least visited state in the union*

now everyone knows your name north dakota
the blogs and all the papers are talking about you even *60 minutes*
i'm collecting your clippings north dakota
the pictures of you from space
      the flares of natural gas in your northern corner
           like an exploding supernova
                a massive city where no city exists
                    a giant red blight upon the land

and those puncture wounds north dakota take care of yourself
the injection sites I've see them on the maps

eleven thousand active wells one every two miles

all your indicators are up   north dakota
　　　four hundred billion barrels, some estimates say

more oil than we have water to extract
　　　more oil than we have atmosphere to burn

north dakota   you could run the table right now   you could write
　your ticket
　　　so, how can i tell you this? north dakota, your politicians

are co-opted (or cowards or bought-out or honest and thwarted)
　　　they're lowering the tax rate for oil companies
　　　　　they're greasing the wheels that need no greasing
　　　　　they're practically giving the water away

north dakota   dear sleeping beauty　　please, wake up
they have opened you up and said, *come in   take everything*

　　　what will become of your sacred places,
　　　what will become of the prairie dog,
　　　the wolf, the wild horses, the eagle,
　　　the meadowlark, the fox, the elk,
　　　the pronghorn antelope, the rare mountain lion,
　　　the roads, the air, the topsoil,
　　　your people, your people,
　　　what will become of the water?

north dakota   who will ever be able to live with you
once this is all over   i'm speaking to you now
as one wildcat girl   to another   be careful   north dakota

The View From 31,000 Feet:

A Philosopher Looks at Fracking

Kathleen Dean Moore

I. 10 PM. 31,000 FEET OVER NORTH DAKOTA

I was flying the late flight home to PDX, seat 8A on a 737.[†] The pilot's voice came over the intercom, loud enough to make me flinch. "We are flying over North Dakota," he announced. "If you look out the right side of the aircraft, you'll see the famous Bakken shale oil fields, where a big fracking operation is underway." I looked down, as directed. Never have I seen such a thing in my life. The entire plain, horizon to horizon, was studded with flames.

My first reaction, a writer's reaction, was to despair of ever adequately describing the scene to readers. Let me try this: You've seen military cemeteries near battlefields, with closely ranked rows of

---

† Please forgive an old advocate the carbon costs of her flights and join her in agitating, against fossil fuel industry lobbyists, for safe, clean ways to get where our climate work calls us. In the meantime, join her in giving ten percent of all travel costs and all speaking fees to anti-oil organizations at every destination.

crosses as far as you can se[...] think, my
god, how is this possible, t[...] another?
Now imagine that you're in[...]d all those
crosses suddenly burst int[...]hane from
drilling rigs, closely ranke[...] can see in
every direction. You think, my god, how is this possible, that humans
could do this to the Earth?

The obvious answer is, what's possible for humans to do depends
on the story we tell ourselves. A culture embodies a worldview, a set
of answers to the fundamental questions of the human condition:
What is the Earth? What is the place of humans on Earth? How, then,
shall we live? A worldview is so pervasive, so built-in to the structure
of our lives that we don't notice or question it, any more than a trout
questions water. Inside the structure of such a story, acts that would
otherwise be unthinkable, become all that can be thought.

So. What possible story permits this systematic violence, to drill
three-to-five kilometers into the face of the Earth, bore horizontally
for several more kilometers, pump poisoned water under pressure
into the casing, and use explosives to blow holes in the casing wall?
This forces the water into the rock to fracture it, releasing gas and oil.
Fracking.

What story makes this okay? I'm thinking the industrial growth
economy is living in a superhero comic book, the sort of cartoon
fantasies of planetary subjugation and mastery that stir the loins of
boys and Wall Street bankers.

The fantasy would have us believe that we humans are the superheroes of the planet, so different from and superior to the rest of
Earth's things that we might have descended from the sky. The fantasy would have us believe we are in charge of the planet, in control,

Says life is like
a comic book,
and humans are
the "superheros"
—sarcasm

th that lies supine and stupid at our feet. a dangerous planet, in endless compe- winners and losers—that's the way of the ling plants and animals and future gen- to live on the toxic trickle-down excess roes. Of course, superheroes are exempt from the rules that govern the rest of the world and the dumb brutes. Within this story, poisoning ground water and smashing ancient rock to get the riches of gas and oil make perfectly good sense.

But the world doesn't work that way, as we are finding. We can't, in fact, destroy our habitat and one another without destroying our-selves. Based on an outdated scientific view of a mechanistic Earth, the superhero worldview is wildly inconsistent with emerging eco-logical and evolutionary understanding of the place of humans on an interconnected planet. Playing out that script has brought the world to a cosmically dangerous place.

II. 3 PM. 25,000 FEET OVER EASTERN UTAH, STARTING THE DESCENT INTO GRAND JUNCTION

It looks as though the entire plateau below the 737 has broken out in chickenpox. The smooth brown face of the land is everywhere pocked with crusty pimple-like discs, connected with narrow white lines—this feverish land, come down with pox. Here and there below the plane, sometimes beside rivers, are clusters of rectangular ponds, bleeding red or yellow or green.

"What in god's name?" I asked the man in the aisle seat.

"Fracking wells and waste ponds," he said, "and it isn't in God's name."

But that's the question, isn't it? By w~~hat~~ [handwritten note: *Not just thinking about humans; thinking about animals and nature.*] they want from the land—not just wh~~at~~ want—with no regard for the living, a~~nd~~ exists in that place? By what right do over a land of night lizards and woodrats under pinyon pines, of canyon wrens that pour their golden scales down red rocks that once were beaches of an ancestral salt sea, a land of small crossroad towns and, in hidden places among the rocks, drawings of water, human hands, and spiraling time?

The justifying story is that God created it all for us, gave it to us, we human beings, and sent us forth to pillage and possess. And so, like an Easter egg hunt, God says, GO, and the children race forth, knocking down the littlest ones, and take everything they can find. That's the story: we can crack this Earth ~~we~~ ~~~~ l, be- cause Creation is God's gift to ~~H~~ [handwritten note: *Solipsism: the view or theory that the self is all that can be known to exist.*] ~~~~ent a thing to be a reasonable creatur~~e~~ ~~~~ ince it enables one to find or make ~~~~ as a mind to do." But there is no reaso~~n~~ ~~~~ nly. Self-centeredness that borders on ~~~~

The story doesn't make any ratio~~nal sense~~ from God's point of view, if I may be so bold as to imagine that God is a Reasonable Creature. If God created the world to *sustain* humans, then surely He didn't intend for one generation to take it all and leave a ransacked and destabilized world for the children of the next generation. And if God created the world to *delight* humans, as the world clearly delighted God Himself—and it was good and it was good, and God saw that it was good, the birds of the air, the fishes of the sea, twenty thousand species of orchids and whales that teach each other to sing—then surely He is startled and dismayed to see His children rampaging over the land, pushing Tonka trucks while they make growling sounds in their small throats, breaking things with careless disregard.

There's a better story than this. Evolutionary and ecological sciences, indigenous traditions, eastern religions, and the human yearning for kinship are all converging in our time on a different worldview. It tells us that the human species is part of ancient networks of living and dying that emerged, through unimaginable expanses of time, from a universe (and perhaps from a God) that shimmers with creativity. Yale historian Mary Evelyn Tucker tells a version of the story:

> Start at the exact beginning—a roaring force from one unknowable moment, this origin moment...the emergence of the first stars, the first galaxies, the first planetary systems. That one moment gave birth over time to the elements. It took another billion years to create the first cell, and from that cell...the planet ignited with Life...multi-cellular life in the bacteria early on and birds and fish and insects....At the same time, Earth began its adventure of conscious self-awareness, from awareness at the cellular level all the way to our own dreaming, meaning-making, language-bedazzled selves. It's thrilling. It's exciting. It's wonder-inducing.

And it's a call to respect and restraint. This world is irreplaceable, essential, beautiful and fearsome, beyond human understanding, infinitely creative. This is the language of the sacred. In the story of the sacred, reckless destruction is a profanity, a blasphemy, a failure of reverence.

III. 5:30 PM. 4,300 FEET, DESCENDING INTO EUGENE, OREGON
In seat 15A on a fifty-passenger CRJ, I'm pressing my forehead to the window, hoping the pilot will swing over the town on his way

to Mahlon Sweet airport. I want to see a fake pipeline that snakes along an entire neighborhood block in the southeast part of town. The neighbors, led by a creative activist named Mary DeMocker, have plastered huge CONDEMNED signs on their little houses and created a long pipeline from what looks, in the newspaper photo, to be hula hoops and garbage bags. The pilot turns away from town to take us over green fields, but I can read about the guerrilla pipeline in the newspaper folded on my lap.

Mary is telling a new story about the high-pressure pipeline that is planned to bring natural gas from the Rockies and Canada through the alfalfa fields and green mountains of southern Oregon, along wild rivers to an unspoiled estuary on the Oregon coast, where it will be shipped to China. Eventually, it will be returned to Oregon in air pollution, climate change, and inexpensive toys. Already the industry is "negotiating" for rights of way across people's land; if people refuse to settle (and so far, ninety percent have refused), the industry will begin condemnation proceedings. By building a fake pipeline in her neighborhood, Mary is making clear that the effects of fracking are not limited to the fire-and-brimstone fracking fields themselves. Fracking is a monster, as David James Duncan and Rick Bass have said, that extends its tentacles, sucking and grabbing, from the fracking fields into the sea and the unsuspecting future.

The story within which this pipeline is even conceivable is, of course, JOBS—family-wage jobs, to use the cynically value-laden phrase. But Mary's story is about a different set of values. Her neighborhood's pipeline warns of damage to farmland, water, iconic mountains and rivers, estuarine ecosystems that nurture children and salmon. It raises a clear voice in defense of the human right to the material conditions of ongoing *life*, including clean water, clean air, and nontoxic soil. It speaks indignantly against the fracking in-dustry's unrestrained taking, this constant *taking*—land, livelihood, public property, private property, highway rights of way, democracy, health, sea beds, birdsong, silence, and the thriving of our children. For god's sake, is there no limit to this taking?

Yes, of course there is a limit. On a finite planet, the extractive, all-consuming fossil-fuel economy is playing out the story of a cos-mic going-out-of-business sale.

IV. ON THE GROUND, CORVALLIS, OREGON

The time when one set of stories, one worldview, grinds up against another is unstable and dangerous. Things fall apart, the center can-not hold. The facts that people encounter, the feelings they directly experience, no longer fit the story they are born to, but the new sto-ry is not yet fully formed, and who can make sense of this tectonic trembling? Feeling the ground slip away, the old story struggles more and more violently for control. The old story becomes bigger and more complicated and insistent to account for discordant facts, even as its foundations shake. It's a profoundly insecure time. It's a time of bullies.

And then something happens. Some big fact. The old story falls apart, and the new story emerges to take its place. Philosophers call it a "paradigm shift," this avulsion, this sudden shift from one foun-dational understanding to another. No one can know where it be-gins: Copernicus's workshop in Poland. Selma, Alabama. Tiananmen Square. The Berlin Wall. The Bakken fracking fields.

North Dakota? I think maybe so. Fracking has taken the old story of human dominion and exceptionalism to its extreme edge. It is a *reductio ad absurdum* of human greed, to crush and squeeze the last drop of oil from the rocks, to take everything until there is nothing left to take, to wring out the washrag to drink the spilled wine—and to claim that this is right, this is smart, this is worthy of us as rational beings. To persist in the taking until the life-supporting systems of the Earth are destroyed? Suddenly, this is revealed as inconceivable. Literally that, unthinkable. Unthinkable, because it can only make sense inside a system of thought now being shattered with every underground fracturing of ancient rock.

A new story is taking its place, a story that matches what we now know about the way the world actually works, a story that validates what we most deeply value and answers the human yearning for connection to one another, to the astonishing Earth, and to an on-going future. In many ways, it's the rediscovery of an ancient, ancestral story. It's an ecological-ethical account of human kinship with a world that is interconnected, interdependent, finite, resilient, and beautiful. Like any worldview, it provides a measure of what is sensible and good.

Because we understand the world's systems and beings to be interconnected, we realize that all flourishing is mutual, and that damage to any part is damage to the whole. This is the foundation of justice. Because we can understand the world as interdependent, we gratefully acknowledge our dependence on one another and on the life-giving systems of the Earth. This is the foundation of compassion. Because we recognize that the Earth is finite, we embrace an ethic of restraint and precaution to replace a destructive ethos of excess. This is the foundation of prudence. Because we understand the planet's systems to be resilient, we are called to take every possible step to stop the harm and undo the damage we have done. This is the foundation of hope. Because the Earth is beautiful, we will refuse to be made into foot soldiers in the oil industry's wars against the Earth. This is the beginning of moral courage.

Ag Land

Wayne Mennecke

The gentleman
roughneck seated
at the bar
wears crude oil
under his cuticles
and after days
of throwing tongs and
toolpushing deep discoveries
from beneath the
North Dakota wheat,
finally wraps himself
around a cold Coors Light.

The Bakken shale oil
pervades underground
north of here,
converting the blue
and brown wide open
into impromptu trailer parks—

home base for extra pairs
of steel-toed boots and
fire-retardant coveralls.

An earthy sigh
through brown afternoon
teeth is felt in his heavy grunt

and storms of rare periodicity
severe with rain
drench the leather hills
with a geographic tongue

tagging the rich territory
and cold smell
of broken
clotted earth
on every inch
of this man's being.

The Occupation

Paul Bogard

There are no unsacred places;
there are only sacred places
and desecrated places.
—Wendell Berry

I wanted to see, so I went. Like most anyone, I had already heard. Even Merriam-Webster had finally heard, adding the word in 2014 along with "hashtag," "unfriend," and "selfie." But me, I live in Minneapolis, and there is no oil and gas exploration here, no "fracking." I grew up surrounded by lush green leaves and blue lakes where we could swim with loons in summer and the Mississippi flowing. This is my home—educated, liberal, overrun with hipster-beards and bicycles. We would never let fracking happen here.

We know it's happening somewhere—the oilrigs, the man-camps, the noise and dust and light. We may even know about the pollution, the stories of spills, the derailed night-trains billowing flames so hot the local fire-guys stand at a distance and watch. But these are rumors of war, news from a faraway land.

So, I went to southeastern Ohio, near the West Virginia border, Appalachia. I went where a bright woman told me, "They all think we're just retards down here." And I felt like I was visiting a country where a foreign force from a land of white pick-ups and only men, stained and unshaven, had come with their heavy machinery to do what they pleased. And I thought this is an America I don't know, that most of us don't.

That bright woman's nam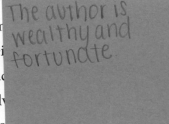ald's; she and her sister Sara are in thei   y shoes, and straight hair past belt bu   he has three missing teeth and one silv   g undercover as we meet and plan o   my lines. Or maybe that's just me, standing quietly as Ted, my host, helps figure out the route. I'm not from here, and I feel out of place. Their accents are Appalachian, and I have to listen hard to understand. I smile and shake hands and give thanks that Ted is here to translate. As we climb into their pickup and start up the highway I jot "hillbillies" in my notebook, a word that says more about me than them. But there's no doubt they're poor, like most people around here.

"This community that I live in is mostly un-educated," says Carrie, sitting in the backseat between Ted and me. "In southeastern Ohio, you're going to find fewer college graduates. You are going to find people that work in factories, that lost their jobs and haven't had a job in three years—most of them longer. They go to church every Sunday. They read their bibles. They believe in God. They believe in paying their taxes and going by the rules. And they think everybody does that."

In other words, a receptive audience for an industry selling easy money.

"The one thing I really would like everyone to know is just how they do this, when they come in," Carrie continues. "When this cap started in 2011, the first thing these companies did is call a meeting in the basement of the local church—and that's the start of the lie, right there. They do that in every community. Then they tell everybody they're going to be rich. They may not say those words, but everybody is high-fiving. They haven't had jobs."

We're in a large white pickup, as though this is the only way to sneak through—like were I in my black VW diesel Sportwagen (forty or more miles-per-gallon easy) I'd be pulled over, questioned, maybe detained.

Carrie and Sara and Jeff tell me the industry goal is to entice as many landowners as possible to sign leases allowing drilling on their property. If any landowners resist, the industry shifts gears, turning neighbor against neighbor, and using a process of "unitization" that allows them to tap the oil and gas lying even under those who don't want drilling on their land.

"Here's the thing that nobody really knows," Carrie says, "just what a predatory industry this is. With unitization, they'll tell you like this, 'You can either sign with us, or you are going to be force-pooled. That's your choice. We are going to take it.'"

How can it feel [handwritten annotation]

"And this is what they won't tell you," Sara turns from the front seat. "Maybe later on down the road, because they've got the rights, they got you in a unit now, they can do this, and this, and this, and this. Anything they want."

Carrie says, "They can kill your mother, and cut her head off if they want to, because that's unitization…"

definition [handwritten annotation]

The word "fracking" is short for "hydraulic fracturing," a process of extracting gas and oil from the ground. The process has been around since the 1940s, but recent advances in technology have led to an explosion of fracking activity across the US. Some people think this the greatest thing ever—finally, we are energy independent! They point to money and jobs gushing into the economy; they wonder how anyone could be against it. Other people, like the public health commissioner of New York, who said he wouldn't want his family to live in a community where fracking was taking place, and the governor of New York, who banned fracking in his state, haven't thought it so great. They point to the potential long-term health costs. "We cannot afford to make a mistake," the commissioner said. "The [significant public health] risks are too great. In fact, they are not even fully known."

So, how does fracking actually work? At Halliburton.com, under "Hydraulic Fracking 101," here's what they say: "Well, it starts with a good bit of water and a lot of sand. Mix those two together, apply a couple thousand pounds of pressure, and introduce them to a reservoir several thousand feet below, often with the help of a small percentage of additives that aid in delivering that solution down the hatch." From there, the blasted water (plus additives) creates tiny fissures in the rock that allow previously inaccessible oil and gas to rush to the well, and voilà, we have a producing well. This process takes, Halliburton says, "3 to 10 days to complete."

Next, "it's time for the operator to remove the water, clearing the way for the newly stimulated well to produce energy for the next 20, 30, 40, even 50 years. The trucks, the pumps, the equipment, and the traffic that were needed to do the job—they're long gone. The operator typically leaves a production valve and collection equipment behind. The rest of the site is remediated, often within 120 days."

The folksy language ("a good bit of water," "down the hatch") makes it sound like these guys are super friendly. Heck, they're only using "a good bit of water" and just a few "additives." The trucks and trucks and more trucks are soon "long gone," and everything is pretty much back to normal in a few months. Except now we have more energy than we ever dreamed possible. What's not to like?

Of course, Halliburton has an interest in making fracking sound simple and clean. They invented hydraulic fracturing in the 1940s and are one of the world's largest suppliers of products and services to the industry. In the United States the name "Halliburton" is well-known because Dick Cheney, Vice President in the George W. Bush administration, was at one time its chief executive. The name "Halliburton" is also familiar because of something called the "Halliburton loophole," which Vice President Cheney ushered into law in 2005. This loophole exempts the fracking industry from key provisions of the Clean Water Act, the Clean Air Act, and the Safe Drinking Water Act, essentially stripping the EPA of its ability to regulate the process. A key aspect of this loophole is that it allows the fracking companies to keep the identity of their "additives" a secret. Their argument is that these additives are proprietary—like McDonald's "special sauce"—and that having to reveal them would hurt competitiveness. They also argue that because fracking is basically safe, why would it need regulation in the first place?

I had heard the Halliburton version of fracking, but then I went to Ohio. "The trucks, the pumps, the equipment, and the traffic that were needed to do the job—they're long gone." That isn't what I saw. What I saw in Ohio is a land under occupation.

In fact, the narrow rural roads are full of trucks, flatbeds hauling heavy machinery, white pickups stuffed with dark men in helmet-like hardhats, the ubiquitous tankers labeled "brine." Most of these trucks sport plates from other states, Texas and Oklahoma especially. Around every corner, another truck of some kind, the gas and oil industry on wheels. Trucks in newly scraped-bare ground lots. Trucks pulled to the sides of roads. Nowhere fracking happens were the roads built for so many trucks. And no one who lives where fracking happens has ever seen so many trucks at once, sometimes dozens an hour. No one has ever heard or smelled anything like the noise, exhaust, and fumes. The trucks Halliburton promised would be "long gone"? They're just down the road at the next new well.

The Halliburton description of fracking is one of reassurance, like, "heck, you'll hardly notice that the industry has come to town." But what it looks like in real life is that the fracking industry has taken over the town.

The same is true with the ground. In fact, the ground has the look of recent battle, torn up and scraped bare, all yet to heal. Long corridors slashed through woods for new pipelines, fresh wounds, fragmentation—forests and fields broken apart. Compressor stations, injection wells, pump jacks, well pads—all of the infrastructure that fracking demands, all of this so new to Ohio. The conquering army has arrived.

The impact of fracking on the ground is tremendous. In a recent study designed to gauge the ecosystem services lost to oil and gas development—such as the ability to grow food, store carbon, support wildlife—scientists found that nearly eight million acres were stripped of vegetation, the equivalent of three Yellowstone National Parks consumed. "For all intents and purposes, these are parking lots," says Brady Allred, an assistant professor of rangeland ecology at the University of Montana. Compared with the size of the US, this acreage might not seem so much. But we are nowhere near the end of the fracking boom; fracking will impact a lot more ground in the next ten, fifteen, twenty years. And because of the roads and other infrastructure needed to support it, each well pad can have an ecological footprint of more than thirty acres. The past ten years, the industry has been drilling fifty thousand wells a year, a trend that many would like to see continue. "Whenever we tell people, they think we're crazy," says Allred. "Nobody has any idea of the magnitude of this."

The day I drive with Carrie, Sara, Jeff, and Ted, we exit the highway and follow back roads until we coast to a hilltop rest. What we see then shocks me. The next hilltop over, maybe one hundred yards away, is sheared, flattened, the bare ground visible where the grass is peeled away. And on this flat pad—like a warehouse thrown up overnight—sits a new compressor station, the first I've seen.

The constant industrial noise, like a factory's churn and whine, is the first thing you notice. The sounds of nature aren't present—no bird songs, crickets, or breeze, just that incessant decibel blur. I have seen industry videos that tout "noise canceling walls" built around compressor stations, but I never saw that in Ohio, in country that until fracking came was quiet.

Then you notice the flames. Called "flares," these flames are "excess" natural gas being burned off. (In North Dakota, so many flares burn that from space at night the Bakken shines as brightly as the nearest largest cities, such as Minneapolis–St. Paul or Chicago.) Shooting from steel pipes that jut above compressor station buildings, the flares remind me of a Greek temple—there might be a chorus in togas nearby—these huge flames topping their pedestals like columned bonfires.

Fences circle most compressor stations, with manned gates where the trucks exit and return. Watching them feels like watching a jail from a distance—somewhere you can't go, somewhere you don't want to. Or, more like watching a military base, the occupiers hidden somewhere inside, slopping down the chow line, laughing at each other's grimy faces, soiled clothes, muddy boots.

Natural gas pipelines need compressor stations at regular intervals to keep the fracked gas moving. In this part of the country, every thirty miles or so another area is chosen, the weight of industry plopped down, and the surface life erased.

At this first compressor station, at the base of the scalped hill, sits Jeff's grandmother's house, small and white. "We was playing here as kids," he says, looking at the compressor station. "This was her and my grandpa's land." The fracking folks wanted this hill and kept after Jeff's grandmother until she finally gave in. *peer pressure*

Imagine having a factory, prison, or military base with flaming spires move in behind wherever you live. Most of us can't, and we wouldn't want to.

But in southeastern Ohio I see the ground we are willing to sacrifice in order to drive our trucks and cars and Sportwagens, in order to cheaply fuel our lives. Far too often these sacrificed areas are in foreign lands, some country we've never heard of and to which we will never travel. Or, these sacrificed areas were long ago lost, ravaged before we were born. What's shocking is when you visit these areas and realize that you are still in present-day America, right now, and that you are witnessing—in the roadside trash, the pollution, the destruction—the result of our constant devouring of earth's resources.

As Jeff says before we turn from the noise and the flames and the decapitated hill, "That's what consumption looks like."

But for all we see above ground, the occupation is at least as widespread under the surface.

We stop at our first injection well. Four enormous drums, industrial barrels twenty-five feet tall, packed together like a giant's stash of beer. I'm not that impressed. No flames, no noise, hardly anyone around. Signs warn us away—private property, etc.—but this injection well and those many others that I'll see don't seem nearly as diabolical as the compressor stations. In fact, they may be more so.

In the Halliburton description of the fracking process, once the oil and gas are flowing, "now it's time for the operator to remove the water" that was used earlier. It isn't just "a good bit of water," though; there are also some "additives." Those additives are chemicals, many of them toxic. When the operator removes the "water," he's bringing up toxic waste.

What chemicals are in this waste? No one knows—no one like you or me, that is. The companies know, but because of the Halliburton loophole, they don't have to tell anyone. And, even though everyone knows the companies are using chemical additives along with their "good bit of water," the waste is considered non-hazardous.

In 1988, the energy industry wrangled a critical change in the federal government's legal definition of waste: all material resulting from the oil and gas drilling process is considered non-hazardous, regardless of its content or toxicity. That's why the tanker trucks clogging the roads of fracking land are labeled "residual waste," or simply "brine," a word that has me thinking of Thanksgiving turkey. "Brine" simply means saturated with salt; it's how my mother treats the bird before cooking it.

When the operator removes this waste, this mystery fluid no one knows the contents of, it has to go somewhere. It's sloshed into tanker trucks and hauled on narrow roads to the nearest injection well, where it's then injected into an old well—back into the ground—and sealed. The fracking industry says not to worry, that it doesn't really matter what's in the waste because it's so safely disposed of, so far below the water table, so away from any danger.

This isn't only happening in Ohio. Nationwide, each year, more than six hundred billion gallons of fracking waste is pumped back into the ground each year. All told, more than 680,000 injection wells dot the country, holding thirty trillion gallons of toxic waste. Why? While fracking waste can be recycled or processed at wastewater treatment facilities, this is far more expensive than simply pumping it into the ground. Also, putting it back under ground removes it from sight. Imagine the complaints if companies were made to create enormous swimming pool-like containers, or rain-gauge-like structures, out in the open where we all could see.

So, while we would never let companies legally dump toxic waste directly into rivers, or spew it onto soil, we allow it to be pumped back deep underground. Until recently, scientists have believed this method of storage to be safe for thousands of years. But that thinking is beginning to change. "Are we heading down a path we might regret in the future?" says Anthony Ingraffea, a Cornell University professor and an outspoken critic of claims that injection wells don't leak. "Yes."

The hundreds of thousands of holes being punched in the ground are changing the earth's geology, adding human-made fractures that allow wastewater to flow more freely. "There's no certainty at all in any of this, and whoever tells you the opposite is not telling you the truth," said Stefan Finsterle, of Lawrence Berkeley National Laboratory. "You have changed the system of pressure and temperature and fracturing, so you don't know how it will behave." In short, critics say, the science that allowed the deep wells of fracking waste hasn't kept up with the current boom. And because all this is happening far below ground, by the time any damage is discovered, it could be too late.

The "too late" that worries scientists most is contaminated groundwater, because once contaminated, groundwater is virtually impossible to clean. In the US, we rely on groundwater in a big way. Collectively more than fifty percent of Americans—currently some one hundred fifty million people—rely on groundwater for their drinking water (in rural areas, ninety-five percent of households, while in urban areas thirty-five percent). And when it comes to agriculture, the numbers are even more staggering: more than eighty percent of our nation's agriculture water needs are met by groundwater.

Again, the oil and gas industry claims there is no danger of contamination from injection wells (or, from surface spills), but many aren't so sure.

"In ten to one hundred years we are going to find out that most of our groundwater is polluted," says Mario Salazar, an engineer who worked for twenty-five years as a technical expert with the EPA's underground injection program in Washington. "A lot of people are going to get sick, and a lot of people may die."

In Ohio, there is growing resistance. More people are realizing that local communities don't benefit from injection wells, for example, and that the only beneficiaries are the well owners and the state, which receive fees paid on the injected waste. Recently, several Ohio communities have enacted laws to control drilling, including Athens, Broadview Heights, Oberlin, Yellow Springs, and Mansfield. Said the Athens city council president: "We're very much concerned about protecting our water supply."

But those concerned about fracking in their communities are finding they have little control. Fracking decisions are made by a Republican-controlled state legislature full of people whose campaigns were heavily financed by the industry and who often live in areas with no fracking. These decisions are enforced by an Ohio Department of Natural Resources that often seems more concerned with protecting industry than the natural resources under its watch. At a recent Ohio DNR open house on fracking, for example, a few dozen mostly middle-aged academics from nearby Kent State were met by fourteen armed Ohio DNR police and a police dog. One man in his eighties told a reporter he had never been to a public meeting "so oversupplied with armed people."

In February 2015 the Ohio Supreme Court, in a four-to-three vote, ruled that cities and counties can neither ban nor regulate fracking through zoning laws or other restrictions. "The Ohio General Assembly has created a zookeeper to feed the elephant in the living room," wrote one dissenting justice. "What the drilling industry has bought and paid for in campaign contributions, they shall receive."

Soon after I returned from Ohio, I had lunch with a friend and told him about my trip. "What more can you say about fracking that hasn't already been said?" he asked. And in many ways that's true. Anyone with an internet connection can find plenty of statistics and articles claiming both bonanza and doom.

But what you can only find by going there is what it feels like on the ground.

I remember that soon after I left the state, the Ohio legislature—while working on a bill to speed up the permitting process for fracking—agreed to hold off for now the urge to open the state parks to gas and oil exploration. It turns out that state forests are already open to fracking, as are—unbelievably—state wildlife areas. And the sense I got was that in time, even the parks would be fair game.

This makes me think about the parks and forests and wildlife areas near my home and what I would do if this occupying force I'd seen in Ohio threatened my trees and lakes and loons and river. I would like to think that I would lock myself to tanker truck tires or pour sugar into pickup gas tanks, that I'd monkey-wrench pump-jacks and burn down man-camps and in every possible way join the resistance.

But resistance against whom? Where does this occupation start, when does it end?

What stays with me is the feeling that not only was this very poor, Appalachian part of southeastern Ohio under occupation, but with its friends in government and industry, and enough voters either tuned out or benefiting from the current situation, this occupation will spread whenever and wherever it desires.

Fracking is unstoppable

Earth Elegy

Stephanie Schultz

I.

Breathe in, breathe out.
Push aside the methanol and mercury
and smell the sweetness of benzene in the air.
Let it relax you and grab a glass of water from the tap.
Don't be afraid of the sparks.
Think of them as cheerleaders,
encouraging you to frack for another day.
Rinse off your dirt and troubles
in a shower of acid and formaldehyde.
Preserve this moment of time.
Soon it will all be over.

II.

You're wondering where all the water is going—
that daily shower in California sucking
the last drops from dried-up Earth.
It's not that. It's the millions of gallons
you use to help shake the soil.

Poor Earth already trembles from shifting plates
and trembles now from chemicals pushed deep down.
Her only defense is to spit new ones back out
in an explosive fit of toxic rage.

III.
What water do we have left?
Just the kind that lights on fire
and whose scent can make us pass out.
The kind that is no longer H2O.
It burns our brains and lungs
and changes who we are.
It gets us thinking about wants and needs,
the here and now and not the future.
It alters our senses and rids us of any we had before.
We start to think this fracking is okay.

Faith on the Front Lines

Louise A. Blum

It is so hot my skin is slick with sweat. My shirt clings to my back with a disagreeable tenacity. The sun bores down with all the subtlety of a drill bit; overhead, a few clouds wrestle half-heartedly for rain and give it up. It is an unseasonably warm day in late May, but then again, aren't all the seasons coming earlier these days? It's hard to remember what the weather is supposed to be. We stand in a line, side by side: before us the road, behind us the vast bowl of Seneca Lake, all around us the rolling hills and vineyards of the New York Finger Lakes. If you kept your eyes closed, you could imagine that all was right with the world. You could forget that beneath the lake lie hundreds of acres of depleted salt caverns and that just behind us, Crestwood Midstream, a Texas-based energy company, is gearing up for work. But of course we are not here to forget. We are here to remind. We form a human blockade before these gates, to prevent the trucks from entering or leaving, to interfere with business, or, at the very least, to bear witness to a crime that is about to be committed: the storage of that liquid propane gas in those abandoned, unlined salt caverns beneath a lake that provides the drinking water for a hundred thousand people.

A constant stream of traffic barrels past; drivers honk vigorously, give us the thumbs up, or, sometimes, a gesture of another kind.

"So why do you do this?" the reporter asks. "Why stand all day in the sun?" My brain struggles to connect some thoughts, but they disperse like the clouds beneath the sun's fierce glare. "What do you hope to accomplish?" he asks.

He's a nice guy; he waits patiently for my response. We had thought that Governor Cuomo's ban on fracking in New York State had put an end to all this. We wouldn't end up like our neighbor, Pennsylvania, its mountains fracked beyond recognition, its streams cloudy, its water poisoned. But the industry's latest response to the claims of pollution has been to propose the use of LPG—that is, liquid petroleum gas—instead of water to frack the wells. Pumping methane, propane, and butane into the earth to fracture rock has been touted as much more "environmentally conscious" than the use of water. Whereas water returns to the surface along with the natural gas, bringing with it all the chemicals that are used in fracking, LPG remains obediently where it's been put: in the earth.

It's hard to wrap one's mind around the environmental consciousness of such a concept.

But it's the perfect way to get around that pesky fracking ban.

Or so they hope.

There are about a dozen of us standing here today. The reporter has been here all day; he's suffered in the sun as well. His question seems the most basic one there is, and yet I don't know how to answer it. What do I hope to accomplish? An end to fossil fuel use? Will standing here on this godforsaken highway, attempting to blockade a multimillion dollar industry really bring an end to the impending catastrophe of climate change?

The reporter smiles at me. Down the line, one of the activists be-gins a song. Unfortunately, it isn't one I know. The blockades at this facility have been ongoing for over six months. Each one has a theme. There have been Birder blockades, Chef blockades, Vintner block-ades, Health Care Workers blockades, Mom blockades, Dad block-ades—we are nothing if not creative. Even Santa Claus got arrested here just before Christmas, prompting an irate letter from one resi-dent citing trauma to his child. Unfortunately his ire was misplaced. Instead of expressing anger with Crestwood for initiating the arrest, he placed the blame on us, the environmentalists. In all the coverage of this issue, those who oppose hydraulic fracturing are continually labeled "environmentalists." Those who support it are referred to as "residents." Never mind that we are residents as well, many for multi-ple generations. The technique is a clever way to paint us as outsiders with agendas, and it works every time.

This particular blockade has been themed "People of Faith." I am not a person of faith; I'm already uneasy, off my game. I know Chris-tianity's come a long ways since the Crusades (and even the 1980s), but as a lesbian, I've learned to be wary around the faithful. When one of my neighbors on the line confesses she's an atheist, I nearly embrace her. I tell her I am too, but the truth is I don't even have the faith for that. Can I really say there is no god? How would I know? Despite a few token pantheists carrying signs that quote Gandhi and the Dalai Lama, there's a heavy emphasis on Judeo-Christianity among these people of faith. There is something unnerving about be-ing surrounded by people in ecclesiastical stoles, and the size of some of those crosses they wear around their necks makes me feel a little faint. The Star of David medallions are only slightly less alarming. I feel like I should come out to them, the way I'm always coming out as a lesbian, but about a much more fundamental difference. I am not a person of faith. I am, in fact, the antithesis. A person beset by doubt.

I've got to hand it to them, however; these people of faith are articulate. "An occupational hazard," one minister comments wryly. They're full of the spirit, too. Every time one of them steps forward to speak, the others pump their fists and call out: "Preach it, sister!" They are great people to put in front of a mic. And they know how to blockade in style: they arrived armed with camp chairs and sun hats, books and sunscreen. The previous week, at the Water Equals Life blockade, we were all so serious we never let go of the banner, never took a break, refused to drink anything because we were so afraid that if we left to pee we'd miss our chance to be arrested. We were so sunburned and dehydrated we couldn't have smiled if we'd tried. If we'd been people of faith we would have been the kind that flagellate themselves. After seven hours in the sun, we had to concede that there would be no deliveries that day. We left dispirited and grim, our feet tired and our backs aching.

The reporter is still standing there, microphone in hand. He's tall and lanky, with grey hair and kind eyes, a ball cap pulled down to shade his face. His question is a fair one: what do I hope to accomplish? I wish I had an answer. The trouble is that deep down I am filled with doubt, and not just about religion, but social change as well. Monumental events have occurred in my lifetime: interracial marriage, same-sex marriage, nuclear disarmament, an end to apartheid, the fall of the Berlin Wall. My mother, born before women had the right to vote, lived just long enough to help elect an African American president. But knowing this doesn't dispel the lingering doubt. There is something so huge about this issue. The energy companies have so much money, so many government subsidies, so much power that (thanks to Dick Cheney, the former CEO of Halliburton) they're exempt from the Clean Water Act. They are soulless in their pursuit of profit. And they have the power of the government behind them: the Federal Energy Regulatory Commission, which has jurisdiction over the storage of LPG, has officially declared that construction can begin immediately, even though geologists have documented the instability of the caverns. Of course, every member of the Commission has ties to the Industry. Why would this surprise me?

And yet it does.

I saw what happened in Pennsylvania with the advent of the fracking industry, welcomed with open arms, given free passage to invade the land, to rape and plunder without penalty or even a severance tax. I know people whose water has been rendered undrinkable, whose land has been decimated, whose lives have become untenable. The shale beneath their feet is not the only thing that's fractured. I've seen families split apart and neighbors turned antagonists by conflicts over lease offers; descendants of miners, who own no land, pitted against those of farmers, who do. And these were people who had so little they'd thought they had nothing left to lose.

There is so little time to change the damage being done by our unrepentant use of fossil fuels—in as little as thirty years, we could render this planet uninhabitable. And my standing in front of this fence is going to stop that?

Around me the People of Faith begin to sing "Amazing Grace," and I join in. Our voices swell up on the first verse, falter on the second. We sing "We Shall Overcome," "America the Beautiful," "This Land is Your Land" (or This Lake is Our Lake), "I'm a Tree on the Water," or something like that. An Iroquois water song that we turn and sing to each of the four directions. I have no idea what the words are. I suggest "We Are the Champions," but no one besides the other atheist has ever heard of Queen. "Seriously?" I ask them again and again. "Freddie Mercury? Where were you in the 70s?" Divinity School is a popular answer.

At fifty-four, I am one of the youngest people here. The weathered farmer to my left is nearly seventy. The woman at the end of the line is ninety. Everyone else is at least in their sixties. They have been standing up for their beliefs—and being arrested for them—a lot longer than I have, and for a lot more issues.

The reporter clears his throat, to prompt me. "An end to climate change?" I try. It comes out sounding more like a question than I'd hoped.

"Seriously," he says.

Sweat trickles down my forehead, pools on my glasses. What do I want? "Perhaps Crestwood will see the light, decide to switch to solar, or wind," I say. It's so lame I nearly roll my eyes.

The reporter smiles again, perhaps a little condescendingly. "*Perhaps, yes*," he says. "But what do you *really* want to accomplish, standing here?"

How has he known to ask *me* this question? Is it so obvious that I am a Person of No Faith? Do I wear my doubt on my face like a brand? The sociologist beside me comes to my rescue. She is articulate beyond reason, and she's not even a preacher. I try to memorize what she is saying, but I am too awestruck by her ability to speak without stammering.

I'm not a complete idiot. I know why we are standing here. We are standing here to block trucks from entering or leaving the facility. We are standing here to physically stop what is happening. We are standing here so Crestwood will have us arrested, so we can clog up the courts and cost them money. So we can call attention to what is happening here. So we can try to prevent disasters such as the one that took place in Kansas, where natural gas stored in salt caverns leaked through underground fissures and caused explosions seven miles away. So we can remind people that not so long ago in a nearby county the collapse of a salt cavern poisoned an aquifer forever. That one of the salt caverns beneath this lake where Crestwood plans to store its gas has already suffered a four hundred thousand ton roof collapse. That Seneca Lake has the highest salinity of any of the Finger Lakes, a clear indication of the fissures that most certainly exist within these caverns. I want to be arrested. Hundreds have been. It is my turn. It is something I can do. It is a concrete action I can take. I have lived and worked in the Twin Tiers of Pennsylvania and New York for nearly half my life. I fell in love with the rivers and the lakes, the hillsides and the trees. I have kayaked every Finger Lake, multiple times. I can put my body in front of a truck. I can go to jail. This is why I am standing here.

This is the simple answer: I want to protect this lake. I believe my actions can help to do that. But then what? Do I want Crestwood to go put its liquid propane gas beneath some other lake? What about the other lakes, the other states, countries, every continent on earth? How can I protect a thing as huge as a planet?

"Are you afraid of being arrested?" the reporter asks the sociologist. She shakes her head. "Absolutely not," she says. I eye her, reverentially. Personally, I am terrified of jail, but I'll do it if I have to.

I am losing faith even in my ability to be arrested. No one has been arrested for the past week and a half because for some time now there have been no trucks for us to stop, most likely because Crestwood has figured out a way around us. We are committed to this form of protest, yet a part of me wants to cross that line and chain myself to the fence. "Oh, they tried that in the very beginning," one of the veteran protesters tells me. "Now they've got injunctions; they can't come within a thousand feet of this place." He shoots me a look. "That means they can't even drive on this road." I stare at him, mesmerized. Route 14 is the only road that runs along the west side of the lake where Crestwood is. This means they have to go all the way around the lake (an eighty-mile circumference) to get to a local winery or a microbrewery, or, I don't know, Canada. We're not trying to be martyrs. We are farmers, vintners, brewers, pastors, teachers, store owners, or, in my case, a vocally challenged writer. This is our land.

But not, apparently, our lake.

Or our water.

Or our road.

I wonder what it is I think the word "faith" means. It has always seemed to me to imply an allegiance of some kind, a tacit agreement not to question whatever the fundamental tenets are. This alone disquiets me. I haven't even said the Pledge of Allegiance since the second grade. Questioning authority comes as naturally to me as breathing.

"You're getting a burn," the woman beside me says. "My bag's over there; I've got a long-sleeved shirt you can wear." A supporter brings us apple slices topped with almond butter, gives us sips of water from a thermos. Another offers crackers and cheese, another fresh asparagus from her garden. I think that there is more than one kind of communion. And more than one way to be political. One of my fellow blockaders tells me to take a break and sit down. I do, and it feels like—well, like heaven. When I return to the line, I ask one of the People of Faith if she's had a break recently. "Why don't you go sit down awhile?" I ask her. She smiles at me gratefully, and hands me her end of the banner.

What sustains me here on this blockade is not religion but collective action—a faith not in the idea of heaven but in the immediacy of earth, in the connection between land and water, in the knowledge that we live in a closed system and that what we have is all we'll ever get and that what we lose is lost forever.

Behind us, a Crestwood pickup truck pulls up. We stretch our banner taut, spread out to fill the driveway, carefully positioned well behind the no trespassing signs. We form a barrier, fragile as our aquifer, formidable as our faith. He won't get through, not on our watch. The door slams and the driver gets out. He looks at us and shakes his head, then pushes a button. We watch the two halves of the chain-link gate slide toward each other, three rows of barbed wire, freshly placed, menacing us from the top, as if we might suddenly decide to climb over, as if we couldn't get there much more easily by kayak, from the other side if we really wanted to. The gate clangs shut, a definitive proclamation, but through its links we can see the lake, its waves sparkling in the sunlight, the second longest of the Finger Lakes and the one with the most water: 4.2 trillion gallons, roughly half of the water in all the Finger Lakes. Six hundred thirty feet deep and thirty-eight miles from end to end, it shines before us, filled with sailboats and jet skis and kayaks, all giving each other space. It is only one gate, easily breached. But we—we are legion. And we will come back. Together, working on all fronts, using all our gifts, we will accomplish change. We will preserve this world, one way or another, for those who will come after us.

This I believe.

The Way of Sorrows

Fiction by John Kenyon

1.

As his car slid along the fresh, gray gravel heaped on the roadbed, Reverend Charles Washburn watched a plume of dust grow in the rearview mirror, loosed from the rocks before dissipating like a wind-drifted contrail. There is no sneaking in the country, he thought, watching his progress marked by the constant quarter-mile ribbon of grit. He returned his gaze to the road ahead and then darted his eyes to the mirror again. A pickup behind him cut through the haze like Moses trying to part the Red Sea. He grabbed his Dictaphone and said as much into it. He could use that in a sermon sometime.

Or rather, next week. While there was no official appeals process, the district superintendent had made it clear he had taken the reverend's request to the bishop, and the answer was still No. *The retirement age is firm,* the email stated. *You turn seventy-two on August 2, so your last service will be July 31.*

That was two weeks away. Two more sermons. Two more chances. He felt guilty, his own desires complicating what should be an orderly process. He had assured his church council that something could be done, and now they would need to accept whatever fill-in the district could find at this late date while they searched for a permanent replacement.

Part of him looked forward to a life in the laity. But he feared he would feel like a criminal sprung after a long sentence. He wasn't accustomed to life on the outside any more than the con, and while the con could re-offend and be sent back, he would be forbidden from even attending his own church, forever locked out. Now there's a topic for a sermon, he thought with a smile.

2.

Sitting at the table in Kyle Hudson's kitchen, Washburn watched the contortions behind the younger man's eyes as he sought to convey his rage in a way that wouldn't upset the minister across from him.

"They just don't f—, they don't care," Kyle said, dropping his gaze to the scarred tabletop.

Kyle was one of the many who had trouble dealing with authority. Not that they rebelled, but they simply didn't know how to act, deference leaving them tongue-tied. Kyle wasn't any different around the preacher now than he had been as a kid. Then, he always watched what he said. The schoolyard taunts and casual curses of the other six days were never to be uttered in front of the reverend on the seventh. But even now, nearing thirty and at a point where such things rarely slipped through his lips even when under stress or after a few too many, he was guarded. He would fumble and stumble, knowing he sounded inarticulate.

Washburn picked up a mason jar of tap water sitting on the table and raised it to eye level. He pulled it close and took a sniff before recoiling with squinted eyes and wrinkled nose.

"You say this can catch fire?"

Kyle nodded and pulled a lighter from the pocket of his work-soiled jeans.

3.

Washburn stepped from his car and checked his reflection in the window. He straightened his collar and pulled on his black jacket. Two weeks from now, he would jump feet-first into retirement, seeking a path toward some form of normalcy. But today, he was in uniform. He wanted to intimidate. The drilling company supervisor, Bart Collins, had agreed to meet with him but asked if they could do so at the trailer being used as an on-site office. Washburn knew the ploy, had used it himself several times. Get someone on your home turf, and it's a significant advantage. When your home turf is a church, the deal is practically closed before a word is said.

He had hoped to do this there, to literally put the fear of God in the man. He knew the supervisor was someone who reported to someone who reported to someone and couldn't completely change the company's plans, but perhaps he could delay, or even move the project away from this spot.

Washburn walked from the parking area and over a rise. As he reached the top, he found himself looking down on a cleared plot of dirt, flattened and groomed. At the edge stood the supervisor's trailer, and in the middle, with nothing near it for several yards in any direction, was a drilling rig. A loud, steady churn filled the air as the drill bit spun, digging its way down through the layers of dirt and rock.

The reverend climbed the steps and entered the trailer. A man behind the lone desk looked up, and then gestured to a seat.

"Sorry about the noise," he said. "How can I help you, Reverend?"

Collins wore a button-down shirt, dark jeans, and work boots. A rim of pressed-down hair marked where a hard hat usually sat on his head. A worker elevated to management, Washburn thought.

"Thank you for meeting with me," Washburn said. "A member of my congregation came to me with a problem, and I hope we can help him solve it."

Collins pursed his lips and widened his eyes as he silently waited for the reverend to continue.

"His place is just on the other side of those trees," Washburn said, pointing to the west beyond the trailer. "And his water has gone bad ever since you folks started your work around here. He has cows, and they're starting to get sick. The place has been in his family for four generations."

The supervisor nodded.

"Not sure what that has to do with us," he said, smiling in a way Washburn found patronizing. "Everything we do is safe and by the book."

Washburn nodded. "Sure, I understand. But every system has flaws, unforeseen occurrences. Isn't it possible—"

"Safe and by the book," Collins repeated.

"Yes, but couldn't you stop and do some tests before you expand?" Washburn said, his voice trailing off.

"Actually, no," the man said. "Lost days are lost money, and we can't afford either."

Washburn leaned forward to raise another issue, but Collins jumped in.

Look," he said, "all kinds of state and federal agencies regulate and monitor our site. I can show you binders full of reports. There is nothing wrong here."

Washburn, feeling outgunned, smiled and stood.

"Of course," he said. "Well, I appreciate your time."

4.

The old woman scoffed at the suggestion.

"Nothing?" she said. "No impact?"

"It's not a joke, mother," Washburn said. "What have I really done?"

The woman turned away from her son and gazed out the window of the nursing home room. At ninety-four she was far from the oldest here but certainly was the most spry. After a moment, she stood and faced her son, who was sitting on the edge of her bed.

"All of the people you have counseled and baptized, married and buried, and set on the righteous path?" she said, pointing a finger at him. "Why, the good Lord Jesus would take you by the ear and give you a good shake to hear you spout such nonsense."

"But that was all just talk," he said. "What have I done?"

She sat on the bed and put a hand on her son's knee.

"Do not let one setback put you in a funk," she said. "You have done great things. And this was the first stumble along this particular path. There will be others before you reach your goal."

Washburn squeezed his mother's hand in thanks.

"I should go," he said. "Ten days to go and a lot of work to do in that time."

5.

On his way out, Washburn stopped to visit with Simon Fields, a member of his congregation who didn't get to services any more. The reverend would pray with him and share news from the church. He also heard the man's complaints, which were usually centered on the food.

"Meat loaf? More like moldy bread loaf! Remember how our mamas used to stretch a package of ground beef by turning the heel of a loaf into crumbs and mixing it all together? Mighty tasty. But these criminals start with a loaf of month-old, green crusty bread, and wipe it on the Styrofoam meat package to pick up some taste and cook it up. Probably throw in the Styrofoam, too, just for more filler! Goddamn, it's awful!"

"Simon, come on now," Washburn said.

"Pardon my language, Reverend, but the Lord himself wouldn't put up with it," Fields said.

Washburn nodded.

"You're probably right," he said. "I'll say something to the administrator."

6.

Washburn flipped through a couple of old *Time* magazines he had liberated from the barbershop so he could read about fracking over lunch at the diner. The cover of the March 2011 issue showed a picture of a chunk of shale with the headline, "This Rock Could Power the World."

Kyle had filled him in a bit—and he had picked up some here and there—but wanted to be better prepared the next time he pleaded his case.

He read about how chemicals were pumped into shale through drilled holes to create cracks to free natural gas. The drilling companies claimed they pumped out the chemicals when they were done, but how do you get something out of all the new cracks that create hundreds, if not thousands of pockets and channels where the chemicals could hide? It seemed perfectly reasonable that they could seep into the groundwater of a neighboring property, as Kyle contended.

The chemicals involved, particularly something called butoxyethanol, were still being studied, but they certainly weren't good for you. This was a farm state, so Washburn knew all about ethanol, and assumed this part of the chemical mix was the reason Kyle could use a glass of drinking water like a camp lantern.

Grace, who had waited on him for years, came over to freshen his coffee. He liked to write his sermons longhand on a legal pad while nursing a cup at the counter.

"You've been eating here a lot lately, Reverend," Grace said. "I thought you fellas had all the home-cooked meals you could stand."

Washburn looked up from his soup.

"I'm retiring soon," he said. "Or rather, being retired. Seems all that goodwill just might have been nothing more than attempts to curry favor with my boss."

"Your boss?" she said. "But you—oh, I get it. That's funny."

7.

Washburn hoped he might know someone out at the drilling site. A personal appeal is difficult to ignore, he knew. He'd learned on his last visit that the supervisor was only on site twice a week. He wanted to avoid Collins and make an appeal directly to the crew doing the work.

He had never been one to adhere strictly to doctrine and assumed that was the reason he had been able to maintain his flock. Rigidness was only welcome in these parts with property lines and bloodlines. Though he avoided reading any Scripture that included the word "begat," his parishioners could recall chapter and verse of their own family trees all the way back to Adam, edited to avoid mention of embarrassing detours taken by their forebears.

That community trait was a source of much of his apprehension about retirement. As a minister, he had a role. Lacking that, he was untethered, someone with few connections to the community.

He parked in the same spot and walked toward the rig. Three men were sitting on the dropped tailgate of an F-150, smoking and talking sports. One of them was Jim Barnes, a man whose pretty young wife brought their two children to Sunday services at least once a month. Washburn decided to focus on him.

"Is that safe to do at a gas drilling rig?" he said, trying for a tone closer to levity than scolding.

Barnes took a long drag to finish his cigarette, then flicked the butt in the direction of the drilling tower.

"Ain't hit nothin' yet, Reverend," he said. "Nothing to burn 'round here, unless the dirt catches."

Washburn smiled and nodded.

"So you're still drilling but aren't to the point where you'll pump in the chemicals?"

One of the other men nodded.

"You got it," he said from around his smoke.

"So, you could still decide not to use them, right?"

"What do you mean?" said the third man.

"I mean, you could decide that they aren't safe and decide against pumping them into the ground," Washburn said.

"Why would we want to do that?" Barnes asked.

Washburn took a step closer. He spoke directly to Barnes.

"Because you have families around here. Your kids drink the water. Your friends and neighbors farm this land."

Barnes jumped down from the tailgate, and Washburn took a step back.

"Trina always comes home spouting your crap about helping your fellow man and turning the other cheek," he said. "Says you think we ought to give our money to poor kids in Africa, or wherever. I barely make enough to buy my girls shoes for school, or to put food on the table. And now you want me to set down my tools? What are my kids supposed to eat? Or wear? This is it around here, man. You want to help, help us find a goddamn job."

Barnes turned and grabbed a scuffed yellow hardhat from the truck bed, then placed it on his head. He walked past Washburn, bumping the reverend's shoulder as he passed.

"Sorry about that, Reverend," said one of the other two men. "But he's right. These are the last jobs in the county. It's this or go hungry."

8.

Washburn had feared—or perhaps hoped for—a mutiny of sorts when he shared with the church council the news from the district supervisor about his forced retirement. But the five women in attendance seemed unmoved. Three stepped up to lead a selection committee that would work with the district on the search and grudgingly agreed when the reverend suggested the men on the council who rarely attended meetings also should be involved.

They took a break for cookies and tea after that and then sat Washburn down for what they really had on their minds.

"Someone needs to do something about that drilling they're doing out by the Hudson place," said Grace Mullins, the youngest member of the council at sixty-eight and always the most vocal.

"Yes, yes." This was Edith Calhoun, the oldest member at a still-sharp eighty-nine, and the one whose support—or lack thereof—could seal a plan's fate.

"I'm on it," Washburn said, trying to put a smile on his face.

"What does that mean—'on it'?" asked Mullins.

"I met with Kyle earlier this week," he said, drawing nods of approval and utterances about what a nice boy Kyle was. "And I have been working with the drilling company."

"Is the drilling still going on?" Calhoun asked.

"Yes, for now," the reverend replied.

"Then the work isn't done."

9.

Another strike against Washburn was that he was one of the most educated people in town at a time when many were turned against the notion of intellect by the same talk radio they sought out as a balm when the world started to seem too complicated. It was a vicious cycle. In some ways, he looked forward to retirement. No longer would he be forced to espouse positions he didn't personally believe. At the same time, he knew this would drive a deeper wedge between him and his community.

But he hoped that intellect would serve him well today. Again in full suit with collar, he was in the waiting room at NaturaCorp, the parent of the firm drilling for natural gas in his area. He had risen early to drive the one hundred seventy miles to the city for a meeting with a vice president in the energy exploration division, the highest rung of the ladder Washburn could reach.

It was a short meeting, with little chance for Washburn to speak. The man read his email the entire time he spouted talking points that were so rote they were recited without inflection. The drilling is minimally invasive. The chemicals are safe. They are retrieved from the shaft. The site is left better than before. Etc., etc.

10.

His final service was as full of celebration as the Methodists would allow, which is to say, not much. He wore a white robe with a bright, green sash, and the full choir augmented by a trumpet and French horn had one extra song planned for the end.

But he hoped his sermon would be the highlight. He layered in passages about Gandhi and Martin Luther King, emphasizing the need to take a stand, that one must answer to God for actions taken against one's fellow man.

He closed with a passage from Leviticus 24 about the need to not stand idly by when witnessing wrong, pounding the pulpit as he recited "fracture for fracture, eye for eye, tooth for tooth," and then sat down. While that verse alone was enough to make clear even to his oft-inattentive flock that he was talking about the need to stop the fracking operation, he hoped the deeper message of the need for the just to prevail against the wicked would resonate.

He had expected applause—this was his last sermon, after all, and surely one of his best—but the extended moment of silence afterward was even better. Let them contemplate *that*, he thought.

When the last notes of music faded from the closing hymn, "Bless-ed Assurance," he walked out to greet his congregants for the final time.

Grace Mullins was first out, as always.

"Wasn't the music just wonderful, Reverend?" she said.

"Yes, it was lovely," he said. "Did you like the message?"

"A little long," she said. "But I suppose you had to use up all of your notes."

As she walked away, more and more of the congregation streamed out, some stopping to shake his hand and wish him luck, others remarking on the beauty of the music. When the last member had passed, he pulled off his robes, left them in the back pew, and headed out the door.

11.

The closest Washburn ever came to being a scofflaw was the shelf of books in his home office that was liberated from the town library. After a few years of being the only person to ever check out something from sparse holdings in the two hundreds, he one day decided to take them all with no intention to return them. The librarian would give a knowing shake of her head when she saw him in the weeks and months after overdue notices began to arrive in the mail, but when she leaped at the chance to be a cataloger at a branch library in the city, recall of his transgression seemed to depart with her.

This, then, would be his most defiant act. Yes, action. This wasn't passing along an old man's complaints about lousy food. It was real.

He lamented that he started so early, on his birthday, of all days. He hadn't really planned, letting passion drive him. The chains sent a chill through his front, the metal rigging of the drill just as cold against his back. At least he could see the sun rising over the hill from his high perch, anticipating the warmth it would bring.

The first workers didn't notice him right away. It wasn't until the supervisor showed that he decided to draw attention to himself.

"Fellas?" he said. "Up here."

They turned as one and looked. The supervisor shielded his eyes against the sun.

"That you, Reverend?"

"Yes. I tried to be reasonable, but now it's time to act," he said.

The supervisor looked at his watch and gave an audible sigh.

"We're planning to inject the chemicals today," he said. "This is going to put us behind schedule."

"Good," Washburn said.

12.

It was the noon hour, and Washburn was tired and thirsty. He hadn't thought about how much energy it took simply to be chained to a metal scaffold.

He watched as a Town Car pulled up at the site. The driver exited and pulled open the rear door. The vice president of energy exploration exited and walked daintily along the dirt to protect what looked like eight hundred dollar shoes.

"You know this won't do a bit of good, don't you?" he said up to Washburn. "We'll cut you down, have you prosecuted for trespassing, and get right back to work. These boys will put in a little overtime to get us back on track. If the media gets wind of this, we'll chalk it up as the work of a lone wacko who seems to be against these fine folks having jobs. Don't even need to embellish on that point. And here, and at hundreds of sites all over the country, we'll keep pulling natural gas out of the ground and selling it to people to heat their homes cheaply, cleanly, and efficiently."

Washburn, glad that chaining himself meant keeping his arms free, clapped loudly.

"Bravo," he said. "If I had been that convincing on Sunday, I might not be the lone wacko out here trying to save us."

13.

Kyle walked up, hat in hand. Washburn beckoned for him to come closer. Kyle grabbed a bar and pulled himself up.

"When are they going to cut you down?" he said.

"They need a special saw, apparently," Washburn said. "At least I did something right."

"You know, when I asked for help, this wasn't what I had in mind."

"Desperate times call for desperate measures, Kyle. Everything else I tried failed. What is it that sportscaster always says? 'Go big or go home'?"

"You watch ESPN?"

"Sure," Washburn said. "Got a beer?"

Kyle was bug-eyed.

"Just kidding," the reverend said. "But I could use something to drink."

Kyle reached into the rucksack on his back and pulled out a plastic bottle of water.

"Thought you might be thirsty. And you sure don't want to drink any water from around here."

Washburn took a long drink. Then he pulled Kyle close and whispered in his ear.

14.

The electric saw operator was getting situated as the first TV satellite trucks pulled up at the site. The vice president scoffed loudly.

"Documenting your own crime, Reverend?" he said. "You know that's how it will play."

Washburn looked down as the camera crews set up.

"Maybe so," he said. "Maybe so."

The saw operator gave the device some juice, and the metal blade screamed as it spun. Washburn called down when the noise stopped.

"Let Kyle here bring me a little something more to drink before you get started," he said. "I won't be able to be heard over the noise of that thing."

The operator looked at the VP, who nodded. Kyle ran over and climbed the tower, then handed Washburn a full bottle, then climbed back down.

Washburn looked down at the cameramen and yelled, "Are you rolling?" All three gave a thumbs up without moving their eyes from their viewfinders.

"Good," Washburn said, as he unscrewed the cap from his bottle. "Kyle here, whose farm is being poisoned by the chemicals being pumped into these wells, just handed me a bottle filled with one of the chemicals from those tanks over there."

The cameras all followed in the direction Washburn pointed, then swung back to the reverend.

"I have been assured at all levels of the company that these chemicals are safe. Well, let's find out."

As he raised the bottle to his lips, the vice president ran to the tower, the supervisor close behind, and they began to climb as the cameras filmed it all.

Vacation Land

Wayne Mennecke

The town stocks its lake
each year with children and trout.
They swim the flecked bottom
between meteors and moon
rocks, large stones concealed
beneath constellations
of floating docks.
Young hands pull hard
on fishing poles.

The fish yank back.

A murk of protest
sidles the rural routes,

bold and red and majuscule
sharp cornered placards

decry fracking and flaring;
a rally in text to save the ground

water animates the commonwealth
interrupts Keystone peace.

Ready to stake the turf with fine print
factions rail against the very idea

of shivering open the earth again
to dispatch poisons

and envenom
our fish and youth still

only in the cradles
of their nurseries.

Frackenstein's Monster:
A History of Unconventional Oil and Gas Technology

(handwritten note: Frackenstein = Frankenstein — a creation that went wrong)

Tyler Priest

The petroleum industry has a gift for reinvention. Over the past one hundred sixty years, geologists and engineers have repeatedly revolutionized the extraction of oil and natural gas from the earth, advancing from cable tools to rotary drill bits, from doodlebugs to three-dimensional seismic, and from land rigs to deepwater platforms. Most innovations did not come as bolts from the blue. Rather, they proceeded incrementally, almost imperceptibly, until observers suddenly realized that the oil and gas industry had become a different kind of creature.

(handwritten margin note: increasing)

In its quest for hydrocarbons, this creature now prowls the American landscape anew, possessing the vision to see into the earth and the power to manipulate deeply embedded rock formations. It can drill down faster and farther than ever, horizontally as well as ver-

(handwritten note: tool)

tically, steering the drill through sharp twists and turns. It navigates by collecting real-time well data about location, pressures, and fluid properties. It sends massive volumes of sand- and chemical-laced water down into a wellbore to fracture and liberate oil and gas from rocks previously thought inaccessible.

Since 2005, the result has been a spectacular expansion of US oil and gas production, reversing decades of decline. Between 2005 and 2015, total US dry natural gas production ballooned from fifty billion cubic feet per day (bcf/d) to seventy-two bcf/d, an *increase* equivalent to the combined 2014 production of Algeria and Canada, two of the top ten gas producers in the world. Most of this rise came from hydraulically fractured shale in Pennsylvania, West Virginia, Texas, Louisiana, and Arkansas, soaring from five bcf/d in 2005 to forty bcf/d in 2015. Domestic oil production, meanwhile, climbed from 5.1 million barrels per day (b/d) in 2005 to 8.7 million b/d in 2015, an *increase* equal to the 2014 annual production from Iraq, the world's sixth largest oil producer. "Tight oil" production from fracking the Bakken formation in North Dakota and the Eagle Ford and Permian Basin regions of Texas accounted for most of this addition. The US oil and gas creature has surged to life again, making the United States the world's largest producer of oil and natural gas and reshaping the global hydrocarbon economy.

Advocating maybe?

The new American oil and gas creation has generated as much fear as celebration. Concerned about harmful environmental effects and disruptive social impacts of unconventional technology, and opposed to any further development of fossil fuel resources, a vocal "anti-fracking" movement has reared up. The word, "frack," beginning with "f" and ending in "ck," has become a curse word, a "linguistic weapon in the shale-gas culture wars."‡ For "fracktivists," the maturing oil and gas creature is not a force for progress but Frackenstein's Monster.

Similar to Mary Shelley's 1818 novel, *Frankenstein: Or, The Modern Prometheus*, hydraulic fracturing has entered the popular imagination as a cautionary tale of frightful technology unleashed upon the land. But as French sociologist and philosopher Bruno Latour observes, "Dr. Frankenstein's crime was not that he invented a creature through some combination of hubris and high technology, but rather he *abandoned the creature to itself.*" Latour goes on to observe, "We confuse the monster for the creator and blame our sins against Nature on our creations." Humans create flawed technologies, not perfect ones. The moral of Shelley's story is that we should not reject our monsters but care for them just like we would our children.

Many Americans might have accepted the Frackenstein Monster if the industry had better cared for it and made it less scary. Leasing and drilling commenced in many places too fast, with too few restraints on unscrupulous operators. It proceeded without baseline studies of possible environmental impacts and the kind of transparency needed to gain public confidence. Attention to environmental controls and appropriate regulations have lagged behind advances in production. In general, the industry has been much better at addressing problems below-ground than above-ground.

Before we decide what to do about Frackenstein's Monster, we must explain the story of its creation, which has a longer and more complicated history than most people realize. Hydraulic fracturing is

---

‡ Many industry partisans insist that "fracking" is correctly spelled "frac'ing." Both are words created by people in the industry to abbreviate "hydraulic fracturing."

one aspect of the story. Equally important, but less often discussed, are the constellation of technologies that made possible deviated or horizontal drilling. In merging fracking with horizontal drilling, the industry's talented if not mad scientists created a technological marvel and changed the course of energy's future. The creature is here to stay. It is too formidable and valuable to kill. The challenge is to make it sociable.

the creature is benefitting energy future. they aren't trying to get rid of it. they are trying to get people to accept it.

THE SETTING

diction

Fracking is a uniquely American invention—for several reasons. First, the unconventional resource base is enormous. It spreads across millions of acres of easily accessible terrain. Second, US laws and policies have been particularly favorable for hydrocarbon extraction, and federal R&D lent crucial backing for the drilling innovations that commercialized fracking in unconventional formations. Finally, the competitive domestic oil and gas industry, consisting of hundreds of small-to-medium-sized companies, lightly touched by government regulation yet often struggling to survive, has had a large appetite for taking risks. Several previously unheralded "independent" firms were in the vanguard of the unconventional revolution.

The scene for this revolution was set during the Cretaceous period, around one hundred million years ago. At that time, a vast shallow sea covered the interior of the North American continent. Microorganisms proliferated in the sun-baked and nutrient-rich waters. Over millions of years, they died and settled onto the silted seafloor, creating mountains of organic material. Eventually, as the ancestral Appalachians and Rocky Mountains eroded, sediment and rock buried and compressed this material along with silt into shale formations. The heat from this compression cooked and transformed the organic material into oil and natural gas. The North American Inland Sea provided the perfect conditions for the creation of extensive shales. These are the source rocks from which oil and gas migrated into conventional sandstone reservoirs in places like Pennsylvania, where oil was first discovered in the United States, and Texas, which became the world capital of oil.

For decades, oilmen dreamed of finding a way to tap into the source rock, but they lacked the technical means of coaxing hydrocarbons from the extremely fine-grained shales. Compared to larger-sized sandstones, shales have much lower porosity (the space between the grains that house oil and gas) and permeability (the ability of a gas or fluid to flow through a porous medium). If a shale pore is the size of a marble, then a sandstone pore has the space of an auditorium. But the promise of extracting hydrocarbons from shale is that they are easy to locate. They are typically several hundred feet thick and extend evenly and contiguously across thousands of square miles. Unlike drilling into folded, faulted, and discontinuous conventional reservoirs, ninety-nine out of every one hundred wells in a known shale deposit is likely to strike petroleum. The difficulty was not in finding the resource but in extracting it.

The United States is a driller's paradise. The number of oil and gas wells that have been drilled and continue to produce in the United States dwarfs every other nation in the world. Between 1949 and 2014, there were 2.5 million oil and gas wells drilled in the United States, more than one-half the global total. This is largely due to the permissive US legal system and policy environment. Unlike most other parts of the world, ownership of mineral rights is not exclusively reserved to the state. Private ownership is widespread and long supported by federal government tax incentives, subsidies, and R&D.

Mineral rights can also be split off from surface ownership. In case of a conflict between the two estates, whoever owns the minerals is dominant. "In legal terms," writes Russell Gold, "the landowner remains the servant while the mineral owner, and the companies that lease these rights, is the master."

more damage

HYDRAULIC FRACTURING

The act of fracturing rock inside a well has been around almost as long as the oil and gas industry itself. In 1865, only a few years after "Colonel" Edwin L. Drake drilled the first commercial oil well in Titusville, Pennsylvania, Colonel Edward A. L. Roberts, who, unlike Drake, was an actual colonel and had served on the Union side in the Civil War, arrived in the area and introduced the idea of dropping explosives into clogged-up or non-productive wells to stimulate oil flow.

Well "shooting" became standard practice in the oil fields and progressed in diverse ways. In 1932, Dow Chemical started experimenting with hydrochloric acid to dissolve rock, a technique known as "pressure parting," which worked in limestones or carbonates, but not sandstones. In the 1930s, Ira McCullough of Los Angeles invented a method of firing bullets to perforate well casing cement. From the late 1950s and through the early 1970s, the oil industry and US Atomic Energy Commission even investigated the possibility of detonating nuclear devices underground to fracture shale. This program ceased due to exorbitant costs and alarm from citizens living near the targeted locations in southern Wyoming.

The use of fluids as a fracturing agent was the brainchild of Riley "Floyd" Farris, a star researcher at Stanolind, the exploration and production subsidiary of Indiana Standard (Amoco). In 1946, Farris and colleague Bob Fast successfully tested Farris's "hydrafrac" theory in the Hugoton natural gas field in southwestern Kansas. To reduce water's friction, along with the number of pumps needed to inject it into the well, Fast added one thousand gallons of napalm-thickened gasoline, followed by a gel breaker, to stimulate the flow of natural gas from a limestone formation. With subsequent wells in East Texas, Farris and Fast mixed in river sand to keep fractures propped open, with positive effects. The technique did not produce gushers, but it proved to be an inexpensive way to extend the life of aging conventional reservoirs. In 1948, Farris patented his hydrafrac process and issued the first license to the Halliburton Oil Well Cementing Company.

Fracking spread swiftly across the oil patch. By 1955, more than one hundred thousand wells had been fracked. Companies experimented with different kinds of fracking fluids, from gelled kerosene, to crude oil, to refined oils. Beginning in 1953, they turned to using more water, with fewer additives. Water was cheaper than crude or gasoline, so it could be pumped economically in larger volumes. The white coats in oil company research labs recommended against water, but field tests indicated otherwise. Injection rates increased with larger horsepower pumps. Improved gelling agents, such as guar crosslinked with borate, were applied. Drillers expanded the range of formations that could be fracked by adding surfactants, which are compounds that lower the surface tension between a liquid and solid, and stabilizing agents like potassium chloride, used to minimize effects on water sensitive constituents like clays. By the 1970s, the introduction of metal-based crosslinking agents further enhanced the viscosity of fracking fluids and enabled the fracturing of higher-temperature wells.

The energy crisis of the early 1970s compelled pathbreaking government research into fracking. In 1976, fears of natural gas shortages motivated Congress to authorize a federal research initiative, the Unconventional Gas Research (UGR) Program, to study technologies for recovering gas from "massive but complex unconventional gas resources, such as "tight" sandstones, Devonian-age shales, coalbed methane, and geopressured aquifers. Funded at around fifteen million dollars per year through 1995, when the program was terminated, the UGR, which became part of the Department of Energy in 1977, worked closely with the industry-sponsored Gas Research Institute (GRI), an R&D organization also created in 1976. The Eastern Gas Shale Program (EGSP) of the UGR pioneered a range of technologies that would later be commercialized in shale development, including "massive hydraulic fracturing," directionally drilled wells, downhole video cameras, nitrogen foam fracturing, and electromagnetic measurement-while-drilling sensors.

UGR researchers published many scientific papers detailing their work in the leading petroleum engineering journals. As oil and gas supplies turned from shortage to glut in the 1980s, few in the industry paid serious attention to this work. One person who did was a Houston-based independent oilman, George Mitchell, who sat on the GRI's board of directors. Mitchell had made his name and launched his company, Mitchell Energy, by discovering the Boonsville Bend gas field in Wise County, north of Fort Worth, Texas. Using Fast and Farris's hydrafracking techniques, he was able to open up the sandstone enough to yield commercial gas wells. Underneath the sandstone, however, lay the five thousand square-mile Barnett Shale, the source rock for Mitchell's gas. The work of the UGR and GRI suggested to Mitchell that this rock might provide an even greater resource.

Encouraged by federal price incentives to produce "unconventional" gas sources, Mitchell Energy attempted its first frack in the Barnett Shale in 1982. Only a trickle of gas came out the well. Not an auspicious beginning, but Mitchell, a steadfast tinkerer, was undeterred. For the next seventeen years, he persisted in drilling test wells into the Barnett, often against the advice of his investors. Finally, in 1998, an enterprising engineer with the company, Nick Steinsberger, tried a different approach. Previously, the company had fracked its shale wells with heavily gelled fluids. Engineers thought gels were necessary to crack the dense shale rocks. The gel did its job, but it also gummed up the cracks and blocked the gas from escaping. Steinsberger proposed a radical and counterintuitive idea. Why not simply use water instead of gel? It was almost as if, as Victor Frankenstein recalls, a light broke in upon Steinsberger from the darkness, "a light so brilliant and wondrous, yet so simple." At the S. H. Griffin #4 well, he pumped in a massive amount of water, with a small amount of sand and surfactants, to see if the pressure would do the trick. After a few days, gas came roaring out. This "slick-water frack" was the critical breakthrough that ignited fracking in the Barnett.

Horizontal Drilling

Fracking did not find wider application until another innovation was combined with the slick-water technique: horizontal drilling. Steinsberger's well was a typical vertical well. It encountered only a couple hundred feet of source rock. If you could turn the well and drill along the length of the shale seam, you could frack thousands of feet of the stuff. In 2001, George Mitchell, already a billionaire in his eighties, sold his company and its fracking discovery for 3.5 billion dollars to the Oklahoma City-based Devon Energy. When Devon successfully coupled horizontal drilling techniques with Mitchell's slick-water fracking, the race to develop unconventional oil and gas reserves began in earnest. Although often mentioned only in passing in stories about fracking, horizontal drilling is the true technological wonder.

Like fracking, the concept of horizontal drilling was nothing new to the oil patch. The first patent for using flexible shafts to rotate drill bits dates back to 1891. Although the prime application was for the dentist's chair, the patent also covered larger scale work. In 1929, the first recorded horizontal well was drilled near Texon, Texas. In subsequent decades, drillers around the world attempted non-straight line, short-radius wells but with only limited success. One problem was the inability to see where you were steering. In drilling a non-vertical well, you had to stop more frequently and take time-consuming surveys before moving on. The other problem was a lack of control over steering the drill. It could often spiral in uncharted directions. A series of interacting innovations, all of which emerged in the wake of the 1970s energy crisis, gradually solved both of these problems and established the commercial viability of horizontal drilling.

The solution to the first problem was finding a way to gather real-time downhole information without having to stop the drill. Traditionally, to collect formation data, drillers would periodically have to pull out the drill and lower a "wireline electric log" into the wellbore. Invented in the 1920s by the French well-services company Schlumberger, this instrument measured electrical (resistivity and conductivity) and acoustic properties. In doing so, it provided inferences about the characteristics of rocks and fluids in the well. Diligent work during the 1960s and 1970s led to a novel advance in well logging, called "mud-pulse telemetry," that transmitted information from the bottom of the well while allowing the drill bit to continue its path of penetration.

Conceived by J. J. Arps in 1964, mud-pulse telemetry used sensors and valves integrated into the drill assembly to convert downhole measurements into a pattern of pulses arranged in a binary code and communicated back to the drill floor. In 1978, after improvements to mud-powered turbine generators and sturdier solid-state electronics, a French-American engineering joint venture, Teleco (which later became part of Baker Hughes), under a contract with the US Department of Energy, introduced the first commercial mud-pulse tool. During the 1980s and 1990s, digital and mechanical refinements to various kinds of "measurement-while-drilling" (MWD) systems employing mud-pulse telemetry provided increasingly fast and reliable information about downhole pressures, temperatures, formation properties (electrical, acoustic, porosity, gamma ray), and wellbore trajectories. MWD improved the speed and accuracy of all kinds of drilling, but it was essential for horizontal wells.

Meanwhile, two other major innovations, along with a host of smaller ones, combined to bring greater power and maneuverability to drilling. Steerable downhole motor systems made their appearance in the late 1980s, and by the late 1990s, "rotary-steerable systems," guided by MWD, vastly increased the speed, reliability, and precision of steerable drilling. In 1982, National OilWell Varco introduced a revolutionary "Top Drive" drilling system, which removed much of the manual labor previously required to drill offshore wells and enabled the handling of longer, heavier sections of drill pipe. By the mid-1990s, portable, AC-powered Top-Drives compact enough to be installed in land-drilling derrick masts were available on the market.

Together with advanced MWD, Top Drives and rotary-steerable systems improved the practicality and economics of horizontal drilling, just as Mitchell Energy unlocked gas from the Barnett Shale.

REANIMATING THE MONSTER

Once word leaked out about Devon's successful marrying of horizontal drilling to slick-water fracking in 2002, a leasing and drilling frenzy commenced in the Barnett, drawing in many other operators. During 2002-2003, more than 1,200 wells were drilled there, a growing percentage of them horizontals. Barnett gas production more than doubled from 0.6 bcf/d in 2002 to 1.4 bcf/d in 2006 (reaching a peak of 6.3 bcf/d in 2011).

Exhilarated by its success and content with its lease position, Devon was in no hurry to expand into other shale regions of the country. But others were, most notably, Aubrey McClendon, the brash, some would say reckless, CEO of another Oklahoma City firm, Chesapeake Energy. After Devon held a coming-out party for Wall Street analysts, writes Gold, Chesapeake "began investing billions of dollars to snap up every drillable acre it could find and kicked the shale boom into overdrive." McClendon first scooped up available acreage in the Barnett, and then in late 2005 he dispatched a battalion of landmen to lock down leases covering the Marcellus Shale in Pennsylvania. By 2008, shale gas operations had swarmed over large swaths of Appalachia. They also seemed to be moving in every direction beyond the Barnett. Southwestern Energy brought the technology to the Fayetteville Shale in Arkansas, and numerous different companies opened other shale basins, notably the Haynesville in Texas-Louisiana and the Woodford in Oklahoma.

Horizontal drilling and fracking had more surprises in store. Conventional wisdom initially held that while fracking might release small gas molecules from tiny cracks and pores in shale, much larger oil molecules would remain trapped. In late 2008, Austin-based Brigham Exploration contradicted this wisdom by producing oil from a ten thousand-foot horizontal well, the Brad Olson 100-15 #1H, from the Bakken formation in North Dakota's Williston Basin. Using "swell packers," giant rubber O-rings that swell up inside the well when exposed to oil, Brigham was able to section off the well and frack the "tight sands" of dolomite with more concentrated force in twenty different stages. Shortly after Brigham's breakthrough, EOG Resources (formerly Enron Oil & Gas), the company that introduced swell packers to North Dakota, demonstrated the efficacy of multistage hydraulic fracturing and horizontal drilling in the giant Eagle Ford shale formation in South Texas. From there, companies used similar technology to revive oil production from the Permian Basin of West Texas and New Mexico.

The unconventional revolution has transformed both oil and gas in the United States, with dramatic effects on the US and global economies. Like every other previous oil and gas boom, the domestic oil and gas industry lately has become a victim of its own success, as oversupply has driven down prices. Pointing to shaky, debt-driven finances and the short lifespan of wells, critics see the end of fracking on the horizon. But unconventional technology is still maturing. Companies are riding out the downturn by continuing to innovate. Microseismic monitoring, for example, has improved the understanding of fracture behavior. Multi-well pad drilling has driven down costs. Wells that are being "refracked," at a fraction of the cost of the initial well, are showing a huge increase in oil and gas recovery. Production is increasing even as the rig count in the field is declining.

The science on the deleterious environmental effects of fracking is still emerging, but mounting evidence points to less harm to water and air than previously alleged. The chemical disclosure registry, FracFocus, founded in 2011 by the Groundwater Protection Council and the Interstate Oil and Gas Compact Commission, has dispelled many of the myths perpetuated about the chemicals used in fracking and the risks to aquifers. A 2015 Syracuse University study convincingly debunked previous research from Duke that linked the existence of methane in Pennsylvania water wells to nearby shale development. Using pre-drill baselines, a dataset a hundred times larger than the Duke studies, and a sampling of almost all the wells in the study area, not just a fraction of them, the Syracuse report established that methane levels in water wells were unrelated to their proximity to oil and gas wells. This came after a 2014 study by researchers at Echelon Consulting, Weatherford Laboratories, and the Pennsylvania Geological Survey that discovered methane in water wells in areas of northeastern Pennsylvania where there was no shale development.

Evidence also points to the relative benefits of shale gas development for fighting climate change. A 2011 Cornell University study suggesting that natural gas produced more harmful emissions than coal was discredited by other studies from Carnegie Mellon, the US Department of Energy, Worldwatch Institute, and MIT, which arrived at the opposite conclusion. A 2014 joint study between the Environmental Defense Fund and the University of Texas-Austin, the first of an ambitious series of methane studies, found that fugitive methane leaks from fracking were much lower than earlier estimates by the

US Environmental Protection Administration. A 2015 publication by air quality consultant Touche Howard made headlines by suggesting that the EDF-UT study underestimated methane releases by relying on a detector that may have been faulty. But the preponderance of evidence, so far, still supports EDF-UT's conclusion that leaks are "well below the threshold for natural gas to retain environmental and climate benefits." According to 2014 findings by the Intergovernmental Panel on Climate Change and the US National Oceanographic and Atmospheric Administration's Earth System Research Laboratory, natural gas produced by fracking has displaced coal in power generation and contributed to a welcome decrease in overall US greenhouse gas emissions.

The oil and gas industry is not hell-bent on ruining the soil, water, and air. Most operators take their environmental responsibilities seriously. Still, like Frankenstein's Monster, the Frackenstein creation has not been adequately socialized. Serious issues confront the industry. These include but are not limited to: noise and surface disruptions from twenty-four-hour drilling near residences; inexcusably poor well designs and cement casings that can lead to gas leaks; troubling disposal practices of massive volumes of water and the unnerving seismic activity associated with them; the sizable flaring of natural gas from unconventional oil wells; the destructive mining of "frac sand" proppants in the Upper Midwest; the dangerous transportation of volatile "light tight oil" by an aging rail system; and the social ills and distortions of boomtown oil and gas activity.

The domestic oil and gas industry's greatest strength, its ability to innovate and move quickly to take advantage of opportunity, is also its greatest weakness. Left unchecked, it can leave regulators and communities in the dust, sowing mistrust along the way. A 2010 interdisciplinary study by MIT, "The Future of Natural Gas," concluded that most problems caused by the industry are manageable through responsible operating practices and sensible, enforceable regulations. But there is so much money on the table and so many valuable energy resources to be claimed that efforts by states to regulate the industry or even by industry to regulate itself are too-often resisted.

We can take one of three approaches to dealing with Frackenstein's Monster. First, we can try to kill it, which some states and countries are attempting to do by banning fracking. This may temporarily solve the "problem." But fracking, like the re-animation of Frankenstein's monster, or Prometheus's gift of fire to mankind (referenced in the title of Shelley's novel), cannot be undone. Fracking is moving to other shale basins around the world and even offshore. Killing the monster is also undesirable, given the environmental advantages of generating electricity from natural gas versus coal and the heavy dependence of the United States on oil and gas for the foreseeable future, regardless of the progress made in renewable energy and conservation.

Another option would be to abandon the monster to its own devices, allowing it to storm into residential communities and the halls of legislatures, like it has in some states. This kind of *laissez-faire* approach is in nobody's interest, not even the industry's, and is not tenable for most communities encroached upon by oil and gas wells.

The last approach is to steer a middle course. We should acknowledge unconventional oil and gas as vital national assets, but we also should place conditions on developing them. Mutual understanding and compromise between the industry and its opponents are necessary to ensure that Frackenstein's Monster and everyone around it live healthy lives. Although not easy, this is really the only choice we have.

Surfacing

Claire Krüesel

I.

Viscosity lowers as temperature rises,
liquids more pliable—willing
to be rushed along
whatever pipe we build them.

True or False: The center of the Earth is very hot.
A student marks False.
I thought it was very cold, she says.

Once, long ago, she was right
and one day she will be right again.

II.

At night, the civilized world blooms gold
to the eyes of roving satellites,
the dark globe
branded by loose pockets
of fire and filament.

The amber body of gasoline
curls into buried drums, to feed
cars and trucks and motorcycles
that illuminate the country
in vanishing glimpses.

The North Dakota Indian Reservations
no longer reserve much, decorous
as charred lace.
The Bakken's fiery tongues
punctuate uncertain fields, hungry now

for oxygen
that will transform the unseen,
that the dinosaurs once breathed.
To each birdlike oil rig
perched on boomtown earth

the worm is a drill-line
to 400 million years ago,
a time machine
humans can't help but call to the surface
for improvements.

III.

One purpose of learning
is to invent. The whipstock
is a curved straw designed
to guzzle
the thick carbon layer of our ancestors

in parallel,
like an infinite road ours for the taking
in all directions,
sunk hands cupping the Earth's stories

while we smolder
its surface, glowy and orbiting
that sense of stillness.

IV.

In geologic cartoons
the Earth's sliced skin reveals an aggregate
of trilobites, dinosaur skulls, femurs,
randomly distributed hollow pebbles, and ferns.

Imagine the wood and metal cartons of cemeteries
added to the image—jumbled,
heaved by an Earth that itches
to grind down those sharp points, to return.

One Well:
Drilling the Bears Ears

Stephen Trimble

I step away from the bladed and dozered scar around the drilling rig. As I move across the top of Cedar Mesa, the disruption at the well site ends with a single stride—as long as I look away. Soft earth replaces rutted mud. Rough-leaved gray-green sagebrush surrounds me and makes a better match for the flawless clarity of the high desert air than the superstructure of the derrick guy-wired erect over its truck bed.

Eastward toward the rim, the sharp fragrance of sage, ambrosial after days of rain, gives way to resiny piñon pine and the juniper-berry scent of gin. This isn't exactly a forest, but the conifers dotting the sagebrush meadows qualify for what we call woodland in Utah—at least ten trees per acre.

One thing proceeds to another. First, one well, then oilfields. First, a barely perceptible gradient, then a canyon.

I pick up a drainage, a subtle incline, then a gully, then a few feet of drop into an eroded stream channel—the South Fork of Fish Creek.

The arroyo slices down through a few feet of soil, twisting downstream to reveal bedrock—Cedar Mesa sandstone, banded Permian sediment from a time before mammals, before dinosaurs. When flash floods come in summer, they roar over these slickrock ledges, grinding with sand and rubble, fluting the stone, moving fresh rubble downstream toward the sea.

The shallow canyon drops a foot to a lower shelf, opens onto a level table of sandstone pocked with shallow rainwater-filled potholes, drops another four feet over a stair-step rim. I clamber down each pour-over.

Spring flowers spatter color under the corkscrew *Bonsai* of the junipers—scarlet Indian paintbrush, yellow wallflower, blossoming cacti: pink and yellow prickly-pear, purple fishhook cactus. I round a corner into a clump of big trees, ponderosa pines, a tangle of willows and green brush. A spring.

Just below the spring, the gentle ramp of rock drops away in a swirl of cross-bedded sandstone and disappears over a cliff, sixty feet down—the headwall of a classic Colorado Plateau canyon. I skirt the rim and look down at the cliffs now rising above a wide canyon bottom, cottonwoods along the stream.

Ravens play in the updrafts. Later, I'll see them flying in groups of twenty, *craaacking* black silhouettes moving across the stormy sky, headed, I'll bet, for a huge communal roost.

I scan the alcoves scalloping the canyon walls. This was Ancestral Puebloan country for nearly two thousand years. I know virtually every bend in a Cedar Mesa canyon yields an archaeological site, and as if on cue, a ruin turns up in the first likely alcove below me. Crumbling but still impressive masonry rises in the shelter of a curving embayment on the south-facing wall of the canyon. Roof beams lie on the jumble of stones. This dwelling is hard to reach, well up the cliff, but it's still likely to have been vandalized by pot hunters—searching for marketable loot maybe a century ago, maybe last week.

I don't need trail instructions, I don't need canyoneering gear. With virtually no effort, I've discovered what I suspected I would discover: I could walk in any direction from the well and quickly find myself in that zone of sacredness where an extraordinary Native presence matches this extraordinary canyon country in spirit.

Cedar Mesa records generations of life here in its stunning inventory of cliff dwellings, rock art, pithouses, and fragments of tools and pottery. The greater Cedar Mesa region shelters more than fifty-six thousand cultural sites that reach back more than twelve thousand years into our past. This remarkable cultural record makes this remote corner of southeastern Utah among the richest archaeological districts in the United States—the nation's most significant unprotected cultural resource. Hikers gravitate to the cliff houses. Archaeologists know that some of the most inconspicuous sites may yield the most important data.

The survey report for the well site reveals seven sites that road-builders and well-drillers must dodge. Indirect effects of development can cause the most harm. The improved road will bring people directly to these sites, with the chance that someone will run their fingers over an ancient pictograph without knowing they can damage the art, pocket an artifact, stumble over a wall, or accidentally use ancient timbers for firewood. We can't measure these indirect effects.

I perch on the rim of this magical canyon, reveling in wildness, in solitude, in my connection to these ancestors of contemporary Pueblo people.

One thing leads to another, and here I am, in wilderness—wild land, for sure, but also land deemed an official "wilderness study area" worthy of designation under the Wilderness Act. The legislation gives us criteria for wilderness, land that retains "its primeval character and influence, without permanent improvements or human habitation." A wilderness "appears to have been affected primarily by the forces of nature, with the imprint of man's work substantially unnoticeable." A wilderness "has outstanding opportunities for solitude or a primitive and unconfined type of recreation." Each of us comes only as "a visitor who does not remain," to a place "where the earth and its community of life are untrammeled."

Here I am, embedded in a tapestry of "untrammeled" landscape and layered history barely a mile from the Hite #1 drilling rig and its fenced wastewater pit, its support wires thrumming in the wind, and its ominous circle of cleared bare ground.

The 2015 Utah State Legislature included Cedar Mesa in an "Energy Zone." The legislators—crusaders for turning over to the state the two-thirds of Utah that's federal land—drafted a resolution declaring grazing and energy and mineral development the "highest and best use" of Cedar Mesa. When ridiculed for this language by appalled citizens, the sponsors softened their language, decreeing that "grazing and environmentally sensitive energy and mineral development" can happen on Cedar Mesa in ways that "protect and preserve scenic and recreational values."

One thing leads to another. The well driller has every intention of industrializing the mesa with dozens of wells. Before we know it, we've confounded the context that gives meaning to these ruins that document centuries of people making the mesa their home.

The Hite #1 drilling rig is the only recent well drilled atop Cedar Mesa. The operator—KP Operations Corporation in nearby Blanding, Utah—may frack the well. Other operators have their eye on other permits to drill on nearby public lands (US Bureau of Land Management lands) and Utah state land.

Conservationists, archaeologists, and Native peoples see the prospect of widespread drilling here as a horrifying threat to wildland values, cultural treasures, and traditional homelands. They have reason to worry, for they don't have to search far to find oilfields farther along on their journey into the frackfuture.

Seventy-five miles north, wells on Big Flat near Moab have industrialized the approach to Canyonlands National Park. But the oil market is awful, and the operator on Big Flat has shut down twenty-five wells and may sell out to cut losses; the disruption remains.

Trek northward for another hundred miles, and you reach the Uinta Basin. Here more than eleven thousand oil and gas wells transformed a major swath of Utah. The busted town of Vernal is a boomtown once again. The same spikes in growth and development that deliver new white F-150 pickups and on-time rent checks create winter ozone levels worse than Los Angeles and spikes in asthma and stillbirths that parallel the leaks in volatile organic compounds from fracked wells.

The boom trumps civil and social harmony. When the local clean air advocates speak up at city council meetings, angry neighbors who drive trucks who sport bumper stickers that say "I ♥ Drilling" have spit on them. Several activists concerned about the effects of drilling and fracking on the community felt so threatened they left town.

Uinta Basin development pushes thousands of wells into wilderness-quality landscapes. Cedar Mesa has one well.

Cedar Mesa also lies at the heart of a proposed 1.9 million-acre Bears Ears protected area. The Bears Ears Coalition has the support of nearly a dozen conservation organizations and twenty-four tribal communities. Named for the twin buttes studding the ridge beyond the Cedar Mesa oil well, a Bears Ears national monument or national conservation area would sweep from the Navajo Nation north through Cedar Mesa to wrap around the east side of Canyonlands National Park. A national preserve here could protect Lockhart Basin and Hatch Point from drilling and fracking—and could even be managed in cooperation with tribes with ancestral ties to the area, including the Navajo (Diné), Ute, San Juan Paiute, the Hopi, Zuni, and other Pueblos.

The canyons, mountains, and mesas of Bears Ears are not a static museum of antiquities. They remain vital as a place of subsistence, spirituality, healing, and contemplation for the Colorado Plateau's Native peoples. Families, elders, and traditional practitioners come quietly to this land to hunt and to gather herbs and firewood, to visit ancestral sites, to perform ceremonies—to "receive healing and nourishment for our spiritual and psychological wellness," in the words of Navajo elder Willie Grayeyes.

One well.

And then, as we see at Canyonlands, it's a procession of twenty-five wells, drilled, linked by pipelines, celebrated by economic boosters, and then shut off during a downturn in oil prices—with the cultural context and integrity of the landscape forever compromised.

Step by step, we jettison restraint, we lose control. Around Vernal, that means a vast network of well pads and roads and fracked oil and gas wells. Ten percent of the methane produced in those gas wells wafts into the airshed over the Uinta Basin—where people and wild-life live and breathe.

One well leads to twenty-five wells leads to a national sacrifice area.

Aldo Leopold grappled with these facts in 1949, when half as many people lived in the United States as do today. He distilled our ethical relationship with the land to an elegantly articulated truth: "A thing is right when it tends to preserve the integrity, stability, and beauty of the biotic community. It is wrong when it tends otherwise."

Philosophers and ecologists have parsed these words for nearly seventy years, and if Leopold were writing now, he might rewrite his ethic to emphasize the dynamic nature of life and the critical need for resilience as we witness the heartbreaking loss of biodiversity—the sixth extinction—and the global consequences of climate change. If he came back to revise *A Sand County Almanac*, Leopold still could rely on integrity as our touchstone. Integrity in a landscape leads to resilience.

"Integrity, stability and beauty," alas, are the last things on the minds of those hoping for a perpetual oil and gas boom. Corporate capitalism is implacable. We can't win the argument to preserve the Bears Ears region for purely ecological or ethical reasons when our greediest opponents don't care, our children are distracted by their technology, and our friends and neighbors are worried about keeping their jobs.

At the same time, we can't write off the value of nature to our psychological and physical well-being. Intensive drilling and fracking disrupts the integrity of natural systems so violently that we cannot know the ultimate consequences. Without experiencing places made sacred by our ancestors' lives interwoven with wildness, what will humans become? What will humans lose? Without interconnected wildlands, dependable springs, and undamaged habitats for wintering, dispersal, and reproduction, what will happen to the native species that bring this land to life?

The native elders who speak on behalf of the Bears Ears can answer these questions. They are deeply conservative and thoughtful people. They choose words that resonate with Leopold's. They emphasize healing over polarization.

> Whenever we build a hogan on a location, we conduct a ceremony to live in harmony with mother earth as long as the sun shines, the wind blows and the river flows. According to this natural law, all the former residential sites are sacred.
> —Mary Johnson, Diné

> ...southeastern Utah was not an empty place that no one wanted but just waiting to be inhabited by European settlers or discovered as a recreation playground, but rather it was and remains our home. We have and still do cherish these lands. We remain hopeful that a time of healing created by our own renewed involvement for these lands may be upon us.
> —Willie Grayeyes, Diné

We can preserve the integrity of our relationship with this dynamic land. We have the power to come to a place where Navajo people, the Diné, would say, "It is finished in beauty"—as they say at the end of their healing Enemy Way ceremony.

In that concluding line of the Navajo prayer for balance and beauty, "it" is life. "It" is ceremony. "It" is our long procession of decisions about places like Cedar Mesa.

"It" must not be finished in disruption.

Energy,

Mort Malkin

not seen except
in light, not heard
outside of sound, but

measured across
dimensions of
whimsy from nano

to mondo. How
precise it seems,
how well controlled we

believe until
[who could have known]
a great oops goes down.

The World Below

Rick Bass

I loved to chase and hunt the oil; I absolutely loved finding it. Pursuing it—mapping it, dreaming it, drilling for it—was such an intense and passionate journey that even the dry holes were exciting. You weren't happy when you missed, but even that was stimulating. I guess you could say it was addictive.

You could say without a shadow of a doubt it was addictive.

I never worked on public lands, sensitive lands. My work was in farmers' soybean fields, drilling only a few thousand feet down into old Paleozoic sandstones with an 8-7/8" borehole. A pinprick. This won't hardly hurt at all.

But I saw some things. I learned some things. And like any of us, I know the sound of a lie.

When the BP well blew out in the Gulf of Mexico, something that wasn't reported in the press was how deep the blowing-out formation was, or if BP even knew from what formation the hydrocarbons were spewing, or how thick the formation was. Typically, the larger reservoirs are deeper, but the fact that this one blew black oil (Deeper horizons generally contain oil that is greenish in color and, at even greater depths, exist as natural gas rather than oil, due to the pressure at those depths.) suggests the reservoir might have been a shallower formation than BP was prepared for. Shallower, and yet larger: maybe the biggest in the world.

Why did that formation, that reservoir, behave so monstrously, with enormous and apparently increasing flow rates? Was an immense salt dome—plumes of salt, ten thousand feet thick—swelling and bulging, flowing like a gel and squeezing this reservoir? Was this reservoir belching its gas in erratic hiccups and burps? We still don't know. The earth is mysterious, the earth is alive—even as we war against it.

Hunting fossil fuels of any sort has always been primitive, as unsophisticated as whaling. In every way, it's seat-of-the-pants work. This is why pipelines always fail. Always. It's hasty and half-assed and done under harsh conditions and on the cheap. They tell us they are in control when nothing could be further from the truth. The earth cannot be controlled. Each year, we know this more and more, and yet each year, we fail to overthrow our fossil fuel imprisonment.

[handwritten margin note: Blames pipeline creators for harsh oil released in ocean]

We always bail out oil corporations. They get the oil, they poison the land; we pay for the clean up, we pay for the oil. The equation is monstrous. And nowhere more so than in fracking.

Industry insists that the formations are sealed off by concrete. This is a lie. Formations are constructed of an infinite number of vertical and horizontal fissures, and that's even before the underground dynamite starts going off. The earth's buried laminae are as porous, as permeable, as skin. What goes into the ground will always find its way to water, which then always finds its way to us, until we have used all the water. Until all the water is gone.

It's not enough to distrust BP, or any large corporation. These days, you have to know how they work: the ins and outs of each industry and the secret heart, secret ethos that governs the movement of each through our stressed history.

One of the penalties of an ecological education, wrote the American ecologist Aldo Leopold seventy years ago, *is that one lives alone in a world of wounds*. The shrimp were on their way toward extinction in the Gulf anyway, due to our channelization of the Mississippi River, the great source of their nutrients. Our flood control of that vast living system is robbing billions of tons of sediment that would otherwise keep building the Louisiana delta and marshes that the shrimp nurseries depend upon, and which serve as a buffer against hurricanes. South Louisiana is sinking fast without this sediment. As Louisiana sinks, the shrimp populations will blaze out with one final pulse of productivity—but there is no more capital; the marshes are living on the debt of the past.

Ruining animals and economies as well

That doesn't make what BP did right, nor Imperial Oil, up in the tar sands. Why is every one of us not clogging the judicial system with peaceful protests and arrests? Why are we allowing such misery to be firehosed into a waiting future that can make no choices, can only receive the toxic fruit of our passivity?

When I remember my days in the oilfield, there's one image that comes to me most often.

I was in my late twenties, working eighty-hour weeks, burning the candle at both ends. We were drilling a deep well down in the

pushing himself past his limit.

swamps of south Louisiana, in a location so far beyond the end of the road that we had to construct our own floating road of lashed-to-gether boards—broad planks of cypress—to go out into the swamp another mile or two, extending our reach. It was a big project.

It was dark, and I was driving through the swamp and through the forest in a heavy rain, going a little too fast. The floating road was slightly underwater in places so often I was bluffing, aiming the company vehicle from point A to point C, trusting that my route would get me there and that I would stay on the floating road. As if my will or desire alone was enough to make it so.

I drifted off, however, and the car nosed down into the swamp.

I can barely recall the strength and nonchalance of the young man I was—the hunger I had for the world. It didn't bother me at all that water was now gushing into the car. It wasn't my car, it was the company's. I was on a mission. I picked up the well logs, the priceless documents I was trying to deliver, put them in my briefcase, climbed out through the window, and continued down the slick board road, ankle-deep in swamp.

I walked for a long time. Finally I saw a faint lone light in the woods, an old shack with one lantern. If the light had not been burning I would never have believed anyone inhabited the leaning shanty.

I hated to do it, but I needed to see if they had a phone. I paused, then rapped on the door.

I had assumed the inhabitants were sleeping soundly—my approach had been soundless—but so instantaneous came the reply to my knock that the two events, my knock and the dweller's subsequent inquiry, seemed simultaneous.

The voice of an old black woman rang like a shot—"State yo' name!"—and was shouted with such authority that I didn't hesitate in the least, but answered her right back, "Rick Bass!"—as if the name of a twenty-five year-old white boy from Hinds County meant anything.

Miraculously—as if I had uttered the one correct phrase that would gain entrance—she opened the door and welcomed me in. For whatever reason.

She didn't have a phone. I couldn't tell if it was a question of access, or if she simply scorned them. I visited a while, then went on up the muddy road, toward the tiny backwoods village several miles distant and the cinder block hotel where I could rent an old beater car from the night clerk, a sled that would get me back to Jackson before daylight, so that the glowing lit world, the world of myth—the world we did not yet know enough not to believe in—could continue.

Looking back, everything about my answer amazes me: the unapologetic cheeriness of it, neither arrogant nor insouciant. I knew it explained nothing but that no explanation was needed. I was on a mission: not quite a hero but a messenger from the gods. If she wanted to have my name—if that was what was most important—she could have it. The night was young, and I would get out of this just fine. I had made it out to the rig all right—the glow of the tower, isolated in that dark forest, looked like the glow that might come from the landing of an extraterrestrial spacecraft, and steam rose from the pipe that was being pulled from the hole, the drill string steaming and smoking like something being born, the roar of diesel engines like that from an army, if not a civilization, a town. I had been there, gathered the treasure, and was headed back.

I had the treasure in hand and drove the logs back to Jackson, several hours north. It seems impossible that not so long ago there were no cell phones or scanners, no computers or even faxes. We had a crude portable instrument called a telecopier that we carried in a briefcase, like a portable nuclear bomb, but its transmission of the logs was blurry and stuttery; the preferred method was for me to just ferry them to the bosses, as if by Pony Express, pulling up in front of their mansions at three, four in the morning, knocking on the door.

They answered in their bathrobes. We would spread the paper logs out on the table like Biblical documents. The light seemed different, back then and at that hour, in the kitchen—a gold light—while we studied the logs and saw, for the first time, the fruit of our labors, the degree of our wealth, with exhaustion limning the edges of our vision. Who would not want to live such a life? We kept the world going. We carried the world on our backs while the world slept, and we kept it going; for as long as we kept going forward, the world kept going forward. Oil kept the world going?

I remember those days so well: the power and heady feeling of being needed, of possessing a valuable and honored skill.

Fracking has nothing to do with the hunt. It's not geology any more, it's just mining. Playing with explosives. Blow up a bunch of crap underground, pump poison down the hole, suck up the gas, then move on. Next explosion. And on, and on, destroying every aquifer. Don't look back, destroy it all. Against fracking...

Fossil fuel corporations possess now—in addition to the right of eminent domain, to seize our private property—the constitutional rights of an individual but none of the responsibilities. Corporations are buying up ad space on the internet under the phrase "oil spill." The industry is contributing billions of dollars to Congresspeople who serve them. The oil companies tell us we can't afford to combat global warming and that we can't afford to not drill in sensitive areas. Such bans will make the cost of oil go up, they cry. But what we are not acknowledging in our addiction is that oil and gas are so very heavily subsidized. For the major oil and gas companies—the corporations' costs are externalized to the consumer, so that our energy consumption, energy addiction, is dependent upon such sleight-of-hand accountings as those that attend to any of the other socialized price supports that right-wingers pretend to find so terrifying. The cost of fracking—the idea that a cup of poisoned, undrinkable water has the same value as a cup of clean water—is one of those huge and many hidden costs. The accounting is false. Part of the secret of "cheap oil," as we are finding out, is that it is not so cheap. Instead, we are paying our giddy debt forward with ferocious momentum.

Even when they drill on US-held properties—public land and government leases owned by the government—the major oil and gas companies refuse to let the government know what's going on: even when the government is a partner in the drilling, via farm-out and override royalty interests, the oil companies refuse to let the government see certain papers and equations, such as the formulas of the fracture fluid the oil companies inject into the well bores and into those public lands, where the fluids make their way into public drinking supplies. It's a trade secret, the oil companies say.

What's going on in these deepwater prospects is reminiscent of gold mining in the 1880s, where crews would turn giant hydraulic hoses on entire mountains and sluice the whole mountain away, washing it downstream, bathing the spoils in acid in order to gather the scant nuggets within. Barbaric, we say of those miners and those times, primitive. Their technology was not commensurate with their appetites. But it never will be. Human appetites have always been ex-

[handwritten margin note: Fracking may be cheap, but it's not really cheap]

[handwritten margin note: Oil companies know they are bring harm to others]

panding at a rate greater than the rate of technological advance; this disparity is what helps fuel technological advance.

In the Gulf, and in the Arctic and in the heartland, the pipelines will always break, the frac fluid will always find its way back to us. In 2014, the White House released a draft report highlighting what geologists such as myself already know: the risks of drilling in America's Arctic could be catastrophic. The Department of the Interior acknowledged that there is a seventy-five percent chance that one or more large oil spills (more than forty-two thousand gallons of oil) would occur if the leases are developed. There is no way to clean up an oil spill in Arctic conditions.

There's so much at risk. America's Arctic Ocean is one of the most unique marine ecosystems in the world—and home to our most beloved marine creatures, including whales, walrus, seals, polar bears, and countless birds. What's more, what happens in the Arctic impacts all of us. The National Climate Assessment found that, "Alaska has warmed twice as fast as the rest of the nation, bringing widespread impacts. Sea ice is rapidly receding and glaciers are shrinking. Thawing permafrost is leading to more wildfire, and affecting infrastructure and wildlife habitat. Rising ocean temperatures and acidification will alter valuable marine fisheries." Fracking is affecting Arctic animals and water negatively

Shell Oil has already tried and failed—ending its 2012 Arctic drilling season with only two holes drilled. It finished that year with one drilling rig running aground off of Kodiak Island, Alaska, its containment dome crushed like a "beer can" during testing, and both of its rigs are under investigation.

We can't trust oil companies to get it right. Nor can they trust themselves. It is time for our government to protect America's Arctic

Ocean. Here, as in the deepwater Gulf, it is unsafe and irresponsible to drill.

In every industry, in every country, our old economic models are falling apart like wet cardboard. The old models hold up for a while, but they are not holding up anymore, and hurricane season is upon us.

Maybe it sounds hypocritical, my nostalgia for the hunt—and maybe I am something of a hypocrite. I have solar panels on my home, I drive an old Subaru—but still, all of our footprints are huge, and our appetites are huge. We want more. We use the right light bulbs, we bicycle, we avoid factory-farmed meat—but we are all wedded to oil.

Every time we blink, we are using oil. The food distribution systems that give us our calories—to blink, to speak, to laugh and love, to rail against the government—come from petroleum. We are choking and drowning on oil; our affluence is short-lived and unsustainable, and now, with the same sudden panic known perhaps to the brown pelicans whose oil-soaked wings will no longer keep them aloft or afloat, we are sinking, overburdened, going under.

Oil is in everything we do.

People are scrambling, trying to rescue us, and we are trying to rescue each other, but we are all going under.

The true price of oil in my estimation is currently somewhere around three hundred dollars a barrel. Too expensive! we cry, even as we are shelling out three hundred twenty-five dollars for it right now. Carrying BP's water. Carrying their buckets of oil-soaked sand. Carrying the trillions of dollars of productivity being lost due to global warming.

Like children, or adolescents, we ignore the consequences of our choices, day after day. It is all imperfectly accounted for; we have all been living too high, hiding the true costs of things.

I left Mississippi almost thirty years ago, moved to northwest Montana for the beauty. I couldn't have landed in more of a bull's-eye of hydrocarbon war if I'd tried.

So much of this revolution, this war, this ecocide, has Montana in its sights. The proposed Keystone XL pipeline, mining the tar sands of Alberta to ship to Asia—while destroying the carbon-absorbing overburden of boreal forest, the great green lungs of North America—threatens to come right through Montana. It must and will be stopped. Inspired by the Bakken oil boom and the coal liquidation in southwestern Montana, the oil and coal executives are lusting to extract as much energy as possible from the Rocky Mountain Front.

Because I grew up as an oil geologist, it's not with the sometimes-reflexive reaction of a typical treehugger that I report from Montana with the news that the future of the world may well depend upon obscure and little-known events that are taking place in wild windy country far from the rest of humankind's notice. In a state with a population of roughly one million, the fate or future of seven billion—and all who come afterward—rests.

The Rocky Mountain Front—the ecological foundations of the east side of Glacier National Park—is being ripped open as if with a hacksaw, in the pursuit of the Bakken Shale, which requires the fracking process to exhume it.

Further, the winding one-lane road through that prairie is being widened into an industrial corridor—in plain sight of our most beautiful national park—to better service the open pit mining of the dirtiest oil on earth, the tar sands' sludge deposits in Alberta. Canada hopes to ship this sludge-oil to Asia via the construction of the proposed Keystone XL pipeline, through the heart of middle America. According to NASA scientist James Hansen, whose science regarding global warming we should have listened to more closely over forty years ago, the development of the tar sands will carry us beyond the threshold where any other mitigation might be effective.

And in another corner of Montana, an equally insidious scam is going on—one which, if allowed to proceed, will also sink this beautiful world, or at least our own species's place in it, along with that of so many other species.

In extreme southeastern Montana, the digging-up of millions of tons of sub-bituminous coal too dirty to burn in this country is occurring. The coal is being sold for pennies-on-the-dollar to China, in order to get that energy market hooked on the dirtiest fossil fuel imaginable—coal too sulfurous and toxic to burn in this country. (And what a farce to believe or pretend that the windborne ribbons of lead and mercury and arsenic will not drift back onto our shores two weeks later; and what an act of great immorality, foisting that toxic coal onto a nation whose citizens lack the means of democratic protest.)

It's an international scheme devised to get developing countries hooked on a cheap and toxic product through subsidies, to encourage infrastructure development—investment in a new generation of dirty coal burning plants throughout the developing world—before cutting off that cheap supply, in order to control the price. A rail line—the Tongue River Railroad, funded in part by Warren Buffet—is being proposed to ferry the coal in open boxcars miles long, from Otter Creek to older, existing rail lines. Cattle ranches that have been in families for generations will be taken by eminent domain. (A few years ago, the Republican-led state legislature passed a bill allowing such takings to occur if they served commerce or energy, or both.)

Otter Creek would not seem to be a dramatic beauty compared to other Montana landscapes—quiet ranching families, a bucolic stream in an otherwise dry land, sandstone buttes, sage, wind, sky—and it's hard to imagine that buried just beneath the surface are the old oxygen-starved marshes where everything rotted before being buried by the slow breath of time. Now, seized by the most ferocious of addictions, we seek to crack open, fracture, and inhale those sulfurous old rotting swamps.

Warren Buffet's coal train—countless chains of mile-long open-topped boxcars trundling steadfastly across the West and then the Pacific Northwest to their ports in Washington and thence to Asia, with the trains' black dust swirling through one community after another—boxcars clanking at all hours of the night at decibels beyond the limits of any ordinance, yet immune to such laws—will result in increased respiratory ailments and other illnesses and will guarantee the rising of sea levels to the point that we could see as many as a billion environmental refugees in our lifetime.

Montana is already shipping its dirty coal to Asia. Otter Creek's additional billion-plus metric tons will simply seal our fates, forcing us into another century of a coal economy.

If you knew what was happening, if you saw that widening pit, and those seemingly innocuous slow-moving trains through Montana, and out of Montana, day after day and month after month and year after year, what would you do?

If you could speak up and out against a slow motion train wreck, you would, wouldn't you?

Surely, armed with the facts from this distant, beautiful land, we will this time choose another course.

I don't understand why everyone in the United States is not hand-cuffing themselves to the gates of power. We can no longer pretend we don't know what is happening. We know what's happening and it's time to act.

At what point then do we, in our inattention, become them? At what point?

This is the dangerous truth: The hungers in the men and women who are working the crane lift-gear levers of those blind husks and blind souls of corporations are every bit as hungry as you or I. They are good at what they do and are on fire with their hunger, and they will track the oil down to the ends of the earth. They have no limits on their powers.

They will find it, and will drill into it, no matter what the depth, no matter what the pressure. They will explode the foundations of this country: the very earth on which we stand.

White Butte

Taylor Brorby

I make a list. Bullion Butte. Camels Hump Butte. Pretty Butte. Tracy Mountain. Sentinel Butte. At the bottom I scrawl White Butte. At 3,506 feet, White Butte is the highest point in North Dakota. I want to climb it. I want to say that I have done what few North Dakotans do—hike and climb buttes. Living in Dickinson, now known as a boomtown, I know that I will need to get out—I will need to get away from the Ford F250s, the "Drill, Baby, Drill!" bumper stickers, and the T-shirts painted with pump jacks reading, "Going Deep and Pumping Hard" and "Frack that Hole." This, I think, is not the North Dakota I know.

In 2013, due to the rampant development of big oil, the State Attorney General proposed legislation that would set aside eighteen geological and manmade features in North Dakota, known as the Eighteen Extraordinary Places. In 2014, returning to North Dakota, I decided to escape from oil development and delve deep into the Badlands in the western half of the state.

Since childhood, I have been afraid of standing too close to the edge of cliffs, outcrops, and lookout points. My knees grow weak and my eyes go in and out of focus, the world waves and whirls around me. At five, I climbed to the top of the state capitol of North Dakota, nineteen stories tall, bounding up the stairs, only to feel nauseous on the top observatory level, surveying the unfolding miles of prairie.

"Mom, are we almost there?" I holler from the backseat of our van. I'm seven and traveling to see my Uncle Kevin and Aunt Kim in Gillette, Wyoming.

"No, Taylor, we're still in North Dakota, and we have a long ways to go."

Humpf. I hate long car rides. After hours of gazing around at the sweeping cropland and prairie grass I become bored. I can't read in the car. (I get nauseous.) I can't take a nap. (I might miss the action.) So I ask my mother for navigational updates, noting the surrounding landscape so that in future travels I can estimate how much time remains until we reach our destination.

"What's that?" I ask, curious at the rising white rock outside of the car window.

My parents and sister have decided to ignore me.

"Ahem. What's that over there?"

"That's White Butte," my dad says, "the highest point in North Dakota."

"It looks pretty small to me," I cluck. I continue to think out loud, noting that my father is keeping his attention on the road, my mother is reading a book, and my sister is listening to Sir Mix-a-Lot on her Walkman.

We wind past White Butte, slowing into the small, twenty-six person town of Amidon, North Dakota. Known as the smallest incorporated county seat, Amidon is home to an antique store and a restaurant, Georgia's & The Owl, which reports that patrons travel up to one hundred fifty miles for its fine Italian cuisine.

Highway 85 swings south, and we continue past White Butte, nearing the southeastern most corner of the Badlands, which, from my vantage point, are just beyond my view.

As we enter Bowman, North Dakota, the last town before South Dakota, my father begins what is known as The Family Ritual.

"Taylor."

"I know, Dad. When you were eighteen and playing baseball here and the bases were loaded, you cranked out an infield grand slam, winning the game. Yeah, I know."

My father deflates.

I live in Dickinson with Peter, a local English professor, his girlfriend, Nancy, and their two pets, a dog named Herman and a cross-eyed Siamese cat named Bailey. Bailey's a nightmare. Every morning he begins his vocal warm-up between four and five, sauntering around the house. Me-ow. And then a little louder. Meee-ow. Followed by what sounds like descending musical scales. Booow, as if impersonating Herman. I eventually sleep with earplugs, attempting to cancel out the morning wakeup routine.

I tell Peter and Nancy my plan to climb buttes and bluffs in western North Dakota. Nancy, who's just recently moved back to the state after living for eighteen years in Asheville, North Carolina, asks if she and Peter could join me sometime. I think it over. I want time to myself. I want to push myself in this dry western landscape, spending time on craggy outcrops, overlooking rippling sagebrush and brown creeks. I crave solitude in a landscape that seems to be overcome by industrialization.

"Let me try one or two buttes by myself first," I say, "I want to see if I like hiking."

As we dive into South Dakota I think the land changes, but really it's just the quality of the roads.

"Mom. What just happened?" I holler.

Confirmation. We've entered South Dakota which, my mother remarks, does not have good roadways.

Imagination fades as we drive through this new landscape. Surely it must be new, I think. After all, it's South—not North—Dakota.

We meet fewer cars on the road. There is a haunting quality to this landscape where I see no fields. We are now in ranching country, marked by rough-hewn land. Prairie grass cuts through the earth, fighting for room amongst clay-ridden soil.

Peter and Nancy can come. After summiting Camel's Hump Butte and Tracy Mountain I decide that they will not slow me down. Memorial Day, I say, will be the day that we climb the highest point in North Dakota, White Butte. Nancy and Peter nod.

Gillette, Wyoming, known as the "Energy Capital of the Nation," is where we travel to visit my mother's brother, Kevin. Kevin works in the coal industry, like my mother. He and his wife, Kim, have one child, a son, Kerry. Kerry is tough—he wrestles, shoves around cousins smaller than him, and speaks like a surfer, saying, "Dude" and "Right on."

Kerry is two years older than my sister, who is ten years older than me. I prepare for this trip by understanding that I will not have a playmate. Some nights I will play my cousin's Super Nintendo, other nights I'll draw in my sketchbook or play cards with the adults, hovering between childhood and adulthood while my sister gets to enjoy adolescence.

I tell Peter and Nancy to be prepared to see rattlesnakes. Riddled throughout southwestern North Dakota, rattlesnakes add a percussive quality to the symphony of sound flowing across the prairie. I've been worried about them during my weekend hikes, fearing what might happen should I be bitten. Wikipedia assures me that seven to eight thousand people are bitten by venomous snakes each year in the United States, and around five victims die. Most deaths, reports Wikipedia, occur between six and forty-eight hours after the bite. Plenty of time, I assure myself, to seek medical treatment.

I haven't seen a rattlesnake yet on my hikes, and since I know Peter and Nancy did not grow up hunting and fishing, I want to remind them to be on the lookout for our scaly friends. We all agree we should not take Herman; none of us want to worry about an Irish Setter dying from a snakebite.

During a game of cards, while I'm drawing alone in my uncle's basement, I sketch White Butte. I rush upstairs to show my mother.

"That's nice, Taylor," she waves, trying to stay focused on what my aunt is telling her.

"No, Mom, you don't get it. I want to climb White Butte."

"Sure, Taylor, sure." She brushes me aside.

I return to the basement, wondering how many steps it takes a seven year-old to climb White Butte. Five thousand? Ten thousand? Maybe if I run it'll take fewer steps! I turn back to my drawing, focusing on the craggy rocks at the top of the butte. I'm an expert at drawing rocks.

We turn off of Highway 85 onto gravel roads. "Taylor, are you sure we can do this?" Nancy asks.

"I've been climbing buttes all summer and haven't gotten in trouble yet."

The truth is I am worried on my afternoon hiking excursions. I don't know what the penalty is for trespassing in North Dakota. Surely, I think, the family that owns the land around White Butte has to be filled with generous people; after all, they own the highest point in North Dakota.

"Don't we need a GPS to get there?" Peter asks.

"It's right there, Peter," I say, pointing to what looks like a low-lying hill. Yes, it is there, but White Butte sprawls out from its tallest point, like a blanket when grabbed in the center and lifted from the ground, creating ridges and valleys. I have no idea how far we will have to walk from the road to get to White Butte, how many rattlesnake holes we'll have to cross before we reach the summit.

Leaving Gillette is never bittersweet for me. Spending days in what feels like a type of limbo, I am ready to go home.

I launch into the van, my Minnesota Twins hat plopped on my head.

"Let's go, Mom!"

My uncle bounds towards me. "Hey, you, big guy, it was so good to see you," he says and squeezes me harder and tighter, giving me a bear hug, his salt-and-pepper whiskers prickling my face. "Come back and see us soon."

As we pull out of the driveway I sigh, knowing that soon we'll return home, back to the world of North Dakota and normalcy.

As we snake along 69th Street Southwest, I tell Peter and Nancy that this is the closest we are probably going to get. I see a farmstead in the distance. Shit. I hope the family is friendly, is used to visitors climbing to the top of White Butte, and aren't the gun-carrying-try-to-outrun-our-bullets type of people.

I park the car.

We unload the car and lather our skin in white coats of sunscreen.

"That doesn't look too hard," Nancy says.

She's right. Though White Butte is North Dakota's tallest point, it is the tallest point due to its elevation from sea level. The butte, up close, is humble.

The first mile to the butte is marked by truck grooves, overgrown in grass. Peter leaves the trail to examine an abandoned farmstead, its wood warped and faded from years of heat and snow, rainwater and sunshine. Peter narrates his experience, saying how this would be the perfect setting for a murder.

The sky turns pink and purple and fuchsia as we enter North Dakota. I tell my parents that I don't want to stop in Bowman for supper, saying I want to stop in Dickinson instead. My sister agrees. What I don't tell anyone is that I want to see White Butte before the sun sets. I want to drink in the stark ridgeway against a lilac sky. "Hurry, Dad, hurry, we're going to miss White Butte."

White Butte, unlike the other buttes of western North Dakota, is cut by a walking path.

"Well, I don't think we have to worry about getting shot," I yell back to Peter and Nancy. "It seems the owners expect hikers on their property."

"Unless this is their private mountain bike path," shouts Peter.

To our left, along the section line, are "posted" signs, signs used to alert hunters, fishermen, hikers that land is not to be entered without the permission of the owner. Faded black ink reads, "No hunting without the written permission of Frank Bulzasky."

Still in the car at 8:45 PM, I claw at the back of my mother's seat. We are nearly to Amidon.

I will get to see my sacred treasure before nightfall, my jewel of the prairie. I lean forward in my seat, squinting to make out the alabaster ridge against the violet sky. As we pass by the butte I press my nose and hands against the window, trying to reach out and touch its rough ridges. I whisper to my sister that some day I will climb White Butte. She turns up her Walkman.

The soil crusting White Butte crumbles beneath our feet. Already in May the earth of western North Dakota is dry. I lead the pack, with Nancy gazing out to the ocean of farmland.

"This is an island on the prairie," she says.

I mull over whether bringing Peter and Nancy was the right decision. Wading through sagebrush, clambering over craggy outcrops, and listening to the flick, flick, flick of notebook pages from the top of buttes is my own personal retreat.

The well-worn trail snakes along the eastern ridge of White Butte, passing through a small grove of trees, littered with cow pies, and interrupted by gopher holes. The path banks right, dipping below the ridge and pressing against orange and green lichen-covered scoria rocks. I touch the rock, press my fingers into the water-worn holes, notice the fine sand sitting in the rocks' pores. How long has the wind and water been at work on White Butte? I wonder.

Before the summit of White Butte, the footpath swerves left against the scoria outcrop, flowing forward, straight towards the meat of the butte. I think of how I've been preparing for this, how I've been yearning to see the rounded curve of the earth from White Butte.

My knees lift toward my chest. Taking higher and higher steps I know the top is just out of sight. Between two rocks stands a silver stake from the Department of Interior, weathered from exposure to ice and snow and sand. "For information write Washington, D.C., Geological Survey."

From the top of White Butte the earth spreads like rippled water. Fields fold away from the base of White Butte and, in the distance, the scoria-ridden outline of the Badlands are in faded relief. Pounded into the rock atop White Butte is another stake from the United States Department of the Interior, declaring White Butte the tallest point in North Dakota. Nestled beside the stake are two green ammo cans filled with two guestbooks, fake $1,000 bills, business cards, and a package of Whoppers, the malted milk balls. Drawings, doodlings, and business information fill the guestbooks. On November 6, 2010, Melissa Bachump wrote: "Open deer season, happy to not have been shot! I own land right next to here. Third [time] coming to this spot, and I love it! Run, run, climb, and glad I didn't die!"

People from Alabama, Kansas, North Carolina, Chicago, Chico have all reached the summit of White Butte.

Mike Morris from New Jersey completed visiting all 50 states when he came to North Dakota on July 9, 2012, and climbed White Butte. The Moody family—Tom, 46; Kelly, 45; Cohen, 14; Kiernan, 12; Claedon, 10; and Kylan, 8—from Pearland, Texas, reached the top a month later. "The Tom," from North Dakota and Tashina, from Portland, summited the tallest peak in North Dakota on August 1,

2013, writing, "Boo-Yah!" and remarked that they climbed the butte "without the use of supplemental oxygen."

I sit on the summit of White Butte, gaze into the distant Badlands, grass pricking across my legs. I think about the future of White Butte in the midst of an oil boom. The panorama contains no view of pump jacks rocking up and down like chickens pecking at scratch. Would the journal entries start reading like a litany of lamentations about the progression of oil development? Would the view—or the land—be brought to ruin?

I look at the ridges, the only geography that breaks the horizon, and trace a rough-hewn land in a world of industrial progress. I want to protect White Butte, I want my nephews to climb this mound of earth and rock and gaze out into the unfolding landscape, run along its ridges of alabaster dirt, and imprint this western landscape upon their minds.

That night, as we return home, I dream of White Butte, carpeted with a black sky and glinting stars.

Perhaps I climbed the rock in an attempt to root myself in place, to write an essay out of love, speaking on behalf of a silent sentinel of the prairie. Perhaps I climbed the rock to satisfy a childhood question, pulling at the back of my brain: What does the world look like from the top of White Butte? Perhaps I climbed the butte to mark a moment in time, conscious of a summer spent driving through my homeland, witnessing the decapitation of buttes, looking as if they were sliced sideways by swords, opened to bleed black blood, to savor a moment listening to the simple sound of switchgrass swaying in the wind.

Towards

Beth Loffreda

"In midair, we have discovered we are already falling inside the abyss."
—Timothy Morton, *Hyperobjects*

"We are a fucking disgrace."
—C. A. Conrad, "The Queer Voice"

During the summer of 2015 when I sat down to write this essay, the sky above Laramie achieved a certain look, a peculiar blurred and staticky quality as if a wall of hard gray hung just behind the fragile blue. It's a look I've learned occurs when there's smoke in the air. I checked InciWeb, which tabulates all of the forest fires in the nation, but there was nothing active in Wyoming or any of our neighboring states. Later I learned the smoke was from fires burning in Canada.

Wyoming could be understood as a long experiment in unsustainability. By this I mean Wyoming's history as a territory and then a state, in other words a recent history, a political confection, a concatenation of interlinked economic, racial, gendered powers. I won't make claims for what came before. Even as I write the phrase "long experiment" though, I think it might be better to say a multitude of unsustainabilities small and large that from a certain vantage looks like a continuous and durable life. That vantage being one of the main contributions of culture to personal experience: it channels and smooths one's unknowing, makes certain untenabilities unremarkable—or at least livable for the time being, which is the time in which a life happens.

Here is a time-being that is simultaneously livable from one angle and untenable from another: my heat came on three times during the July in which I was finishing this essay. My house is heated by natural gas; I cook with it. My home's electricity is almost entirely derived from burned coal and natural gas. My kitchen lights are on, and my laptop is plugged in and charging. I walk to work but drive several times a week, 15 or 40 miles, to the nearby mountains to hike and bike. I have a 2006 Nissan Xterra and a 1995 Ford F-150, neither of which can manage 25 mpg, highway. I don't water my lawn, but I have a lawn. Most of the vegetables I eat are trucked from Colorado and California. The growing season here is very short, and it is not difficult to look around most any month of the year and think there would be more hospitable environments for human life, but nevertheless life is conveyed here in a mildly-subsistent version of how it is conveyed everywhere else in America: fewer Walmarts, fewer supermarkets, no malls, but still we're in the network. Amazon Prime's two-day delivery is reliably accomplished. I teach at the University of Wyoming where there is no state income tax and instead the state's budget and thus my salary that pays for my heated house and vegetables and Prime deliveries, are heavily reliant on severance taxes on natural resource extraction—coal, gas, oil, uranium—and on power production. In 2013 Wyoming ranked second in the nation for its all-source CO_2 emission rate because of the latter activity. This summer a study of the greater Yellowstone ecosystem argued that due to climate warming a regular and catastrophic cycle of forest fire will likely lead to the transformation of most of Yellowstone into grassland well before the end of the century. The mountains that I drive to in order to hike and bike have been decimated by the pine beetle, a species buoyed by drought and warming and which in some nearby areas has killed over 90 percent of the lodgepole pines. The beetle's kill rate has declined in recent years, the Forest Service notes, due to "susceptible host depletion." Which means there are no more trees to die.

Inside what I am describing is a daily life I like as much as I find it a fucking disgrace. This is the enmeshment I don't know how to think all the way through: how we go about our days as if the precipice isn't there, as if we haven't already fallen off of it. Which has its particular intensity in Wyoming, as the energy industry, gas and oil and coal, drilling and fracking and burning, permeates every aspect of life here: ecology, politics, culture, education. The lobby of the School of Energy Resources on my campus is adorned with the names of fossil fuel companies. The School's work is deeply devoted to what it calls enhanced forms of fuel recovery, terminology into which fracking dissolves without a sound. The signs of the "play" are everywhere. The other day I read a university press release that employed this word to describe the work experience of a new hire, his time in the Bakken and Marcellus shale "plays." This word kills me. Its dismally ironic erasure of the ecological violence necessary to wresting the remnants of the long dead out of the ground to burn; the spread into all linguistic arenas of the exotic forms of risk that began regularly crashing economies in the new millennium. And also its acknowledgment of the theatrical, that one product of these activities is the masking of the abyssal fall with a feeling of narrative continuity, the sense of a future: life is what it will be, roughly. My entire life—by which I mean the way I live and pay for my days—is in large part underwritten by the play. It must be something akin to what it was like to live as a white person in the days of westward expansion: no matter one's personal beliefs and activities, one was carried along on a current that projected a future that was in fact predicated on certain cascading and unequally-enveloping destructions.

Certain communities feel the untenabilities first, experience their sharpening into a crisis. There are towns in Wyoming that already reside on that nearing horizon where the abyss, no matter the play, is already unmasked. You end up on that horizon these days if you are unlucky enough to live on ground above oil or gas and if you're inside a political situation willing to demolish whatever meaning once attached to your citizenhood, if such meaning ever existed, in favor of other forms of capital. Pavillion is a particularly infamous example, featured in the documentary *Gasland*, which tracked the impacts of fracking on small American communities. Pavillion is a town of just over 230 people in west-central Wyoming. In 2011 a preliminary study by the EPA linked dirty water outside the town to nearby fracking activities by the Encana Corporation. Water samples collected for the study held methane, benzene, arsenic, and 2-BEp, among other contaminants. The report was met by intense criticism from the energy industry and conservative politicians, as well as some Pavillion residents; in response, the EPA withdrew from the investigation and handed it over to the state. Encana contributed 1.5 million dollars to support the state's investigation. Wyoming offered cisterns to residents. The federal Agency for Toxic Substances and Disease Registry advised residents not to drink tap water, or cook or bathe with it. Many in town are divided against one another, those who want the justice of an answer and those who want the justice of continuing employment and unravaged property values. Today the full investigation still drags on. Encana and other members of the energy industry assert that their activities are safe and that to reveal their proprietary blends of fracking chemicals would harm their competitiveness. People still live in Pavillion, for the time being. The time being the life in which you shouldn't bathe in or drink the water and yet everything is fine. That's crazy-making. That's the horizon drawing near, and soon it will be crazy-making for all of us, if it isn't already.

That nearing horizon might also be an old past catching up with us too. By which I mean there's a rhetoric people in energy-industry-dependent places like Wyoming hear a lot: some things need to give. We need these industries, and what they need needs to become our priority too. The sound of that rhetoric is a paternalistic kind of realism, a pragmatism that disguises its own violence in condescension: you can't have everything you want. It's the very old sound of men in power. Some things need to give.

A few years ago I went to Casper, Wyoming, for a conference. I was put up at a hotel that, when I arrived, appeared to be a complex of buildings, poorly lit, pocked with bars. I arrived at the hotel late, and when I walked into the lobby to check in I felt immediately if obscurely that I had entered the kind of situation that if you are a woman you not-infrequently enter, in which men remind you that you are safe only because they allow you to be: i.e., the kind of situation that reminds you of your essential situation, that you are unsafe. You wouldn't have been able to nail the sensation to a witnessable fact: a statement, a gesture, an obvious aggression. The violence was purely ambient. It made me feel a little crazy. Nothing was going to happen, but it was in the air that it could—that the social contract, such as it is, that I moved through the world believing kept me relatively safe in hotel lobbies was a fragile and revocable thing. When I turned to leave the lobby I saw a sign for the "lingerie nights" the hotel was hosting. Outside, groups of men hung out in the parking lots. I did not see another woman anywhere. It felt ineffably bad. The next morning one of the conference hosts said the hotel was often used by men from the oil and gas fields on their days off, in town with money to spend. In the daylight it seemed merely to be a hotel; I felt newly crazy regarding the kind of crazy I'd felt the night before.

Last winter a student of mine, the daughter of a woman who owns a small-town Wyoming bar, talked briefly with me about the influx of male workers with energy-derived money: the effect she described was in essence a certain unavoidably-felt if unmetricable sexual degradation. Students in other classes, waitresses back in their hometowns, described the same thing: the more cash in hand, the more diminishment of respect. A deep reminder: that one is in service to, that one can be rendered an object. A deep reminder of how certain accelerations rot out the social contract between men and women, such as it is, particularly in places where the contract is already degraded (as in: Wyoming has the largest gender wage gap in the country). Certain accelerations: in the rate of resource exploitation and CO_2 accumulation, in the economic and social asymmetry between men and women, in the acceleration of development everyone knows won't last—that last point being, I think, not immaterial, that the death, the end, the bust, the collapse of those other accelerations is written into their every aspect. I do not mean to say anything as simple as the claim that an unprincipled exploitation of the land leads to other unprincipled exploitations. And it is of course true that the poor treatment of women happens in places without an energy boom. That it happens everywhere does not, however, eradicate its particular recent expressions here. How often, when energy money turns up, do women re-learn in a variety of drably quotidian ways, their worth?

A current research project at my university's School for Energy Research involves biogenic natural gas. Some coal-bed methane is the product of sub-surface microbes; the thought is that finding ways to promote microbial life in old coal seams and other fossil fuel reservoirs will allow the revival, to use the language of the school, of "economically depleted hydrocarbon reserves," in order to bring them "back into production and extend their economic life." It's a life support system for fracking and the larger industry of which it is a part, and thus a life support system for my current life and my state's life, a grace period, a little more smoothed-out future for our untenability. It's a revival that may smuggle another revival into the future with it, may carry forward that rotting-out social contract and its refreshed misogyny, if we're not careful anyway. Some things may need to keep giving. Some people may already be further down in the abyss than others.

An orbital tour of cities at night

Rachel Morgan

will reveal design by oxen and cart
or automobile. The lividity of light
tells what gas man burns to prolong
the day. One lamp left on, so dark
homes are not entered. An email
fills the bedroom, a floodlight's sleep.
Even from distance, a fishing boat's
all-around white light anchors to space.

In the fracking fields burn-off glows
and roads connect, but lanes and places
lead nowhere. It's true the wheat glows.

Oil Town Palimpsest,
or A Brief Material History of Frackland

Stephanie LeMenager

At the California Oil Museum in 2012 in Santa Paula, California, two docents are talking about the labor rights conflicts in Michigan and a concurrent strike at the Port of Los Angeles. "I've got a friend in construction who moved to Arizona, one of those right-to-work states," says one docent, an older man. "He says he can't make a living there." Then he adds, "But those girls who clerk at the Port of Los Angeles shouldn't get six figures, if that's true."

The other docent, a middle-aged woman, bustles to the gift counter to rearrange some Unocal oil tanker toy trucks, whose blue and orange boxes advertise authentic "lighted headlights" and "PVC tires." She says, "My ex-husband's in Michigan. He's a union guy."

At this point I'm standing about five feet from the docents, trying not to listen to them, on the trail of the modern oil ecology that led my hometown of Ventura, California, to become a frack site. Our

Monterey shale formation promises a mother lode of oil and natural gas—mostly oil. Placing fracking within the history of oil exploration in the region is important to me, as is understanding how the unmanageable risks of energy production become normalized and even invisible to those of us who live with it. As the docents chat, I'm reading a text box in front of a scale model of a petrochemical refinery located about three miles from my house in Ventura, which is roughly twenty miles from Santa Paula, the site of the museum. "In the early 1950s, Shell Oil Company constructed a urea fertilizer plant on a ninety-six-acre site located several miles northwest of downtown Ventura," the text box says. "Urea," it explains, "is a concentrated nitrogen-based fertilizer" whose manufacture depends heavily on natural gas. Shell piped in the gas from the Ventura Oil Field, which extends from the hills north of my home into an industrial district of Ventura Avenue, my neighborhood's main drag. The field started in 1915 after the General Petroleum Corporation—now ExxonMobil—made a discovery there. Memories of the field's origins are scattered widely in county archives and print, much of it industry history.

Particularly vivid memories can be found in an interview with "Pretz" Hertel, recorded by a county museum docent in the late 1970s. "Pretz"—short for "Pretzel," the nickname given him during World War I because of his German ancestry—came to the Ventura oil patch in 1921. He worked as a petroleum geologist for Shell, after receiving a degree in geology from Stanford. In the 1880s, Pretz notes, the Ventura field had been a ranch, one of many apricot, walnut, and cattle properties in the area. A man named A. B. Barnard drilled a well on his property that "started spittin' out…salt water." Then "a little bit of gas comin' along with it." Abandoning the idea of watering his orchard, Barnard put up a sign—at the time, an ironic one, reading "Oil, gas, and salt here."

To orient ourselves to this liquid geography, let's imagine a map. Consider that Barnard's ranch and the Ventura oil field transect and inhabit the Ventura River watershed, which moves through a valley surrounded by high hills. The hills to the southeast support a seven-mile-long raised aqueduct. The county's historic preservation society believes that the aqueduct was built by Chumash Indians (known as "neophytes" in the California Mission culture) who had been trained by skilled Mexican masons who had either read the Roman architect Vitruvius or been instructed in his masonry techniques by the *padres* at the Mission San Buenaventura. The aqueduct begins within the northern quadrant of the oil district, where the trickly San Antonio Creek intersects with the Ventura River, and it terminates at the old mission, located southeast of oil country, about a half mile from the Pacific coast. The petrochemical plant—the one built to produce urea in the 1950s—sits almost atop the Ventura River. This has been an unhappy proximity. The archives of the *Ventura County Star Free Press* record accidents, spills. In 1977, an accident at the plant fatally burned one worker and injured four others. By that time the urea plant was converted into a gasoline refinery by USA Petrochem, who bought the plant from Shell in 1972. Court records reveal a lawsuit brought against USA Petrochem by a local environmental group in the early 1980s, when the plant was considered for retrofitting so that it could again produce fertilizer. Thanks in part to the Clean Air Act, the environmentalists won the day, the retrofitting never happened, and the refinery itself ceased operations in 1984—one year shy of the one-hundred-year anniversary of Barnard's oil discovery on his Ventura ranch.

What drew me to the California Oil Museum was what appeared to be a new sign posted at the now decrepit USA Petrochem facility, coupled with the news that an incident of fracking was verified in the hills near my home. The Petrochem facility became a symptom of my own fatal ignorance, a complement to the lack of regulatory oversight that fracking has called attention to but that has been an aspect of American energy production since the nineteenth century. I noticed the sign at USA Petrochem one afternoon when I casually rode my bike onto the edge of the old refinery to take some photographs. It read: EPA SUPERFUND REMOVAL SITE. A quick search of local newspaper archives revealed that the Environmental Protection Agency's criminal investigation division had begun looking into charges that USA Petrochem illegally stored toxic and flammable petroleum waste on this site. An inspector on an unannounced visit in 2011 reported seeing what appeared to be petroleum leaking onto the ground from cut pipes and "about 46,872 gallons" (a fabulously precise estimate) of sludge in tanks. The open concrete tanks, leakage, and contamination of the Ventura River were acute concerns, almost thirty years after the site shut down. As to why an apparently brand-new sign appeared at the refinery with the EPAs name and the word Superfund on it, an EPA staff person I contacted said, "I don't know." The two docents at the Oil Museum mentioned only that "gangs" and "homeless" hang out there. They hadn't heard about the recent investigation.

The docents directed me away from unpleasant current events to the museum's cable-drill rig exhibit room, where I read about drilling techniques in California circa 1900. Fundamentally, this museum is about the ordinary and largely accepted horrors exemplified by the old petrochem refinery, even as it also narrates a proud heritage of bold innovation. Oil history is inevitably a history of high-risk technological experiment, of the perceived crisis of getting oil out of the ground because of its super-utility—a crisis repeatedly met by experiments meant to push technology to catch up with the challenge of getting at the oil and the accidents accompanying these experiments, deep in earth. The majority of artifacts in the California Oil Museum's cable-drill exhibit are "fishers," fittings that attach to the drill shaft and are meant to pull out objects, like bits, that might break off in the process of drilling. The sheer variety of fishers on display attests to how many times things went at least a little bit wrong. Sometimes what fell into the pit was people, like the fictional Joe Gundha who smothers in the drill pit in Upton Sinclair's 1927 novel *Oil!*, the basis for the Paul Thomas Anderson film *There Will Be Blood*. Parts of that film were shot in the upstairs rooms of the California Oil Museum, whose building is the former business office of Union Oil. One of the earliest pipelines to carry California crude to the Pacific Coast, like the one we see Daniel Day-Lewis surveying in Anderson's film, was recently removed from a nearby municipal golf course. "I don't think anything was in those old pipes," a docent told me, adding that relic pipelines can be found all over our region. Tens of thousands of feet of derelict pipeline carpet the Gulf of Mexico, I would learn, later. The liquid lives of water and oil fatally intermingle under our feet, out of sight.

The question of how to materialize the ecology of an oil district quickly becomes thinking about leaking, about the quiet, slow accidents that become too ordinary to conceive as accident or threat. (I use the verb "materialize" here to mean both "to make material or represent" and "to cause something to appear in bodily form," because it's been hard to represent fracking, and oil recovery more broadly, as about real bodies working in real time.) As drought overtakes the (fracked) American West, I am plagued by the specific problem of how not to forget, in the process of merely living as an American modern, that the water table is porous and penetrable, particularly when it lies as near to the surface as it does in my old hometown. The water table in Ventura has been as shallow as ten feet below the surface, although currently it's estimated at thirty-five feet. A recent Environmental Impact Report (EIR) treating the historic North Ventura Avenue oil district within the larger city of Ventura uses fire insurance maps to identify "49 addresses that may have historically impacted the shallow soils or groundwater of the study area." Appendix 4.7 of the EIR, listing "recognized environmental conditions," is 811 pages long. Reading it, I learn that there are thirteen sites near my neighborhood that have been "on the road" to the National Priorities List (NPL), then delisted. There are also sixty-four sites classified as "ERNS," which stands for the "Emergency Response Notification System." At these addresses, reports were made to the EPA of releases of hazardous substances. A list of street-by-street properties includes a few saddled with the potentially playful acronym "LUST," indicating a leaking underground storage tank. And all of these incidents took place *before* the recovery and waste storage processes we call fracking.

As Susanne Antonetta wrote caustically in *Body Toxic*, her intimately materialized memoir of hazardous waste interpenetrating her own cells and the landscapes of southern New Jersey, we Americans like to make lists. With Whitmanian bombast, we make lists like the NPL that then become a primary and sometimes a sole form of action. As I became more interested in my neighborhood's water systems, I ceased to be surprised by the inconsistency of official designations given to toxic sites, and by the number of such sites. At least the EPA can be commended for responding to the county's belated report that they were "having trouble" with the old oil refinery. Approximately one hundred fifty old tanks had been removed from the Ventura Avenue area, where I used to live, as of 2009. Grassroots organizing on the "westside," my part of town, just south of the heaviest industry, resulted in efforts on the part of the city and county to imagine, and implement, improvement. The city-sponsored booklet *Transforming Urban Environments for a Post-Peak Oil Future* includes fully realized "scenarios," much like speculative fiction, that beautifully sketch designs for a community where fifty percent of the food supply is grown within city limits and seventy-five percent of urban irrigation needs are supplied by gray water and roof water. But those plans were never realized, as the so-called shale revolution that brought fracking to town pre-empted legitimate estimates that we'd surpassed our peak production years for easier oil. Precisely where the urban ecology appears most likely to materialize is where, too, it is most likely to disappear in the often contradictory accounts of diverse public actors.

The bodies of discourse that I call by the approximate names (1) "environmental policy discourse"—including documents such as EIRs and the EPA archives—and (2) "civic history and planning"— including documents like historic context reports and surveys, the city's peak oil plan, and recommendations for historic preservation— contain dissonant plots. If you want to understand what oil has been and means in your town, you have to play the role of detective—and you may become disoriented in the process. Consider this confusing fact: some of the same sites listed as potentially hazardous in the latest EIR for my area appear in a "historic context and survey report" also commissioned by the city as places of noteworthy "historic integrity." My own home, built to accommodate oil workers in 1929, is designated with a status code of 5D3, meaning that it's slated to become a "contributor" to a historic district (theme: 1920s Working Class Streetscape). The same primary archival sources were used to make this historic designation as were used, by another consulting firm, to report brownfields in the same neighborhood. The USA Petrochem Plant appears in the historic context survey as an exemplary architectural "form" of the post-World War II period. A quick search of the Web turns up the old Ventura refinery within an almost pornographic image series of industrial ruins. Admittedly, old energy infrastructure lures me, too. Places like the refinery are the shadow-cities in the palimpsest of the modern.

How do we acknowledge toxic heritage? Whether both toxicity and industrial or labor history can be recognized as players in a historical–ecological relationship worthy of commemoration is important. Of course there's nothing wrong with instilling pride in a still largely working-class, semi-industrial district. The grassroots boosters of Ventura's "westside" have looked to historicity as one means of attracting investment to a community that has been written off by some city residents—not just because of its semi-industrial character but also because its current residents are primarily Latino. The historian Richard White eloquently described work as that which "involves human beings with the world so thoroughly that they can never be disentangled" from it. Old worksites, regardless of their toxic load, have an emotional resonance. They are scenes of world-making. In White's analysis of how the Columbia River was used to harness hydropower, "energy" becomes a way to talk about how humans and nonhumans work together. Yet power, in its most anti-social forms, also comes into being as the result of commanding energy, which ultimately means commanding life.

This leads me back to labor, the point at which we entered our conversation about the effort to materialize modern ecologies, with the discussion of labor politics in Michigan by the docents at the California Oil Museum. Labor sits at the seam of ecology and history. Laboring bodies (human and otherwise) rearranged each other in order to bring modernity, as material practice, into being. After I visited the California Oil Museum, I went to Texas and to Fort McMurray, Alberta, looking avidly for more oil history, in regions now remade by fracking and tar sands mining. During that time, America's "Motor City," Detroit, declared bankruptcy—and in its still painful death throes, a whole era of envisioning American efficiency, speed, and solid, working class jobs also dissolved. With the rust-belt keenly suffering, fracking marks just one of many nodes in the Tough Oil sector (including oil sands mining, transshipment work via oil trains and trucks, pipeline building) that looks like salvation—a way back to good industrial jobs, except without the environmental regulations, fair industry taxes, and in some cases even the labor rights that were hard-won in the twentieth century. The over-reporting of jobs created by fracking has been widely studied. Transient labor—typically performed by skilled drilling crews from Texas and Oklahoma—takes the place of more permanent, local work. Yet even in Texas energy-related jobs make up only 2.5 percent of the state's employment. Michigan, Ohio, Pennsylvania, Texas, Oklahoma, North Dakota, California's San Joaquin Valley, Ventura—these all are key points of reference for environmentalists and for labor activists and historians.

A history without ecology is one that fundamentally disregards working people and other bodies (animals, water, oil) capable of remaking worlds through physical force. It's equally important to remember that ecology isn't segregated from history, that ecology doesn't live in the primeval woods. The ecology of an oil town can teach us to remember often obscured laborers in the making of modern life such as, again, water. I can't help but return to water as California groans under a severe, four-year drought, and as I consider the billions of gallons of water used to frack wells nationwide, with most of these wells in places experiencing water scarcity.

Susanne Antonetta relates the problem of energy in the twentieth century, which for her centers around nuclear energy and its unresolved toxic waste crisis, to the "docetism" of her Christian Scientist grandmother. Like Mark Twain, Antonetta recognizes Mary Baker Eddy's faith as complicit with American ideologies of progress. For if bodies are simply matter and matter doesn't matter (the central tenet of "docetism" that underlies Christian Science, as Antonetta understands it) then what leeches into the ground from our waste storage tanks or runs into the storm drains from our paved streets doesn't matter, either. All that does matter is energy, the efficient rearrangement of matter toward the acute goal of power. Energy is a metaphysical ideology. Richard White recognized this plot, moving through bodies at work to energy and power, as one that ultimately depleted the cultural and natural reserves of the Columbia watershed. Now fracking plagues the Ventura River watershed, as I've noted. Soon after I first heard of a verified fracking incident in my neighborhood, a tony winery in Santa Barbara County was reportedly fracked, with the vineyard owner claiming that a pipeline of contaminated, industry-produced water ran right through his grapes. This latter story garnered attention because it uncomfortably mixed up two environmental genres: the story of local, artisanal food production and the sacrifice of the rural outlands to toxic degradation.

Fracking is troubling in part because it has no clear storyline, hovering somewhere in the vicinity of chemical contamination, climate change, and underhanded resource exploitation like the rerouting of water from the Owens Valley depicted in *Chinatown*. The fact that fracking hasn't easily fit into already familiar environmental storylines has made it harder to account for. This lack of accountability was made law in the famous "Halliburton loophole" in the Energy Policy Act of 2005, which liberated fracking from the Safe Drinking Water Act and other federal regulations, including the Clean Air Act, the Clean Water Act, and the Community Right to Know Act. Yet fracking doesn't really represent a discontinuous rupture with the histories of petroleum and natural gas extraction. For not only has fracking been happening for about seventy years, albeit with lesser degrees of toxicity in the produced water and without the horizontal onshore/offshore drilling at great depths that causes particular concern in southern California, but also it's a technique that in many respects only extends the misrecognition of liquid systems as immaterial that we see in petroleum production from the beginning, with its profound disregard for the water table—so permeable, so close. Even if frack chemicals do not contaminate groundwater when they're injected thousands of feet below the water table, as some studies suggest, studies have shown that natural gas leaks near the surface of frack wells can get into our drinking water and into the atmosphere itself, making fracked natural gas a dirty fuel, not a clean one. The seismic consequences of fracking are now being recognized even by industry, and with Oklahoma's seismicity rates increasing by six hundred times historic levels, seismically sensitive areas like southern California are on alert. Then, of course, there is the question of fracking as a producer, or exacerbator, of drought.

The under-imagined vertical geographies of LUSTs and quake faults and pipelines that run through our municipal golf courses make up the material contexts that ground fracking in environmental history and story. Memories of old oil infrastructures from workers on the ground give us a sense of how where we came from landed us where we are. A segment of Pretz Hertel's interview about historic oil mentions a water-intensive secondary recovery technique called "flooding" taking place in Ventura in the 1940s causing "serious" landslides. According to Hertel, his company "fixed" the problem by filling in the canyons below the drill sites so that the sliding land would have nowhere to go. I used to live just one house away from the high hills that form the Ventura River watershed's eastern boundaries, and when I moved into my home neighbors alerted me to the possibility of landslides. In the late 1980s, the city sent a notice to residents of my street and a few others that we might be in a slide zone— apparently this followed a slide to the north of us at a clay-mining facility serving the oil industry. My former next-door neighbor told me that if I saw the trees moving down the hillside near our homes, I ought to remember to "stop, drop, and roll." Later, she informed me that she suffers from a delusional disorder. I would counter that we're all a bit delusional, hunkering beneath frack zones that are geologically sensitive hillsides, mining oil in seismically unstable oceans, and going on every day, driving, consuming the multiform products of petroleum feedstock, recycling plastics that must be shipped to China to be broken down.

Two years ago, I left Ventura to take a job in Oregon, hoping against hope that I'd entered Ecotopia. At least the book was set in my new neck of the woods. Now I kayak in reservoirs drained so low for farming that fish float belly up in them. The fish also die here because it's simply too hot in summer. And in the newspaper I read about oil trains, crossing the rivers toward the seaports of the Northwest, coming from the Bakken shale. Fracking teaches that energy, as an ideology and economic mover, has made us forget ourselves. By "ourselves," I mean all the tender bodies whose relationships are at the core of energy and without whose work there will be no world to move or desire.

Fire on the Mountain

Fiction by Sarah Lyn Eaton

"Shit." Donna saw the air wavering above the well and bit down hard on her lip. She tried to pick up speed, but her legs were stiff in the pre-dawn air. She spied the crack in the well cap before she neared it. It was worse than the last one. She narrowed her eyes, piercing through the mist of the property for a flash of bright cornflower wool, hoping Blue Louie wasn't lighting up in the nearby woods. Tottering back to the house, she flipped the red switch on the outer wall. Lights above the barn flashed red, visible to the whole property. No one would be using flint, matches, or lighters until the well cap was fixed.

"Damn," Donna muttered, shaking her head. "Third crack this month." She flung a fist at the dark sky. Every year it got harder to make a life on the mountain. Everything was more expensive, the cost of the taxes on her view, of fabric for new coveralls and rubber to replace worn-down boots, even the price of a good hard cider was near impossible to manage more than once a year. Donna wet her lips at the thought and sighed. Everything cost water. Even hard work spent blood, sweat, or tears. Often all three. There wasn't enough water or money to fix the cap. Especially when they had to shut the ranch down every time the gas pushed out.

"Saw the lights burn just in time," Blue Louie scowled, coming around the side of the house with an unlit blunt in his hand. He winced as he leaned against the wall, and Donna knew his arthritis was flaring up—not that he'd ever complain out loud. He'd worked for her dad and practically raised her. She never once heard him complain. Blue Louie threw an eye to the well. "Another split?"

"Afraid so. You and Jake will have to fix it. I have to get to the station. They won't hold our water if we're not there to get it."

Blue Louie nodded. "Can we fix it good or do we got to patch it again?"

Donna blew a breath out while she thought about it. "Ask Lincoln for some aid. His farm's close enough that it would serve him to help us do it right. You'll have to wake Jake. I got to get the oxen hitched and start down if I want to get my place in queue."

"Leave the cap to me." Blue Louie slid the blunt into his pocket and turned into the house.

Donna counted to seven and moved on to her tasks for the day. The woman walked slowly to the barn, stretching her tired muscles as she went. She wasn't old yet. Her hair was only lightly peppered with threads of silver. But she'd been working the ranch every day of her life, and the years were long ones.

The ranch had been prosperous farmland in her mother's family, before her parents were conceived. Her Gram had told her bedtime tales about fresh vegetables growing out of the dirt in rows, as far as the eye could see. Such stories. Donna couldn't imagine just plucking food from the earth and biting into it without first testing for contamination. She smiled, remembering her Gram, as she opened the barn door.

Her grandfather had seen the future written in the fracturing earth and turned to raising cattle and oxen for milk and labor. Donna's parents had been forced to scale the numbers down when the rationing grew more restrictive. Donna only kept a couple of cows for milk and cheese. And she only raised enough oxen she knew would sell. Thankfully, workforce was always in demand.

Lately, Donna and her son Jake had been skimping on their own water consumption to maintain the best oxen for market, counting on the rain cisterns to sustain themselves. But the spring rain had been fickle, and those cisterns were low. Times were rough on the mountain all around. She combed her fingers through her hair, allowing another soft smile for the shower she'd get in town. She'd pay a fair coin for it, but it'd be worth every cent.

She picked out six of her finest animals and hitched them quickly to the large water cistern. The oxen were the only reason those who stayed on the mountain were able to remain there. They were the only way to get the water up the mountain. It would be a long day, but she considered the drive in to town with such magnificent specimens as free advertising. She scowled as the sky turned a lighter shade of dark. If they didn't start for town before the sun was up, they'd never make it in time.

The light was breaking in the sky as Donna drove the oxen into town, balancing on the top of the cistern. She would have to walk them back on foot once the tank was full. They pulled into the train station at the edge of town where a small crowd had gathered already. Donna

sighed at her queue placement until she spied the Sheehan girl, Sadie,
waving at her from where she stood atop a crate, fifth in line.

"Miss Donna! Over here!" Sadie was only nine years old but
smarter than any other kid Donna had known, even her own self.
It was a shame that Sadie was too young to be a match for her son
Jake, who'd been sickly since he was born. Someday, Sadie would be
a formidable ranch owner.

"You starting your own business without consulting me?" Donna
teased.

"I came out this morn and told everyone I was in line as your
representative," Sadie flashed a grin, revealing a missing tooth along
her bottom jaw.

"Well, as my representative, do you think I could barter more
of your time so as I could sneak into Rosetta's for a quick shower?"
Donna finished tying the oxen to their queue post.

"It'd have to be quick—that's the longest shower they got!" Sadie
laughed proudly. "I'll take care of the oxen." The girl bent down,
cooing over the big oxen at the front. "None'll bother us. Everyone
knows these big beautiful oxen belong to you. Available for sale at
Cumberland Farms!"

"I don't pay you near enough." Donna patted the oxen on the
rump before scurrying across the road to the Suds and Duds. A large
group of dusty-robed pilgrims sat in the lobby for prayer time. Donna rolled her eyes and walked up to the counter, where plump and
young Rosetta folded laundry. "I hope they're buying while they're
praying," Donna snorted.

"More of them come through as more places dry up, looking for
some meaning to their lives. I try hiring them on for a spell, to work

in the steamhouse, but no one's interested in hard work anymore." Rosetta's eyes crinkled against rosy cheeks. "Usual for you?"

"I'd be grateful. Brought my own soap this time," Donna held up her small bag, "though yours is finer." *And my coin's a bit tight.* Donna sighed. Rosetta's soap smelled of wild lemongrass.

"Listen," Rosetta lowered her voice and leaned forward. "There's rumor going about that the prices are going up again. I'll be jammed up. Let's you and me do each other favors. You bring me what milk you can when you come into town and you can get your shower on the house, soap and towel included."

Donna considered it. Rosetta was always quick with kindness, but she never offered services for free. "If you mean that, it would be a blessing. I don't ever have much more than a couple of jars extra, but I could throw in a head of cheese or two as well. It's not a lot to trade but they're yours if you like."

"That's a couple of jars and cheese I won't have to purchase. Most people don't want coin anymore. All anyone wants to trade in is water, which I don't have to spare." And she didn't. You couldn't run a bath and laundry house without water. She handed Donna a room key, eyeballing a new customer. It was always busy at Rosetta's on Water Day. "Let's start next month."

"Sounds good." Donna walked to the back hallway where the showers were. Stall three, the shower head sat over a grate, with a tray beneath it to catch the water runoff, which was filtered and reused until it classified as grey water, which was used to wash clothes in the steamhouse. The older—but not old—woman disrobed and rubbed her soap across dry skin. She spent three glorious minutes underwater, scrubbing her scalp and skin until it glowed. Once a month was better than never.

The pilgrims had moved on by the time she came back through the lobby and slipped the room key onto the counter. Donna hurried across the road and pushed through the mob that thronged the station. Thankfully Sadie stood on her crate above them, one eye on the oxen and another keeping lookout for Donna. She stuck her thumb up, and Sadie waved an all clear. Donna walked up to the tracks to visit with her friend, Sergeant Morelock.

"Got a present for you," she said, patting the bag of Blue Louie's weed in her pocket. He waved her away, void of his usual charm. "Everything all right?"

Morelock cursed and motioned her forward. "Not a good day, Donna."

"How so?"

"Word is there won't be enough water to meet the town quota." He scowled out at the throng of pilgrims. "And you won't be the only ones fighting for it. Everyone here has a script for their share."

"Shit," Donna cursed. "I need enough water to keep my oxen hydrated."

"Maybe it's time to turn your work farm into a meat farm." Morelock shrugged sympathetically.

"Everything costs water. Even that," she sighed. Blood, sweat, and tears. Donna's heart fell. They were fighting to scrape by as it was. Once upon at time, there had been water to drink, water to bathe, water to swim in, and water to waste, and the mountain had prospered. It was why Donna's family hadn't left when the water was contaminated. They couldn't imagine things were better where the water was scarcer.

Donna slipped the Sergeant his bag of weed. "No special favors necessary. Sounds like we're both going to be having a bad day."

"You're good people, Donna."

"Just remember that later if I'm one of the angry throng. It's not personal." Only then did she notice the other guards silently lining the walls. Others in the crowd noticed them, too. Only the pilgrims seemed undisturbed by their presence. Donna wandered back over to Sadie.

"Everything okay?" the girl asked. Her dark hair was cut short, mussed up to hide the home job. Sadie's father was a Recycler and spent long shifts in the old landfills. It was a job with security—the landfills were massive—but it was a hard job for a single parent. "All right?" Sadie repeated.

Donna shrugged. "It is what it is." She looked around. A few stalls down in the queue, Toby from Lincoln's farm caught her eye.

"Go on. I got you," Sadie said, shooing her away. She was a gift Donna would find a way to repay.

"Donna." The man touched the edge of his hat in greeting as she wandered over. "What's the word?"

"Just a rumor." She hitched her pants up, keeping her voice low. "Bout more rationing." Toby grunted a curse.

"Suppose we're all in the same boat," he ground his teeth together, tugging on his ponytail.

"Some worse than others," Donna admitted. "Sent Blue Louie over to ask Lincoln for help with a new well cap." Toby whistled through his teeth.

"I'm sorry to hear that."

"Possible we aren't going to get that help?"

"More than possible," Toby nodded. "You know we would. But we found our own leak. Gas build-up is getting stronger."

"Looking for a way out," Donna surmised.

"Yup."

"Fuck." Donna felt her insides twist. "Thanks for the heads up."

"Wish I had better news."

"Me, too."

The whistle bell tolled, signaling the imminent arrival of the train. Donna hurried back over to where Sadie stood. When the train pulled up the cheer was lighter than usual. Folks had been waiting for this train long enough to notice when it pulled in lighter than usual by how easily it stopped.

They called the first farm up, and Sergeant Morelock spoke to them privately. Bob Foster swore and threw his hat to the ground, gesturing angrily. The other soldiers stepped forward to create an armed barrier between the crowd and the train.

"Times are tough, ain't they, Miss Donna?" Sadie whispered.

"Yup," she nodded. She pulled out her food rations and handed half of them to Sadie.

"That's too much," Sadie frowned.

"Some for your dad too," Donna insisted. "When times are bad I get generous."

"That don't make sense." Sadie furrowed her brow while she pocketed the food.

"No it don't."

Donna watched as Bob Foster drove his cart up to the outside of the train. It must be real bad if they were making sure no one waiting could see what was being delivered. When they called her name, Sadie untied the oxen from their mount.

"Ready for the spiel?" Sergeant Morelock asked as Donna approached.

"How much am I losing?"

"About fifty gallons."

"That's impossible!"

"Others are losing more."

Donna bit back the words she wanted to share with her friend and swallowed hard. "Is this permanent?"

"I don't know," Morelock shrugged.

"What happened?"

"Someone tapped into the old plumbing systems and rerouted a bunch of water from the reservoir."

"Thought those pipes were sealed up?" Donna's surprise was genuine.

"Someone cut into a pipeline. Must have had plans to the system. I appreciate your calmness, Donna."

"Like I said, just remember me next time."

"You'll be first to queue," he assured her. "They'll load you at the backside of car five."

"Thanks." Donna motioned to Sadie, who followed her along the back of the train, leading the oxen.

"Bad news?" Sadie asked.

"Bad news. Could be worse." Donna bit the inside of her cheek before she could curse herself. *But it probably will get worse. Can't make water from thin air.*

As the men climbed up to attach the hose to the cart, Sadie wandered up the tracks, looking for a bead on new work. Donna saw her stop at the last car where the individual households picked up their rations. She returned with business.

"Got a proposition for you," Sadie offered.

"Shoot," Donna said, opening to negotiations with a smile on her lips.

"The pilgrims are looking to go up the mountain. They're looking for the 'fire-air born from water' and say it's up there." Sadie shrugged. "They're willing to split their water ration with anyone willing to permit them access. I said I knew a gal."

Donna knew they meant the gas coming from her well. The people who didn't live with it were always fascinated by it. "I gotta feed them?"

"No. They want to share food with you." Sadie shrugged again and crooked her fingers in the air like quotation marks. "It's their way."

"No strings?"

"Not that they say."

Donna rocked back on her heels, considering it. "What do you want?"

"Figure my dad and I could rate a share of the water."

"I'll double what you get today," Donna agreed. What could she say? Donna was coming home with less water than she needed and a bunch of pilgrims. She was feeling generous. Sadie's face lit up, and she ran back to co-ordinate with the pilgrims. Donna leaned against her water cart.

What a day.

Blue Louie and Jake were still working at the well when Donna pulled in with her strange parade of oxen, water cart, Sadie, and a few dozen pilgrims. Jake grinned in disbelief. Donna shrugged. A few dozen pilgrims would add up to a lot of water.

"Bad news, Donna," Blue Louie called out, but she waved her hand dismissively.

"Saw Toby at the station. More bad news down there, I'm afraid."

"That why the pilgrims?"

"Yup." They were already busy behind her, setting up tents for the night.

"We almost got the patch done." Jake pointed the seal out to her. "But a minute ago another started on the other side."

"Might be time," Blue Louie said heavily. Donna shook her head and clenched a fist. *Fuck. Damn. Shit.* She didn't notice one of the pilgrims sidling up beside her.

"Did I hear you've had trouble with your well cap?" The man bowed his head respectively. She guessed he was about her age.

"All landowners have," Blue Louie said defensively. "They keep cracking."

"My grand-dad said it wasn't our job to maintain them. That it was part of some deal. Our government disagrees with that assertion." Donna opened her arms. "So here we are, fighting with fire-air."

"The cap cracks because Mother is trying to help you," the pilgrim said. Up close he now seemed older than her, well-kept beneath his dusty robe.

"How so?" Jake frowned.

"If you trap the methane improperly, the build-up could cause an explosion. At the source point, clouds of methane are not that dangerous."

"How do you know that?" Jake's tone was suspicious. So was Donna. She'd only heard her Grampa call the fire-air by that name.

"I know something about the drills that created the fire-air. Do you mind?" Donna gestured for him to go ahead. He extended a long tube into the air. He hit a button and a flame emerged from the end. Donna, Jake, and Blue Louie scurried backwards. They spied the wavering air lift up from the cap and a flame burst, burning off in the air above them with a loud crackling pop. The pilgrims stopped their work and cheered, a look of awe masked across their faces. It ran through Donna's veins unsettlingly, but she pushed the thought away.

"My brothers and sisters and I can help you," the pilgrim said. He turned the small flame off.

"How so?" Donna stared at the group behind him.

"We can pipe the methane away from the well. It won't make the well water usable, but it will save your home." His face and voice were sincere enough.

Some help. Donna scowled inside. "And how much will that cost me?"

"Nothing," the pilgrim insisted. "Just permission to camp on your land while we work."

"Nothing costs nothing." *Everything costs water,* she thought. "What about the materials?"

"We can send for them. And we're prepared to pay you. Each worker will pay you a liter of water a week. We'll even dig and build our own compost latrine."

Blue Louie laughed out loud. "Universal mercy," he proclaimed to the sky.

"Why on earth would you pay me?" Donna waited for the strings to appear.

"We have use for the methane. We'd be paying you to let us siphon it off. Think of it as an investment on our end."

"You won't have enough water."

"Between me and you, we'll never have enough for everyone again. We can't all move to Canada, eh?" He chuckled. The northern border had been nailed down tighter than a cemetery vault since America started rationing. The pilgrim gestured to his brethren. "We are descendants of the old drillers. This work is our penance. We have learned to survive on very little."

"What will you do with the methane?"

"Do you need to know that?" the pilgrim asked seriously.

Donna hesitated. *Yes*, her ancestors rallied in her head. Ghosts on the land tried to rise and answer for her in a warning of patterns repeating. Of gift horses and Trojan warriors.

But the ancestors couldn't pay for the feed or water her animals needed. That she and her son and Blue Louie required. With extra income, she might actually be able to make use of her overflow cistern and have some savings. And she wouldn't have to worry anymore about where Blue Louie lit up his blunts. *Do I need to know?*

"Suppose not," she said, extending her hand, grateful for an answer to the day's problems.

What We Take for Granted

Scott Slovic

Water. Clean water. Water on demand, each time we turn on a faucet or press a knob on a drinking fountain. The other week, the fountain went out in the English Department where I work, occasioning a minor crisis. Workmen thronged the hallway, removing the old apparatus and, eventually, installing a new machine for the thirsty masses. No cost was spared to make drinking water available to the students and professors who inhabit the old academic building.

Meanwhile, when I pull up a map of fracking locations on the internet, I see that tremendous swathes of the United States are currently being plumbed for hydrocarbons, fracked for money and energy, despite the risk to water resources for local residents. The entire region from Ohio to New York State and down through Virginia, a giant fracking zone—Texas and Louisiana, Colorado and Wyoming. The four largest urban concentrations in this country—New York City, Houston, Chicago, and Los Angeles—are all marked in red on the map I have before me, indicating the threat to public health, and particularly to water resources, posed by nearby fracking operations.

A few years ago, I had an opportunity to join an exciting university in Morgantown, West Virginia. The department was excellent, the ideal job—I would have had all the time I needed to focus on my own research. But as I traveled from the airport in Pittsburgh, I watched with increasing uneasiness as I passed one fracking site after another, brightly lit gouges in the land, industrial equipment poised to extract shale gas from deep underground. During my brief visit to Morgantown, industrial smokestacks made visible an ambiance of contamination, reminding me of the underground tampering that was taking place throughout the nearby mountains. I have seen video clips showing water from kitchen faucets burst into flame in neighboring Pennsylvania, read news stories about chemical spills in West Virginia rivers. My short foray into fracking country and my contemplation of a move to such a location gave me nightmares. I turned down the job.

Here in northern Idaho, I live in a region that is not entirely supportive of higher education and work at an underfunded campus. But the air is clean most of the time (except during wildfire season), the water relatively untainted. I live in a small town where I hardly need to drive—my hybrid car sits for weeks at a time in the driveway, its battery occasionally dying from non-use during the winter. I walk to work. I don't worry about the water—indeed, I take the water for granted. Or, rather, I would do so had I not visited the fracking zone back east and realized the alternative to this clean and safe part of the country.

But even in Moscow, the water must be treated, often even filtered to remove the natural sulfur. To experience the unique gift of untreated, unfiltered water, you have to go deep into the mountains of central Idaho. When I teach environmental writing in the University of Idaho's Semester in the Wild Program each fall, I live with the students at the Taylor Wilderness Research Station in the middle of the Frank Church–River of No Return Wilderness, located on Big Creek, seven miles from the confluence with the Middle Fork of the Salmon River. The research station gets its water from Pioneer Creek, a frigid torrent that rushes down from Dave Lewis Peak through the old homestead that became a university research station in 1970.

This past October, my students and I were thinking about argumentative writing—how a writer takes a stance and makes certain claims to authority. One of the pieces we read, an essay using a systematic strategy of point-by-point, numbered examples, was David Orr's "Reflections on Water and Oil." Orr argues that oil and water "have had contrary effects on our minds," oil undermining intelligence and water enhancing it. He suggests ultimately that our heedless pursuit of oil—and the money and technologies associated with it—seems to come from "the belief that we can make an end run around nature and get away with it."

Indeed, it is all too easy for any of us to turn on the faucet at home, see more or less potable water come out, and assume that all is fine, that we have "gotten away" with our petroleum-based culture. We turn on the ignition in our cars with scarcely a thought about what we're burning—where the fuel came from, at what cost, and to what cumulative effect on the planet. We are a species capable of imagining the big picture, of putting our lives and actions in perspective—yet we're prone as well to put our heads down, ostrich-like, and try not to worry. We like to take things, such as today's apparent normalcy and safety, for granted.

But we do have the potential to perceive and recoil from danger, as I found myself doing when I visited fracking country two years ago. And we have the capacity, as well, to relish the purity and health of our lives in unpolluted nature. David Orr wrote his essay on water and oil in the fracking region of Ohio, concluding that we might better understand the very essence of our lives as humans "when the waters again run clear and their life is restored [so that] we might see ourselves whole."

When my students and I finished reading this line while sitting on the front porch of a cabin in the Idaho mountains, we paused and walked over to Pioneer Creek, where we plunged a metal cup into the pristine water, untouched by shale oil or the dozens of chemicals (from hydrochloric acid to 2-Butoxyethanol) thrust into the ground in pursuit of oil, untouched even by Giardia, and we passed the cup around, ten of us seeking a primal appreciation for the essential ingredient of our lives. Pure water.

Far from fracking country, we made a conscious effort not to take ourselves or our planet for granted.

Fracking and Its Two-Pronged Problem

Frederick L. Kirschenmann

Eventually you will reach a point where you must invest as much energy to pump the oil as you will get out of it.
—Dale Allen Pfeiffer

The practice of hydraulic fracturing, or "fracking," has created at least a two-pronged problem.

First, in the shorter-term, the increased global production of oil, and the decreasing price of fuel, creates an illusion in our culture, which leads us to believe that energy can still be cheap and abundant, that unlimited economic growth is still possible, and therefore that our industrial economy—which evolved as a result of cheap, petroleum energy—can now continue and thrive indefinitely. Second, in the longer-term, it extends the practice of burning fossil fuels and, therefore, the amount of greenhouse gases we inject into the atmosphere, which has a potentially foreboding consequence for the future of the human species on our planet.

The delusion that our oil economy, sustained with hydraulic fracturing, can now continue indefinitely, also leads us to dismiss many of the short-term social, economic, and ecological costs associated with fracking. According to an increasing number of observers such costs are already apparent, but for many of us the attractiveness of cheap energy is too appealing to consider such damages—damages that are likely already being done to our water, our land, our wildlife, our air, ourselves.

The social disruptions that this short-term "oil boom" have cost are significant. Unless you live in ecologies like the Bakken Shale region of North Dakota, you probably are not immediately experiencing some of these costs. However, the costs, for many, are real, and they will have long-term economic impacts. Some reports indicate that certain species of wildlife, like the sage grouse and the pallid sturgeon, will likely go extinct from the damage fracking is causing to the environment in certain regions of North Dakota. A diversity of wild species is what has made North Dakota an attractive environment for hunters who bring considerable, ongoing economic benefits to the state. Consequently, it is not improbable that fracking will eventually make North Dakota less attractive to sportsmen.

Furthermore, the exploding rail cars and hemorrhaging pipelines, used to transport the oil, continue to cause considerable, costly damage to the landscape, as well as many communities—not only in North Dakota but surrounding regions as well. According to reports, the clean-up of the Yellowstone River due to the Exxon spill has already cost one hundred thirty-five million dollars and still counting. The costs of many other spills have run into the billions.

What can happen to the farmland of farmers where the pipelines have been installed was made clear in a 2013 article about Steve Jensen, a wheat farmer in northwestern North Dakota. While harvesting his wheat, Jensen discovered an oil spill from a ruptured pipeline. The rupture, likely caused by a lightning strike, spilled 865,200 gallons of oil on his wheat field, making a large portion of his field unsuitable for crop production, and after a year of cleanup work (twenty-four hours a day, seven days a week) the oil still has not been cleaned from the field. And as any farmer knows it will likely be years before the soil can be restored to full health—if ever.

Certainly the beauty and serenity of the Badlands, which have been a significant tourist attraction for North Dakota, is not likely to be sustained once more pipelines are installed, given such predictable disasters.

Another, related cost of the perpetuation of the oil economy made possible by fracking is the transformation of our farmland. It is the continuing availability of relatively cheap oil that sustains the highly specialized, monoculture farming systems that now dominate the landscape and incentivizes farmers to raise more livestock in confinement, instead of on perennial grasses, to produce more corn to feed the animals, and to develop more ethanol to produce more fuel.

When my father and mother began farming on our farm in North Dakota in 1930, they personally experienced the pain of the dustbowl, caused not just by the weather, but also by the way farmers farmed—plowing up too much of the native prairie to plant more crops. The extent to which grasslands are now being plowed up to convert to cropland, especially in combination with the impact of climate change, is almost certainly positioning us for another major dust bowl in our near future.

The combination of these costs, together with the ecological damage to farmland, can have significant long-term economic damage, especially in regions like the Bakken Shale in North Dakota. Such damage will not be recouped by any short term economic gains from the increased oil production, especially since most of the oil wealth produced by fracking goes out of state to investors. Whatever economic benefits that may accrue to local communities from increased oil production, such as increased jobs, are few and very short-term, often go to imported laborers, and certainly do not compensate for the longer-term damages to land, water, and wildlife.

In addition to all of these observable damages from fracking, there are now additional, possible impairments that may be caused by fracking. One is the increase of "man-made earthquakes." Another is the potential long-term impact that the incredible amounts of water required for fracking could have on future communities.

Yet, devastating and disheartening as these short-term damages are, they are minuscule compared to the much more comprehensive, global destruction the perpetuation of the oil economy will have on our planet. As the most recent International Panel on Climate Change (IPCC) report pointed out, we now only have about fifteen years to put a cap on carbon and begin to sequester the carbon that we have already accumulated in the atmosphere to avoid irreparable damage to the planet. Consequently, as many ecologists have already reminded us, it is in our interest—and certainly in the interest of our grandchildren—to keep the remaining fossil fuels in the ground.

We appear to have forgotten that the era of our oil economy is a very short period in the timeline of human history. The first producing oil well in the United States was in Titusville, Pennsylvania, in 1859 and, naturally, it took several decades to transition to an oil economy. So our oil economy is only about hundred years old, and while none of us probably want to go back to a pre-oil economy, we do need to design and transition to a post-oil economy. Such a transition is inevitable, both because of the rapid depletion of oil, and because of the devastating consequences of putting more greenhouse gases into the atmosphere.

This transformation to a post-oil economy will be complex and will take time to develop. Consequently, it would make much more sense to now sparingly use some of the remaining fossil fuels as transition fuel to create our post-oil energy economy than to use it to extract as much short-term wealth and convenience as possible.

The design of such an alternative energy system will be essential to our future—and certainly to the future of our grandchildren. Continuing to extract oil as rapidly as possible to keep the oil economy going for a few more years can only be described as a kind of insanity.

Our failure to recognize this problem and begin the transition to a post-oil economy is the first of the two-pronged challenge that fracking has imposed on us. A second, more foreboding challenge is acknowledging the long-term damage that the continued burning of fossil fuels will impose on the planet. The fifteen-year timeframe that the IPCC warned us about is a tipping point beyond which it will likely be impossible to restore the health of our living ecosphere on which the survival of the human species ultimately depends. I think we sometimes tend to forget that 99.9 percent of all of the species that ever existed on our planet earth are now extinct. As evolutionary biologists remind us, conditions change over time that make it impossible for certain species to survive. For several million years now the ecosphere of the planet has been favorable to the evolution and survival of the human species on our planet. However, if we continue to produce more greenhouse gases and inject them into the atmosphere, climate scientists poignantly warn us that conditions for human survival on the planet will become questionable.

All that said, it simply is in all of our interests to end the fracking as soon as possible and to put all of our wisdom, technologies, and entrepreneurial skills into designing our post-oil economy and communities.

The good news in all of this is that according to many of our sociologists and psychologists this transition could actually improve our quality of life. As Tim Kasser has pointed out, based on numerous psychological studies, our current consumptive lifestyle, made possible by our oil economy, has actually produced a very poor quality of life. A less consumptive society, in which we cooperate in our communities to develop what Marjorie Kelly calls, a "generative economy" would actually produce a better quality of life than what we currently have. Instead of encouraging us to extract as much wealth from our communities for ourselves as possible (as our current oil economy does), such a cultural shift could lead us to focus instead on the "common flourishing of life" in our communities. We already see a few eco-villages, intentional communities, and "food hubs" in which people have made some progress moving in these directions.

Besides, as Dale Allen Pfeiffer and many other energy experts remind us, we will soon reach a point where it will cost more energy to extract the remaining fossil fuels than the energy we get out of them. In other words, the energy return on energy invested will not be sufficient to continue fracking. So does it not simply make good common sense to begin the process of making the transition to a post-oil economy now, instead of delaying that inevitable challenge by extracting a few more barrels of oil through fracking?

Epic Fail

Robert Jensen

Ecologically, we humans are an epic fail.

In internet-speak, that term can be used derisively or sympathetically. A failure of grand proportions can be labeled "epic" either to mock or to offer condolences to someone who fails so completely.

Both the unkind and the compassionate uses are appropriate in this context; we humans should be able both to laugh at, and feel sorry for, ourselves as a species. Judged on the criterion of ecological sustainability, we are an unprecedented epic fail, and our failure deepens daily. As we understand that scope of the failure, we will be both painfully aware of how difficult the challenges we face really are and frustrated with the limits of our culture's imagination.

Nowhere is the epic nature of our failure more evident than the extraction of what is often called "extreme energy"—the pursuit of hydrocarbons in the tar sands, mountain-top removal, deep-water drilling, and hydraulic fracturing. The manic pursuit of these technologies is a glaring example of our failure, yet the dominant culture cannot imagine a way to stop.

First, let me be clear: My observations do not rest on a definitive conclusion about the more contentious debates about the safety of a practice such as fracking; at this point, our understanding of the threats posed by fracking is emerging, and no consensus among those with relevant expertise has emerged. Reasonable people can disagree, and reasonable people have assessed the specific risks about specific practices differently. Acknowledging that, I believe a sensible proposal would be to stop all fracking, or at least place a moratorium on new fracking, until there is evidence that it is safe. This is simply a plea for the precautionary principle, which places the burden of proof on those supporting an action to demonstrate it is safe, rather than placing on critics the burden of proving that the action is clearly a threat to public safety or health.

The widespread denial or minimizing of the proven and potential dangers of such extraction techniques, which are more expensive and dangerous than earlier methods used to reach more easily exploitable pools of hydrocarbons, is troubling. But even more frightening is a deeper denial that lies at the heart of the search for fuel: As a society, we cannot seem to imagine a low-energy future, and, therefore, we stumble forward toward disaster. No one can predict the exact timing or exact unfolding of specific disasters, but we can be reasonably sure disasters will happen along the way, while our burning of the extracted fossil fuels moves us well past the point of irreversible climate destabilization.

In short: we can't know whether we will blow up or burn up the living world first through the extreme extraction of fossil fuels.

Epic fail.

We should linger on this epic fail for a moment, neither to laugh at nor feel sorry for ourselves but rather to confront the grief that we may—and inevitably must—feel, not only for humans but for the larger living world. For most of human history our many failures, no matter how tragic, were localized and potentially reversible. Now, we face the global and relatively permanent consequences of the human assault on all Creation. Today, we face a reality no other humans have ever had to face in history: It is likely that the ecosphere will not be able to sustain large-scale human presence into the indefinite future, and in the process of destroying our home we will desecrate the entire planet. Using terms such as "Creation" and "desecrate" is not intended to slip into theological terrain but rather to signal the importance of these matters. As Wendell Berry has put it:

> There are no unsacred places;
> there are only sacred places
> and desecrated places.

Perhaps that seems a bit too heavy an introduction. So, let's pause to acknowledge the irony in all this: We are in this predicament because we're smart. Cursed by our intelligence, humans are generally oblivious to what makes us truly unique while at the same time drunk on our sense of being uniquely important. Of course we are special (No other species can match our cognitive or linguistic abilities.), but at the same time we are just one more species among millions (all of which are dependent on ecosystems that are far more complex than any species, including humans, could ever hope to understand fully). As a result of this confusion, we seem bent on destroying the beauty of being human and the beauty of the larger living world.

OK, that didn't really lighten the mood. So, let's start again, trying to understand how we got here. It's helpful to remember that life on Earth is the scramble for energy-rich carbon. In this endeavor, species expand and contract, depending on a variety of ecological factors. Populations of various species rise and fall, generally kept in check by the complex interactions in ecosystems. No species has ever contemplated the global implications of this quest for carbon until now, and it is only in recent decades that some members of this one especially smart species have suggested that we do something unprecedented in Earth history: consciously contract.

If we are so special (in regard to our ability to think at a level unique to our species), we should be able to recognize that we aren't special (in regard to facing the same laws of physics and chemistry that all other species face). At this point in history, that awareness leads me to one unavoidable conclusion: We have to reshape human life to live with a lot less energy. That is, if we want to maintain a large-scale human presence on the planet, the conventional "lifestyle" of the more affluent sectors of the planet (including, but not limited to, the United States) must change. That means the consumption norms of contemporary capitalism must change; the growth model of contemporary capitalism must change; the profit motive of contemporary capitalism must change. Given that contemporary capitalism is defined by mass consumption, endless growth, and profit, this means we must scrap the norms (especially the celebration of greed), mechanisms (especially modern markets), and institutions (especially the corporation) of capitalism.

We have trouble, as a culture, imagining that contraction in energy consumption, and we have trouble imagining the end of capitalism. The critic Fredric Jameson, (attributing it to "someone once said") has written, "It is easier to imagine the end of the world than to imagine the end of capitalism."

But that's only part of the problem—for some, it may be easier to imagine the end of the world than to imagine the end of air conditioning.

So, summing up the problem: Lately humans have dominated the planetary competition for energy-rich carbon, and that domination is undermining life on Earth. We're #1 for now, and it turns out that being #1 in this fashion means that over the long haul we lose big. And, increasingly, the long haul looks like it's going to be a short trip. Our grandest failure is the product of our greatest success.

So, our task is to face a simple question that has serious consequences: Is the human with the big brain an evolutionary dead end? Is *Homo sapiens'* domination of Earth coming to an end, not in some imagined science-fiction future but as the result of today's processes of resource extraction and waste generation? If so, what are we going to do with our species' time remaining?

The trajectory of the multiple, cascading ecological crises that define our world cannot be predicted with precision, but the trend lines are clear enough. Our task is not to figure out how to maintain the illusion of human control of the ecosphere—and it always was an illusion, even when we seemed to be more successful—but instead, borrowing from my friend Jim Koplin, "to learn to leave the planet gracefully."

There are steps we can take to make our departure from the planet's center stage more graceful, and we owe such a graceful departure to ourselves and the larger living world. But before we focus on those steps, we need to spend time analyzing how we got to this point in history. When facing the scope and depth of these ecological crises, many people want to move immediately to a discussion of actions that can be taken to "solve" problems, which I believe is a crucial error. Avoiding the reasons for our epic fail tends to lead to "solutions" that are ineffective or counterproductive. There are problems without solutions, at least solutions that are based on the same assumptions and that work within the same systems out of which the problems arose.

It's time to think about life beyond solutions, which requires us not only to confront the reasons for our epic fail but also to deal with the despair that inevitably flows from such honesty. That process is as much emotional as intellectual and is possible only if we have compassion for ourselves and each other, grounded in a love for our specific home places that are part of the larger planetary home.

If it seems odd to inject the idea of love into this harsh analysis, consider Dostoevsky's insight that "love in action is a harsh and dreadful thing compared with love in dreams." We have many dreadful realities to face, none of which will be resolved by dreaming.

None of this need be depressing. While it's true that I don't spend a lot of time skipping down the sunny side of the street whistling a happy tune, I'm one of the most mentally healthy people I know. If that seems counterintuitive—that someone focused on the unsustainable nature of our society would make such a claim of psychological stability—consider all the intellectual and emotional energy I don't have to spend on denial. All around us is the evidence of the irreversible collapse of our ecosystems, piling up in ways that are impossible to ignore, and yet most people expend enormous energy to keep themselves from these realities. Freed of that (or, at least, mostly freed most days), I need not waste time on the delusional systems that humans create for avoidance.

What do I mean by delusional systems? Think about all the arguments—typically influenced by a superficial understanding of science that privileges physics and molecular biology over the far more important work of ecologists—that rely on technological fundamentalism, the idea that we can always invent our way out of our troubles simply because we want to. That's delusional, which can be demonstrated by asking simple questions: Given that many of our most intractable ecological crises are the result of the unintended consequences of high-energy/high-technology, why would we invest our hopes in more of the same? Why would we look for solutions to our problems by embracing the naïve assumptions that have deepened the problems? When our success at extracting fossil fuels inadvertently creates ecosystem damage at the extraction point and a climate crisis globally, what do we do? Intensify the search for more fossil fuels. We become fracking fundamentalists.

Since I don't have to construct and maintain these kinds of delusions, I'm freed up to deal with reality. That is difficult, but that freedom makes it easier to set aside the culture's obsession with pleasure-indulgence and pain-avoidance in favor of accepting the inevitable grief and the struggling for deeper joy. That is where we live, "the human estate of grief and joy," to borrow from Wendell Berry, and it is there that we can accept reality and begin to build a different world.

A STATE OF PROFOUND GRIEF

Jim Koplin, the one who wanted us to learn to leave the planet gracefully, did just that on December 15, 2012, at the age of seventy-nine, dying as he had lived, gracefully. Jim was the first person I met who was willing to face these issues squarely, and it was through my twenty-four years of conversation with him that I came to understand these multiple, cascading ecological crises (That's his phrase, which I have been using ever since I first heard it.). More than anyone in my circle of friends and comrades, he continued to face these realities and challenged others to do the same. As a result, he woke up every day in a state of profound grief.

I remember him using that phrase in a conversation a few days after the attacks of September 11, 2001. I had thrown myself immediately into the antiwar movement's organizing efforts to block the US invasions that would come after that attack. Jim participated on the edge of that movement, but his own work remained focused on long-term community building, efforts aimed not at specific political ends but at creating networks of people with shared values who could be part of the "saving remnant" he believed necessary for a dramatically different future. Jim was not callous about the loss of life on that day, but he also was not afraid to point out the casualties from the attack were not all that unusual in a world structured by the domination/subordination dynamic. Jim told me when he woke up on September 12, he didn't feel appreciably different than he had the previous day. "I wake up every morning in a state of profound grief," he said.

I first assumed that Jim was poking at me to make a point, but as we talked I realized he meant it quite literally. I had always known that Jim deeply felt the pain in the world and the pain of the world, in a way that was hard to articulate. This is what it means to face the world honestly, he was telling me, to not turn away from that pain. He also believed we had an obligation to maintain our sanity and stability so that we can act responsibly on behalf of justice and sustainability.

Jim had fashioned a way of frugal living in progressive communities that worked for him, but he always said there was no template for how to live these values in this world. He believed in embracing the grief, not just because it was the right thing to do but because it made possible a fuller embrace of the joy. When I think of him, I most remember the hours we spent talking about these ideas, which typically would take us, in a single conversation, from quiet despair to giddy laughter. Others often told us that our ideas about these subjects were depressing, but neither Jim nor I ever were depressed by the subject. It was, for us, a way we loved each other and held onto a love for the world.

This is the point in this kind of essay where the writer steps back from the edge and reminds readers of all the reasons for hope. But I long ago gave up that kind of hope-mongering. Rather than search for a pithy ending of my own, I'll go back to Dostoevsky's *The Brothers Karamazov*, and the section out of which the "love in action" line comes:

> If you do not attain happiness, always remember that you are on the right road, and try not to leave it. Above all, avoid falsehood, every kind of falsehood, especially falseness to yourself. Watch over your own deceitfulness and look into it every hour, every minute. Avoid being scornful, both to others and to yourself. What seems to you bad within you will grow purer from the very fact of your observing it in yourself. Avoid fear, too, though fear is only the consequence of every sort of falsehood. Never be frightened at your own faintheartedness in attaining love. Don't be frightened overmuch even at your evil actions. I am sorry I can say nothing more consoling to you, for love in action is a harsh and dreadful thing compared with love in dreams. Love in dreams is greedy for immediate action, rapidly performed and in the sight of all. Men will even give their lives if only the ordeal does not last long but is soon over, with all looking on and applauding as though on the stage. But active love is labor and fortitude, and for some people too, perhaps a complete science.

A Feminist's Guide to Fighting Pipelines

Ahna Kruzic and Angie Carter

Another world is not only possible, she is on her way.
On a quiet day, I can hear her breathing.
—Arundhati Roy

PROVISIONS, OR WHAT YOU'LL NEED TO GET STARTED (AND TO KEEP YOU GOING):

☙A tribe: Your sisters, your brothers, your elders, your allies. Find them next door. Find them far away. Commune with them. Practice. Together you will hold one another accountable, find strength, heal wounds, laugh. You do not do this alone. You do not do this as two together. You do this as many, as more, as a growing movement.

❧Inspiration: What we are trying to do right now has not been done before, is unfinished, is underway. Something to inspire the unknown is necessary.

❧Love: Yes, you hate the destruction, the exploitation, the commodification, the corporation. But it is because you love this fierce world, your beloveds' places in it, the challenge that comes with change, the hope that you might help to make it better, to make it just.

❧Rage: Righteous rage to fuel you to say the things they say you shouldn't, to stand up in places where they say you can't. Most importantly, to build the fire to bring others in. Rage to tell the polluters, the manarchists, the doubters, the compromisers, the profiteers, the tycoons. Halliburton, ExxonMobil, Energy Transfer Partners, Mayflower, Bridger, Sandpiper—no more.

❧Memory: Honor the countless before you whose names you do not know, whose names were not recorded. Remember the trafficked, the silenced, the vanished, and the forgotten. The crusaders and the truth speakers. Carry them with you. Feel their weight not as rocks carried on your back but hands pushing you on, pushing you further, pushing. Think of this as a birth, a becoming, the beginning.

❧Risk: What you are doing now has not been done before. You do not have a guarantee that what you're doing this time will work, but you do know your rage and hope will drive change. It has to. Those before us gambled on a future that couldn't be predicted. As a result, people of color, women, Native Americans, LGBTQ, those with disabilities, and others have more rights and respect than they once did. Though there is so much more to win, you're doing that now, every day.

STEP ONE: BUILD COMMUNITY

❥ Build community with purposive inclusivity, but go beyond inclusivity.

❥ Meet people where they're at, and create space for people to make their own connections. Move beyond teaching rhetoric and talking points. If we put our hearts into building relationships and real coalitions, we are doing more than fighting the pipelines in our backyards. We are standing against commodification, exploitation, racism, capitalism, and patriarchy.

❥ Use your local values as tools. Find those values that enable you to say no to the proposed pipeline, to extreme energy, to the colonization of our future. More importantly, say yes to neighboring. Livelihoods. Family. Values. Love. Together, build a new narrative. Amplify it. Do not be afraid to privilege the voices that need to be heard. Live and learn in your narrative, together.

STEP TWO: MOVE BEYOND THE HERE AND NOW

❥ Reach beyond your local context. It's not just one pipeline. It's all pipelines. It's the oil industry. It's commodification, exploitation, racism, capitalism, and patriarchy. Destruction. War. Victory does not come when the pipeline project moves or is shut down. Winning is bigger. If your pipeline is stopped, we're still facing total destruction or almost total destruction. This is about generations from now and the world in which they will fight and love and eat and pray and, at night, dream. They are your light. Follow them. Forge the paths to reach them.

❥ This is not a political campaign. There is no single target. Though we don't know exactly how we'll win, we must trust that today's, tomorrow's, and next week's struggle will get us there.

→Connect to existing regional movements; build real coalitions united by hope for the future. A farmers organization protects their agricultural heritage and legacy. A religious group works to stop the human trafficking industry in the Bakken region of North Dakota. A neighborhood alliance forms to preserve landowner rights. A grand-mothers' organization presses for protections for future generations. Students call for divestment from the fossil fuel industry. You may not all agree about the path forward, but you all believe in a shared future.

→There is we and there is us, and these are built stronger from each unique story, challenge, perspective, journey, and life. *I, me,* and *my* are an important part of us, but there is no *alone.*

STEP THREE: CARE FOR YOURSELF

→You will work with people with more privilege than you. Sometimes they will be people you respect, admire, and learn from. Sometimes they might take credit for your work. Steal your thunder. Take up too much space at a meeting. Yell at you. Question your identity and experience and lived knowledge. Expect this because it will happen. Many times. Do not question yourself because of it. Privilege and its associated authority does not grant omniscience. Do not apologize for their privilege. Step aside, not back, to let them leave or pass.

→Apologize. Forgive. You will make mistakes, and so will others. You make them out of anger, in frustration, in fatigue, out of privilege or habit. Others will, too. It is no surprise that we are anxious, intolerant, allergic: our earth is sick, poisoned, grieving. Focus on the work, on what you must do today, do tomorrow, do next week.

❧You will need to change, to shift, to slough off the layers of what they said you should do, said you should be. You have not been trained to do this; no one has. It is hard; it hurts. You will fail and try and sometimes, you will get it right. Let it go. Keep going.

❧Do what inspires you and drives you, even and especially if it requires checking out. Stepping back and caring for yourself is critical. This struggle is centuries-long; it could outlive you. Checking out to feed your spirit, to find validation or encouragement, whatever that looks like, enables you to continue tomorrow, next week, next year.

❧See *Provisions*.

STEP FOUR: IMAGINE THE IMPOSSIBLE

❧Be brave enough to believe in the world your heart knows is possible. It is okay that you don't know what it looks like or how we'll get there. Learn from those before you, those with you. Remind yourself we have not yet known a world without exploitation. But somewhere, deep in your bones, you know that we will find it. Or build it.

❧Trust that through the undoing, the dismantling, the collapse, we will learn to remake and will remember to question, to honor, to debate and disagree and come together again.

❧Share this. Post this. Highlight and cross out and revise this. Make it yours. A guide is a living thing, evolving as we learn and know and do better. There are wrongs we have not even learned to see yet that have not yet been named. There is so much more to learn, to change, to do.

The Story of Staying

Jan Bindas-Tenny

A NORTHWESTERN MIGRATION

There are primarily two kinds of people in the waiting area for a flight to Williston, North Dakota: the company men and the roughnecks. The roughnecks are white men with steel-toed boots and baseball caps slick on their heads like onion skins—they might even wear these hats in the shower. They are tattooed white men staring into their smart phones with muddy-bottomed jeans. The company men are skinnier white and east Asian men with leather loafers and Mac computers; they hunch on conference calls with headphones. I am the only woman.

Jobs on an oil rig: Roughneck, Toolpusher, Derrickhand, Worm, Roustabout, Ginsel, Mud Logger, Company Man. Everyone sleeps on the rig; the mud logger wakes at 11 PM for a 5-Hour Energy drink breakfast before the night shift.

Crops that used to grow in North Dakota: wheat, barley, oats, alfalfa. Specialty crops that now grow in North Dakota: beans, canola, flax, safflower, lentils.

Flying into Williston, North Dakota, at 1 AM is like flying into Paris or Dallas. If I squint my eyes to make them blurry, the light from the oil rigs and natural gas flares on the prairie glow the same orange as a suburban cul-de-sac. The rigs are small Eiffel Towers. The flares are jet engines. I push myself against the window.

Man camps in Williston clutter the outskirts of town with white recreational vehicles crowded on rectangular patches of grass. Many have plywood skirting; most are quiet on the outside. Some unfold a spiderweb of rectangular metal cabins, a future vision of settlement on Mars.

Things people say to me in Williston: Their supply and demand is going to bite them in the butt. How many years do I have left? We need people to group up and help each other. Most of us make too much to qualify for assistance. I never used to lock the doors. I do a lot of hollering. There is a lot of dust. It's a natural disaster.

The census can't handle the numbers. What they're sure about is that the population started at twelve thousand before this round of drilling in 2008. Some say the population is thirty thousand now, fifty thousand, going to be a hundred soon. Some say the ratio is 50:1 men to women. Some say the ratio is 5:1 men to women. The man camps are hard to count. As are the people sleeping in their cars at Walmart. Hard to keep track of who is squatting what awning.

Other things people say to me in Williston: There was an eviction notice on my door. They waited until dark to send some high school kid to tape it up. Ten people got eviction notices that first month. I wasn't living high on the hog. There's a little bit of Indian in us— Ojibwe tribe. My brother's a jerk. He won't mow the grass. There's somebody sleeping under the trailer next door. I own some rights, but I won't let them drill on it. I'm sick of oil.

Coffee shops in Williston: Meg-A-Latte (owned by Meg in two locations: one on Million Dollar Way and the other in the megachurch called New Hope Wesleyan with its big TV screens, electric guitars, young pastors in flannel shirts, and everyone in the movie theater-type pews with grande machiattos in their drink holders), C Cups Espresso (as in bra size), Boomtown Babes Espresso (bright pink shack along Route 2 where men in trucks can drive through to check out the "babe-ristas"), Daily Addiction Coffee House (my favorite, located on Main Street).

Strip clubs in Williston: Whispers and Heartbreakers. Where to find a sex worker in Williston: Bubbles Laundromat, backpages.com. Things politicians want to talk about: sex trafficking. Things politicians don't want to talk about: eviction notices taped to the doors of the long-term trailer park residents.

WE HAVE ENOUGH OIL WELLS

I drive out to Carole's ranch on a Saturday morning. What a savanna, what big swaying wheat, to be driving through the North Dakota fields on a morning in June, broke, awake, almost ridiculously awed, with nowhere to be but here. An endlessly humming landscape, still fields spin with trucks, dust, pumpjacks, and oil rigs. The oil horses bow and rise like persistent supplicants. The blue sky rips the grasslands wide open.

Carole drinks her coffee on the cold porch, smokes cigarettes in the fog, patrols her land from the control tower of her small red house, a watchdog ready to snarl at interlopers. Carole learned to raise cattle first, then to manage an oil field. She's a fourth generation rancher outside of Watford City, North Dakota. Carole invites me to join her on the porch. By the door she tacks a sign in all caps:

BEFORE YOU KNOCK ON THIS DOOR,
PLEASE READ AND FOLLOW DIRECTIONS
ACCORDINGLY.

1. WE BELIEVE IN THE LORD AND WORSHIP
HIM IN OUR OWN CHURCH. WE ARE NOT
INTERESTED IN YOUR RELIGION, THANK YOU
VERY MUCH. GOOD BYE.

2. WE HAVE ENOUGH VACUUM CLEANERS, SO
WE DON'T NEED YOURS. GOOD BYE.

3. WE HAVE ENOUGH INSURANCE TO COVER
OUR NEEDS AND WE PAY THROUGH THE TEETH
FOR IT SO WE DON'T NEED WHAT YOU ARE
SELLING. GOOD BYE.

4. DO NOT ASK TO SURVEY. GOOD BYE

5. WE HUNT OUR OWN COYOTES. THERE IS NO
ROOM FOR MORE HUNTERS, SO DON'T EVEN
ASK. BTW, THE DEER AND PHEASANTS ARE
PETS, SO DON'T ASK TO HUNT THEM EITHER.
GOODBYE.

6. WE DON'T HAVE ANY LAND FOR SALE. GOOD
BYE.

7. WE DO NOT NEED OUR DRIVEWAY PAVED.
GOOD BYE.

8. WE DON'T NEED A PICTURE OF THE YARD. IF
WE WANT AN AERIAL PICTURE, I'LL HAVE MY
UNCLE TAKE ME FOR A RIDE IN HIS AIRPLANE.
GOOD BYE.

9. WE HAVE ENOUGH OIL WELLS AND PIPELINES AND OUR LAND HAS BEEN DEVALUED ENOUGH. WE DON'T NEED OR WANT ANY MORE. PLEASE LEAVE BEFORE WE HAVE YOU ARRESTED FOR TRESPASSING, OR WE SIC THE CAT ON YOU.

10. IF YOU ARE A FRIEND AND HAVE COME TO VISIT, BY ALL MEANS, KNOCK ON THE DOOR! WE WILL INVITE YOU IN AND MAKE A POT OF COFFEE OR A MEAL AND VISIT.

I examine her face, the deep creases around her eyes, young sparkling irises, heavy cheeks and a short blond haircut, the transitional lenses of her glasses blue-gray in the daylight beside her hooded sweatshirt. We sit facing out on the land in folding chairs. It's raining and cold. I'm chilly in a jean jacket, not prepared for summer in the north country. She asks if I want coffee and if I mind if she smokes. Yes and no, I say. Hot coffee on a cold day, cold hands around a hot mug, and the rain dropping splashy puddles on the porch just out of reach, Carole tells me she is sick of the hype.

"Are they telling people what it costs to live here? Are they telling them about the trespassing and the traffic and dumping? People have no respect. They were never taught respect. Everybody wants a piece of the Bakken, and they're all going to cut corners if you let them, big or small."

Carole inherited the land from her parents, who inherited the land from her grandparents, who inherited the land from her great grandparents. Now Carole leases the land to her tenant for ranching, and space and mineral access to the oil companies who operate four oil pads or "locations" on her property. She receives money in the mail based on production rates, but not all the extra cash from the production comes her way. The money spreads out between various distant relatives who live in Boston and Detroit, Virgina and North Carolina. Owning land in North Dakota does not mean you own the right to profit off the crude sucked up from your section of ground. Mineral rights were severed from land rights during the first oil boom in the 1950s, and the mineral rights to Carole's land were divided years ago. Her grandparents deeded the mineral rights back to her great grandparents at their request, which Carole thinks was likely more of a demand, but she wasn't there so doesn't know. There are many distant relative mineral owners, but as Carole explains, "I am the only one who has to give anything up so we can get royalties. The fact is that I had to give up twenty-five acres of land that I will never see back in production for crops or grazing in my lifetime."

We pile into Carole's Dodge Ram. Her green bucolic hills are pockmarked with reddish brown oil patches and shifting steel. Cattle swarm the fence. Tossed up and down by the pitted gravel road, leaning forward into the jolting breaks, my stomach queasy from the turns, I listen to Carole's headaches with the oil company. She takes a drag off her cigarette heedless of the bumpy ride that's rattling my brain. As we pull up to the location, the pumpjack looms larger than I expect. The pumpjack is the symbol for you to visualize the industry. Every pumpjack has the same world beneath it in the end: the layers of shale, the explosives, guar, sand and water, the black carcasses of ancient animals and plants, the broken families, disputed documents handed down the generations, the monthly checks, the flaming ground water. Yes, you can go underground and exhume the details.

Danny, the construction foreman for the oil company pulls up, a smiling middle-aged man in a muddy white truck with a wedding ring on his finger. He stops out of courtesy to Carole. Immediately she starts barking. Not angrily, or with real rage, simply sparring, sportingly, to show him who is boss. She yells about the erosion, alfalfa vs. wheat grass, about the fence. Danny attempts to calm her by talking about his wife and his horses back in Washington State. As we pull away Carole grumbles, "I told them to move the fence, they didn't listen to me. They are slowly learning to listen to me."

We drive farther down the road beyond the boundary of her land, to a new set of hills, turn left at a grain silo, right at the dilapidated frontier shack, right again, past a trailer park Carole calls "Little Mexico," and onto the highway. Carole is probably wealthy, of course, wealthy by a rancher's standards but not one percent wealthy. Not Dubai tycoon wealthy.

After Carole buys me lunch, I drive away. Looping back to town, I pass an abandoned school house with chipping white paint, a new red dirt oil pad directly behind, the up and down, up and down of the pumpjack as it pulls.

Origin Story

The armored jawless fish of the late Devonian period and early Mississippian crawled to the shoreline of silty embayments, warm deltas, and inland lakes for a few short breaths then back underwater nearly four hundred million years ago. Imagine the endless water. The plants waving like water-logged caterpillars in the Age of the Fishes.

The phytoplankton, so small and floating like a chlorophyll blanket on the shallow seas, named for the Greek: wanderer plant. In a permanent back float, the small spirals, arrows, and elbows of green sucking up sunlight until death. Then they sunk. On the seafloor, corpses in a silty coffin, their proteins quickly melting to slime. Fats last forever. Small lipid bubbles covered over by sediment bits on top of sediment bits. The marriage of kerogen and fat procreated the hydrocarbon predecessors for crude oil.

In 1953 on Henry O. Bakken's land, a drill hit the middle layer of shale two miles down, and the first bubbles of light-sweet crude hit the surface six months later. Henry married that year, became a millionaire the next. Named after Henry, the Bakken Formation occupies two hundred thousand square miles in the ancient seabed of the Williston Basin. Many estimate that it contains between three to four billion barrels of oil.

The story of North Dakota oil is a story of lust and abandon. In the 1950s oil companies drilled vertically, sometimes into dry holes, sometimes striking it lucky. But wells always eventually ran dry and stopped pulling. The companies disappeared to Alaska or Texas, the roughnecks left, buildings emptied, and rusting pumpjacks rested still. In the 1980s another round of drilling began with the development of horizontal technology. Again, the wells reached capacity and ran dry. In 2008, technology combined the practice of horizontal drilling with underground explosives, what we now call fracking, to dig the most productive wells in this sordid history of North Dakota's boom and re-boom. Now, the Bakken produces one million barrels of crude per day.

Lorin Bakken, Henry's son, still lives on the old homestead, doesn't own a car and keeps to himself.

"On the one hand…it's good," says Lorin. "On the other hand you miss the way it used to be, too."

SHORTAGE OF LAND

Barbara Vondell picks me up at the Meg-a-Latte, her blond hair blowing around in the wind as we walk to her blue pickup truck.

Energetic, verbose, grandmotherly, and smiling, Barbara asks me if I want a tour around town. The Williston that I see, the Williston that I pace up and down, is not the Williston that Barbara, who was born here, describes with excited hand gestures. She takes me to the west side where the skeletons of new apartment buildings, the upside-down windows, and modular bedrooms stack at irregular angles like broken limbs waiting to be realigned. The places where the alfalfa is cut back and the gravel leveled off suggest the beginning of a cul-de-sac or an oil pad. Barbara walked her dogs up here off-leash but not anymore. She says, all this, so many of us nearly homeless, fifteen thousand new apartments but half of them empty. The rents are too high. The rent here is the highest in the country right now, higher than San Francisco: three thousand dollars for a two-bedroom. Barbara explains that out-of-town developers own most of the new lots, buy up ranch land, and bought all the apartment buildings in town. Developers sit on them empty, waiting. Money talks. The city has to do something, she says. The city has to stop the developers from raising the rent, but when I say rent control, everybody shudders. Nobody wants Washington telling us what to do. Their supply and demand is going to bite them in the butt, though.

Grandmother to ten, great-grandmother to two, Barbara shares a trailer in the FM Court with her elderly Alzheimer's ridden mother and four dogs. FM is the latest to sell. Before it, Elm Estates and Schatz went. Glenn Villa is close behind. Once owned by local families who lived on-site, the trailer courts sold for between eight to ten million dollars each. The Schatzes and the Glenns hightailed it out of town, likely to the Black Hills to prefab mansions to live in some peace and quiet. A realty investment company based in Scottsdale, Arizona—ReNUE Properties—holds the deeds. Barbara traced all the paperwork to a series of LLCs, an investment company in Alberta, Canada, called Sound Capital then back to ReNUE in Scottsdale. She hands me a stack of court documents with the company names highlighted. ReNUE operates through a Fargo property management company and sent a high school kid to tape up eviction notices on everyone's door. The lot rent for Williston trailer homes went from twenty-five years of three hundred dollars per month to seven hundred fifty or eight hundred fifty dollars this summer with rumors that it will go to fifteen hundred dollars at the end of this year. Barbara started a Facebook group called "The People of Williston Have Had Enough" with seventeen hundred members. She led a protest on Million Dollar Way when the first trailer court rents tripled.

The residents own their trailers but rent the land. Trailer courts often operate as unregulated low-income housing, but in a market flooded with oil work and nowhere to stay, the winks and nods of how things always were give way to capitalism. Barbara says it's extortion. If she wants to sell, she has to move the trailer. Who in their right mind is going to buy a trailer with no land? If she abandons, ReNUE will sue. Everytime someone leaves, ReNUE trucks in a shiny new mobile home and fills it with oil workers who pay twenty-five hundred dollars per month. Barbara pays the rent or ends up bankrupt.

Barbara takes me to meet Jo Anne, a seventy-six year-old live-wire with deep creases around her eyes, work pants, and a short haircut. Jo Anne starts yelling as soon as we pull up. I want to quit the grocery store, she yells at Barbara. She works there stacking shelves. Barbara holds her hand. I want to retire, she yells again. She bows her head. If God gives us only what we can handle, he must think we are more than women.

The Myth of North Dakota

Late 1800s:

1. Williston is largely a tent city inhabited by riffraff and scoundrels intent on making a quick buck from the some ten thousand workers employed to build the bridges, grade the roadbed, dig out the cuts, and lay the track.

2. This is the new land of Canaan, an ideal society emerging in a new inland empire.

3. Sometimes called "Little Muddy," Williston is a rip roaring hell-raising town.

4. The company decides to lure prospective settlers by advertising for them to "come and see."

5. Grand rush for the Indian Territory! Over fifteen thousand acres of land now open for settlement. Now is the chance to procure a home.

6. The goal is to attract full families for long-term settlement—not simply more men on temporary work visits.

The story of North Dakota has been, in one sense, the story of people leaving. The "Myth of North Dakota" builds on three ideas: the myth of the garden, the "work and win" philosophy that promises realization of the American Dream through hard work, and an image of an empire in the making, settled by good and just people.

2010s:

1. Williston is largely a tent city inhabited by riffraff and scoundrels intent on making a quick buck from the some ten thousand workers employed to dig oil wells.

2. It's time to find the good life in North Dakota.

3. A recent poll ranking the happiest states declares North Dakota as the number one spot.

4. We have the lowest unemployment rate in the country with literally thousands of jobs available.

5. The number of tents in Davidson Park is growing, and now a family of three has moved in.

6. "Business is awesome," she said on a recent Wednesday as she surveyed a growing line of trucks filled with men waiting to place their orders. "I mean, you get cute girls in here that actually know how to make coffee…business is so booming."

Natural Disaster

Barbara invites me to a meeting at Spring Lake Park later that evening. She says I'll meet more trailer court residents on the edge of eviction. The early evening sun backlights Barbara, and while she raises her voice and points her finger at the crowd, she shakes her head, an alleyway preacher, a neighborhood politician rallying her troops, with little training or formal schooling. About forty people are present, some with walkers, some coughing, others pacing the perimeter. Jo Anne, at the picnic table, takes vigorous notes with wide eyes, listening to Barbara's rising tone, nodding her head up and down up and down.

I'm like the rebel, says Barbara. We want to try to do a documentary to tell our stories, try to make it as public as possible.

A man in his forties with glasses shouts out that he called Jon Stewart, Colbert, and Ellen. Barbara continues that the problem lies with the city's inability to say no to the developers, that the developers are taking over this city. Barbara knows how to say no. I was a mean mom, she says. I said no. You gotta say no. If they jack our rent to fifteen hundred dollars, we're all going to have to abandon our homes, and why don't we want rent control?

It is a natural disaster, says another young man. Where is FEMA? When there is a flood, the government shows up. When there is an earthquake, there they are. What about us?

A woman in the back stands up and offers her ranch outside of town with two hundred twenty acres of land. She says people can move their trailers out if they want. We don't have water and sewer, but we have space.

I kick into my old labor organizer mode. I'm whispering things to Barbara. Plan an action, I say. Set a goal. Give everyone an assignment. The group decides they should hold a town hall meeting to interrogate city and state officials. They will amass hundreds of people! By the end of the meeting everyone is clapping and shouting. They each take assignments: who they can talk to in their trailer courts about the town hall meeting, who will draft the letter inviting the governor, who will find a space. Several of the women say they won't talk to the oil workers, not to them. They won't understand. They are the problem. Melissa, a young mother in the back, stands up and says she thinks we need to talk to the oil workers, the guys in the man camps. They are struggling too. Not them, most of the group replies. Melissa counters that with them, we might have more impact. The issue never really gets settled.

At sunset it is over. The meeting is finished. I drive my rental car down the dirt road, see the sky's reflection on the lake, and stop again. The shore is empty, no fishermen on the grass. A few children are screaming their feet into the air on the swings. I look back at the picnic tables to see the old women and their canes, husbands guiding their elbows into cars. A discoid cloud blocks the sun sending a sprinkler of rays all around. I snap a photo.

THE STORY OF LEAVING

As I pack my things, I get a long text from one of the trailer home residents, the kind of text that comes in four different parts out of order. She says, despite all of this, even though I may be homeless soon, I'm happy to know all these people. Before this happened, I didn't even talk to my neighbors. Now we talk all the time.

Cultural theorist Lauren Berlant says that our persistent desire for the American Dream is both continually dissatisfying and always unattainable. The fantasy of the good life always meets the reality of "a bad life that wears out the subjects who nonetheless—and at the same time—find their conditions of possibility within it." She calls this paradox cruel optimism. Never satisfied, always clambering. In this place where the American Dream is supposed to be abundant, everyone seems to sleep in the cold with a tiny blanket stretched thin in an attempt to cover cold toes. Any way the blanket gets pulled, frigid limbs ice over, never enough. Anna Deveare Smith quotes Cornel West in her performance project *Twilight: Los Angeles*, that white people "have their own form of sadness. Tends to be linked to the American Dream." Ann Cvetkovich elaborates in her book *Depression: A Public Feeling* that by linking sadness to the failure of the American Dream, West "suggests that sadness comes when the belief that one should be happy or protected turns out to be wrong" and hopefulness gets punctured. As gas prices drop later in 2014 and into 2015, I read about oil companies pulling out of Williston. Man camps pack up leaving trammeled grass and piles of discarded plywood skirting. Barbara tells me she plans to move her mother out of the trailer court soon. The rent is too high. Boom, bust, boom.

While I'm waiting to board the plane, a woman comes to the microphone to say that our flight has been delayed. We don't know how long, she says, could be hours. Everyone sighs a giant waiting-room-wide sigh. I start to pace up and down the hall. A drunk guy in a dirty tank top talks on his cell phone loudly, I need to get the fuck out of here! The man next to me has a pumpjack tattoo on his bicep: the Martian head and long neck, the tripod legs, the steel cord extending below ground. He's shaking his leg up and down, up down so violently the whole bench seat moves, and my head bobs with him, making it hard to see.

Prophecy

Mark Trechock

North of the lake the Colossus of Oil
holds aloft a fireball of gas
like an Olympic torch wafting sulfur
to salute the record-breaking pumpers.

Midnight, the trucks still rumbling
down the two-lane past Lakeview Wrecking,
where their final resting place awaits,
gas flares in the distance like untended bonfires,
six, no seven to the west,
no time to let our gaze linger,
as we roll through the diesel-powered traffic
past the colossus and its eternal flame.

Sudden headlights appear in our lane
down from the crest of a hill.
We slow and descend to the gravel shoulder
like subjects curtseying in obeisance.

"At the end of the Bible," says Jay,
who was schooled in King James apocalyptic,
"it says night will be no more."

The Shining:
A Night in the Heart of Energy Independence

Jeremy Miller

Flames glow like cats' eyes on the snowy horizon. In the nearer distance, grain silos and white fields appear through my salt-stained windshield. The days are growing shorter, and I can feel my eyes rolling back, my lids descending like heavy curtains.

It's November 2012, and I've come to North Dakota's Bakken on a writing assignment. My final destination, like that of so many writers, is Williston, North Dakota, a town of somewhere between fifteen thousand and thirty thousand residents along the Missouri River, transformed overnight into the throbbing center of the Bakken oil boom. Ostensibly, my job is to write about students attending several newly created oil-training programs across the state. But I am most interested in seeing the communities bursting at the seams with an eclectic cast of new characters. The noise, the fire, the chaos—the color of the new frontier—all are elements I seek to capture. But for days, the sun has remained hidden behind clouds, rendering the landscape in a palette of gray. Along with the color, my energy is leaching away. I need a place to sleep.

This drive toward the epicenter of US petroleum production began five hours earlier, in Grand Forks, on North Dakota's eastern border. On the outskirts of town, ice-glazed hay bales lay scattered in snow-covered fields. The round swirls appeared almost impressionistic against the flat evening light, as if out of a Brueghel painting. I pressed on, past Devil's Lake, stopping for lunch in a small town claiming to be the geographical center point of North America. The sun came out briefly as I pulled out of the snowy lot and turned on the radio. Through the static came an interview featuring a politician lauding North Dakota's "economic miracle." The state had the lowest unemployment rate in the country, a fact the commentator attributed to the nearly one million barrels being siphoned daily out of the depths of the Bakken. A news report that followed discussed a report from the International Energy Agency, which asserted that by 2015 the United States would become the world's largest oil producer. I drove on, past a big box discount store, its parking lot pocked with icy puddles. Out front, a garish neon sign jutted into the sky: HOME OF ECONOMY.

An hour or so further West, in the town of Minot, the mechanics of that economic miracle became visible. The snow that was so white in the east was here rendered a sooty brown, lying in piles at the feet of the low brick buildings downtown. I'd clearly crossed that mythical line of moisture, the one hundredth meridian. Gone were the birches and pines that stipple the state's eastern half. The land gave way to bare buttes and the beige stubble of the short grass prairie.

Like the snow, rush hour traffic began to accumulate, most of it comprised of tankers and white pickup trucks, many of them emblazoned in red lettering with that familiar name, HALLIBURTON. Scattered among the Fords, Dodges, and Chevys were long processions of oil tankers, which ran together into a great mobile pipeline, their engine breaks thrumming like jackhammers. I continued on, weaving cautiously between the big rigs, over the vast and undulating plains. As the sun descended, solitary flares—each a single flue combusting natural gas liberated from the deep oil wells—flickered on the roadside. Though still more than fifty miles away from the oil boom's de facto heart of Williston, I had clearly penetrated a major artery.

A couple hours later, I find myself on the darkening streets of Stanley, a once quiet farming town of fourteen hundred which, like Williston, has morphed rapidly into a hub of petroleum production. Proof lay in the hundreds of wells encircling the town—each with their attendant flares—and the dozens of NO VACANCY signs pulsing red in the night. I've heard about the mass influx to the region but refuse to believe that there is not a single affordable room anywhere. I take a chance on what looks like a budget hotel, the non-functioning vacancy sign out front offering a modicum of hope. In the lot, massive and muddy white trucks jostle together like animals at a feeding trough. Beside them, my small rental appears roughly the size of a field mouse.

The gritty odor of petroleum permeates the small lobby, and the plush carpet is smudged with tar tracks. A sign, apparently a disregarded one, states that boot covers are mandatory. A short, bespectacled man behind the desk shakes his head before I even have a chance to say "hello." In addition to there being no rooms available in his establishment, there are few if any vacancies within a fifty-mile radius. "You know there's an oil boom, right?" he asks with no small tinge of sarcasm. For the next two hours, I drive through freezing temperatures, from motel to motel, in vain.

My thoughts begin to turn to the morose. I ponder the growing possibility of hunkering down for the night in my small car, just as hundreds of pilgrims to the oil patch have done over the past few years. In Dante's *Inferno*, I recall, the innermost level of hell is not boiling but freezing. As Dante and Virgil cross the frozen River Cocytus, stepping over the heads of traitors locked in the ice, Dante laments, "I beheld a thousand faces made doglike by the cold; hence frozen ponds cause me to shudder now, and always will."

As I ponder the various tableaus my frozen body might be discovered in the next morning, I remember the business card in my breast pocket, which I'd put there as a sort of failsafe in case I can't find other accommodations. TARGET LOGISTICS reads the embossed blue lettering. The card was given to me a few days earlier by Lance Yarborough, a petroleum engineering professor at the University of North Dakota, in Grand Forks. Yarborough warned me about the scant accommodations and said he knew the manager from his "industry" days, scrawling his name in my notebook. "He's a good guy," said Yarborough as he flicked the white rectangle toward me. "Just give him a call and tell him Lance at the university told you to stop in. It's expensive, but he might be able to give you some kind of a discount."

A quick web search reveals that Target Logistics is not a hotelier in the sense of a Hilton or Radisson but a "workforce housing company...provid[ing] those working in remote, austere, or hostile environments with affordable turnkey accommodations." Like numerous other companies such as Supreme Group and Kellogg, Brown and Root, Target Logistics benefited from government contracts—all told accounting for hundreds of billions of dollars—building bases and barracks during the twelve-year war in Iraq. By all accounts, Target Logistics was a relatively minor player in Iraq. But it proved highly adaptable once the war ended, turning its eyes to the great industrial front expanding on the northern plains. Earlier in 2012, the company began constructing "man camps"—rows of prefab temporary huts now widespread across northwestern North Dakota—for the thousands of workers who'd converged on the region. Target Logistics also built a few larger lodgings like the one I was now seeking. These so-called long-term living facilities, Yarborough told me, were not of the "barracks" variety but designed with executives in mind.

I finally find this particular "hotel" at the end of a road so recently graded that large sections are still dirt. The building is a boxy structure, perhaps best described as a cross between a suburban condominium complex and a minimum-security prison. Unlike the other motels I've visited, the lot is not jammed with mud-stained pickups but holds a large number of sedans, the bulk of them high-horsepowered and US made. Inside, the air is not tinged with the scent of crude oil but the unmistakable odor of off-gassing cheap carpeting.

A sullen faced woman behind the front desk nods when I ask if there are vacancies. She says her cheapest room is two hundred dollars per night. I pull the card and my notebook from my pocket, reading the name given to me by Yarborough. "Would it be possible to call him?" I ask, flashing a quick smile. "Lance said he might be willing to give me a small discount."

She looks at me listlessly. "The price is the price," she replies. "We're usually jam-packed. We don't discount." Then, sensing my desperation, perhaps, she slides a clipboard with a list of banned activities toward me. *No smoking. No fighting. No weapons. No foul language. No unregistered guests in the room. No drugs. No alcohol.* Perhaps North Dakota had become the new frontier, but this was no rowdy saloon inn. The building was clearly designed with security and control in mind. It was an enforced quiet, an island of manufactured calm in a sea of extractive frenzy.

I look over my shoulder, contemplating heading out again into darkness and the scrum of elephantine oil vehicles. With temperatures plunging, I assent, putting my initials next to the long list of banned activities while hoping my editor will agree to cover the additional expense of the "oil patch premium." As I sign the receipt, I note the name at the top of the invoice. It reads, THE STANLEY HOTEL.

"The Stanley Hotel?" I snicker, thinking of Jack Nicholson rampaging through austere halls, bloodstained axe in hand, in Stanley Kubrick's 1980 film adaptation of Stephen King's novel *The Shining*. I look for a smile, a wink, some hint that the name is not merely a fluke of geography but a conscious nod to King's renowned novel—and perhaps, by extension, an ironic acknowledgment of the industrial juggernaut carving up the prairie.

She offers no response. Perhaps she's a literalist. The hotel in the book—and the movie for that matter—is called The Overlook. The exterior shots of the hotel Kubrick used were those of the Timberline Hotel, at the foot of Mt. Hood, in Oregon. Nonetheless, the novel was inspired after Stephen King stayed in the Stanley's infamous room 217, outside of which the author reportedly encountered the ghost of a small child. The specter, which has been seen by others, reportedly wanders the halls in search of his mother. For that reason, Colorado's Stanley Hotel—often called the most haunted place in the country—is a metonym for King's tale of madness and the supernatural.

She swipes my credit card. The machine returns a reassuring beep. "Thanks, Mr. Miller. Enjoy your stay," she says without emotion, sliding a plastic key card across the desk.

"I scanned more narrowly the real aspect of the building," wrote Edgar Allen Poe in *The Fall of the House of Usher*:

> Its principal feature seemed to be that of an excessive antiquity. The discoloration of ages had been great. Minute fungi overspread the whole exterior, hanging in a fine tangled web-work from the eaves. Yet all this was apart from any extraordinary dilapidation. No portion of the masonry had fallen; and there appeared to be a wild inconsistency between its still perfect adaptation of parts, and the crumbling condition of the individual stones.

The haunted house and its cousin, the haunted hotel, are mainstays of contemporary horror. But they are based on a formula established a century and a half ago, in the Gothic novel. Exemplars of the genre are well known: Mary Shelley's *Frankenstein*, Bram Stoker's *Dracula* and Elizabeth Gaskell's *A Dark Night's Work*. These tales, which often take place in dark castles or subterranean passageways, are known for their dark atmospherics and characters hen-pecked by primal anxiety and fear. In the best of these stories, setting merges seamlessly with psychology. In Poe's description of the grim exterior of the building we feel the mounting psychological tension, the "wild inconsistency" of the mansion's crumbling stone and its still solid structure. Horror thrives on paradox, entropy, negative potentiality—the ruin hidden in the mansion, the monster lurking in the prince, the ax-murderer glowering in the husband, the industrial wasteland concealed in the prairie.

As I make my way to my room through soft fluorescent light, I note the sterile, compartmentalized feel of the place, so very different than Poe's fractured mansion. The carpet bears no intricate patterns but is a tidy gray berber. The walls are adorned with large glossy images of pump jacks, pipelines and other pieces of oil-production machinery. (The carefully curated artwork, I assume, has been chosen to stir the imagination of the clientele in the same way a Monet or Matisse hanging in a small bed and breakfast in Bordeaux might remind visitors of the sights that lured them to the French countryside.)

In spite of the "tasteful" décor, there is something distinctly unsettling about the place. Access to all sections of the building requires the use of a key card. I swipe mine through the narrow slot and enter a long, silent hallway leading past the workout room, which is clean, brightly lit, and filled with brand new exercise machines. Though nobody is inside, the television is tuned to CNBC, the hieroglyphic "crawl" of financial markets slithering like an infinite serpent along the bottom of the screen.

The confines of my room are benignly modern—in keeping with the rest of the hotel—complete with obligatory flat-screen television and Scandinavian knock-off furniture. A gray duvet covers a queen-sized bed flanked by two sleek lamps. Because of the ample sound-proofing and insulation, I hear nothing other than the gentle hiss of the heating system and the low murmurations of the television. While the temperature outside is in the teens—with a wind chill pushing the mercury further down—the temperature inside remains a steady and comfortable sixty-eight degrees Fahrenheit.

My thoughts once again turn to the "other" Stanley Hotel, in my home state of Colorado, which squats under gray crags at the entrance to Rocky Mountain National Park, an hour and a half north of Denver. The hotel, which opened in 1909 by automobile magnate Freelan Oscar Stanley, is sprawling and palatial, its façade adorned with grand balconies, rotary windows, and white colonnades; the interior is accentuated with dark wood and intricate latticework. I remember visiting the hotel as a child and smelling the old wood in the atrium and running my hand over the cold, soot-caked flagstone of the fireplace in the lobby. To my mind, the space seemed not merely of another era—it appeared to have been built by members of a different race altogether.

"The past is a foreign country," the British novelist L. P. Hartley wrote, "they do things differently there." Indeed, the historic Victorian hotels scattered across the West bewilder us not merely because of their decadence but because of their utter improbability. Indeed, stumbling onto the shell of a once great hotel in a place like Leadville, Colorado, or Butte, Montana, or Goldfield, Nevada, can feel something like discovering a crash-landed spaceship. Most were built with the intent of extracting profit from the extractors themselves. However, more abstract motivations seem to have driven their construction—an urge (foreign though it may be to us nowadays) to build spaces that would endure once the temporary revenue streams of the boomtown inevitably dried up.

In these unfamiliar and unlikely halls, the mind hums with resonances and vibrations of the past, as I once learned at a beautiful old inn in McCloud, California, a former mill town situated on the southern slopes of Mount Shasta. From the 1890s to the 1940s, the building was a company store in a company town run by the Mc-Cloud River Lumber Company, known locally as "Mother McCloud" because of its singular dominance. The rooms of the old mercantile were lovingly restored—ornate Victorian light fixtures, rough pine wainscoting, claw foot tubs. Several times throughout the night my sleep was interrupted by an antiquated system that would loudly cough to life, refusing to acknowledge my attempts to lower the temperature by way of a digital thermostat. In the small hours of night, I awoke sweating and swearing, hearing what sounded like the metallic whine of saws. The pressed tin ceiling of the room was slanted and silver, and the floral patterns above looked like the impressions in a huge waffle iron poised to press down upon me.

If there is an antithesis to the atmosphere of a Victorian hotel, it is surely found at the latter Stanley—an aesthetic sensibility one might call late twentieth century American suburban. Where the older Stanley's blueprint was guided by an eccentric and singular vision, the newer Stanley adheres unthinkingly to tract housing design concepts and modern code specifications.

Perhaps new generations of horror writers will find material in the sepulchral banality of these spaces. But I quickly realize my unease is less the product of what is inside the hotel than what is outside it. In Williston, the violent crime rate has nearly quintupled in the last decade. In 2013, a few months after my visit, the body of a fifty-eight year old rancher named Jack Sjol was found in a shallow grave with multiple gunshot wounds. Females in the oil patch report being stalked and sexually harassed by oil workers incessantly. Rape is epidemic.

In addition to mounting crime against people, there are also the growing scars on the prairie—testament to mankind's tremendous penchant for violence against the land. Like the inhuman villains from Alfred Hitchcock's *The Birds* or Arthur Herzog's *The Swarm*, oil infrastructure appears with frightening speed. Mazes of roads and pipelines cut across the prairie, fragmenting habitat. Oil wells now press to the margins of Theodore Roosevelt National Park and the Elkhorn Ranch, where Roosevelt is said to have devised the ideas that would eventually give rise to the National Park System.

As in the best horror, the carnage being inflicted on the Bakken is not only widespread it is also decadent. Nowhere is that decadence more prominent than in the thousands of gas flares lighting up the prairie. As much as one third of the state's entire production, according to the Energy Information Agency, is simply burned away. From space, the pointillism of tens of thousands of flares in western North Dakota merges into a great city of fire spanning half the state. While oil companies relentlessly push to drill in other major natural gas fields, such as the Northeast's Marcellus formation and Utah's Uintah Basin, enough gas is going up in flames in the Bakken each day to heat a half-million homes. In 2012, the US earned the dubious distinction of being one of the world's top natural gas flaring nations (along with Russia, Iraq, and Nigeria) according to the World Bank, largely because oil companies in North Dakota have deemed it unprofitable to build the infrastructure needed to capture the gas. This destruction of land, water, and air, mind you, is justified as a necessary cost of achieving "energy independence," the mythical idea that we can reduce our dependence on foreign oil by drilling more at home. Energy independence, of course, is a mere handmaiden to this country's impossible paradigm of economic growth, an exercise obsessed with building more and more edifices like the Stanley Hotel, monuments to pace, sameness, and sprawl.

I sit down at the small desk, plug in my laptop, and begin to transcribe the notes I've collected over the previous days. But I can't remain focused on the task. My eyes wander around the room finally settling on the window. Small flakes drift past. To ease my anxiety, I quickly drink the contraband beer I've smuggled into the room in my backpack. Because I haven't eaten since lunch, the alcohol rapidly goes to work, spreading like a low-grade fire through my body. My thoughts turn to my wife and kids on the west coast. Are they safe and warm, huddled together tightly on the couch, bathed in television light?

Quickly, I button my coat and venture through the silent halls and into the cold. Outside, snow falls softly. The air thrums with the sound of engines, but there is a lower pulsing, almost a vibration, as if the air itself is being funneled through the gears of some enormous and inscrutable machine.

The only option for food within walking distance is a gas station. Under fluorescent lights, the white beasts congregate. A man in a ball cap and soiled overalls steers a gas nozzle into the haunches of his Ford, clearing his sinuses with great force before launching a glob of mucus onto the pavement. Inside the convenience store, I probe through the refrigerator case, grabbing a soda and a turkey sandwich encased in heavy plastic. A young woman behind the counter, probably in her early twenties, averts her eyes when I step up to pay.

"Twelve fifty-five," she says. Her eyes widen as I put my credit card on the counter. "Denver!" she says with giddy excitement, gesturing to the logo of a credit union in Denver. "That's where I want to go. I'm saving up."

"Oh yeah?" I replied, explaining it was my hometown but that I haven't lived there in years. "Nostalgia. I need to get a new bank account, I suppose."

"It's a great city," she says, explaining that she has friends living near Washington Park, downtown, and hopes eventually to be able to move in with them.

In spite of the line forming behind me, I continue the conversation. It is the first genuine human interaction I've had all day. I have the feeling the sentiment is mutual. "But isn't this the place to be, you know, for jobs? Aren't people lining up to get in here?"

She tilts her head back a little, letting out a laugh of wariness beyond her years. Then her eyes meet mine. "I can't wait to get out of here."

The earnestness of her words rattles me. "You aren't thinking of moving here, are you?" she asks.

"No, just visiting. I'm staying at the hotel across the way," I reply, pointing at the featureless box barely visible in the darkness.

"Good," she says. Her next declaration is made with intent and loudly enough for the oil-stained men in line to hear: "Get out of here as fast as you can. It's hell."

Back at my room, I swipe my keycard and toss the plastic bag on the bed. Then I open the curtain, looking out at the long convoy of trucks massed on Highway 2. Farther out, pump jacks and drill rigs roar and gas flares shimmer like banners along an endless war front. I stay at the window, watching the snow and ice accumulate on the sill. I nudge closer, pressing my head against the glass. Even through the insulated glazing, the cold is palpable and chills my forehead. "Now the darkness was shot with swirling whiteness," King wrote in one of *The Shining*'s few lyrical passages. "A coughing, whooping sound and bending, tortured shadows that resolved themselves into fir trees at night, being pushed by a screaming gale. Snow swirled and danced. Snow everywhere."

The ghosts are out there, too, I thought, gathering in that austere expanse of ice and steel. Some are already wandering; some are yet to be discovered; and others still are waiting to be born.

The Extravagance of Vice

Fiction by Antonia Felix

By the time Scott Hale opened Sunny's Snacks and Laundry on Highway 85 jutting north out of Williston, North Dakota, the sleepy farm road had become a rumbling, truck-choked throughway lined with strip malls, motels, and apartment buildings. Small as it was, Sunny's was located far enough north of the densest sections to stand out among competing mini-marts, and since Scott only sold chips, soda pop, and other non-perishables as well as sandwiches and donuts he bought elsewhere every morning, the more discerning diners on the oil patch knew better than to waste their time stopping by. Truckers tended to avoid the place, too, preferring the wider selection and free showers at the truck stop a half mile further up the road. Scott had hung red neon signs stating NO TOBACCO, NO LOTTO, and NO LIQUOR in the front windows to warn the tanker drivers that pulling in would be a lost cause. Scott's cousin and roommate, Ted, who got paid by the load driving a water truck between oil pads and storage wells, revealed more than once how something like an unnecessary stop could ruin a whole day and an entire disposition.

Originally an ice cream stand built by Scott's grandfather, the store and laundry gave Scott something to do while counting down the clock for his real life to begin. He knew exactly what that life would look like, and it didn't involve a snack bar and laundry covered in soot. He did enjoy the laid-back lifestyle of his little enterprise, however, since the biggest crisis on any given day was a jammed coin slot or a cup edging to the front of a shelf and shattering to the floor due to the vibration of the truck traffic. Sand trucks, oil tankers, fresh water tankers, produced water tankers, fracking fluid tankers—the thousands of trucks necessary to get just one well up and running made trucking the roaring heart of Williston and beyond. But Scott's regulars, most of them, did not drive trucks, and they appeared in no hurry as they pulled into his parking lot. They knew what to expect: the tinkling bell on the door, smell of popcorn and coffee, country music like their grandparents' liked it playing low on a boombox, tables on green linoleum, and filmy windows that Scott deliberately left dirty in order to soften the view of the pumpjacks and mayhem. They also expected to see the shop's namesake, Sunny, the yellow cat, curled up in a window on the back counter. If they looked forward to these familiarities they were usually satisfied, since Scott had not moved a table or switched out so much as a brand of pop in the two years since he opened.

Scott could see his home from the windows above the coffee urns. Parked behind a billboard a few yards away, his two-bedroom RV was one of about two dozen scattered around a makeshift trailer park. The Williston entrepreneur who re-tapped a water well and brought in an electric line to create "Prairie Court" did not bother to haul away the rusty parts lying around from an abandoned gas well that had belched its last methane in the 1940s. Once they got used to the obstacles, the residents stepped to and from their trailers like ordinance specialists casually walking through a marked mine field. Scott could afford something better—much better, in fact—but his lodging in Williston was only temporary. Christine would soon be home, and she did not know it yet, but she could not stay in her hometown. And since *she* could not stay, *they* could not stay. His customers were unaware that this meant that the shop's days were numbered. There was no point in advertising the fact. They had enough miseries to contend with without contemplating Sunny's going dark.

At just twenty-one Scott was well set for the life he planned to propose to Chris. They would build a one-story ranch house with a wrap-around porch, and the new sheep barn would contain every amenity Chris could dream up, including heat. The land was already bought, fifty acres of pasture on a teardrop-shaped lake in Kidder County, far enough east of the Bakken oil fields' gas flares that the night sky was still dark. The first time he laid eyes on the land he was so certain Chris would love it that he wrote out a check on the hood of his pickup and handed it to the Realtor. On the way home he stopped to buy software for designing the house, had it gift wrapped at the card store, and slipped it under the seat.

Scott's regulars knew Chris from her photos taped to the cash register, the one on the left showing a delicately featured, unsmiling face half-hidden in the shadow of a cap. Dressed in Army fatigues, she leaned against the door of a military Humvee, flashing a peace sign. Neatly printed at the bottom, she had written: IT AIN'T ALL BAD IN JALALABAD. Her grave expression gave the peace-sign gesture an unmistakably aggressive edge. In contrast, the photo at the right displayed her in a green halter gown standing next to Scott, dressed in a tuxedo and, at six feet tall, accentuating Chris's slight five-foot-three frame. Her smile glowed white and genuine, and her auburn braid trailed over one shoulder. It was the night of Scott's senior prom, 2011, when Chris was a junior and two years away from enlisting.

Scott had moved the photos from the side of the register to the front to avoid glancing at them. School, parents, both families camping in the badlands every summer, her farm, his farm, the town that became an infested hell before their eyes: all of that was in the past. His days were now filled with replacing all that was destroyed, including the losses still unknown to her. That news would have to wait because she already had too much to bear. Her letters unleashed obscene sorrows. One fellow private, a woman from Chris's regiment who, like her, raised sheep back home, was killed by a grenade lobbed at them a minute after they strolled out of the bazaar carrying bags of fruit. *I blacked out for awhile and when I woke up she was blown apart. One of her arms was lying across my knees and her legs were out in the street…* Chris got lucky that day and was barely hurt—just a few bruises on her back where she fell against some rocks. She was a private, a supply clerk who filled out forms and put boxes on shelves, but in an earlier letter she told him that in her first week in Afghanistan she knew she was as vulnerable to attack as a soldier on patrol.

Her latest letter mentioned a more serious injury without going into much detail about the attack that caused it. She blacked out that time, too, and when she woke up she was in surgery back at FOB Connolly. The doctors gave her a local when they removed the shrapnel embedded in her pelvis, and she listened to their banter in a groggy haze throughout the procedure. When it was over, a medic told her she was fine. She could finish out the last month of her deployment at her desk. *They said they got it all, but that if I bleed when I am not supposed to bleed, I should let them know.* Scott focused his attention on the new pictures of Chris blooming in his mind: Chris on their porch facing the lake, Chris taking pictures of her forty sheep grazing by the water, Chris's two dogs ready to rush out to the pasture at one word.

The picture would gain more substance, take on the flesh of sacred desire if he could visit the place one more time before Chris came home. He told Tim he would close up the store for a day if he would drive out to the property with him, but Tim was not eager to veer from his lucrative sixteen-hour days. And arranging a last-minute rendezvous with his parents was too complicated—even though they loved Christine and loved his plans—since they now lived in Grand Forks on the other side of the state. When a real estate developer offered a small fortune for their acreage near the city limits, they rejoiced that grace had intervened to provide an escape. They couldn't handle Williston exploding as if the world's biggest circus had come to town and decided to stay. At this circus, the carnies and the roadies and the audience kept moving in with only one thing in mind: making as much money as possible and then getting out.

Scott's parents gave him two-thirds of their windfall, grateful to be able to provide their only child with some security, and he accepted it with half of his heart. It was blood money, after all, reaped from a system that drew profit from slaughtering the land, above and below, and using Biblical proportions of water to do so. Every detail about the boom was a story of excess, which made it unnatural and brutal enough for people with the deepest homesteading roots to flee. There was no such excess in the wildernesses of the North Dakota badlands in which Scott spent so many weekends and summers and holidays—no hoarding anything more than required for an upcoming winter, no extravagant dens or nests, no prolonged noise. The only thing in excessive supply was beauty.

Scott contemplated these things as he wiped down the washing machines and mopped up the floor. The glut of abuse that wore down a person's spirit—pipeline breaks that spewed thousands of gallons of oil into fields or dumped a slime of radioactive wastewater into a stream—was an extravagance of vice. He had witnessed the permanent damage of a brine spill, where toxic water, twenty times saltier than the sea and laced with acids, sulfur, and radioactive bits of Earth that had been asleep far below the surface, had escaped from a quarter-sized hole in a pipe. Brine spills were like plagues dreamed up by a god to tame an unruly tribe; they sterilized the land, leached the life out of it for good.

He saw a few of these sterile patches of land each time he drove out to Theodore Roosevelt National Park. His favorite hiking territory in the North Unit rumbled from the trucks that encircled the parkland. New roads carried tanker trucks hauling water, sand, wastewater, and oil in and out of the well pads that pressed up against the perimeter of the park like viruses trying to penetrate a cell. On his last trip to the park he passed a feral horse lying on the gravel shoulder, road kill from a truck, its dappled corpse left to bloat in the sun. The undying methane flares on the well pads, testaments to the waste that calls itself good business, burned off gas that came up with the oil because the company CEOs did not want to cut into their profits to capture, transport, and bring it to market. These torches surrounding the park became part of the Bakken's blazing network, a checkered pattern that flamed with such ferocity that it could be seen from space.

For all the waste, destruction, and ugliness, the oil boom gave Scott a fortune that, had he turned it down, would have brought his parents more despair. He held their gift in his bank account, envisioned the life it would bring, and blessed it with the other half of his heart.

Chris showed up at the store on a Tuesday afternoon in July. Scott had his back to the door as he looked out the window toward the RV park where a girl who looked about eighteen was crouched down by the furthest trailer, wiping her eyes with her arms. Over the past few months he saw men drive up to her door every half hour or so. Earning her own blood money, he figured, but holding herself together better than some of the other bruised and doped-up girls who sat at his tables folding their laundry. He scratched the cat's ears and turned around. Chris was steps away from the counter now, duffel bag slung over her back, loose fatigues making her appear even smaller. He froze. *You're a week early. We're not ready.* She dropped the bag to the floor, and he came around and embraced her.

She wrapped her arms around his waist. He looked at her face, which was more chiseled now and tanned below her eyes, bringing out the freckles on her nose and cheeks. The muscles at the hinges of her jaw were hard and shapely. She was beautiful. *You're alive. You love me. I hope you are stronger than you look.*

"I took a taxi from the airport. I wanted to surprise you." She eyed the cat and sprung over the counter to pick him up. Holding Sunny tight, she walked back to Scott.

"Welcome home," he said.

The customers in the front room who were watching this reunion began to clap and stand up. People filed in from the laundry room in the back, and each customer came forward to shake Chris's hand or give her a hug. One of Scott's neighbors, a woman in her sixties whom he had come to know well since she spent the good part of every day in the shop, squeezed Chris's hand and started to cry. "Bless you, my girl," she said. Chris thanked her. Another woman's two little boys tugged on her pants and asked if she had a gun. She said yes and then crouched down to face them. "And you know what?" she said. They smiled and wriggled around each other. "I'm not afraid to use it if I have to." They smiled some more until their mother led them away. When everyone returned to their tables, Scott led Chris to Sunny's window and lifted her onto the counter so they could talk eye to eye. "Do you mind staying here for a little while so I can close up? Then we'll go see your folks, if you want."

She wiped a circle in the window with her elbow and asked him why most of his customers were so sad.

"They're probably just moved to see you," he said. "People get emotional seeing a soldier in uniform." *The truth is, they are sad for you.* There would be time later to explain how they learned what lie ahead for her, how Tim had shot off his mouth in the store one morning because he was mad, mad to be a trucker when other truckers did bad, stupid shit.

She looked out the dirty window again. "Your place is back there, right?"

"Yes." *And Tim doesn't get home until five AM.*

He turned off the music and casually announced that he was closing up as soon as the last customers finished their laundry, and the shop quickly thinned out. A half hour later he locked the door and they walked next door to "Prairie Court," sidestepping the rusty scrap.

The next morning he walked out to the kitchen to find Chris staring at the map taped to the door that detailed the North Dakota section of the Bakken shale formation. Williston stood in the upper left of an area covered with ten thousand wells that in the past few years had spread into the National Grasslands to the west and the Fort Berthold Indian Reservation to the east. She squinted at one section and asked him about the short line attached to each dot that marked a well. He explained that the line represented the horizontal section of a well, the segment that did the fracking. "Each well goes straight down about nine thousand feet to the shale layer," he said, standing behind her with his arms around her shoulders, "and then curve and goes horizontal for a few thousand feet more." She tilted her head. "I've never seen a map like this before," she said. "Little circles with tails. They look like tadpoles."

She then passed her finger along the three green patches of Theodore Roosevelt National Park, each bordered in red dots. "I knew there would be more wells, a lot more, but I wasn't expecting this. The land looked like another planet when I flew over it yesterday. Those white rectangles are everywhere. It's going to take a while for this to sink in."

"This is just part of it," he said. "The map doesn't show the thousands of miles of underground pipe that's carrying fracking fluid and brine to a few hundred storage containers and wells. Only a handful of them are inspected, the ones within city limits. Otherwise, no one is checking them for leaks."

"I thought the state had to inspect these things," she said.

He laughed. "The state isn't going to tell these guys what to do. Last year they were almost unanimous in voting down a bill that would regulate these pipelines—it was a joke." *No one is watching out for us. It's time to move on.* "There are a lot of spills," he said. "They're pumping out about a million barrels of oil a day now, and the system can't handle it. The worst that can happen is brine spilling from an underground pipe, a well bore, or a truck. It's a killer that keeps on killing, a lot harder to clean up than an oil spill. And it's happening somewhere out here every day."

"Is that what happened to your farm? Is that why your parents sold it?"

"No, but it was probably only a matter of time because they had a couple dozen pipelines on their land, like many farmers do. No, they got out because they got sick of the floor shaking day and night from the trucks, from the constant stink and daylight of the gas flares, and from suddenly having to live in a city, a city that's one big, filthy truck stop full of men who live in their rigs and order up prostitutes on their cell phones. This was my mom and dad's *home.* Now it's a pit."

She rested the back of her head on his chest and pointed at a spot near Williston. "Lots of wells near our farm; I bet it looks different. I hope they didn't sell all the spring lambs yet. And I can't wait to dive into the pond—it's almost as hot here as it was over there." She turned around and kissed him.

He hadn't worked out how to tell her. He thought he had another week to sort it out. But is it possible to soften that kind of blow?

She pulled away and flicked a nearby plastic cup into the sink. "You don't plan on living in this thing forever, do you?" she asked. "I *like* you, but I don't think this is going to work." She grinned at him.

"I've got a plan. You'll find out. Tomorrow."

He made breakfast, and afterward they threw her duffel bag into the truck and headed out to her parent's farm. He watched her scan the fields and dusty air that clung above the roads cut out for the well pads. He rolled up the windows and turned on the air conditioning to tone down the stench of sulfur and the noise. When they turned onto the deserted farm road leading to the Dermott place, he pulled over and stopped. A mile up the road she would see for herself why they couldn't stay, and he had to prepare her for it.

"What is it?" she asked.

"I have to tell you something before we get there."

She straightened up. "Is my dad okay? Is it my mom?"

He stared ahead and felt the road shake through his boots. The cold air pouring from the dash made his nose start to run. He saw them riding their bikes up this road with Tim when they were kids. Tim was always a length or two ahead, pumping his pedals in jerks, working harder than he had to. He and Chris followed behind, side by side. One July afternoon like this, with the heat making waves in the fields and the sky and the cicadas buzzing, Chris stopped to look at a black butterfly that had landed on the gravel. They were only seven years old, maybe younger. They dropped their bikes and crouched down by the butterfly. It flew up a few inches and then dropped back down. "It's a grasshopper!" Chris cried. "A grasshopper that can fly!" They looked at its big eyes and jagged back legs. "God made a new invention," she said. "Grasshoppers that fly." It was new to them, so it was new to the world. Creation was unfolding before their eyes. He kept staring ahead. "There was a spill, Chris. It was bad."

She waited. "How bad?"

"It was a brine spill from a truck. Intentional. They never found the guy because it happened at night—"

"What do you mean, intentional? Who would want to wreck my parents' farm? They don't have an enemy in the world. What are you saying, Scott?"

"Some truckers, once in a while, don't want to wait at a well storage site, so they dump their load in some out-of-the-way place and go back to pick up another. It's illegal, of course. And it's evil. But it happens. And it happened here four weeks ago."

"And they never caught him."

"No."

"You said the brine spill is the worst that can happen."

"They're working on it. They rinsed the pasture with fresh water and are replacing all the topsoil."

"But you said the brine kills everything, forever."

"We'll just have to see, Chris."

He was winging it and failing. Maybe her parents would do a better job. He had called them the night before, ducking outside with his cell phone after Chris had fallen asleep to tell them that she had come home a week early. They wanted to know how much he had told her. He promised to break the news, part of it, at least, in the morning before they drove up to see them.

They slowly rolled on and turned left onto the gravel lane that formed the western border of the Dermott farm, two hundred acres settled by Chris's great-grandparents in the 1870s. The white farmhouse stood at the top of the driveway, but its façade, usually colorful this time of year with flower boxes at the windows, was instead an ominous hulk with its windows boarded over with plywood. The blinded house faced a section of pasture in which an unattended backhoe stood next to a mound of dirt covered in blotches of white and yellow that twinkled in the sun. Farther down the pasture, nearly out of view, stood the pond. When they got out of the truck the air carried the buzz of motors and pumpjacks and planes. The side door of the house opened with a creak, and then the screen door. Jack, Chris's dad, waved them in.

The house was dark and cool inside and smelled of meatloaf. Angie, Chris's mom, switched on the light above the kitchen table and took her daughter in her arms. They stood there for quite some time, and then Jack took his turn. They wanted to know if she was all right, and she said she was. The doctors checked on her before she left, she told them, and she was fully recovered. Jack and Angie glanced at each other, and then Angie asked everyone to sit down. The table was set with white china and cloth napkins. Scott could not see what Angie was doing over by the stove, since the light over the table enveloped them in a singular glow that blocked out the rest of the room. She returned with a platter of meatloaf and a bowl of boiled potatoes. "You look like you've lost some weight," she said to Chris. "Not that you needed to. Are you sure you're all right?"

"I'm fine, Mom. Really."

"We're very glad to hear that," said Jack. After Angie sat down Jack said grace and they started in. Scott tried to keep the conversation light for as long as he could, telling them about some of the characters who came into the store and giving them a rundown of the wildlife he saw on his last hike in the badlands: bull snakes, mule deer, bald eagles, prairie dogs. He left out the bit about the dead horse on the side of the road. But the small talk could go on for only so long, and after Angie and Chris cleared the dishes they found themselves sitting at an empty table. Chris wanted to know about the windows.

"Your mother could not look out at that pasture," said Jack. "She had a real hard time watching what was going on out there, so I made it easier on her."

Chris said she wanted to take a walk and find the herd and sit by the pond. Angie put her hand on her shoulder and said, "There is no herd, dear." She looked into her daughter's face. "And the dogs are gone, too." Chris looked at her father.

"The spill that Scott told you about got into the pond," he told her, "and we didn't discover it in time that morning to keep the sheep and dogs away." He spoke matter of factly, as if reporting a bicycle theft to the police. "When we went down to the pond after breakfast we saw the colors in the water and the white crust around the edges and in the grass. The ground was wet. There were truck tracks in the pasture next to the driveway and an indentation where the water must have drained out, so we knew it was a tanker truck."

"And the sheep?" Chris asked.

"Some of the lambs were lying down, obviously sick. The brine from these wells is full of salt and acid and radium and diesel and God knows what else. We couldn't let them burn from the inside out, so we called the vet and had them all put down. It was the only thing to do. Even if some of them had not drank anything, the grass was so contaminated that they would have gotten sick from just a few hours of eating that."

"I see," said Chris.

"No one would buy contaminated sheep," said Angie, "but we weren't even thinking about that. We couldn't let them suffer."

Scott watched Chris clench her jaw. When he moved his leg to touch hers beneath the table, he felt her leg fretfully bouncing up and down.

"I know this farm was your future," Jack said to Chris. "We feel real bad about that. We kept all your letters, and we know how many plans you had for the place. You did a lot of research about breeding and shearing and new markets for wool and such things in your spare time, and we know that when you get your own place you will do real well with it. And you know we're going to help you as much as we can." Angie reached over to a side table and brought out a shoebox crammed tight with letters.

Scott stared at the box. He couldn't bear to look at Chris because he knew her eyes were full of terror. *This farm is the only thing that kept her sane these past nine months. We should have lied, said that all the sheep had been sold and her parents were gone for the summer, told her anything to keep her away from this place. She's not ready for this.* He looked up at Jack. "That must have been real hard for you both," he said, forgetting where they were in the conversation and flashing back to the image of Doc Bromberg stepping through a pasture of fallen sheep with a syringe. Scott knew that pasture as well as his own, had run across it for years as a kid and played and rolled down the gentle slope to the edge of the pond where he and Chris and Tim would lie in the sun and then jump in the water to float around in inner tubes and find faces in the clouds. Now it was parched and dead, along with at least forty sheep, including the two ewes that had been Chris's pets since she was twelve years old. And Buck and Penny, two fine Australian Shepherds that were with them even longer.

Jack said that since they could not prove who committed the crime they had to pay for the cleanup themselves. The state would not take any responsibility. They found a company that could come out to start draining the pond the next day, but they hadn't made a lot of progress yet removing the topsoil. State inspectors came out to take samples and they were still waiting for the report. If the brine had time to leak into the water table, the land was even more useless. They had to move on and would start by packing up the house, putting everything in storage, and staying with Chris's aunt and uncle in Denver for a while. *You should have left two weeks ago and spared her this.*

Chris's leg continued to jerk. Scott grasped her hand on top of the table. "You don't have to worry about Chris," he told them. "I wanted to surprise her, but I'll tell all of you now. I bought some land out in Kidder County, a real nice spot on a spring-fed lake. I plan on building a house and a barn on it, if Chris likes the idea. There is an auction out there every two weeks in the summer, so we'll be able to buy as many sheep as we want. My parents got a lot of money for their property, as you probably heard, and they wanted to make sure that Chris and I have everything we need. Well, we do." Chris nodded her head as if picturing and approving of each step of this plan.

"What do you think, dear?" Angie asked her.

"It sounds great," she said. "I can't wait to see it."

Scott's heart began to race. He knew the most discrete shades of meaning in every tone of her voice, and her timbre that moment was not that of relief or happiness or even enthusiasm. Her voice was as politely bland as a customer ordering a refill of coffee. She didn't mean it; she barely knew what she was saying. She was thinking about something else. And she looked like she was about to jump out of her skin.

Scott thanked the Dermotts for lunch, and Chris walked him back to his pickup. She wanted to spend the night with her folks, and he understood that. She kissed him and it was natural and honest, leaving no doubt that they were *together*. "You be good," she said. He decided to hold off on the gift-wrapped box under the seat until tomorrow and left for Sunny's.

Two hours later he tried to call, but Chris did not pick up, so he called her mother. She explained that Chris was exhausted and sound asleep in her room. He kept the store open the rest of the day and into the night, and Tim strolled in at about ten o'clock when the place was empty. Scott locked the door behind him and turned off the outside lights. They pulled up a couple of chairs by the cash register and Tim put two cans of beer on the counter. "So, how is she?"

"I think she's in trouble."

"What do you—"

"We shouldn't have told her. She was in a war zone until yesterday for Christ's sake—what were we thinking?" He broke down and crossed his arms over his face.

"Christ, Scott."

"Her parents tried so hard to be calm when they explained everything, but my God, it destroyed her. She wrote them hundreds of letters about what she planned to do with the farm. It meant everything to her. It probably kept her alive."

"I know she saw a lot of gruesome shit. She was real shook up when her sergeant and his men got blown up in the convoy last month," Tim said.

"What?"

"She didn't tell you?"

"She wrote to me about her friend who got ripped apart by a hand grenade...Jesus! What else hasn't she told me?" He was screaming.

"She's been through hell, Scott. She was riding in that supply line convoy last month when the truck in front of her got blasted by a missile. I think the sergeant had been kind of a father figure to her, a real good guy. That's when she got hit with the shrapnel."

"When did she tell you this?"

"She called me sometimes."

"She called me, too, but she didn't tell me about the missile or the sergeant or any of it. She said she got hit by the shrapnel when she was standing by the gate of the base watching a training exercise that went wrong. Why didn't she tell me the truth?"

Tim pulled another two beers out of a paper bag. "Maybe she was afraid that if you knew everything she'd been through you'd think she was damaged goods."

Scott tapped the side of his beer can. "She would have to be pretty messed up to think that."

"If she's in bad shape, she should see someone."

"No shit," said Scott.

"Where is she now?"

"With her folks. She was pretty shaken up when I left her this afternoon, even though she tried to hide it. Her mom told me a few hours ago that she was asleep. Maybe she still is."

Tim leaned forward in his chair. "I don't care how tired she is, why didn't she come back with you today? That doesn't sound like Chris. You two have been inseparable your whole damn lives and all she's talked about and written about is how she can't wait to be with you. She came here yesterday, Scott. She spent the night with you over in our wreck and didn't even think about seeing her mom and dad until she absolutely had to."

"So why did she want to stay out there tonight?"

"Right. Why?"

"Tim, she told a couple of kids yesterday that she had a gun."

"The Dermotts have always had rifles and shotguns on their place, just like every other farmer around here. And all the gals—even my *mom* keeps a girly little pistol in her sock drawer, and I bet Angie and Chris do, too."

"Maybe she went out looking for the asshole who ruined her life. Did she ask you if you had any idea who it could be?"

"No," said Tim. "Not a word."

"It would make sense that she would come to you about it. To find out if you had heard anything from other truckers."

"It would, but she didn't."

They drank their beer and Chris's words echoed in Scott's head: *Be good…be good…be good.* "That was the last thing she said to me when she left for Afghanistan," he said. "Christ!"

"What?"

"When I left her today she said, 'Be good.' That's the way Chris says goodbye, a real goodbye that means she's not sure she's ever going to see someone again."

They stared at each other for a moment and then ran out to Scott's truck and drove across both lanes of the highway straight into a field until they came to a back road that would get them close to Dermott's place. Fifteen minutes later they were scrambling up the farm's gravel driveway. Scott jumped out and pounded on the side door. It was nearly midnight, and it took Jack a few minutes to come downstairs. "Where is she?" Scott didn't wait for an answer but ran upstairs to the last room on the right and switched on the light. The yellow bedspread was perfectly flat and the duffel bag sat neatly on top of the low dresser. He swung open the closet and swept his arm through the clothes, then ran back down and out of the house. He raced toward the pond and stopped short when he neared the edge. Even in the dark the salt-eaten, empty pond bed was so white that it looked like a crater of the moon. Another whiteness drew him further along the perimeter to the left.

Tim caught up to him with a flashlight that bounced circles on the ground. "Turn that thing off," Scott said quietly. He continued staring at the milky figure on the ground. They stepped closer and saw the white cotton nightgown flowing to her bare feet and the pillowcase over her head, blotched with a stain as dark as the grass. The pistol rested in her left hand near her head. They dropped to their knees, and in a moment the crickets started up again.

Peace Garden State

Wayne Mennecke

Welcome to fly-over country,
land of people on their way
to someplace else.
Beneath its sweet clover

dark pools gather
and prospectors
for a new life flood in
from California, Idaho, Michigan.

Here the employed thrive
on the roundup of shale oil;
the departed vent methane
from the bowels of geology.

The living dead earth up remote
dull buttes with hammers and knives
tapping unsexy resources
in search of dinosaur curiosities
venture without fortune.

Anyone can be a landman
and secure mineral rights
to hectares of local extinctions

until there's nothing left to claim.
They will horn in on sacred hearths
and creak open the earth closets
along Little Missouri River

where the leavings of antelope
hang like skullcaps in dead air.
A century of deathblows,
generations of bison teeth

heaped long ago
molder in desiccate fields,
spaces where buttes once stood
witnesses to petroleum's revival

in these trafficked lands: this is
the nature of the bone boom wilderness,
of buffalo commons
turned oil boomtown

where stewards of this empire
shelved their arrow heads
and pelt scrapers
when the skins ran out.

Last Call:
Frack Wells, Wood Frogs, and Leopold's Ethic

Stephanie Mills

I come from a mining family—although they were engineers involved in digging hard rock for minerals and metals, not drillers for oil and gas. None of my antecedents had a Golconda or Bonanza experience. My granddad discovered no gold nuggets or mother lodes. Throughout the twentieth century he and then my dad abetted the slow, persistent, careful as possible gutting of the earth to produce the sinews of industrial civilization: coal, iron, lead, zinc, and copper, equipping the ore processors, mills, and smelters.

When, at the family dinner table, I would condemn the environmental destruction mining caused, these mining men would sternly remind me that the demand and applications for these commodities were universal. Without them, life as we knew it would be unimaginable. Our life wouldn't go without coal and uranium mines and electrical generating plants, to say nothing of oil and gas pipelines, tankers, refineries, and internal combustion engines. Because there's no such thing as the sustainable extraction and consumption of any finite resource, the mining and petroleum industries have never pretended that there could be. They're in the irrevocable entropy business, just doing their jobs.

The petroleum industry, dealing with fluids, is different technically from mining, but it, too, is a flaming one-way trip, with the additional impact of yielding substances whose combustion is among the leading causes of the greenhouse effect and climate chaos. The fossil fuel business is a particularly daring technological and industrial endeavor; shorn of any pesky ecological context, it's something of a wonder. It is also audacious, globe-girdling, rapacious, relentless, speculative, and hugely complex. While it doesn't provide much employment, no doubt there are some skilled, decent, reasonable people working in it, as in any industry. Demons "R" Us. CEOs, lobbyists, scientists shilling, PR apparatchiks, purchased politicians: a Carbon Pandemonium of pushers, pushing planet doom. If extreme energy extraction like high volume horizontal hydraulic fracturing is what it takes to keep the oil and gas game going, it will proceed—unless thwarted somehow.

Fracking is a venture that can be implacably aggressive, employing totalitarian tactics such as the secrecy about the formulas of chemicals being blasted into the earth to lubricate the fractures. After these brews have done their subterranean job and been pumped up and trucked off to be disposed of by being injected into deep wells, they quite possibly infiltrate aquifers. They may be spilled on drill sites or susceptible to leaking from holding sumps and tanks. Ignorance of this chemistry and the possible health consequences of exposure to it leaves community members, care givers, and first responders in the dark as to what they're dealing with if and when the infrastructure fails.

Although I have no direct experience with fracking, absent a ban on it and given an up tick in the price of natural gas, that could change any day. The gas-bearing Antrim Shale underlies most of Michigan, and ten conventional wells have been drilled and capped just a couple of miles away from my home. A few years ago landsmen cruised our townships, acquiring mineral leases or drilling rights. Having a fracked well in my back yard would finalize the erosion of the rare privilege that is this beloved country life and issue my visa to Gas Land.

With its towering thirst, menace to human health, pipelines, and energy hunger, fracking is nightmarish. It's like strategic bombing of civilian populations, causing sudden disruption and displacement of communities, fragmentation of landscapes, destruction of property values, and rural livelihoods.

Even before the gas starts to flow, tremendous energy must be expended in producing and deploying the pipes and running the drill rigs to sink the myriad of miles-deep wells of the shale gas/oil boom. The natural gas energy returned on the fossil fuel energy spent in the apparatus and activity of fracking is costly in every sense.

Fracking aims at deposits of deep, diffuse, shale-bound petroleum and natural gas. The earth has a lot of these deposits, and there's a frenzy to frack the fuels out of them, but the net energy yield, the rapid falling-off of well production, mounting opposition, and the threat of terminal climate chaos if these and other remaining fossil fuels are burnt all mean that it's a shaky endeavor. Could increased activism administer a coup de grâce and keep it in the ground?

Fracking is not exactly unprecedented. This isn't to argue in its favor but to say that it's on a continuum: We got here by increments on the industrial civilization conveyor belt. If the fossil fuel spree had begun with such a devastating, ruinous extraction process, would even the monopolists, the wildcatters, the captains of industry, the oil and gas men, the utilities, and we ordinary folks with ordinary appetites for comfort and ease have thought twice? Probably not. Empire in America made its way west via broad axe and two-man saw, river-scouring log drives, soil-sterilizing slash fires, prairie-destroying plows, buffalo-slaughtering railroads, passenger pigeon massacres, and genocidal American Indian relocations, treaty abrogations, and wars.

If fracking with all its thirst and poisons and boomtowns and methane leakage and pipelines and planet-frying greenhouse gas emissions had, in 1850, been marketed as nature-conquering progress that promised wonders and ease, any quibbles about its long-term consequences would have been inaudible. Such enterprises are the late-stage metabolism of growth-predicated economies and imperial societies that become radically dependent on—and encased by—their technologies of exploitation, production, and consumption. This has been the accustomed pattern of globalized industrial civilization.

INTERLUDE

I live up north in Michigan's Lower Peninsula, land that sustained small, seasonal populations of hunter-gatherers, one Big Cut of hardwoods followed by marginally successful farming on the thin, cleared soils. With some woodland re-growth came the development of a tourist and second home economy—and a multitude of Little Cuts: continued high-grading of the broadleaf trees, intermittent pulp cutting of pine plantations and poplar stands. With some scenic and preindustrial exceptions, the human story here has been one of subtly mining and degrading the terrain. Even so, it remains pretty by and large, especially as contrasted with the Ag Belt and Rust Belt farther south.

Thirty years ago, when I arrived here from San Francisco, I used to be able to roam not just my wooded acres but my friendly next door neighbor's and became enmeshed with the land. Then the neighbors moved. Their acres got sold, fenced, and pervaded by deer blinds, ATVs, snowmobiles, and heavy trucks carving two-tracks whither they would. The land became occupied, violated territory, and I was growing older. I began taking my constitutionals by the roadside.

At first I went on the roads east and north. Then I learned that the big landowner whose fields I passed that way was known for a lifetime of mean craziness and bad news in his wake—no one whose notice you'd want to attract. Lately he's mining his land, liquidating his forest assets, logging his holdings near and far. This is not only a twisted rural personality to dodge, but his economically rational behavior towards his trees is earsplitting and tragic to witness.

Tacking, I headed west and north. That route, which served me for several years, took me past a frog pond that every spring became a holy site. The second the ice thawed, life returned and the songs began: red-winged blackbirds, then wood frogs, then peepers; the complete riot, a joy supreme erupting from the long sere winter landscape.

Last summer some banker bought a big lot upslope from the wee wetland and commenced "developing" the site for his spacious American Gothic-style country home. They cut down some pines by the road, thus evicting a nest of barely-fledged kingbirds. They scraped the lot's soil bare, preparation for an emerald green spray-on lawn. As the edifice rose, plastic sheeting that had swaddled the masons' late-season work on the stone chimney got shredded by the bitter winter winds and blew all over the place.

The other day the squire moved in and cut down more trees, these the spindly ashes and willows around the little pond. That day, the frogs went mute. The whole event affected me like a mugging, or the death of a close friend. It infuriated me, too. Sic transit pastoral idyll. To behold all this oafishness, for there to be yet another household on the road, thus more traffic and less wildlife to enjoy on my asphalt afternoon pilgrimages I found existentially depressing. These perfectly legal, presumably reasonable and certainly conventional actions on the part of this landowner made me heartsick. (Not that I haven't found it necessary to cut a few pines down at my place. Fire safety was *my* justification. Demons "R" Us.)

Of course, running out of amenable places to walk qualifies as a high-class problem. It is at the tolerable end of the land violation continuum that proceeds through biofuel acreage and wetland fill through shopping malls and slumburbs to frack fields, tar sands, and coal-stripped sacrifice zones. Yet, like fracking, the developer's or householder's stripping away of vegetation and living habitat plays its part in climate change and the sixth great extinction crisis as well.

THE UPSHOT

Sometimes, it seems to me that Aldo Leopold said almost everything about land that needed to be said, the self-evident truths—or truths that become self-evident upon reading or hearing them perfectly stated, as the Land Ethic: "A thing is right when it tends to preserve the integrity, stability, and beauty of the biotic community. It is wrong when it tends otherwise."

If more of us had a sense of love for and belonging to nature, if we knew our natural communities as our neighbors and understood their selfless service to the whole of life and thus ourselves, would we partake enough of that natural resilience to learn to do without some comfort and convenience? Could our communities be hardy and cooperative enough not to be fractured by the promise of a few jobs and the cash from a lease sale? Could we regain enough sanity to say no and hell no to propositions that not only bid fair to destroy land and air, but water, too?

Much ugliness and desecration has resulted from regarding land as a commodity to be possessed and trafficked in rather than as a community to which we belong, a living community whose every member—kingbird and peeper, red-winged blackbird and wood frog, red osier and gray dogwood, water strider and skeeter—is equally evolved, vitally necessary, lovely in its way, and entitled to respect.

Resistance to fracking is extensive and increasingly effective. Anything is possible. Citizen movements with their eloquent nonviolent direct actions and daring, carefully crafted legal assertions of community rights, could unleash a sea change, and not a moment too soon. Our society just might arrive at sanity before we've demolished our present ecosphere, and we might manifest a will to work in concert with, rather than against, nature.

What if shale gas and oil were left unfracked and unburned under the ground? What if that precious dwindling conventional fuel energy was used sparingly and judiciously to facilitate a transition to a different way of life? What would it take to make that happen? How do we get enough of us to care about nature? How do we get enough of us to organize politically, and in effective ways? How do we reconnect with neighbors for mutual aid? How do we regain the strengths and skills necessary to function in the environments to come?

As we make our way to a non-ecocidal future, we need to understand that while it will be necessary to utilize some remaining resources to deploy technologies for capturing renewable energy, these technologies themselves are not without their adverse environmental effects. What's more, they can't simply replace or equal fossil fuels in their energy density or their other unique physical characteristics. Fossil fuel dependency is deeply structured into global industrial civilization, and overcoming it, as we must, implies dramatic cultural change. In the end, we need to kick the techno fix habit and return to more modest means, to lifeways in keeping with nature. It will be difficult but possible, and ultimately for the better.

Life is whole. "In short, a land ethic," wrote Leopold, "changes the role of *Homo sapiens* from conqueror of the land-community to plain member and citizen of it. It implies respect for fellow-members, and also respect for the community as such."

Can we finally come to understand that flouting the Land Ethic is a mortal threat to all beings, ourselves included? When we begin to regard land as a community to which we belong rather than a commodity that can be possessed, careless, greed-stoked travesties like fracking will be rightly seen as sociopathy, and even the smaller, more commonplace injuries like low-density exurban sprawl won't pass unquestioned. Finally relinquishing infernal, insatiable conquest, can *Homo sapiens* atone?

Double Run

Jacqueline Robb

I've learned to never order trout at a restaurant. Though I was tricked once by neat rows of trout on ice at my local fish market, never again. Their taste, at best, is only a vague resemblance of what I remember from childhood.

My dad always carried the trout he'd caught in an old wicker creel. They came straight from a clear mountain stream to our kitchen. He'd swing open the lid to show off the morning's catch, his quiet smile saying, "Would you look at that!" Brookies, my dad called them, native to cold water streams, the state fish. They were red speckled trout nestled in ferns he'd kept damp with creek water. The fish would go from creel to newspapers on the kitchen sink to be cleaned. Then my mother rolled them in corn meal and gently sautéed them in butter in a cast iron pan.

"The best meal I've ever had in my life," my niece once said, sharing her memory of one of those long ago lunches. I had nodded, the delicate smell and taste of that sweet trout vivid in my memory too. That this tribute had come from a granddaughter who had turned vegetarian made me smile.

When I was old enough to walk the creek, I learned to fish in Double Run, one of my dad's favorite spots. A small mountain stream, it runs frothing and bubbling down the hillside into Loyalsock Creek, which drains into the Susquehanna River, the center of one of the largest watersheds in the country. That, in turn, empties into the Chesapeake Bay, and from there into the Atlantic Ocean.

Double Run is a patchwork of small white waterfalls, flat rippled stretches, and deep pools that sometimes hold a thick water-soaked log. Those were the best spots, imagining granddaddy trout, too smart to be caught, lurking under the logs. To tempt them, we baited our hooks with worms, jabbing one end on, then the other to make a knot too hard, we hoped, to tug off. My dad gave me the prime spot by the log while he worked his way upstream.

I stood on the edge of the creek bank, fishing rod in hand, trying hard not to move or make a sound to alert any fish that I was there. Sometimes I felt a silent underwater tug, sharpened by holding the line in my fingers, my cue to give a sharp upward tug back. Sometimes that upward tug ended in the lively heaviness of a snagged fish straining against being reeled in. Other times, I felt only the empty hook drifting along the current. But always there was the forest, the stream, and my dad, in a place where the sight of even another fisherman was unusual. A place that felt it was the way it had always been, pure and untouched by the outside world.

This afternoon, the beginning of a weekend in late September, my adult daughter and I are on the road. Near the end of a five-hour drive back to this place where I grew up—a place that she loves, too—we exit the busy interstate and are soon driving up the valley, mountains on both sides, a stretch of road where my shoulders always relax in an automatic response to where I am.

Today, though, it is different. The narrow, winding road, usually almost deserted with at most a few scattered cars and trucks, is full of traffic. A steady stream of tankers and pickup trucks is rolling along on the other side of the yellow line that divides the road.

"What's going on?" my daughter asks.

It's quitting time on a Friday afternoon, I realize. For the only new industry in the area—fracking. "It's the frackers," I tell her. Frackers and their tanker trucks streaming out of their drilling areas for the weekend. Streaming out of this rural area that has the distinction of having only one traffic light in the whole county. While this arrangement worked just fine while I was growing up, seeing the fracking traffic today, I wonder what changes are ahead.

The clouds are grey and heavy overhead as we drive up the mountain and turn off on an even smaller blacktop road that leads to a little stone cottage we are renting for this fall weekend. It is on a parcel of privately owned land, one hundred acres of mostly old fields and woods, with a converted barn and small lodge farther up the gravel road.

"You're in for some wet weather," the manager says as she checks us in. "All that flooding last week from the storm, and now there's more rain coming." She hands us our keys. "Call if you need any more firewood. Oh, and don't be surprised if you hear a helicopter buzzing around in the morning. It's the frackers."

Frackers. I open my mouth, then close it again. I still feel rattled by all the tanker trucks and drilling rigs we just saw. But I know there are at least two sides to that word. Ironically, this undeveloped area is hungry for jobs—including those attached to the booming industry of extracting natural gas—but the area also relies on tourists who are drawn to the pristine beauty of its land, raising the question of a disastrous collision at some point down the road. But I don't live here anymore. Which seems, in the minds of the people who do, to lessen my right to take a stand.

Still, I worry when I think about the pressurized fluids the frackers use, a sort of slurry of water and chemical additives, when they drill down into the earth. Particularly when I am here in the mountains where the streams and lakes have remained unchanged over generations.

In the morning, it's raining, the kind of steady rain that usually signals an all day affair. No matter, we put on our raingear and drive down to the local state park. Our plan is to walk but also to take a look at the flood damage. In the center of the park, orange traffic signs close roads to the town below the park and to the cabins along the creek where we stayed the summer my daughter and her twin brother had their first float down the creek in old inner tubes.

This morning, through the rain, I see thick trees and saplings that have toppled sideways or into the water along what used to be the edge of the creek. The creek banks are pushed back by the flooding, thick deposits of rock and gravelly dirt on what was the forest floor. And somehow the most unsettling sight of all, the heavy wooden tables where we picnicked are now tipped on their sides or even upside down, moved several feet by the flooding water.

"Look," my daughter points. "The trail's closed, too." She faces the lower end of Double Run, where it empties into the Loyalsock. My dad favored the upper, more rugged end of the stream, where there wasn't a trail. Today, though, we planned to take the path instead of sliding down the hillside to get to the stream. But the trunk and branches of a thick hemlock block the way while making a natural bridge over the water.

My daughter shakes her head. "Papa was always so patient with Chris and me. I would get my line snagged, then something would go wrong with his." She laughs. "I don't think he ever even got his line in the water when he took us both fishing."

We climb up and over the tree trunk. Ahead, more trees and branches are strewn over the trail. Frothy white water roars down the creek bed. I wonder if the trout are hiding deep in the pools, staying out of the way of the swift current. It is clearly not a day for fishing or hiking up along the usually peaceful stream.

A picture from one of those twin fishing treks sits at home on my son's bookcase. Framed, it has made two moves with us though now it is viewed only during my children's visits home for holidays. My daughter in her little blue jacket stands beside her even then taller brother, both of them grinning, proudly holding up their catch. Congruently, there is (somewhere) a small black and white picture of me, probably a little younger than their pictured selves. Same grin, with my thumb hooked in the gills of my catch of the day. And further back in time, another black and white picture from my parents' old photo album. My dad, looking much younger than I ever remember seeing him, in a cocky younger man sort of pose, pipe in his mouth, showing off his Double Run catch of the day.

The next morning, the rain stops. I pour coffee, then lay kindling for a fire. An odd sound registers, a distant humming, first faint then more distinct. It grows into a loud mechanical buzzing that thunders right overhead. The frackers.

I run outside. A silvery helicopter is tacking back and forth over the fields beside the cottage, a thick cable suspended from its belly. It hangs straight down with a rectangular metal box attached to the bottom, a box that stays smoothly horizontal as it passes just yards above the ground. Sensing equipment. Looking for more places to drill. I hear myself screaming, sounds alternating with words. I wave my arms over my head. "Go away. Go away." Even though I know I can't be heard over the whirling buzz, I keep on. Jogging frantically in place, I shift to face the helicopter as I yell. Its path does not change. Turning at the road, it continues to go back and forth across the fields. Finally, it whirls around and heads down over the hill, its sound shifting to a muted buzz, then silence.

My daughter waits for me by the cottage. "Oh, Mom," she says.

The shock of it—that concrete, looming image that fracking is here, right here in the middle of the beauty where I grew up—is too much. I hug her and weep.

I can't get Double Run and the other waters it is connected to out of my mind. The flood damage we saw yesterday was bad. This area, though, has weathered hurricanes, flooding, and even a tornado. The land has always righted itself, proving its ability to absorb and repair damage, damage from natural events. But fracking feels different. Unknown. Even with all its scientific data, man is at the helm, not nature.

Aldo Leopold in the Foreword to his classic *Sand County Almanac,* wrote decades ago: "Like winds and sunsets, wild things were taken for granted until progress began to do away with them. Now we face the question whether a still higher 'standard of living' is worth its cost in things natural, wild, and free."

In my mind, I see my dad, creel still in hand, pausing only briefly to consider this before he answers.

Empires

Michele Johnson

ExxonMobil states that hydrofracking is a new development in natural gas extraction.

The fracking process was first patented under the name "Hydrafrac" by the Halliburton Oil Well Cementing Company in 1949.

A friend of mine used to work for Halliburton, fracking wells. He jokingly refers to Halliburton as "The Evil Empire." ✳

A UK Parliamentary study found that hydraulic fracturing poses no more risk to the environment or water supplies than any other oil and gas production technique.

Hydrofracking has been used in more than one million wells since the 1940's.

Tim Yeo MP, chairman of the UK Parliament's House of Commons Energy and Climate Change Committee, said, "There has been a lot of hot air recently about the dangers of shale gas drilling, but our inquiry found no evidence to support the main concern—that UK water supplies would be put at risk. There appears to be nothing inherently dangerous about the process of 'fracking' itself and as long as the integrity of the well is maintained shale gas extraction should be safe."

Some dude in Fort Lupton, Colorado, thought his drinking water smelled funky. He put a cigarette lighter to it and poof!—the water lit on fire.

The process of hydraulic fracturing has never been regulated under the Safe Drinking Water Act.

The American Petroleum Institute says, "numerous protective measures are in place at well sites" and "federal statues regulate every step" of the process.

According to a Yale University survey, people living less than a kilometer away from natural-gas wells were more than twice as likely to report upper-respiratory and skin problems than those that live farther away.

The subsurface formations that undergo fracture stimulation reside thousands and thousands of feet below formations that carry potable water.

The Garfield County Hydrogeologic Study examined the methane problem on Colorado's Western Slope. The study concluded that gas drilling has degraded water in dozens of water wells. The scientists didn't determine which gas wells caused the problem or say exactly how the gas reached the water, but they indicated that a system of interconnected natural fractures and faults could stretch from deep underground gas layers to the surface. They called for more research into how the industry's practice of forcefully fracturing those deep layers might increase the risk of contaminants making their way up into an aquifer.

Imagine eight Empire State buildings, piled tip-to-toe on top of each other and buried into the earth. That is how deep the average hydrofracture is located.

That friend of mine—the former Halliburton employee—now works for someone else, fracking wells on the western slope of Colorado.

The oil and gas industry defends its construction technology, saying it keeps gas and drilling fluids—including any chemicals used for hydraulic fracturing—safely trapped in layers of steel and concrete. Even if some escapes, they say, thousands of feet of rock make it almost impossible for it to migrate into drinking water aquifers.

The American Petroleum Institute concluded, "There are zero confirmed cases of groundwater contamination connected to the fracturing operation in one million wells hydraulically fractured over the past sixty years."

Judith Jordan, the oil and gas liaison for Colorado's Garfield County stated, "It is highly unlikely that methane would have migrated through natural faults and fractures and coincidentally arrived in domestic wells at the same time oil and gas development started, after having been down there...for over sixty-five million years."

Occam's razor is a problem-solving principle that states that, among competing hypotheses that predict equally well, the one with the fewest assumptions should be selected.

A study released in January 2015 by the Seismological Society of America confirms that hydraulic fracturing activity associated with natural gas drilling in the Ohio portion of the Marcellus Shale induced a "rare seismic sequence" in March 2014.

Put more simply: Fracking caused an earthquake.

> I assume the dude in Ft. Lupton did not want his kitchen sink water to catch on fire.

> I assume the people working for Halliburton do not really like the term, *The Evil Empire*, but I also suppose it makes them snicker in the way that Austin Powers movies make them snicker.

> I assume no one wants to purposefully pollute groundwater or cause an earthquake or break out in embarrassing rashes or perform Houdini party tricks on the water that they drink.

The "Halliburton Loophole" refers to legislation introduced in the 2005 Energy Policy Act that exempts hydraulic fracturing and oil and gas drilling from certain sections of the Safe Drinking Water Act and the Clean Water Act. The Halliburton Loophole represents a significant reduction in federal oversight of drilling and fracking operations.

Former Vice President Dick Cheney recommended the insertion of the Safe Drinking Water Act and Clean Water Act exemptions into the 2005 Energy Act. Cheney was a former executive of Halliburton.

According to Forbes, low-level seismicity is actually detected during fracking operations all the time but at magnitudes that are virtually imperceptible to most people.

The year was 1972. I remember waking up, my mother and brothers all sitting at the kitchen table prattling about the way the whole house had shook the night before, how the walls waved and dishes clanked. It had been a 2.5 magnitude earthquake. I'd missed it all.

According to the Colorado Oil & Gas Conservation Commission "Dissolved methane in well water appears to be biogenic [naturally occurring] in origin."

According to *Propublica*, drinking water with methane, the largest component of natural gas, isn't necessarily harmful. The gas itself isn't toxic—the Environmental Protection Agency doesn't even regulate it—and it escapes from water quickly, like bubbles in a soda. But the gas becomes dangerous when it evaporates out of the water and into peoples' homes, where it can become flammable. It can also suffocate those who breathe it.

Methane smells like poop.

Near Cleveland, Ohio, a house exploded in late 2007 after gas seeped into its water well. The Ohio Department of Natural Resources blamed a nearby gas well's faulty cement casing and hydraulic fracturing for pushing methane into an aquifer and causing the explosion.

I wonder, did the people in the Ohio house feel the shake beneath their feet? Or was it imperceptible, like the cold December night in 1972 when I slept, tucked underneath my Muppets sheets while my brothers and my mother watched the wonder of it all—the walls that moved and the beds that shook?

I assume no one wants their house to smell like poop.

I assume no one wants their house to blow up.

I assume my well water is safe to drink.

I assume no one is always right, all of the time.

I have more faith in simple answers than I do in complicated ones.

Strata = a layer or series of layers of rock in the ground

Vivian Wagner

I started noticing the lines of tanker trucks at a deep injection well along I-70, not far from my southeastern Ohio village. They'd wait, their diesel engines idling and their lights on, to pump their fracking waste underground. Sometimes I'd drive by quickly on the interstate, looking over my shoulder at the trucks for as long as I dared before turning my attention back to the road. Other times, I'd drive by slowly on State Route 40, trying to see the drivers inside the trucks, trying to understand who they were and what they were doing. Trying, perhaps, to get their attention.

I felt deeply at odds with this well. To begin with, why was it called a "well"? That seemed to be the opposite of its true identity. A friend joked that we should call it, instead, an "unwell." It didn't bring forth fresh water. Rather, it "accepted"—in the industry's strange language of gifting—loads of toxic water from gas wells throughout the Marcellus and Utica shale regions. The trucks seemed an affront to me, a direct threat, a way that the hydraulic fracturing boom had suddenly entered my small, safe space. This well drilled down into the earth just a few miles from me, and the rock layers it hit stretched underneath my own home, my neighborhood, my village. I'd known that Ohio was quickly becoming ground zero for fracking, part of what the industry strangely terms the Utica and Marcellus shale "plays," but this well brought it close to home. This was my backyard. This was my earth.

The year before, I'd watched the well go in. I'd figured it had something to do with fracking, but at the time I didn't know about injection wells. The property had an old farmhouse and barn, and apparently the owner had either leased or sold the land to a gas company for this purpose. Soon, bulldozers plowed past the decaying barn and through the grass and wildflowers to the top of the small hill, clearing and flattening the land. Over several weeks, workers installed a tall, skeletal drilling rig, outfitted with dizzyingly bright lights. A day and night-long commotion commenced. They drilled down, down, down, into deep layers of rock, far below the water table, far below anything we could ever even imagine at the surface of the earth.

The earth is a planet of layers, of history written into the rocks. These layers tell the story of seas coming in and retreating, of plants growing and dying, of seashells and limestone, of tremendous pressure, of coal forming, of gases trapped, of water finding its course in secret underground tunnels and seeps. These layers of igneous, sedimentary, and metamorphic rocks tell the history of the state in a more detailed way than anything on the surface ever could. And except for brief glimpses you can catch along highways where dynamite blasts cut into the pages of this rich and complicated book, or in creek and river gorges where the water has worn down through the layers, these rocks are usually hidden from sight.

Certain spots in Ohio are suited for injection wells, because of the presumed sturdiness of the rock layers and the protection they afford from seeps or breakthroughs. According to the geologists who work for the drilling companies and the Ohio Department of Natural

Resources, which regulates Class II disposal wells, injecting millions of gallons of wastewater into these areas is relatively safe because the poisoned water goes so deep, far beneath the ground water, down through impervious rock layers, to a porous layer that can absorb it all. Essentially, the wastewater disappears. Thousands of years might pass before any untoward effect from such dumping takes place. That's if everything goes well, if nothing spills, if nothing breaks. If things don't go well—which sometimes happens, due to drilling error or equipment failure or just the randomness that happens with any physical process—there can be breakthroughs, leaks, emergencies. There are numerous cases across the country of such spills, though the soil absorbs mistakes, hides evidence, heals itself as best as it can.

Never know when something might go wrong

I pondered these issues, as yet at the edges of my consciousness, while I watched the installation of the injection well. When the initial drilling finally finished, the scaffolding and lights came down. A small drab green building and an innocuous-looking cement pad replaced the drilling apparatus. The dirt around the pad was smoothed out and reseeded with grass. If I didn't know any better, I might have mistaken it for some kind of industrial gas station. The building kept a little light on by its door, a light that looked for all the world like a porch light, as if it were keeping alive the spirit of the farmhouse that had first been on this land, a farmhouse that most likely kept its light on through the night since it had been built on the major thoroughfare of the National Road. In the early years, it might have been a lamp kept burning by a small, old-fashioned gas well on the farm. Later, it would have been an electric bulb when the rural cooperative brought electricity in. The little building had brownish green tanks set up alongside it, with pipes and intake valves sticking out the top. A small road led up to the area. It was all neat and tidy, with the light, the door, the pad. It looked like it was open at least through the late night hours, and perhaps it actually accepted material twenty-four hours a day. Every time I drove past, the trucks were there, waiting.

I watched all of this as an outsider, but increasingly I felt like an insider. I started becoming aware of the heft and roll of hills and rock layers. I started wondering about the connection between this well and my own land, my own rocks, my own water. I started trying to visualize the wastewater and brine flowing through the deep, cool darkness to unseen places. Perhaps some of it had reached as far as my house, thousands of feet down below my yard and garden and street. I started imagining I could feel it down there, shifting the soil, moving the rocks. I started worrying about the slope of the land, about all the unseen layers beneath me.

Two years ago, in the hot California desert, when the well was first drilled along the interstate, my father shot himself. He was alone in his house. A neighbor heard the shot and called the police. I got a call from my sister that night, telling me what had happened. When I arrived a few days later, his room was stripped, all the furniture and the carpet removed as hazardous waste. All that remained was a deep blue spot where the cleanup company tried and failed to scrub his blood from the cement. It had soaked down, too deep to be removed.

I don't know what to do with this fact of my father's death, with this spot. It's toxic. It's hidden. It's unspeakable. It's not safe.

Relating to waste they inject in wells

Fracking involves drilling a gas well, injecting it with a mixture of water, sand, and chemicals, and using that mixture to create small fissures in the rock layer that release gases. The sand opens these fissures so that the gas flows out. It's a process that a geologist friend compares to getting blood out of a stone, and in some ways that's exactly what it does. It releases gases that would otherwise be trapped indelibly in the rock layer and forces them to come to the surface.

Fracking wells start with a rig that drills down into deep layers of rock. Geologists and engineers on the gas company's staff do a site survey beforehand to determine exactly where the well will be placed, how deep it will have to go. After they drill the well, workers install a wild mess of tangled pipes on the surface, some of them for injecting fluids, some for removing gas, some for separating the gas and oil from the leftover brine. Millions of gallons of brine can get pumped into a single well, but only some of the brine comes back up to the surface. Much of it stays behind in a watery grave. The brine that comes out is sometimes held in outside storage pits, where it evaporates into the air. Other times, it gets trucked away to injection wells like the one near my village. Sometimes, it accidentally spills onto the ground, soaking quickly and surreptitiously into the unseen layers below.

Fracking is a violent process of change, transformation, and forced release. Fracturing breaks apart, creates fissures, opens up. Bones fracture. Glass fractures. Skulls fracture and let go. Fracturing happens when pressure is brought to bear on a solid material, something that doesn't bend. It's from the Latin *fractura*, which means to break. It suggests something more severe than breaking, though. Fracturing can't be undone, can't be fixed.

Fractures can be small, but many small fractures add up to create a large breakage, a falling apart. Water is damaging, even as it's life-giving. Under pressure, mixed with sand and chemicals, it breaks apart. It creates fissures. It destroys.

The gas, on its own, is soft, barely there. Even the language used to describe gas makes it seem unobtrusive. We speak of pockets of gas, as if the earth were a garment, as if the pockets were simple things, decorating it, holding valuables like keys or stones. And the process of fracturing releases this gas, as if it's happy to be out, happy to be free of its confines.

It would be nice if we could leave the gas there, untouched, unreleased. It would be nice if we could leave the rocks there, unfractured. Leave the water there, in the streams. Leave the ground there, undrilled.

I wish I didn't feel so fractured. I wish there were some way to tell this story without resorting to strange language—but even my sentences break. The fissures will have to tell the tale.

The inscrutable blue spot on the cement in my dad's room speaks a language I don't understand. Even though new carpet has been installed over the cement's sand and rock, reseeding it with respectability, the spot remains, speaking silently of its layers. Of its meanings. Of its depth. Of its inability, finally, to be cleaned up.

Tercet for Kitty

Karla Linn Merrifield

Insomniac nightmares, too, ferry our pain:
fracking's toxic chemicals, coal-scorched mercury.
Yet, with the despair of Aeschylus comes wisdom vainly.

The Tree of Life Holds the Scales of Justice

Carolyn Raffensperger

A couple of years ago I traveled to Chicago to get continuing legal education credits from the Illinois Bar Association's Environment Section. I was licensed as a lawyer in Illinois in 1994 after years of law school, passing the bar exam, and then affirming that I would uphold the Constitution. Sitting in my old law school's auditorium I listened to speaker after speaker talk about how the cuts in the federal budget meant that the US Environmental Protection Agency had no money to give Illinois for monitoring air and water quality or for enforcing environmental laws. Paradoxically, the new exciting project that all the lawyers were talking about was the proposed consensus legislation that would allow fracking to go forward "safely" in Illinois.

Almost all of the lawyers in the room with the exception of a few renegades like me were defense lawyers, meaning they defended polluting corporations. That day, they got all the tips they needed from the federal and state agencies on how best to get around environmental laws and continue business as usual.

About two months later I sat with my friend, the remarkable writer and activist Sandra Steingraber, in the Illinois capitol building as the legislature rammed through that legislation permitting fracking in the state of Illinois. It was a giveaway to the oil and gas industry since the State had no money to ramp up the legal infrastructure to enforce regulations even if they were the safest in the nation, which of course they are not.

I turned in my Illinois law license. I simply could not be a part of the disconnect between law and justice. Too often the law seems to be a way to justify injustice, whether it is racial profiling, or anointing corporations as people and giving them the same rights as humans, or permitting the pollution of the sky, rivers and babies.

At the time of the fracking legislation I no longer lived in the state, but I had a long history in Illinois. While I was in law school I had the rare experience of being one of three commissioners charged with determining whether a site in southeastern Illinois was suitable for the region's low-level radioactive waste. Ultimately the other two commissioners and I voted down the site and dramatically changed federal radioactive waste policy: there have been no new low-level radioactive waste facilities sited anywhere in the United States.

Our Siting Commission was taken out into the field one day to show us how the geologists mapped the underground geology. The question was whether the geology could contain the waste if we sited the facility above it. The geologists used sound to map the below world. They put microphones down two holes and send a sound from one to the other. But what was astounding to me were the sounds that the Earth herself made. There were rumbles, and sighs, and cracks. I asked the geologist if the Earth sang.

A tribe in North Dakota, whose reservation has been ravaged by fracking, says that the law is Song. Why? Because Song cannot lie. In this indigenous worldview law and justice are the same.

US law now has an enormous gap between law and justice. I suspect that a lot of that gap is because the law is no longer based on truth. When the law creates legal fictions such as "corporations are people," we get absurd and unjust outcomes. Essentially, the law is based on a lie.

As a lawyer I've long struggled with the question of what is law. My favorite answer is that it is the set of rules that a community agrees to live by. Of course the key question is who is my community? If we make law to protect legal fictions like corporations but neglect the community of the natural world, we will end up destroying the life support system on which we all depend. As Janine Benyus, the founder of the field called Biomimicry says, as humans we have "one vote in a parliament of 30 million (maybe even 100 million), a species among species." Justice means we take into account every vote.

Injustice springs from ignoring the rights of the community. Whose vote do we include and whose do we exclude? Consider this: those fictional corporation people have all the rights of human people under our law, but the rivers and the living things deep below the Earth and the future generations of all creatures lack rights that come even close to say Exxon or Energy Transfer Partners—the pipeline company trying to pipe oil from the Indian reservation in North Dakota through my yard and into Illinois. So we include oil companies but exclude the Earth and all of her creatures from the law. This is unjust.

Nature's justice is immutable—if we pollute the water, we pollute ourselves. If we destroy all the pollinators, the soil, and the air, then we shall not eat. If we take away the Earth's capacity to renew, restore, and heal, then we doom ourselves to illness.

The closest thing we get in the law to nature's kind of justice is through legal rights, the kind of inalienable rights that we associate with the freedom of speech, religion, and owning a gun. Ironically, we have a greater right to own a gun than we do to breathe clean air and drink clean water. The problem with most of Western law is that environmental law is a species of free-market, private property law. We buy and sell the permits to pollute. We do cost-benefit analyses on fracking the Bakken oil fields, or the Marcellus and Eagle Ford Shales, and then balance the costs of fracking, such as destroying drinking water and causing asthma and miscarriages, against the economic gains of fracking. Guess which side wins with blind Lady Justice?

One night I dreamed that the Tree of Life held the Scales of Justice. Justice is not a blind woman weighing things in a scale trying to achieve a balance. Justice is a community of all the Earth's beings singing a call to future generations, to the ones below the Earth's surface and to the flying and swimming ones. Only a law that includes the rivers, forests, prairies, ocean, sky—and all that is contained within them—is just.

Yes, the Earth sings. She sings a love song to the Tree of Life.

In the fall of 2014 nearly five hundred women and men gathered at the Future First Women's Congress for Future Generations. They gathered evidence from speakers like Sandra Steingraber and others who described the threats of fracking and extreme energy production. Many in the room were dealing with frac sand mining along the upper Mississippi or pipelines stretching from the tar sands or the Bakken oil fields in North Dakota. They decided to stand for justice and be the voice of water. Sunday morning at the close of Women's Congress, the extraordinary singer Rachel Bagby sang parts of the *Declaration of the Rights of All Waters* as I read it. We were singing our alliance and allegiance to our wider community. We were adding our vote to the parliament of all species. This is what we sang:

> We, the women and men of the second Women's Congress, have gathered on behalf of the waters of the world. Water speaks as one voice. She weaves together and through the lands of the world, has deep seas above and below the surface, flows from the mountaintops and in the veins of every living being. She has spoken and we are opening our ears to listen. The song she sings is one of deep anguish. She is calling upon us to be her guardian.

> We, the waters of the world and all who rely on us, must have our voices heard loudly and clearly. No longer is there an option to neglect or betray us—for our survival is entangled with yours.

> **As the Ocean I have a right**

> To be clean, healthy and unpolluted: free of pesticides, chemicals, and toxicity

> To be wild and free

> To be powerful and playful, rageful, and joyful

314

To freely connect with, and welcome in, other bodies of water

To allow my intrinsic inbreath and outbreath to flow freely

To create, nourish and replenish life, and to take life, in sacred balance

To maintain and regenerate my inherent, teeming diversity

To maintain my natural and rightful temperature and pH balance

To be respected for my inherent value and beauty, and to not be commoditized

To be in relationship with all that is in the sky: to give water to clouds, to make tides with the moon

To be recognized with gratitude as the sacred source of life

To be protected as a part of the Commons, in perpetuity

As Lakes I have a right

To be loved, honored and respected as a full participant in the water cycle

To reflect the brilliant sky

To maintain my natural and rightful temperature and volume

To offer abundance for all beings who are dependent on me

To be clean, healthy, unpolluted, and free of invasive species

To receive clean, unpolluted water from the clouds and the bodies that replenish me

To change shape, form and phase; to lap gently and wave wildly

To meet untrammeled shores with my waves

To be recognized and honored as majestic, sacred, and great

To be protected as a part of the Commons, in perpetuity

As Rivers I have a right

To flow freely without impediment by dikes, dams, and human-made channels

To be honored for my natural rhythms of flooding and retraction

To be clean and unpolluted

To be in intimate relationship with the land and with time, as a shaper of the earth

To connect to other beings and bodies of the watershed, including the ocean

To receive clean, unpolluted waters from the creeks, streams, tributaries, and rain clouds that feed me, and to give clean, unpolluted waters to the water bodies that I feed

To maintain my natural and rightful temperature and levels

To be enlivened with sunlight and embraced by moonlight

To support all the birds, fish, mammals, plants, and beings in the ecosystem around me

To be recognized as beautiful, sacred, blessed, and life-giving

To meander gently and to rush fiercely

To be protected as a part of the Commons, in perpetuity

As the Waters Above I have a right

To fulfill our role as a full participant in the water cycle

To travel through clean air, absorbing, and releasing clean water

To rumble, roar, and sing

To dance in our own way with the sun

To receive the prayers of the people, and to reflect the yearning of the human heart

To be free from the pain and horror of the human-made abomination—the mushroom cloud

To move, grow, and release water based on our own inherent rhythms

To be protected as a part of the Commons, in perpetuity

As the Waters Below I have a right

To be respected, listened to and understood

To be honored and unexploited

To be free of contamination

To be carefully preserved, not wasted, knowing the immensity of time it took to create me

To be held as sacred, and honored as the divine life giver that I am

To be protected as a part of the Commons, in perpetuity

As Humans we have responsibilities

To honor, love, respect, and acknowledge all water bodies as wild, free, powerful, essential components of an interconnected water cycle that is living and the source and sanctuary of ALL LIFE

To have empathy, compassion, and reverence for the integral boundaries and relationships of these water bodies

To learn from these water bodies by heeding the warnings from beings and systems under duress, and to act with urgency to repair and restore these water bodies

To take active responsibility to educate ourselves, children, and decision-makers to better understand the interconnectedness of the water cycle. Part of this responsibility is to revive traditional wisdom from communities that hold intimate and long-term knowledge of the interconnectedness of these water bodies, and to act on and learn from their wisdom

To uphold existing laws and policies to protect these water bodies, and to create new laws and policies and new institutions to safeguard these waters, such as to create Guardians and to elect people who will defend the aforementioned rights

To protect these water bodies by not damaging their ecosystem or the ecosystems from above and below which feed them

To treat other humans with justice and fairness, giving and sharing water with respect for the needs of each person and our mutual dependence on water. Each commoner has an equal right to share in the Commons

To withdraw our consent from practices that do not fulfill our responsibilities to uphold the rights of all waters and to give our free, prior and informed consent to practices that repair, restore and protect the waters

To cultivate relationships with the waters, shared across all cultures, of partnership rather than domination

This Song. This Law. This Tree of Life. Justice.

Yucatán

Mark Trechock

The last time I went to Mexico,
I rode the bus through the Yucatán,
its riverless forest plain and persistent sweat,
the branches weighted with patient vultures,
past the Pemex refinery smoke,
on to the Mayan stone constructions
and the lonely calendar that outlasted them.

The guide with moist-looking skin
said it was all about water,
enough for jungle but not for empire.
A little less rain, a few more babies,
fights breaking out at the cistern,
and the bargain with nature was broken,
the thread back to his ancestors lost.

Back in my own flat, waterless plain,
I hear the Bjelland pasture spring went dry,
first time since homesteading according to Fjelde.
He heard it from Bjelland himself,
who called him up from Arizona.

He lives there now; his oil well came in.
Three million gallons of fracking water.
Fifty thousand dollars the first month.

The Town That ♥s Drilling

David Gessner

I greet you from the land of the giant white trucks. I sit here, typing away, barricaded behind the door of the last available hotel room—the smell of smoke oozing from every fiber of polyester bedspread and carpet of this non-smoking room—in Vernal, Utah. Outside on the crowded streets, hundreds of Rams and Rangers and Silverados prowl, most displaying Texas, Wyoming, and Oklahoma plates. They are driven by twentysomething men who, like their trucks, are almost all white and who congregate outside my door, talking loudly and smoking relentlessly and, quite honestly, scaring me a little. I chain-lock the door and crank up the TV.

The drivers of the trucks are here for the same reason I am: the boom in drilling for oil and natural gas. The vast, dry lands south of Vernal hold about half of the state's active rigs and present a veritable smörgåsbord of opportunities for energy extraction: shale aplenty, fracking for both oil and natural gas, and even the state's very own poised-to-open tar sands. Uintah County has been Utah's main oil producer for more than seventy years. As far back as 1918, *National*

Geographic extolled the area's potential: "Campers and hunters in building fires against pieces of the rock had been surprised to find that they ignited, that they contain oil." In other words, what is happening here is no nouveau drilling dalliance, no young sweetheart in first flush, freshly wooed, like the Bakken Field in North Dakota, but an on-again, off-again affair that has been going on for decades.

This affair interests me, with all the salacious details of how Big Oil sidles up to a town, flirts with it, and wins it over. Not to mention what happens if—or, more accurately, when—the wooer decides to ditch the wooed.

In Vernal, population nine thousand, evidence of earlier wooing abounds. A quick ride around town reveals Big Oil's equivalent of a dozen roses or a box of candy. There are shiny new schools and municipal buildings and ballparks. The Western Park Convention Center, covering thirty-two acres, is one of the largest buildings of its kind in the West. Not every town hosts a golf tournament called Petroleum Days or throws a music festival—like last summer's weekend-long Country Explosion—co-sponsored by a maker of centrifuges and mud/gas separators. Then there's the Uintah Basin Applied Technology College, a beautiful sandstone building with the streamlined look of a brand-new upscale airport.

On my first visit to Vernal, in the heat of July, I peeked in on a class called Well Control, where a movie was being shown that, unlike the grainy safety films of my youth, had the production values of a Spielberg movie. There were models of oil derricks in the lobby, with the name Anadarko, the giant Texas oil company that is one of the area's main employers, prominently displayed. In this case, Anadarko's particular bouquet was a 1.5 million dollar gift for construction and faculty endowment.

It was a short drive over to the rec center, a looming spectacle of oaken beams and concrete and great sheets of glass that revealed within Olympic-size pools and running tracks and climbing walls and squash courts. It looked as if Frank Lloyd Wright and Frank Shorter had gotten together to build their dream house. This building points to one of the less obvious ways the town has been wooed. While Anadarko alone paid fourteen million dollars in county property taxes last year, the total income for Vernal and Uintah County from oil and gas far exceeds this number, as a result of sales tax, production taxes, mining royalties, and lease payments on federal land. In other words, the building is not a gift outright but the metaphoric equivalent of Big Oil saying, "Here, honey, go buy yourself something nice."

Companies like Anadarko must incorporate the impacts of drilling into the cost of doing business. A community center can have lasting benefit, but the companies drilling in Utah should also install the pollution controls that keep the air clean to breathe, so that Vernal residents are healthy enough to enjoy it. Anadarko has taken some of these pollution control steps. Other companies need to follow suit. They should also invest in meaningful reclamation where they have drilled. When the last bulldozers and drilling rigs have left, companies should be able to say this land is as good as, and in some cases better than, before.

On that first day back in July, I drove from the rec center to Main Street, rejoining the white truck parade past classic strip malls and an abundance of hotels. (The Holiday Inn, many locals would tell me, was rented out for a year in advance by Halliburton—before it was even completed.) At the chamber of commerce, when I mentioned concerns about the environmental consequences of the boom, a young woman smiled at me from behind the counter and said, "It's an oil field town and everyone makes money from the oil field. Tree-huggers should go somewhere else." From there I climbed back in my car and was drawn like a magnet to a big sign that said: I ♥ Drilling! It pointed toward a small shop called Covers & Camo that made custom seat covers and was bedecked with stickers and filled with souvenirs, all professing love for the pursuit of gas and oil. Inside, wearing a big straw hat and a T-shirt sporting the same words that adorned the sign outside, was George Burnett, the affable, slightly manic owner. I was surprised to learn that his business really had nothing to do with drilling.

George had opened his first shop, Mr. Trim Seat Covers, back in Provo, Utah, twenty-five years before. But then the economy started to crater and no one could afford a truck, let alone covers for the seats of a truck. A friend told him about Vernal, where the latest oil and gas boom would mean not just plenty of trucks but truck owners with money to spend. Business was slow at first, but then George found his gimmick: I ♥ Drilling! He put up his signs, made his T-shirts, and suddenly was the talk of the town, all the drivers honking their horns as they passed his shop. Only a few gave him what he called "the single-finger salute."

George pointed to his pride and joy: an old black-and-white photo he'd had blown up and made into a poster. It showed three women in hard hats and one-piece bathing suits riding on a truck bed that featured an undeniably phallic ten-foot-tall wooden oil derrick with black papier-mâché oil gushing out of its top. The photo was of the 1953 Oil Progress Parade down Main Street, an event that George had exactly recreated the previous summer, right down to the derrick, the one-pieces, and the vintage truck. At the top of the list of funders was Halliburton.

For all Vernal's riches, there is some fear that boom is becoming bust, with oil prices falling and natural gas abundant. If so, it won't be the first time. Since its initial boom, in 1948, Vernal has been riding these waves up and down, the boom of the early 1980s crashing hard and then rising again only to crash in the early 2000s. During these dark times, no matter how hard the town ♥ed oil, oil didn't ♥ them back. If a lesson was to be learned, it would seem to be one of caution, but as soon as oil returned, the town threw itself back into the industry's big arms. That was the George W. Bush boom, which included a last-minute gift of almost three thousand more permits. This turned into the Obama boom, which continues to this moment. But for all the bunting and cheers, some people are wary. Did oil really ♥ them? They had been burned before.

From George's Covers & Camo to the Dinosaur Brew Haus is less than a fifty-yard walk, and I learned there that not everyone in Vernal is as gung ho about oil as George Burnett. The place was bustling as I jockeyed my way through the crowd. My working method as a writer over the past few years has boiled down to the first line of a joke: a man walks into a bar. I've found drinking with the locals to be a good way to take a town's temperature, and, sure enough, before I'd had two sips of beer, I was listening to a tall, bearded man describe the joys of fracking.

"What the eco types will tell you is that it contaminates the water," he yelled over the din. "But if you know anything at all about it, you know that the water's here. And the gas is here." He held one hand down low and another above to illustrate.

I listened to him for a while, not voicing my doubts, until he got bored with proselytizing and moved on. Almost immediately I found myself talking to the next guy down the bar, who turned out to be a geologist. Though he, too, worked in the oil fields, he was skeptical when I told him the theory I'd just heard.

"That's great," he said. "But just ask that guy one question. What happens if there is an earthquake?" He didn't seem to be actually predicting one as much as tweaking those who spoke with the fervor of certainty.

After a while the crowd thinned out, and I took a seat near the wall, scribbling notes on napkins. Above me was a picture of a rugged man, gray at the temples, obviously a river guide, in a scene of craggy rock and white water. Eavesdropping on the table next to me, I learned that there were still people who had been drawn to Vernal not for oil but for water. Most of the party were river guides, and when I asked about the photo, one of them told me it was a legendary local riverman, Don Hatch. The young woman at the chamber of commerce had said that treehuggers should get out of town, but here was a table full of them, mixing with the roughnecks.

"Nobody graduates from high school in Vernal anymore," said Jeff Hommel, one of the guides. "They think they don't need to since they can make seventy to eighty thousand dollars out in the oil fields."

Looking at my napkins from the night, I find one name scribbled several times: Herm Hoops. I was told that he was an old-time river rat who, unlike most, was frank about what oil had done to the town. "He spoke out at the last town meeting," one napkin says. And after that, barely legible: "People wanted to kill him."

I wasn't able to track down Herm Hoops on that first trip to Vernal, which is one of the reasons I've come back. Returning, my first stop was the Dinosaur Brew Haus, where I met a man named Rich, who works out on the oil fields. He contained in one person the odd mix of oil and water I'd noticed on my last visit. An ATV instructor, kayaker, scuba diver, and former ski patrol emergency medical technician, he'd moved west seven years before from upstate New York in search of adventure and opportunity in the booming oil fields, just as earlier adventurous easterners had been drawn westward to search for gold, beaver, silver, uranium, you name it. Rich now spent his days driving from drill site to drill site, where his perfectly metaphorical job was to separate oil from water in the condensate tanks next to the wellheads.

"Some days I don't see a single person," he said. "It's dangerous. When the weather's bad that red dirt turns to snot. We had five water tankers roll over last year. But it's by far the best money I ever made in my life."

In his late forties, Rich is older than the standard caricature of the oil field worker. He likes Vernal, lives near the rec center, but prefers to get his exercise by exploring the surrounding canyons, lakes, and arches by foot, ATV, and dirt bike. When I told him I had never been on an ATV, he asked if I wanted to go for a ride the next morning, and I, to my own surprise, said yes.

Which is how I ended up trying to tame a wild ATV. Rich said that the shifting and driving were simple, and I'm sure they were to him. But I managed to fall off after only about one hundred yards, accelerating when I meant to brake, and then the willful machine decided to run over my leg. It was not, as I first suspected, broken, and I made it a good half hour before falling off again, diving for safety as the ATV turned over.

"You performed a textbook roll," Rich said. It was the single compliment he would pay me over the course of the ride.

The more I got to know Rich, the more I liked him. Earlier we had hiked up to see Moonshine Arch, and I noted that he, unlike me, did so rapidly and without a single gasp for air. He was a fit, adventurous single man, and I could understand the appeal of heading out to the oil fields to cash in for a while, the way my friends went to Alaska to fish when we were in our twenties. As for the ATVs, Rich again subverted the caricature. Safety-conscious, he outfitted us in helmets and chest pads. We didn't drink anything stronger than water, and when we stopped he would say, "Isn't it great to be out here in such a beautiful place?"

If you ask current residents what exactly Big Oil has given them, the answer is usually jobs. And it's true: jobs have been gained, hundreds of them, and Uintah County has the lowest unemployment rate in the state at 3.9 percent. But most of these jobs are for transient outsiders. Jobs in services, oil and gas mining, and government have all increased dramatically in the past ten years, but only mining and government pay better than the national average; service wages lag far behind.

For Rich, however, it was a good deal all around. He considered himself a nature lover—"being out in it" was one reason he gave for loving the job. The larger repercussions of what he was doing didn't concern him. He was simply there to do a job, cash in, get out. What was the big deal?

Herm Hoops, when I finally got to see him later that afternoon, had an answer to that question. After saying good-bye to Rich, I drove out east of Vernal, past a life-size pink dinosaur, to Herm's house. A big man with a thick beard and an easy manner, he greeted me in his driveway wearing just shorts and a T-shirt despite the afternoon chill.

Part of the big deal, Herm explained, is that by doing his job, Rich makes it hard for others, like Herm, a river rafter, to do *theirs*.

"When I take people down to raft Desolation Canyon, the single thing they talk about now is the number of oil wells they see. That's not what they paid for. They paid to get away from it all. Not be in the thick of it. They say oil is good for business. Not for my business."

We sat in Herm's living room, a cozy place with a lit Christmas tree, a glass case featuring Civil War figurines, two kittens that crawled all over me, and a fine view of the sun's late red glow on Split Mountain in Dinosaur National Monument.

"When I first came here in the Seventies, it was a beautiful place," Herm said. "A lazy Main Street lined with cottonwoods. The old booms had faded, and the two top businesses in town were agriculture and tourism. People came to see the dinosaur quarry at the park. People came to float on the river."

He held out his large hands, palms up. "And what are we left with now?"

Certainly not tourism. A tourist would be hard pressed to find a hotel room in Vernal. In fact, while oil jobs and the services that support them have been rising, the numbers of people employed in agriculture and recreation have fallen dramatically.

And then there were the busts. Herm remembers the last one. Storage lockers of people's possessions being auctioned off. Houses foreclosed. He is not against drilling, he told me, but what is lacking is perspective and long-term thinking. The problem is exemplified by the archetypal Vernal high school student who drops out, lured by the chance to make money working in the oil fields, and buys a house, a big truck, some ATVs.

"What happens if that job goes away?" Herm asked. "He is left with no education, many debts." In fact, at the public meeting where Herm questioned the oil orthodoxy, a boy just like that stood up and said, "If we don't keep drilling, how will I pay for everything?"

Herm wasn't trying to drive oil out of town. He was merely suggesting that Vernal proceed with some restraint and consider investing in the future. For that he was greeted with fury, even death threats.

Over the past forty years Herm had seen Big Oil bring its gifts, and its gifts were shiny. But he had also seen oil and chemicals foaming and floating down the Green River. He had seen rising crime, prostitution, and spousal abuse and a culture defined by the twenty-something males who come to work the oil fields. (Utah has a higher incidence of rape than the national average, and Vernal has a much higher rate than the state as a whole.) Air quality has dramatically worsened; last winter's ozone levels in the county rivaled those of Los Angeles.

All this has made Herm a little less giddy than most about Vernal's prospects.

"I've been through it before," he said. "They come into your neighborhood. They change your neighborhood. Then they move away. And we're left to pick up the pieces and pay the bills."

As I drove back into town I brooded. I had tried to keep an open mind about the relationship between Big Oil and Vernal, and I couldn't deny the many obvious benefits oil money brought. I've even felt at moments, when talking to Rich or George or amid the bustle of the Brew Haus, that there is really nothing wrong with riding a wave, with accepting "reality." Why be a spoiler at the party?

Maybe because the party always ends.

I came to Vernal to write about an oil town but also for another reason. For the last four years I have been working on a book about the great western writers and environmentalists Edward Abbey and Wallace Stegner. Vernal is just the kind of place that Abbey would have abhorred and Stegner would have seen as representative of the boomer mentality that has always been a large part of the self-destructive ethos of the American West.

But today, in Vernal, instead of turning to Abbey and Stegner, I look to one of their predecessors, Bernard DeVoto. I've brought a book of DeVoto's along on my second trip to Vernal, and its pages bristle with energy, insisting on being read. DeVoto was an intellectual descendant of Major John Wesley Powell, the famous geologist who, in 1869, became the first European to float down the Colorado River through the Grand Canyon. Both Powell and DeVoto were forerunners of thinkers such as Stegner, Abbey, and Marc Reisner, whose *Cadillac Desert* tells the dark story of water manipulation in the arid West. Together these writers have created a counter-narrative of the region. DeVoto was writing in the 1940s and 1950s, but the enemies he faced might as easily have been from the 1850s or from today. Those enemies said that the land was vast, and that taking what that vast land had to offer was a westerner's birthright. That was and remains a hard argument to fight against.

DeVoto didn't care if it was hard. He had watched too many places be cored out. Too many places where the citizenry was seduced by the dream of riches, only to be left empty in the end. Locals might convince themselves that it was a mutual commitment. We ♥ each other. But despite the companies' promises, there was never any true commitment to the places they were emptying of fuels or minerals.

DeVoto asked a simple question: can you show me a single time when a company didn't leave after taking all it wanted or needed?

Here in five words is his summary of the extractive industries: "All mining exhausts the deposit."

Those words are as relevant today as they were in 1947. But while I admire DeVoto's sweep and scope, I usually admire it from afar. When the man I am walks into a bar and talks to people, he understands why those people do what they do. They want money for schools, money for big white trucks, money for themselves and their kids. They want petroleum golf tournaments and fancy rec centers. Like most of us, they see things in the short term.

Largeness of thought does not come naturally to most of us. But there are times when the big picture is hard to avoid, and in Vernal I had a rare opportunity. I got to gaze down at the town from far above in a small plane piloted by Bruce Gordon of EcoFlight, a nonprofit organization that sponsors flights over the western landscape. It was a startling experience: what was theoretical became actual. These were the places, these were the fields where the white trucks went during the day before coming back to rest at night in front of all those hotel rooms.

"Most people driving through just see a few sites from the road and have no idea," Bruce said. "But from up here you can see the extent of it."

We are fooled by the land's vastness; we can't believe it can be ruined. But this is a failure of the imagination. Scar this dry landscape, and the scars remain.

Not ten minutes outside of Vernal the land quickly rose and grew wilder, with the Green River—Powell's river and Herm's—carving beautiful and snakelike through a sere landscape of purple and yellow. All that great, empty, unpeopled space, still looking like, as Wallace Stegner called it, "the geography of hope."

But on second glance you saw the straight, squared lines that didn't quite fit in nature, the rectangles that turned out to be the hundreds of drilling pads and evaporation ponds that dotted the area. The land was scarred; in places it looked as if someone had taken a knife to a beautiful woman's face.

With me in the small plane were two staff members of the Southern Utah Wilderness Alliance, Ray Bloxham and Steve Bloch. "They used to say that the vegetation would eventually reclaim the sites," Steve said through the headset. "But scientists no longer think so. Not enough water for the vegetation to regrow."

Not enough water. The mantra of the West. As the flight continued, down to the Book Cliffs and Desolation Canyon, we saw hundreds more rectangles. Rectangles up in the high, forested mountains where black bears roam in the greatest concentration in the state. Rectangles near the Sand Wash, where rafters who put in to retrace Powell's journey were now serenaded by an industrial hum. Rectangles near the unique Fremont defensive armaments on rock spires by the river, and rectangles near the largest known Ute petroglyph panel in upper Desolation Canyon.

To get from rectangle to rectangle, the giant white trucks needed roads. So what had once been roadless wilderness was now a spider web. These were the roads that my new friend Rich spent his days driving, and they were everywhere. One of them, Seep Ridge Road, will lead to the new tar sands right at the foot of the beautiful and previously isolated Book Cliffs. This particular road will be forty-nine miles long and paved, the land scraped one hundred feet wide to provide for a fifty-five mile-an-hour, two-lane highway.

The geography of hopelessness. I scribbled those words in my journal. I thought of how Stegner and DeVoto knew that water was the most precious resource of all, and how below me the Green River and the White River ran through what had been raw wilderness and was now industrial hive.

I asked Steve, who owned the land we had looked down at? It was mostly public land, he said, some administered by the Bureau of Land Management and some by the US Forest Service. In other words, *we own* this land. It belongs to all of us; it's our land, our heritage.

You would be wise not to make that case too loudly in Vernal. I wouldn't want to walk out on my hotel balcony and announce that this land is my land, public land that the oil companies are coring out for profit. "*Your land*?" most people in Vernal would respond incredulously.

It's *our* land, they would say. *Our* birthright. And, they might add, if we want to trade our birthright for a climbing wall or a fancy petroleum college, then we damn well will.

It is an argument that is hard to counter. And I have no doubt it will ring out here forever. Or at least until the wooing is over and Vernal, along with its oil and gas, lies exhausted.

Shift

Wayne Mennecke

We meet in the garage
at his lab bench of broken projects and rough drafts.

The self-taught paleontologist demonstrates
how to make museum quality resin casts of dinosaur bones.

Doug uses towers of Legos
framing a fossil within the bricks

then pours silicon,
viscid like melted cheese

down into the column. Four hours later
the bone is released from the rubber negative

and color tinted resin mixed with catalyst
are poured into the silicon mold.

In four minutes the resin hardens
as a perfect copy of the original fossil.

This he imparts on us
educator to educators

volunteer to volunteers
inventor to disciples.

We meet at the bar for drinks years later.
He works the Bakken dark pools now

trading fossils for tight oil and a guaranteed payday
plying at towers, extracting cores

fracturing shale,
still an agent of discovery

detached from career
family and ex-wife.

Our group glorifies new dig sites,
chats up current paleo research

and future publications,
but tonight Doug sits

curing with surrender
at the bar's edge

eyes searching out rapture
in an open faced grilled cheese sandwich.

Sand in My Backyard

Jon Jensen

I have sand in my backyard. My kids love to play in the sand, building miniature roads and cities, a whole world of their own creation, their fantasies playing out on the landscape. But my kids are not the only ones who love the sand and want to use it to live out their fantasies. After millennia underground the sand in my area is suddenly valuable, a commodity that corporations covet even more than kids. Now the dumptrucks don't say Tonka on the side—and the fantasies being lived out are all too real and threaten to devastate the landscape as if a big bully came to kick in the mini-cities of children's sand boxes.

Fracking isn't just about oil—it's also sand and water, people and community—and the destruction from fracking has come home to my backyard, the beautiful bluffs and hills of Northeast Iowa. And the questions raised by fracking are not just for North Dakota and Texas; these questions are crucial for all people and all places.

What do we make of this new "sand grab" that accompanies hydraulic fracturing? How do I protect my backyard without spoiling other places? How can I make sense of the complexity of (and my own complicity in) this latest folly of our industrial, fossil fuel culture? What are the alternatives, short and long-term, that can take us in a new direction, lead us past fracking to create a real, lasting, and resilient culture that builds communities rather than destroying them?

These are the questions that keep me awake at night, that haunt my dreams and drive me deeper into the Driftless Region that is my backyard not in search of sand but of answers.

Fracking has many impacts, some of which extend well beyond the drilling sites. Like all environmental problems, these impacts are experienced locally and vary by region. Water quality in Pennsylvania. Social unrest in North Dakota. Increased seismic activity in Oklahoma. The list could go on and on.

Where I live in the Driftless Region of the Upper Mississippi Valley we are far from any fracking sites, but the impacts are here as well. Our region, defined by rolling hills and bluffs, evidence that the glaciers missed us and left no glacial "drift" behind, may not have oil and gas but we do have sand. This may not seem special—there is sand everywhere; it's one of the basic geological building blocks of our earth. But our sand is different; our sand is special. No offense but our sand is better than your sand—at least if you want to crack open rock and hold it open to extract fossil fuels.

While the Driftless Region may be defined geologically by the absence of glacial events, the region is increasingly defined economically by the presence of sand mining. The St. Peter and Jordan sandstone found near the surface in areas throughout southwest Wisconsin, southeast Minnesota, and northeast Iowa is the latest hot commodity for our industrial economy, hell-bent on destroying the

Earth as quickly as possible in the name of cheap energy and quick profits. This sandstone contains what the industry calls "high-quality silica sand" and the surrounding communities increasingly call "frac sand."

This special sand is extra hard and just the right size for propping open the cracks or fractures that are the result of the high pressure injections of water, chemicals, and, yes, sand. These "injection liquids" for hydraulic fracturing are not just water but a "chemical soup," a very sandy chemical soup. That sand comes from my backyard, the area that I call home, a beautiful area that is increasingly dotted with open pit mines.

Like all mining, the sand industry had its "boom time" with exponential growth in the number of mines and amount of sand. Wisconsin gives a taste of this boom. In 2010 only five sand mines existed in the state and most of them were operational for decades. By 2013, over one hundred sand mines were open, most serving the fracking industry and operating on a scale and schedule that overwhelmed the surrounding communities and countryside.

In addition to their impacts on the land—converting beautiful countryside to industrial wasteland—these mines pose a threat to public health. Silica dust causes lung ailments, from acute silicosis, which can be fatal, to asthma and other chronic conditions more difficult to track and causally identify. If the dust doesn't get you, watch out for acrylamide, a chemical byproduct from sand processing that is a known neurotoxin and probable carcinogen. Its presence in the wastewater at sand processing sites should be a concern to rural communities, a bit of shrapnel from the collateral damage that never gets counted in the cost-benefit of industrial mining.

Then there are the trucks—hundreds, thousands of them pounding the rural roads and disturbing the countryside. The impacts on roads are being studied, but we must expand the analysis and consider the big picture. How much embodied energy is in the transportation infrastructure necessary for this mining? What are the public health costs from the diesel particulates inhaled by rural residents who live along truck routes? How do we account for the safety issues that inevitably accompany large-scale trucking? Who measures the losses in quality of life, the noise pollution, the impacts on wildlife, and the countless intangibles?

The mines, especially in Wisconsin, crept into the countryside largely unnoticed at first, but now the opposition has grown and organized. Iowa is the last state to be invaded by this sand grab. Not much of Iowa has this special sand, only a little corner, just three of Iowa's ninety-nine counties have significant quantities of frac sand. Geologists call this region the Paleozoic Plateau; tourists and locals call it "God's country"; sand companies call it "pay day." Now activists call it a battle zone.

Here in Northeast Iowa, groups have organized locally to fight new mines under the heading of "protectors." In Winneshiek County where I live, the protectors are a local group of citizens "dedicated to protecting the natural resources and public health of Winneshiek County." Young and old, these citizen environmentalists organized to fight back against fracking, to stop the sand mining, to say to the corporations: "not here" and "you can't have our sand." Here the protectors secured a moratorium on new mining permits. They organized and protested, fighting the corporations that threaten what we care about and value.

The image of protectors is powerful; these are the fighters who will defend our homeland from the threats of industrial mining. Defense, protection, fighting back are all common themes of the environmental movement. The threats change—pollution, extinction, logging, mining, etc.—but the need to fight, to protect, to save nature is consistent.

The protectors are out there fighting all aspects of fracking and all the environmental problems from mountaintop removal in West Virginia to old growth logging in the Pacific Northwest. This is what environmentalists do—they fight back against the despoilers; they are the good guys protecting nature from the corrupt corporations.

We all should join them, join the good fight to stop fracking, stop sand mining, protect our homes and stop the despoilers.

This essay could end here. We know what to do—let's just do it.

But it's not that simple. While we need protectors and we need to stop fracking, we also need to go deeper, to take a closer look and make sure that we aren't guilty of the oversimplification that is part of the problem with fracking.

There are at least three problems with the protectors' response, the environmental response, to the issue of sand mining. It fails to acknowledge our own complicity in the system, risks oversimplifying the causes, and falls short of the imperative to offer a viable and compelling alternative. Let's start with complicity.

We are all, even the protectors who organize in opposition to it, deeply complicit in the economy and systems that support and drive the fracking industry. We drive cars that run on fracked oil, heat our homes with fracked natural gas, and wash our clothes with hot water from fossil fuels. At a deeper level, we depend upon an industrial economy that demands cheap energy and spews out the profits that we depend on; they pay my students' tuition and provide my salary.

To be complicit is not the same as being to blame or responsible. But it is a type of responsibility. We must oppose fracking, but we must be careful not to do so blindly. We must recognize our own moral entanglement in the larger systems that drive the fracking industry and work to change the system, not simply stop the consequences.

Am I a hypocrite if I oppose fracking but also drive a car running on gasoline that may have come from fracked oil? Not necessarily, but simply posing the question illustrates the ways that it is problematic to see this as "us vs. them," the evil despoilers of the environment against the protectors of nature. We are all destroyers of the environment. We are all complicit in the structures and systems that create and sustain the industrial economy. We are all miners. No one lives in our society without causing harm. Once we fully grasp this complicity, it should be clear that it is not enough simply to fight; we must change the game.

Opposition to sand mining has to deal with charges of NIMBY, merely wanting to make sure that the mining is "Not In My Back Yard." This attitude is seen as a type of selfishness, wanting my place to be pristine but not caring what happens elsewhere. Are we only trying to protect our place but ignoring the impacts on other places?

To charges of NIMBY I start by pleading guilty: I don't want this mining in my backyard. This is a beautiful place; it's my place, and I love it. I will not apologize for loving this place and wanting to protect it from influences that threaten its beauty and health. But the larger question here is important: What happens when a local community is successful in protecting itself from a threat? Does it simply push that same threat, in this case a sand mine, onto another community, perhaps one with fewer resources? That may be a win for me but it's not a win in any larger sense. The protection is minimal at best.

Without a larger response, fighting back in one place is likely to push the mining to somewhere else, most likely to a community that is poorer or less organized. This is why the environmental response has often not worked in the past and is not likely to work here. We need a fuller response, a different way of seeing this issue, this time, this predicament.

This is not true just for fracking or sand mining, the same is true for most "environmental" issues. Environmentalists like to see things as black and white. It's us and them, the good guys and bad guys, the evil fossil fuel industry vs. the good greens.

Environmentalism with this narrative is about stopping bad stuff, and there is no shortage of bad stuff that needs to be stopped. We need to halt the destruction of people and planet; we need to protect our communities to defend ourselves and all life. But if we widen our lens, pan out from a narrow focus we begin to see a different picture, a new view that makes the black and white blurry and raises questions about how we got here and whether we can really protect "the environment" from the transgressors. We think of the environment as a "thing" that needs to be protected instead of seeing ourselves as part of the larger system. We fail to recognize the ways that we are tied up in the larger systems that produce fracking and sand mining, that we are complicit in the same economy and systems that lead inevitably to this destruction.

Maybe it is time to step back and take another look. We can start with the realization that frac sand mining, and fracking in general, is simply the logical conclusion of a set of assumptions and systems that have been in place for decades.

It is helpful to articulate some of the assumptions behind this mining so we do not, in the end, merely halt this evil to find ourselves facing another, perhaps worse evil, in its place. Fracking assumes that

- places, especially rural places, are dispensable;

- profit is the only important factor in deciding whether to pursue an activity;

- any activity that produces jobs is a good thing regardless of the impacts;

- nothing is sacred except for economic growth; and

- local communities are not capable of making decisions about their own land and which activities to allow on this land.

Even beginning to articulate this list illustrates the ways that fracking, like so many of the problems we face as a society, is the result of short-sightedness, or a lack of vision. In the short-term, it seems like a good idea; it is another way to meet our society's "need" for fossil fuels. But a longer term perspective gives a very different look; it allows us to see other issues—water and seismic concerns, community impacts, and the deeper issues of culture and economy that led us here. We need new vision to see clearly; we need a wide angle that illuminates new perspectives and alternatives.

While opposition to sand mining in the short-term is essential, it is not sufficient. This opposition must be accompanied by a long-term perspective that grasps the power structures involved and the way that this sand mining is the working out of a system, a system in which we are complicit.

We also need to make this issue personal, not simply by getting involved in the opposition but by internalizing and personalizing the larger questions of energy usage, consumption, and lifestyle. We must put our own lives in order to ensure we have integrity and right livelihood behind our larger, public opposition. We cannot avoid doing harm; it's simply not possible within the systems of our society. But we can make sure we work to minimize our dependence on fossil fuels and our buying into the larger industrial economy. As Wendell Berry powerfully notes in his essay, "Think Little," this work cannot be merely public or political:

> If we are to hope to correct our abuses...then we are
> going to have to go far beyond public protest and
> political action. We are going to have to rebuild the
> substance and the integrity of private life in this country.
> … A man who is willing to undertake the discipline and
> the difficulty of mending his own ways is worth more
> to the conservation movement than a hundred who are
> insisting merely than the government and the industries
> mend their ways.

We also need a countervailing narrative, a different way of picturing our world and our way of relating to the planet and to individual places. We need to see ourselves living without fossil fuels, without dependence on mining jobs, and economic growth. The environmental movement has generally failed with this task. They/we have focused on protecting and preserving and on halting bad actions but have not often articulated the alternative.

Much good is happening on both of these fronts. Individuals are working to put their houses in order, to ensure that the household is as much an arena for action as the courthouse. At the same time, communities are recognizing that a transition beyond fossil fuels is possible; transcending industrialism in favor of a local economy that builds and maintains sustainable, resilient communities is not something to be feared but to be embraced and celebrated.

None of this means that the protectors are wrong. In fact their work is essential. Without the protectors, little else is possible; they buy the time and space to take this deeper look and provide this fuller response. But fighting back is not an endpoint; it is a necessary first step, making room for this new vision, this larger approach.

Opposition can catalyze and drive the necessary shifts in values and systems that lead to real change. Fighting back can be the first step toward alternative ways of thinking and innovative new practices. Protection of our home places might inspire new ways of living in these places, new economies, cultures, and systems. Here in Northeast Iowa, that larger approach is embodied in the work of groups like the Winneshiek Energy District and the Community Rights Alliance, creating a new energy economy and asserting the rights of communities to determine their own fate.

Maybe it's time we environmentalists returned to the sandbox along with the kids. Not to mine the sand or even to build protective walls to keep out the bullies. But to dream with the sand, to design and build, create and think freely. What if we had a local economy so strong that trucking jobs did not seem attractive to the rural poor? What if we designed communities that were walkable and bikeable so that cars seemed unnecessary and the demand for oil plummeted? What if we strengthened local, democratic politics so communities determined their own fates and had the power to stop industrial mining? What if we had a society that did not depend on fossil fuels?

Sound too good to be true? A farfetched dream? Perhaps but that's the point of the sandbox; it's a place for dreaming big dreams, for creating new worlds and imagining new ways of being. Kids protect their sandboxes from bullies, those who would destroy. But more importantly, they protect their creations because they know the power of vision to transform the world. Our opposition to fracking is essential, but protection alone is not enough. We need vision and perspective, deep understanding, new systems, and practical solutions. We need the sand in our backyards because the sandbox is the place of the dreams and vision that will really stop the fracking.

A Stranger in a Bar

Michelle Donahue

He yells with gravel
in his throat, a tongue that
tastes of soot & other
blackened things, voice a
rumble that joins the jukebox,
the clang of change in his dark-
wash jeans, work boots
thumping as he dances.

Later. It is dark & quiet,
we sit face-to-face in a booth
in the back & he begins his
story, voice booming
with the clanks of glass, then
low, a wave's crash:
loud as it crests, soft as
it falls to whispers.

His hands—hard beaten,
weathered—leave sweat

on the table. He bobs his
head, shakes that greasy hair,
as familiar words tap from his
tongue: *pumpjack, seismic, basin*
shaft. I pick at his silent stretches,
the dark space between breaths.

I wonder at that rise & fall,
how words gather, escape
from lips unheard. I know
nothing, a man delivering
a story like glass: transparent
until broken, seen only
as shards, from a glimpse
of that splintered edge.

The Ultimate Out of Balance

Fiction by Maryann Lesert

We came to know that fracking can look uglier and uglier depending on who, ultimately, is in charge. From the rusty sheet metal welded to the framework of their 136-foot-tall monster of a drill rig to the messes they left behind, Dillon sites, we soon discovered, were pure carelessness and slop.

When we arrived at the Wheeler well site, the gates were open and the security trailer was gone. The last time we'd visited, the wellhead was surrounded by trucks, hoses dangling, limp, as a huge tension-arm fed flexible tubing down into the well bore. Clean-out pipe, the supervisor had told us. Now, the long triangular gates were wide open and everything was gone: no metal coils snaking across the ground, no compressors or diesel engines or light racks, nothing but a vast, flat swath of flesh-colored dirt.

Sonja appeared at my side. "It's a wasteland," she said.

"Fricking *the* Wasteland," Kate bobbed.

It's possible that T. S. Eliot himself wouldn't have been able to imagine such a thing: the black plastic liner torn and lying in clumps, the mustard yellow and rust-colored stains wherever the dirt was exposed, the waxy sheen on the surface of the drought-dry earth, and all of it set across the road from the Amish farm where the family's oldest son drove a horse drawn rake through the field. He stopped to say hello and told us that just that morning a slew of trucks had come and hauled everything away. Everything except the chemical barrels and jugs left here and there, hoses left open to the ground where evidence of their contents fanned out in salty stains. Everything except the torn black liner that was supposed to provide a barrier against spills, and our favorite find: a small plastic box labeled *Five Minute Escape Pack*.

It was ecological apocalypse on a six-to-ten-acre scale.

We stumbled around the site for two hours that afternoon, taking pictures.

Though Sonja and Kate were former students, after a summer of visiting frack well sites together the three of us were becoming research partners. Sonja was working on her senior thesis, the sensory story of fracking, and Kate kept us connected to people, writing songs about the people and places affected by fracking. We took pictures for the articles I was writing. Get-the-word out pieces to let people know that fracking had come to Michigan, and as our friends in Pennsylvania warned, it had taken the industry only two to three years to fundamentally change our forests.

It was August, in the middle of a months-long drought that had been scorching crops with ninety-degree heat, and the sky above was roiling with cold blue clouds that refused to let go of their moisture.

Sonja and I knelt in front of chemical barrels, photographing labels and tearing off any packing slips we found. Kate replenished our silver colloidal soaked handkerchiefs covering our noses and mouths and wandered about the site, taking video of the frogs that blended in with the pasty green water, their backs matching the green-white sheen of the water pooled around the entrance gate.

Three plastic barrels, each with their own hazardous symbols, were left sitting out in the hot August sun, even though the symbols indicated various degrees of combustibility when exposed to heat and sunlight. Warnings included hazardous vapors and inhalation dangers, chemicals listed that could eat through the soft tissue linings of the lungs or the esophagus. Left out in the full sun, for how long? And for how much longer?

But nothing prepared us for the sewage-looking mote around the pit that spanned the back edge of the well pad.

The black plastic liner that was supposed to be cleanly draped over the edges of the pit was torn in too many places to photograph. It was obvious from the bull-dozed pile of dried and stained run-off that the liner had ripped often. Shredded pieces of black plastic were laced within piles of crusted dirt. Dried erosion tracks ran down the side of the pit's dirt walls, ending in salt stains and dirt that looked as if plastic coated its surface.

Haas, the head of the Michigan Department of Environmental Quality's Oil and Gas Division, always made a point to laud Michigan's storage regulations, which did not allow flowback to be stored and evaporated from open pits.

But when the flowback came back up quickly, during those first few stages of fracking, it had to go somewhere.

"That's one thing Michigan got right," he always said. "Flowback has to be stored in tanks. There's no open flow back pits here."

But this pit, obviously, had held flowback water or gelling agents or acids or salts or chemicals at some point. The signs were everywhere, especially in the watery mote that surrounded the pit.

Oily, yeasty, organic-looking shapes floated in clumps that coagulated like sewage on the surface of the water. In the middle of a drought, there was a mote several feet deep that rippled with a current in the wind. Yet those puffy, sewage-like shapes held their form under water. Layers of purple-brown and pasty-yellow clumps covered the mote bottom, and where the edges of the mote met the sun-scalded earth, the dirt curled up like layers of carved balsa wood. Supposedly plain old dirt and water stood in stiff, curled wisps.

What we saw all over that sight—rust and mustard powders, combustion symbols on the barrels and jugs left behind, the ripples of oily organic waste floating and sculpting the depths of that awful mote—was nothing natural or safe or supervised.

It was a wasteland, the Wheeler Wasteland, as we came to call it.

Kate cooed at the frogs submerged in the pasty green puddles as we left. "Oh, buddies, you gotta get out of there."

"The frogs," she shook her head, "they're always the first sign."

After several long minutes of watching them, one of the three frogs that clung to the edge of the mud sank away, sliding down the slope and into the milky-green water.

Kate was still talking about the frogs when I steered the car into the long, banked curve that took us past the State-Rudmond site and Dillon's one hundred thirty-six-foot-tall monster of a drill rig rising over the tree line in the middle of the Au Sable State Forest.

The spectre of that drill rig rising up through the clear cut in the woods struck me with awe and despair, and as we walked up the access drive, past the guard shack on site, I knew the guard would be after us, but I also knew on state land, our land, we could walk right up to the gate and we could not be arrested.

But none of that mattered. After what we saw at the Wheeler site, all three of us were bold with the need to document and share.

The well site was bathed in an exaltingly hot orange light, a wrong light that lit up each metal rung and each bulbous tank head and the towering upward climb of the rig itself with a glow of brilliant color: hot whites, bold yellows, pure blues, all set against the most turquoise blue sky.

I was sun-bleached myself, dulled and taxed after our disturbing work at Wheeler, making the spread of rust and colors and noise difficult to process under such a bold, beautiful sky. The drill rig rose from a tumult of orange and white rounds, rusting joints and valves, navy-blue glycol tanks and metallic, cone shaped vats. Battleship gray scaffolding made up the two story structure around the base of the rig. Seeing it from the side where we were, we could see right down to the hole, to the way the drill housing sank into the surface casing, and the huge rusty iron legs of the drill rig splayed out like the base of the Eiffel Tower. The bright yellow drill housing and its coils and hoses rose and fell with clouds of puffing chugs from the diesel motors that sat propped around the base of the rig.

I stood there trying to comprehend the screeching of the rig, the drill bit grinding through the rock down below, the blazing yellows and blues and rusted joints of it all—and all of that color and sound seemed to meld together to create a shimmer of a man walking toward me.

I knew the guard was behind me. I heard him yelling, and I knew Sonja and Kate had stepped in to give me time to photograph. I heard

Sonja's voice, calm and steady, say, "Put your fist down, and we'll answer you."

I turned back for a moment to see the guard's dark hair and his hunched shoulders, him facing Sonja with Kate off to the side, his fist lowering but his fingers still tightly clasped. I heard the whole conversation, but at that point, I was mesmerized by the vision.

There was a man vaporizing from the base of the drill rig, and I lowered my camera to watch. His long fire retardant jacket wavered in slices, yet I knew he was real. I watched him take shape as if he had been blown up and out of that well bore, as if he was now blown forward by the intense whisper-screams of the rock.

He moved in such a hitched, skeletal way that it looked as if there were pistons firing off behind his hips and knees, popping his joints and pushing him forward.

I looked to my camera and back up and he was gone.

Later, we wondered if the heat and fumes had somehow created that wavering mirage of a man that neither Kate nor Sonja saw. With the sun shining down at a severe, golden angle upon all of those hoses and coils and tanks, all the grating and weld marks, two stories of sheet metal and stairways and bright colored signs, the base of that rig had turned into a kaleidoscope of colors—patches and smears of bold blues and yellows that began to blend and breathe and move. And overwhelmed by the grinding screech of the drill rig, I wondered if my own tired, sunburned eyes had assembled a man of mirage as I tried to resolve foreground from background and all of that unbearable noise.

We had all had experiences before. When Kate and I drove in behind a tanker spreading brine the first time we'd seen the Wheeler site, we knew the smell was getting to us, but we were getting great pictures. Later, standing downwind from the well pad, I was aware that I was breathing in too much hydrogen sulfide. The flags had been up at yellow that day, and in the heat and humidity, I could feel and taste puffs of concentrated presence on the wind. Kate and I knew we had to leave when our lips and fingertips began to tingle.

For days my skin felt as if it had been sandpapered with pure heat—as if the sun mixed with that oily sulfury smell was abrasive itself. That's when Kate started mixing gallons of silver colloidal water and bringing along water jugs of various acidities. Water treatments the Japanese used for radiation and chemical exposure.

Then, there was that night Kate said she would never forget.

We'd been out on the State-Lexford site for several hours, and I had been so determined to capture the mess behind the drill rig that I crawled through the vine laced ferns, going back into the woods and sneaking up over the berm, over and over, getting shots from all angles.

When I was discovered by the drill rig supervisor, I decided to stay and talk, to be exactly who and what I was. I leveled with him, and we had an hour-long conversation about drill rigs he'd worked on in Louisiana and Pennsylvania, in the Middle East and the Ukraine, where the people were some of the friendliest he'd ever met.

He was the one who told me about the guys on the floor, how they had the real shit jobs, the taken for granted jobs. He didn't go so far as to talk about the lost fingers and mangled hands, but he expressed real human empathy, and as the western horizon started to periwinkle, we shook hands.

Later that evening, as Kate and Sonja reviewed what we'd seen and done that day, I stared into the fire and sighed. I felt sadness, true sadness, and I admitted it.

The two of them were laughing at me for coming clean with the guy, for admitting my intent to write about what I was seeing and smelling and learning. When he came toward us as we crouched down and worked our way through the woods, Kate and Sonja had angled away, and I had stayed, giving them time to sneak off.

But as he and I stood and talked, the feeling that good people with good intentions were blasting the earth below us with horrible chemicals and sand mined at great cost brought on that awful sense that there was no stopping the process.

And so, as we talked about his wife being a physician's assistant, how she'd come to the Ukraine with him and spent a year working in an orphanage, we did bond in the most basic way. We were all doing a job, doing the best we could.

Of course, he also tried to tell me they were painting the rig, getting it ready for a visit from investors, and that's what was causing the pungent smell that was making me feel light-headed. The enamel paint, he said, gave off that strong smell.

But as night fell, I knew I wasn't feeling right, and so did Sonja.

"I think you got gassed, Teach," she said, looking at me as we sat around the fire.

Time passed in slow and quick spurts, and I seemed to be unable to take a deep, satisfying breath. When night came, Kate seemed to understand that something more than a slight exposure problem was going on. "Maybe we should all get in one tent tonight."

We'd brought two tents, Kate's four-person and my tiny two-person that was so short you had to crawl into it. I zipped myself in, telling them, "Nah, I'll be fine." But I wasn't.

For some reason, I was gripped by strong currents of irrational fear. My tent was tucked into a flat spot surrounded by huge old oak trees, but I kept imagining, each time I started to drift off to sleep, that there was a pickup truck careening through the park, heading straight for my tent. When I sat up, looking up through the tent fabric, I realized that another camper's light was shining in the distance. Perhaps I had felt that light through my closed eyelids and imagined being run over. But as soon as I tucked myself back into my sleeping bag and closed my eyes, the truck would head right for me again.

Down the Road

Mark Trechock

Heading west on the interstate
through oil country toward Montana,
passing the ground laid bare for Best Buy
and newcomers' condominiums
whose prices will rival Manhattan
until the next bust and evacuation
for whatever boom comes then,
uranium or gravel or fresh water,
to whatever unsuspecting place,
passing the oil trucks headed to the Bakken,
the dual-wheeled pickups with company logos
and license plates from far away,
passing the eight-acre scoria pad cut out of a wheat field
to accommodate the drilling rig and its odor of fracking fluids,
the pad not likely to go back to wheat
in the farmer's lifetime or his heir's,
passing the grain elevator they want to tear down
for a place to deliver fracking chemicals,
passing the sign, a shade the color of a tree trunk,
welcoming us to the national park,
passing descendants of Coronado's horses,
never packed and never ridden,

looking down from a bluff,

passing a winglike metal fabrication

churning west on a wide load semi

destined, we speculate, for an Oregon wind farm,

passing wheel after wheel after wheel,

whose contact with the pavement

produces the insistent chant,

Gotta move gotta move gotta move.

Three Rivers Quartet

Andrea Peacock

1. Cattle v. Conoco

For nearly two decades, Chris Velasquez and his dad ran cattle on a grazing allotment called the Rosa, rolling high desert lands in northern New Mexico, punctuated by bluffs and arroyos, ringed by mesas. In a way, it's what's left of Velasquez's ancestral homeland. "We used to live where the Pine River and the San Juan meet up here, then when they built the lake, it either was drown or move," he says. In 1962, the Bureau of Reclamation completed a dam stretching three-quarters of a mile across the San Juan River. The idea was to control flooding and provide irrigation water for the Navajo tribe. It also displaced Velasquez's community. "All my ancestors on my mom's side, well on my dad's side too, came from right up here," he says. "My grandpa and my grandma on my mom's side, they were the second farm below the dam. They got chased out too. From right here on, all the people who lived here—they were all Spanish people—relocated. Threw them to the four winds. Scattered them all over the place."

The Velasquez family wasn't blown far: his dad bought a place near Blanco, New Mexico, the nearest town with a name, a short drive west and south of their former home. The entire clan now lives and ranches on about 320 acres they share with seventeen gas wells. "My dad's the one that started the ranch, but we've always had animals," he says. It was the former owners who sold the mineral rights back in the 1930s or 40s. "So they've been after this area for a long time," he says. "They've been hammering it, it didn't happen overnight. They had a vision for it."

Velasquez speaks with the short, clipped phrases common in the rural West, as though words, like everything else in this dry, windy land, need conserving. He's taking a break today, driving my husband and me around the Rosa in his diesel pickup. He babies the vehicle, easing along miles of dirt and gravel roads mined with potholes, washouts, and bad grading at an almost frustratingly slow pace. He's got to take care of it, not like he can afford to replace it, he says, glaring as roughnecks and water trucks roar past.

The gas industry pumps three billion cubic feet of natural gas every day out of the San Juan Basin, which straddles the New Mexico–Colorado border. Only about seven percent of the land in this part of New Mexico is private, the rest divided between the state, feds, and tribes. As of winter 2010, the San Juan gas field ranked second in production volume only to the Powder River Basin of Wyoming. Some three thousand compressors run twenty-four hours a day, seven days a week pressurizing gas from about twenty-three thousand wells, lighting up the canyons and hilltops in all directions. Gas companies have punched in two and half miles of road for every square mile of land—that's fifty-four hundred miles worth—nearly all dirt roads through wild country.

Though ConocoPhillips is the largest, more than one hundred thirty companies lease through the Bureau of Land Management here, subcontracting out everything from road construction to water hauling, putting hundreds of operators with trucks on these back roads every day of the year. While the field was officially discovered in 1927, this was ground zero for coal-bed methane (gas extracted from between layers of coal seams—held in place by water, released when the water is drawn out), and business boomed in the 1980s, industrializing the otherwise rural landscape.

Velasquez and his family trucked cattle to the Rosa each summer. His daughters spent their childhoods on horseback, camping out, wrangling. He points out abandoned homesites near natural springs, fishing holes that were rich with native squawfish before the dam, canyons containing rock art and Anasazi ruins, places of adventure from his childhood. Velasquez set aside ten thousand of those acres for wildlife conservation in 1996, a winter closure to give the mule deer some respite after his girls watched hunters on off-road vehicles chase a small herd into a pond where they nearly drowned. "My youngest daughter would call them the murderers," he says. "They can hunt on here, but they have to walk. They can't drive their vehicles. And there was some pissed off hunters."

Velasquez was a model rancher and had a good working relationship with the BLM. In 1995 the agency nominated him for an Excellence in Range Management award, which he won. He and another rancher, Linn Blancett of Aztec, served on the Oil and Gas Ranchers Working Group.

The BLM office out of Farmington, New Mexico, manages leases for all the federal land in this portion of the basin, accounting for most of the active wells (the rest under state or private lease). In advance of drilling, the BLM normally undertakes a massive planning effort, setting guidelines so exploration and production won't unduly affect wildlife, destroy archaeological sites, dirty the air and water; so roads will be correctly built and maintained, wells placed appropriately for the terrain. And giving the public a chance to review and comment in advance of the dozers and drilling rigs. Or at least that was the process until the 2005 Energy Policy Act, in which the Bush Administration pushed through Congress a five-year pilot project called "categorical exclusions" in which the oil and gas industries were exempt from federal environmental laws.

Farmington BLM director Steve Henke says his office still performed all those analyses, they just did so outside the public eye. "It was a full environmental review with the same components of an environmental assessment with the exception that we didn't formally document and analyze alternatives," he says. "And we handled most of that just out in the field with that discussion, saying, 'We're close to an arch site, or we're in a bald eagle area or a winter restriction area or, you staked this on a slope that's just not acceptable, we need to move it.'"

Henke says he'd bet no one could look at any particular set of well pads and tell which was approved with a formal environmental review and which went forward under President Bush's "categorical exclusion" experiment.

Chris Velasquez would agree, though not for the reasons Henke intends. His experience on the Rosa, he says, has led him to believe that the rules on paper—BLM regulations, state wildlife guidelines, the industry's own "Good Neighbor" program—are regularly ignored in the field.

Our tour with Velasquez comes a few days after Henke and I talk. We start out on a chilly February morning, during the wet winter of 2010 when road conditions were at their worst. We have a hard time finding any site that appears to meet all BLM requirements. Velasquez points out the violations as though they are personal insults: inadequate and fallen fences, open gates, puddles and catch basins of viscous liquid, leaky pipes everywhere. Ruts in the roads approach and exceed six inches, the point at which BLM regs state they should be shut down and fixed.

Henke tells me his team of thirty inspectors intends to attempt to get out to each well pad once every three years and has been coming pretty close to that goal lately. If someone calls with a complaint, they'll check it out. But jurisdiction and oversight are complex. The BLM keeps track of things like fencing and road conditions, while the state tracks air and water quality. Folks with complaints have a hard time figuring out whom to call. And then the companies themselves are always merging, buying, and selling leases. As one woman put it, "You start out reporting this cattle guard and they say, 'Well, it's not ours, call BP.' And BP says, 'Well, it's not ours. Call Conoco.' And they say, 'Well, it's not ours. Call Williams.' You go around the circle and when you get to this one there, they say 'It's not ours, call Conoco.' Where you started, you know."

When I mention the conditions I witnessed on the Rosa to the acting director of the New Mexico Oil and Gas Association—the state's main industry group—Deborah Seligman asks me why I didn't report the violations. "Did you write them down? You took pictures. Did you call them?"

If we saw one hundred wells that day, I reply, is it my job to track down and notify each company? Whose job is it? I ask her. Is it the rancher's job? Because, I'm thinking, he's already got a job.

In 2005, Velasquez and Blancett walked out on the BLM ranchers' working group. It was, Velasquez says, a waste of their time. "I used to spend a lot of time with the guys from the BLM," he says. "I thought I was doing good, we were making progress. I found out I was just chasing my tail."

"We were fighting the same thing over and over again. They'd tell us in the meetings, 'Well, we got everything taken care of.' Okay, let's go out and look at it. I'll be darned if the first time we stopped here, it hit them right in the nose. 'Oh it shouldn't be like that. We're going to get it fixed. Next time you come out here it's gonna be fixed. We're gonna have it done.' Yeah right.

"We were the only suckers who weren't getting paid."

A year later, Velasquez gave up on the Rosa as well. Basically, he says, cattle and gas development on this scale can't co-exist. There's the constant traffic of water-hauling and maintenance trucks, heavy machinery scraping away at the muddy roads, drilling and fracturing rigs. Animals get hit. They drink from temporary reserve pits, catch basins, and puddles containing the byproducts of gas production: methanol, glycol, antifreeze used to defrost transmission pipes.

Velasquez documented his animals lost on average a sixth of their weight in four years. He took pictures of cows and calves losing hair at their muzzles, a sign they'd been drinking polluted water. He had the herd tested for petroleum products—a four thousand five hundred dollar endeavor—and found all but two were positive for at least trace amounts. He sent pond water to a lab when he suspected it had been contaminated after a nearby reserve pit overflowed its berm. When eight of his cattle died in one week, he footed the bill for the autopsy (five hundred fifty dollars for one animal). "When they opened her up, her liver had turned light pink, and it disintegrated as soon as the air hit it. It was like mushy at first when you pick it up with your fingers, then it just went through your fingers. Dissolved," he says. "And it's a slow death, it's not something that they can die right away from. They kind of walk around there, with their head down until finally they lay down and die. All their organs quit on them."

When twenty of his cows got into some glycol or methanol-laced water, he lost that year's calves. He shows me the test results, the receipts for all this, as well as the response from Phillips Petroleum when—eighteen months after the year of the lost calves—they sent him a check for nine thousand nine hundred dollars for the "alleged" poisoning. "This is just a small token for what they've done," he says. "They've contaminated my entire outfit. They'll pay, but they won't admit wrongdoing."

Phillips, now merged into ConocoPhillips, declined to be interviewed but sent an email stating, "as the largest operator/producer in the basin, ConocoPhillips constantly seeks ways to mitigate the impact of drilling and production."

Velasquez's frustration isn't just a matter of the hits to his pocketbook. He points out, as we drive deeper into the Rosa, how the sagebrush, juniper and piñon trees get smaller, scragglier, and eventually, deader. Mule deer populations are down, he is sure, though both the state and the feds have no data on the matter—they have no pre-drilling baseline data, so no one is keeping track in any kind of statistically meaningful way, wildlife specialists from both the BLM and New Mexico Fish and Game tell me.

We come across the carcass of an emaciated fawn by the side of the road, not scavenged by coyotes. "See when they drink that methanol and that glycol, the coyotes and the wildlife won't eat it, they know it's contaminated," Velasquez says. As a former road maintenance employee of San Juan County, he's got the expertise to grouse at the condition of the roads. "This company, they've extracted enough gas just out of the Rosa to have this road paved and done correctly. See how the roads, the water just piles up in the middle like this? That's where the erosion and sediment comes in… When the mud gets real heavy they'll bring in them big dozers like V-8s or V-9s, and they'll plow that road until they find dry ground, and they'll just shove that dirt completely off the road."

His frustration has built over the years, the result of dozens of accidents, slights, and insults. He tells of the time a semi-sized rig climbing a steep grade locked onto his horse trailer so neither could move. The supervisor should have been ahead on the road, he says, making sure the way was clear. Another day, a water truck driver coming fast around a curve slammed on his breaks and slid sideways. "It damn near landed on top of us. I was so damn scared I couldn't even open the door to get out and chew him out." Twenty years ago, Velasquez locked the gate leading to his private land, closing out a bulldozer driver who wanted to use the road as a shortcut to a project on BLM land. The company called the sheriff, and Velasquez was sure he'd go to jail. In a repeat performance in 2009, the dozer driver thought he might just push through the gate anyway. "They were trying to figure out if they could run me over with that blade they had," he says. "The sheriff told them, 'You better not. You're asking for trouble if you do that.'"

Velasquez dotes on his grandson, a blue-eyed toddler with his own hat and pony who lives next door; he loves to ride on the tractor with his granddad. "I've got plans for him," Velasquez says. "I don't know how much of it will be left, but he'll take over what we've got. If he wants it." Whatever the boy decides, the Rosa won't be part of his future. Velasquez sold off his share in 2006, a sacrifice to the gods of the gas patch.

2. Charlene Anderson's Commute

Prosperity clearly resides in Farmington, New Mexico. Even in the middle of the Great Recession, locally owned stores (an independent book shop!) line the downtown streets, and the long commercial strip of national chains appears to be thriving. The town has a first-rate hospital and library, an opulent recreation center on a hilltop with eight lighted tennis courts, and a slick museum dedicated to local history (the current exhibit: "From Dinosaurs to Drill Bits"). The roads are clogged with expensive, mud-splattered pickup trucks, most sporting the ubiquitous tall flags that enable drivers to see one another coming through the hills and curves of the back roads of the gas patch.

Planted at the intersection of three rivers—the San Juan, the Animas, and the Plata—Farmington isn't on the way to anywhere. There is no interstate highway, no major airport. If it weren't for oil and gas—and all the water haulers, mud loggers, welders, drill-bit venders, contract archaeologists, and well-service companies that come with it—Farmington's main commerce would be selling groceries to rural folks on the weekends.

It's early 2010, national demand for gas has flagged a bit, and that has folks here worried the boom that began with the coal-bed methane craze in the 1980s might finally go bust. So it's not easy to find people willing to criticize oil and gas here. For one thing, it's a pretty good living. For another, the big companies especially are generous with their largess. But finally, as Charlene Anderson puts it, "It's really hard to making a living without kissing their ass."

Anderson is a graphic designer who lives just outside Farmington. She's got a good working relationship with XTO, the gas company with leases near her property; she pretty much has to, as they sat their well in the middle of her driveway. All the resulting traffic has turned her road into a four-wheelin' adventure drive every time she needs to get in or out. Even when it's dry, she says, you don't really need to steer because of the ruts. On wet days, she comes out the other end covered in mud. "It was really bad one day, so I have Ed [her husband] in my ear on the telephone and said 'Honey, I need a pep talk. I'm out driving today and it's bad.' 'Drive it like you stole it, Char,' he says."

Charlene and Ed's home is just far enough outside of town to feel rural. It sits two miles down a dirt road across a sagebrush flat, where Charlene now also battles Russian thistle—an invasive weed encouraged by all the extra gas-related traffic. She can't spray it, due to Ed's health issues (sensitivity to chemicals). So she rails against it, along with the trashed road, the bad air, and human shortcomings that make the whole situation possible.

"The changes are just so incremental," she says. "It took me about a year, and even me, now I'm used to there being three or four wells. So we have this crappy airshed, power plants, oil and gas, a lot of cars without emission controls.

"You come here and say you're from someplace else—not Montana. Some place where there are people and roads. You would say, 'What the hell is her problem?' Because it looks empty, and it looks pretty nice. Well this is fine compared to Houston, but I don't think Houston is something you should measure from.

"I think collectively we've lost track of measuring from something that is good."

We're driving pretty fast as Charlene talks, her little Honda bouncing in and out of ruts—otherwise we'll get bogged down in the mud. She pulls over at the gas well that straddles the road to her house. One day, the company was out here working, and the whole thing was blocked off. She had a project due and arrived at the well pad to see the UPS truck on the other side waiting for her. The gas workers ferried her nine packages across, and she sure appreciated it. It hasn't happened since, but she worries: what if it had been an emergency? And what if there were a hydrogen sulfide leak?

"One of the things I'm supposed to do on my list of being a good wife is calling XTO and saying 'We'd like a wind sock so we can look out and see which way the wind is blowing.'"

And that's part of the crux of her dilemma, of our dilemma: natural gas is about as clean as fossil fuels get. As Charlene and I talk, the Winter Olympics are playing on television sponsored by endless advertisements touting clean natural gas. "If you compare it to coal, well what kind of comparison is that? That's like comparing cat shit to dog shit, I'm not sure which is worse. Cat shit is smaller, and they hide it. We're told it's all perfectly clean, but it's not clean when we're perfectly downwind of it.

"And my god, here we are just wasting it. This is a really cool resource—it's great, it's a pharmaceutical resource, it's polymers, really cool plastics. I mean, all this neat stuff comes from it, and we're lighting it on fire for heating. I'm not asking everyone to wear long underwear—though I am personally wearing long underwear—but we've been dinking around as a country for decades."

Like a lot of folks who actually live with oil and gas, Charlene has a firm grasp on the hypocrisies of her position, as well as the greater social delusions the rest of us share. "It's like smoking. If you went to the doctor, he would never hesitate to say, 'Stop smoking now.' No choice. That's the message. It's not like, maybe tomorrow, or you should do a little better.

"That's the message with energy. It's nice to say 'we need to be more efficient,' but that's a halfway approach. Energy Star? Where things are maybe twenty percent better but your fridge is twice as big? That's not working."

By the time we've traveled the length of Charlene's drive, it's about time to turn around and get back to the pavement. I don't get to meet Ed because he lives in Ajo, Arizona, moved there in 2007 after the gas-related pollution knocked him on his butt pretty much on a daily basis. So while Charlene spends a lot of time thinking critically about the larger dynamics of energy politics, for her it's personal. "I seriously love this person I married, and it kind of pisses me off I can't live with him."

3. Sug McNall's Tour of Hell

The gas companies haven't sprinkled nearly so much sugar outside Farmington city limits, and the farther one gets from town, the louder the critics get. A lot of farmers and ranchers in rural San Juan County, as it turns out, don't share their urban cousins' enthusiasm for living in a gas field. Even Dorothy Nobis, who heads up Farmington's Chamber of Commerce, acknowledges the conflict. "Farmers and ranchers are not successful because they roll over and play dead; they're passionate about what they do. And they have a commitment to it that is equally true of the oil and gas industry. So you have two groups who believe that what they're doing is maybe more important than what the other guy is doing." It's not just about making a living, she agrees, but a clash between two different ways of life.

Tweeti Blancett is infamous in these parts as the Republican rancher, the Bush campaign volunteer who won't let the gas companies push her around. She and her husband Linn ranch just outside of Aztec, about half an hour east of Farmington. She's not intimidated by the BLM or the weight of ConocoPhillips, which owns the mineral rights under the Blancett ranch. Her unusual background makes her one of the first people journalists contact when writing about the gas industry here. When I make that call, she invites me to a meeting at the hotel she owns in town.

"We're the Four Grams," she says, introducing me to the group of middle-aged women who have gathered in the dining room of the decidedly feminine Step Back Inn (think doilies and lace), to swap information. "Chris is an honorary Gram." Which seems appropriate given the way Velasquez's eyes light up when he talks about his grandson.

Jan Rees is a birder and tells me her current interest is the health of local bald eagle and southwestern willow flycatcher populations. Shirley "Sug" McNall grew up on a nearby ranch. She was knocked unconscious five years ago by hydrogen sulfide coming from a well near her home: "I went out to get my paper and almost didn't make it home," she says. The fourth Gram, who asked to remain anonymous, is the unofficial group's unofficial records keeper.

Then there's Katee McClure, a reporter for the local paper whose interest was piqued when a gas company buried toxic waste just outside her workshop.

"I have two wells on my property," McClure says. "I had no reason to distrust the oil and gas company. My husband, who is a carpenter, always said, 'Don't watch guys work, they don't like it. Just offer them some drinks and walk away.'" So McClure took the workers tea and sodas, then found out they later covered up a toxic spill without a word. "It's not acres away, it's right under my nose. And I'm thinking, what have they done out on the BLM, out on the public lands where no one is watching?"

Sug is one tough woman. The kind who speaks her mind, who doesn't back down from a righteous battle. As a seventeen-year-old nursing student, she took on an instructor—a Catholic priest—who couldn't keep his hands off the young women in his class. "I guess it was Michael Jordan who said, 'If you see something wrong, strap on your armor and go to battle.' So that's me, and I'm getting kind of old and tired, but you can't lay down. They'll eat you."

Sug's family homesteaded 740 acres on nearby Crouch Mesa in the early 1900s. They were farmers and ranchers, and they prospered. She figures she's got several hundred relatives in the area, people she doesn't even know. Her first husband worked more than two decades in the gas patch before he got laid off and died at age forty-four, so "just about everything I own is because of oil and gas," she says. "But that doesn't make it right, what they're doing."

Sug put together this Tour of Hell sometime around 2003 or 2004 for a seminar on toxics in the community. It was her idea of entertainment, and she's recycled it since for filmmakers like Debra Anderson (*Split Estate*) and Josh Fox (*Gasland*) and journalists like me.

She picks me up at Blancett's motel at 8 AM in a blue two-seater pick-up, the back end covered in bumper stickers. One of our first stops: McCoy Elementary, where her daughter works and her grandkids went to school. A small bridge across a wooded creek links the school to the rest of the world. Behind the playground sit two XTO wells and storage tanks. "There are five hundred kids in there. That tank, it's four hundred feet away—we've measured it. This tank emits fumes, it's gone into the classrooms," she says. "One of my good friends was a teacher there. She complained about the gas fumes in the classroom to the administration and they told her to live with it. This is our bread and butter."

If something were to happen—a blowout, a seep of deadly hydrogen sulfide—if the bridge were out, there'd be no way to get emergency equipment in, nor buses to move the kids out.

Aztec, Farmington, and Bloomfield all have rules about how close to a house or a school a well can be situated—mostly somewhere between one hundred and four hundred feet. In unincorporated San Juan County, there are no such regulations. What Sug intends to show me next is how the county's poor pay the highest cost for the region's boom. We set out for Crouch Mesa, an industrial landscape set among a mishmash of trailer parks and low-end subdivisions.

"This land, I remember when it was nothing but rolling hills, and we ran our cattle out here," she says. Her folks sold it off to developers, and in a reverse sort of gentrification, the Mesa now houses the county's poorest residents: an estimated six thousand people live here.

"Most of the people who live here are green carders or Navajos," she says. They don't take the newspaper, and they don't read legal notices printed in it. They're afraid of what will happen if they ask questions or make trouble. "Nobody seems to think they have any rights, and I say it's a socio-economic thing because you don't see crap like this in Farmington."

The crap she's talking about is endless miles of pipeline, the constant humming of compressor stations, wells sitting across the street from tiny, boxy houses, a one hundred acre pipe yard that stretches for blocks, settling ponds for contaminated water, bone yards for abandoned equipment, rusty holding tanks, and everywhere signs warning of hazardous materials.

At one end of the mesa, a California corporation runs a sixty-three acre landfarm, taking in debris from spills, tank bottom sludge and drilling mud among other materials. It's all pretty highly-contaminated stuff, but the theory is exposure to a variety of "yeast, fungi, protozoa, and bacteria" accelerates natural recycling of petroleum contaminated hazardous waste. It's called bioremediation. "Just as mold will gradually consume a loaf of bread, certain microbes in the right conditions will also consume petroleum products," reads the website from this particular landfarm, run by Industrial Ecosystems Inc.

The problem is, no one is monitoring what sorts of waste might be migrating off-site—neither down off the mesa through surface or groundwater runoff into the Animas River, nor what's blowing around in the dust, what the neighbors downwind—just across the street—might be breathing.

Down off the mesa, we hit another trailer park, this one with a gas well and high-pressure line seated between two homes just like another single-wide. "As you can see, these people are sort of at a disadvantage," Sug drawls. "Nobody thinks they have any rights. So they're kind of trashy, I used to be trailer trash too. But they're human. And we're on a pipeline, a high pressure pipeline right in the middle of their houses."

Sug and I take a break from our tour to munch on peanut butter sandwiches in the parking lot of a local grocery store. Sug asks if I have a headache yet, and I'm surprised that she knows this. It's normal, she says. Everyone she brings on this tour gets a headache—in fact, most people who live around gas production live with headaches of unknown origin.

She tells me her activism is a source of conflict in her family, and that too is common. "I can't even have family gatherings with my sister and brother-in-law and nephews because of what I do. Environmentalists are a dirty word to them. I keep telling my sister, every time she sees an eagle or drinks clean water, she ought to kiss my butt," she laughs.

Back on the road, we stop by a pastoral farm, an old hayfield, that was ripped apart to make way for a pipeline and never put back together right; when the heavy equipment crossed the road, the vibrations cracked the walls in the owner's house.

As Sug's tour loops back around toward Aztec, we crest a ridge revealing below us the vision of the Hell she's been promising all afternoon. "I call this the Ring of Fire," she says. "This is called the Blanco Hub. Refineries, treating stations, whatever you want to call it. If you wanted to knock out a lot of the energy for Texas, Arizona, California, this would be the place to do it."

There are at least eight facilities spread out below us in the valley, belching fire and smoke, lit up like a small city: a nest of compressor stations, refineries, and pipelines. When Sug rolls down her window, the roar of machinery fills the car. It doesn't get much quieter when she rolls it back up again.

We coast down the hill and pull over into the shadow of a giant ConocoPhillips facility. We're in a Catholic cemetery, occupying a space about the size of a moderate retail parking lot. "I always end my tour with this," Sug says. "It's just another one of those not-right things."

4. ARMENTA'S LAMENT

The gas rigs on the ridge above the West Ruins of Aztec Ruins National Monument pose a unique challenge, says superintendent Dennis Carruth. The point of visiting such a place, he says, is to understand how people once lived in this landscape. That act of imagination becomes awfully difficult in the gas patch.

Anasazi people built this village along the north shore of the Animas River during a two hundred fifty-year span, beginning nearly one thousand years ago. As a community, the people were connected to those who lived at nearby Chaco, through trade and shared culture.

The monument itself contains three hundred acres of stone and adobe rooms, a maze of multi-story living and storage space, burials, irrigation canals, courtyards, even one Great Kiva, a large circular structure built for ceremonial use. The builders hauled ponderosa pine, Douglas fir, spruce, and aspen from the mountains to use as beams, and some of these original logs remain. Only one of the three complexes within the park has been excavated; a second sits undisturbed. The third, the North Ruins, lies partially under a road and three well pads belonging to XTO Energy and Mañana Gas Inc. of Albuquerque.

The gas leases preceded the North Ruins inclusion in the park, Carruth says. For Aztec to expand back in 1988, both New Mexico's senators had to be on board. The deal was struck on the condition that Congress leave the mineral rights alone, he says.

Parts of the North Ruins have likely been destroyed by gas activity. "It's a multi-roomed feature with a lot of kivas and other structures around it. The road cuts through, and the pad is on the edge of that site too," he says. Archaeologists have pieced together this much information based on above-ground surveys. "Then there's this block where we don't know anything, that the gas pad is on. It overlaps that site, so we don't actually know where its original boundary is."

The Monument has been able to mitigate impacts to the North Ruins a little by requiring extra padding on the road. But, as Carruth says, "It's a little bit like closing the barn gate after the cow is out. You have a giant oil pad on top of a cultural resource. You can look at opportunities to maybe pad the road, to minimize traffic, sound mitigation."

While visitors are often simultaneously surprised to see gas rigs within the boundaries of a World Heritage Site like Aztec, and understanding of the needs that led to this odd pairing, Carruth says policies that exchange history for energy are short-sighted.

"It's part of the story of man, and it's actually like tearing out a couple chapters. Then you won't understand what's in those chapters," he says. "They're gone. Or how you got to the chapter you're in right now, to give it context and meaning."

Gilbert Armenta is among many of the living remnants of these mingled cultures. "Let's go back two thousand years," he says, when I ask what this place was like before gas was discovered in the river valleys occupied now by the Bloomfield–Aztec–Farmington triangle known as the Tri-Cities. "My people were already here. One thousand years ago, instead of being nomadic, they started building pueblos, started living in the more communal state. Probably seven hundred years ago, the drought came, just like it does now, probably worse then… That would bring us up to maybe, oh, 1400, early 1500s. Then the other side of my family started coming in. The Europeans, which would be the Spaniards looking for gold."

His great-grandfather, who settled near present-day Bloomfield, New Mexico, in 1845, purchased a Cochiti Pueblo slave woman from Ute Indian traders who became Armenta's great-grandmother. As Spaniards ceded power to Mexicans, then Anglos beat down the Navajo, the local economy shifted from trade to sheep to agriculture.

"The Anglos had introduced orchards on a big scale," he says. "The whole valley was covered in orchards, anywhere from two or three acres, to three hundred or four hundred acres. From apples, to pears, to peaches, you name it." In the late 1800s, more than one thousand farms blanketed the valley. People raised broomcorn, pinto beans, wheat, and alfalfa. Two canneries processed fruit. A train hauled excess produce and livestock for export. There were small coal mines, a few oil wells; a canal dug to run a turbine provided enough power for lights each evening. "The turbine would make what they call 'brown light.' You would put the switch on and it was kind of like a candle, maybe better than a candle," he says. "The power plant would run basically from sundown to 'Hey, it's time to go to bed.' Ten or eleven at night. Then they'd turn the power plant off, and you were going to go to bed anyway."

Money wasn't an issue, he says, because everyone had work; everyone was fed. The Depression passed with hardly any notice. In Armenta's recounting, the valley is an agricultural Eden with minerals underground poised to play the part of the snake.

The idea of a split estate, where ownership of a particular patch of earth does not include the minerals beneath it, is not intuitive. Rather, it's a remnant legal device with roots in English law. "It came from the king of England who wanted the profits, you know, the rents from the minerals," explains Timothy Fitzgerald, an economics professor at Montana State University who studies the way our culture handles the costs and balances of resource development. "He was happy to have his subjects live on the surface, but if they found hard-rock minerals, then he wanted a piece of the action."

Fitzgerald contrasts this with Spanish law where both the surface and subsurface were reserved for the king, and with the early American practice of conveying the entire estate to private individuals, part of the great democratic experiment.

Once people in the United States realized what sort of coal wealth was lying underground, he says, it made sense for individuals to sell the digging rights to those with the knowledge and tools to do the job efficiently. When it came to the vast open space of the West, this arrangement made further economic sense as the minerals tended to dwarf in value whatever the surface owner might have had in mind so far as making a living. The government got in on the deal with the Coal Lands Act, the Agricultural Entry Act, and the Stock Raising Act of the early 1900s, all modifying the intent of the original Homestead Act so that mineral ownership remained with the government, which could then lease those rights as it chose.

A hundred years ago, the wilderness and plains of the West must have seemed endless. Wildcatters could plop down a well just about anywhere and not ruin anyone's view. Things are different nowadays, in terms of both the way we live on the land and the manner in which industry goes about its business, putting local communities and oil and gas companies on a course of inescapable conflict.

"If you go back in time, there's just a little hole in the ground, right? Run a little well stem down it, throw a little cement on top," Fitzgerald says. "It was pretty simple. Put a horsehead pump on the surface...You don't have pipelines running everywhere, you're not really fracturing anything."

Hydraulic fracturing—called "fracking" for short—involves setting off explosive charges far underground, pumping in a toxic stew of liquids and sand, to open and prop up passages for gas to flow through to a well. It's a technology that's been around for close to seventy years but has only been used effectively on a large scale for the last couple decades. Combined with directional drilling, fracking has opened up all kinds of possibilities for gas extraction from shale, a fine-grained sedimentary rock. The Marcellus Shale in New York and Pennsylvania, the Barnett Shale in Texas, and the Bakken Shale in North Dakota have gotten a lot of attention, but there's potential pretty much any place with shale. Fitzgerald marvels at the technology. "They're taking gas out of stuff that's like that," he says and knocks on the hard wood of his desk.

The problem is, we're not just taking gas out of empty rangeland any more. Fitzgerald uses the example of leases along the Yellowstone River, the longest undamned river in the United States, and a world-class trout stream. "Obviously if we drill one well, we're going to destroy a blue-ribbon fishery," he says. "Well, maybe, maybe not. But clearly a blue-ribbon fishery has a lot different value than just somebody's grain field. And it's got a lot different spatial dimension to it. We can't just save one little piece."

Gilbert Armenta's parents were among those lucky folks who owned the rights to the ground under their feet. When his father came back from fighting in World War II, the Armentas were approached by a landman (the gas company employee charged with handling landowners). "He said, 'Mr. and Mrs. Armenta, if you sign this lease, we'll give you twenty-five dollars. And we'll give you so much for the gas once we drill it. But don't worry, in five years—if we don't do nothing—you keep the leases, you keep the money and we're out of your hair.'" They took the deal, and five years passed with no drilling. So when the company came back again with the same deal, the Armentas thought nothing of signing a new lease. Only this time the company—Standline Oil—farmed out its lease to Southern Union Production, which dug a hole. "If you read the lease," Armenta says, "the lease says once a hole goes in, the lease is now forever. It has no end…That same well they drilled back in 1952 is still producing today."

It's one of a dozen wells on Armenta's land, including one right outside and down a short ridge from his dining room. Though the pads themselves only take up 2.5 acres a piece, they are situated so as to make irrigation impossible. On several occasions, a well blew oil all over his hayfield and into an irrigation canal. The compressors run every day, all day, all night, pumping natural gas through a pipeline at two thousand to three thousand pounds of pressure, running on the gas as it's extracted (unmetered, free for the company). Where the Armenta family should hear nothing but birds, maybe the sound of the San Juan River off in the distance, instead the roar of machinery drowns out everything. The fumes seep into their bedroom at night, he says, when the wind is calm. He still pays property taxes on that land, but the layout of well pads and associated apparatus has made it useless for growing anything but a little cattle feed. And since his parents—the original leaseholders—are dead, the Armenta family is paid nothing.

In 2006, gas company XTO began negotiating with Armenta to put in another coal-bed methane well. Armenta made sure the company was aware of his family cemetery, where his great-grandparents are buried, sitting on a bluff next to the proposed well pad. He asked them to fence it off, and instead they said they'd fence in the well. Armenta came home one day to find the markers all gone, a porta-potty and pile of gravel sitting in their place. XTO had pushed the top of the cemetery off the bluff.

When he couldn't get any response from XTO, Armenta put up a fence around the graves; XTO responded by suing him for putting up a fence on "their" property. (After consideration, XTO withdrew their lawsuit and offered him a check, ostensibly as payment for something else.) All Armenta wants, he says, are new headstones. And an apology.

He knows he's not going to get one.

Rachael Moore, spokesperson for Exxon (which bought XTO in 2010), characterizes the incident as a "commercial dispute that was resolved in XTO's favor in 2008." She says further, "We are a responsible operator and refute any accusations that suggest otherwise."

Folks like Dorothy Nobis of the Farmington Chamber of Commerce and Deborah Seligman of the New Mexico Oil and Gas Association, point out that the Tri-Cities communities are thriving because of oil and gas. Nobis talks of the industry's charitable donations, alludes to the hospital, museum, and network of parks and recreation centers enjoyed by Farmington families because of the gas companies' largesse. "They put a lot of money into the boys and girls clubs, youth sports, in parks and recreation, in just about everything you can think of that will make the quality of life better here," she says.

Seligman agrees. "I love to see what oil and gas has generated within the communities of San Juan County," she says. "When I first went into Farmington twenty years ago…there was nothing on that road. You went into town and the choice of hotels was an old Ramada Inn, the old Best Western, and a Holiday Inn. That was it. And there was one grocery store. The increased business—the Wal-Marts, the T.J.Maxxes, the Lowe's…I mean that was a need. So what would the impact be if oil and gas wasn't there?

"You know, I love wilderness just as much as the next person, but is wilderness going to sustain a community?"

The worth of a strip mall, however, is in the eye of the beholder. The tracks for the little train that used to transport local produce to the wider world have been ripped out. The sheep are gone, Armenta says, so are the flour mills. Orchards and farms were transformed into subdivisions to house the influx of immigrants coming to work the gas field. Even Nobis admits the community has a drug and crime problem. When New Mexico repealed the death penalty in 2009, the two men sitting on death row were both from San Juan County.

"Now everybody, everybody, is dependent on oil and gas," Armenta says. "So when you go from being an independent, full-employed population to being almost half unemployed… They say oil and gas has been good to the people. It's been good to Wal-Mart. I know that. 'Cause the little mom and pop stores that were here when I was young and growing up have disappeared."

Armenta sees his family history, his community's plight, in the larger context of a culture gone mad with waste and greed. "We have these monster machines that eat up the earth, day after day, twenty-four hours a day, seven days a week, just butchering the earth to get down to that coal. To feed the hungry power plants that have no end in sight. Their appetite is so huge, they will just never get enough.

"What has oil and gas done for me?" he asks. "In 1967, it killed my father in a pipeline explosion. In 1969, two years later, my uncle was killed hauling pipe out to the oil field. In 1975, my middle uncle was killed in a plant explosion. Right here in Bloomfield. Three brothers from the same company. That's what oil and gas has done for me.

"When my father was killed, we were still kind of young. My father had life insurance. Twenty thousand dollar life insurance. They told my mom, if you want a lump sum, you can have ten thousand dollars. If you want the twenty thousand dollar, you got to draw it out in ten years. So for ten years she drew out ninety-five dollars a month. In order to make it, she went on welfare. That's what oil and gas has done for me.

"They say, 'Oil and gas has done a lot for you guys.' Not for me."

Greed

Linda Hogan

In spring, how desperate the first sprouts reach for water, mineral,
the first tendrils and roots greediest of all.

The starving stand in shadows awaiting the end of any banquet.

My infant takes his first breath, then hungers for more milk, more air.

And then the pain of taking away is never gone.

Without end there is the want of something that can never be.

The pain of such desire is more desire.
Some take from all the others.
They are still earth creatures,
the hungry child,
taken from the table,
the breast,
even earth's great and fertile fields
flowering and then letting go of the seed.
All have forgotten what hides in the shadows
where they once did.

But then, the greediest of all
envy the immortals
who return the envy as they long for a body.
All their earth senses they desire,
the taste of sweet milk, fresh fruit.
But gravity has its own desire
to call us into the ground.

How I wish words could return to the mouth
like music to the flute, or breath,
as it was in the beginning,
remembering the nourishment that began this precious
world, but always remembering that even when the tide went out
the waves still came toward us, carrying some generous yield.

Something yet holds purchase, holds sway
in a world filled with green trust, even the blade
of grass recalls how
to grow back its original blade.
But I don't know what tide is arriving
from the greed of American soil.
Just like for mineral,
now the search between rock, flint,
shale.

Hear No Evil

Stefanie Brook Trout

I.

We don't want to hear about fracking simply because we don't like
the language. It's unpleasant to hear about pumpjacks and fracking
fluid. It's distasteful. Frankly, it's too sexual, and not in the shiny,
symmetrical, and airbrushed kind of way that breaks the internet but
in the vulgar way that focuses on the parts of fucking we don't like
to think about: The sweaty, furious pumping. The fluids staining the
bedsheets. The way we turn into animals. The hunger. The vulnera-
bility. We like sex, but we don't like the mess that it creates.

II.

We don't want to hear about fracking because we don't like how the
language makes us think of, just for a moment, nonconsensual sex.
We don't even like to say the word, rape. We don't like talking about
real rape, much less metaphorical rape. We try to redefine rape, to
rank it from worst to least bad. We are trying to figure out what rape
is legitimate and who was asking for it. We try to joke about rape, or
to laugh at jokes about rape, because we don't want anyone to think
we can't take a good rape joke. And the parallel is too far a stretch
anyway. Hyperbolic. The land can't give consent, so it can't not give

consent. And if it could give consent, it probably would. It's given us everything else we ever wanted from it.

III.

We don't want to hear about fracking because it's not in our backyard. We don't want pumpjacks on our land. We don't want fracking fluids in our watershed. We don't want to drink the contaminated water flaming out of the faucet. But as long as it's somewhere else, hidden somewhere that we don't have to see it, then we love fracking. Fracking means jobs. Fracking means energy independence. Fracking means bridge fuel. Fracking means we don't have to make sacrifices; we don't have to change a thing. Fracking is the future. As long as it's not in our backyard. In fact, why not do it somewhere we've already written off? Like North Dakota. Hell, it might even make the place a little better.

IV.

We don't want to hear about fracking because it's just one more thing for the environmentalists to gripe about. The environmentalists always need something to gripe about, and if it weren't this, it would be something else. We're tired of the griping. We're tired of the debate. We're tired of being asked to choose between the wastey ways we love so much and the future. We're tired of being made to feel ashamed when we refuse to do anything. This is your battle, not ours. We have other things to worry about: job security, a second mortgage, finding a leak at the bottom of our swimming pool. We don't care much for politics. We vote—we're good citizens—but after the results are in, we don't want to worry about what's good or bad for the future. We work hard, and we deserve to live without worry. At the end of the day, we want to drink margaritas and grill hot dogs and water our lawns with underground sprinklers. It's not our job to worry about fracking, and if it's your job to worry about fracking, then keep us out of it. Better yet, get a real job. We hear Halliburton is hiring.

V.

We don't want to hear about fracking because we don't like your alternative. If the solution could somehow be linked to consumerism, if we could do the things we love without fracking, we might be more inclined to listen. But you are asking too much. Your valuation of the future is too high.

VI.

We don't want to hear about fracking because gas prices are down, and we are happy. We remember four dollars a gallon. We remember austerity. We had to trade in for a more fuel efficient SUV. But now we can fill up our yachts and jet skis and run the AC while heating the pool all summer long. Did you hear us? We are happy. How dare you damn "fractivists" try to take that away from us?

VII.

We don't want to hear about fracking because it's been going on for decades, and what's the big deal anyway? We don't care about the difference between vertical and horizontal drilling. The fossil fuels are there for the taking. We'd be fools to squander them. If we contaminate our fresh water, then we'll just buy bottled. And the increased demand for bottled water will create jobs. Win/win.

VIII.

We don't want to hear about fracking because we hear two different sets of facts, and we don't want to have to think critically to get our own answers. We don't know whom to trust, so we don't trust anyone. But we'll take the cheap energy. Put it on the future's tab.

IX.

We don't want to hear about fracking because it's time Chicken Little buttoned his beak. You always say the sky is falling, and as far as we can tell, the sky is still there. We know there are several different endings to the Chicken Little folktale, and we choose to believe the ending we want. We choose to hear whatever supports the status quo. If that means we get eaten by a fox or that the sky really collapses on our heads, there's nothing we could do about it anyway. It's too late. We might as well enjoy the time we have left.

X.

We don't want to hear about fracking because we know it's only a matter of time before it rips our world apart, and when it does, we want to be able to say "We didn't know" and actually mean it. How dare you try to make us liars by forcing us to see the truth before we are ready? (We are never ready.)

Why Not Frack

Bill McKibben

In one sense, the analysts who forecasted that "peak oil"—i.e., the point at which the rate of global petroleum extraction will begin to decline—would be reached over the last few years were correct. The planet is running short of the easy stuff, where you stick a drill in the ground and crude comes bubbling to the surface. The great oil fields of Saudi Arabia and Mexico have begun to dwindle; one result has been a rising price for energy.

We could, as a civilization, have taken that dwindling supply and rising price as a signal to convert to sun, wind, and other noncarbon forms of energy—it would have made eminent sense, most of all because it would have aided in the fight against global warming, the most difficult challenge the planet faces. Instead, we've taken it as a signal to scour the world for more hydrocarbons. And it turns out that they're there—vast quantities of coal and oil and gas, buried deep or trapped in tight rock formations or mixed with other minerals.

Getting at them requires ripping apart the earth: for instance, by heating up the ground so that the oil in the tar sands formation of Canada can flow to the surface. Or by tearing holes in the crust a mile beneath the surface of the sea, as BP was doing in the Gulf of Mexico when the Deepwater Horizon well exploded. Or by literally removing mountaintops to get at coal, as has become commonplace across the southern Appalachians.

Or by "fracking" the subsurface geology in order to make natural gas flow through new cracks. The word is short for "hydraulic fracturing" and in the words of Seamus McGraw, it works like this: having drilled a hole perhaps a mile deep, and then a horizontal branch perhaps half a mile in length, you send down a kind of subterranean pipe bomb, a small package of ball-bearing-like shrapnel and light explosives. The package is detonated, and the shrapnel pierces the bore hole, opening up small perforations in the pipe. They then pump up to seven million gallons of a substance known as slick water to fracture the shale and release the gas. It blasts through those perforations in the pipe into the shale at such force—more than nine thousand pounds of pressure per square inch—that it shatters the shale for a few yards on either side of the pipe, allowing the gas embedded in it to rise under its own pressure and escape.

This new technique allowed the industry to exploit terrain that it had previously considered impenetrable. It was used first in the late 1990s in what's called the Barnett Shale in Texas, and is also being widely used to liberate oil from beneath the Bakken Shale in North Dakota. But the industry's biggest excitement has come in the East, where a boom has been underway for several years in the so-called Marcellus Shale that runs from West Virginia into upstate New York. This gas-trapping shale formation has been estimated to hold as much gas as the whole United States consumes in a century. (The estimates are highly contested; some analysts are insisting that new data show them to be considerably smaller, though still vast, and indeed at the end of January 2012 the federal government slashed its earlier predictions in half.)

The gas is also ideally situated along the route of many existing natural gas pipelines and near the heavy-consumption eastern megalopolis. If you're an energy company, it's about the best place on the planet to find a huge pool of gas—it's like discovering an underground deposit of beer directly beneath Yankee Stadium. Because of the potential profits, the agents of various companies have fanned out across the back roads of the region in a remarkable land rush, seeking to lock up drilling rights on the hitherto not-very-valuable acreage of marginal dairy farms and cut-over woodlots.

The emerging movements against fracking, and the science that informs them, raise three key concerns. In ascending order of importance they are:

First, how much damage is being done to water wells and underground aquifers from methane migration and the chemicals mixed with water and then injected into fracking wells under high pressure? You might call this the "flaming faucet" question, and it has understandably and rightly galvanized many of the local people fighting fracking. The industry claims that there's no problem—that the cement casings they put in the wells keep the chemicals out of layers of soil where drinking water might be found. But rigorous scientific study has been scant, in part because since 2005 (at the urging of then Vice President Dick Cheney, whose former company Halliburton is a major player in the fracking boom), drilling companies have been exempt from federal safe drinking water statutes and hence not required to list the chemicals they push down wells.

Preliminary research from Duke University seemed to indicate that indeed methane was showing up in drinking water; in December 2011, the EPA released its first thorough study, conducted in the Wyoming town of Pavilion, where residents had reported brown, undrinkable water after nearby fracking operations. The EPA concluded that the presence in the water of synthetic compounds such as glycol ethers and the assortment of "other organic components" were "the result of direct mixing of hydraulic fracking fluids with ground water," and told local residents to stop drinking from their wells.

The company involved insisted that the EPA had introduced the contaminants itself; Oklahoma Senator James Inhofe, best known for decrying global warming as a "hoax," added that the EPA report was part of "President Obama's war on fossil fuels." But the evidence from Pavilion was a powerful indictment of the industry, and it led several leading doctors to call for a moratorium on fracking pending more health research. "We don't have a great handle on the toxicology of fracking chemicals," said Vikas Kapil, chief medical officer at the National Center for Environmental Health, an arm of the Centers for Disease Control.

December 2011, then, was a tough month for the fracking industry, and it ended on a particularly low note—on New Year's Eve a magnitude 4.0 earthquake in Youngstown, Ohio, was blamed on the injection of high-pressure fracking water along a seismic fault, a phenomenon also documented in Arkansas and Oklahoma.

A second concern has to do with the damage being done to rivers and streams—and the water supply for homes and industries—by the briny soup that pours out of the fracking wells in large volume. Most of the chemical-laced slick water injected down the well will stay below ground, but for every million gallons, 200,000 to 400,000 gallons will be regurgitated back to the surface, bringing with it, Seamus McGraw writes, "not only the chemicals it included in the first place, but traces of the oil-laced drilling mud, and all the other noxious stuff that was already trapped down there in the rock: iron and chromium, radium and salt—lots of salt."

The question is what to do with that volume of bad water. If it leaks into small streams, disaster results: the classic case is Dunkard Creek, which rambles for forty miles along the Pennsylvania–West Virginia border. In Tom Wilber's words, "its clear, green eddies and swimming holes, shaded by hemlock and sycamore trees, attracted generations of anglers, paddlers, picnickers, and nature lovers" who enjoyed the 161 aquatic species found in its waters.

In September 2009, however, pretty much everything died in the course of a few days—everything except an invasive microscopic algae that normally lives in estuaries along the Texas coast. This bloom of "golden algae" that killed everything else was a mystery—how could a species that usually lives in brackish water on the ocean's edge have survived in a freshwater Appalachian creek? The answer emerged swiftly: drilling companies had been illegally dumping wastewater in the region, turning it into brine.

Instead of simply dumping the water, the companies could have sent it to the local sewage treatment plant—but these were generally not set up to handle high volumes of briny water. Along the Monangahela River, for instance, when treatment plants started accepting tanker trucks loaded with waste-water, "workers at a steel mill and a power plant in Greene County were the first to notice something strange: river water began corroding equipment." The state eventually had to put the Monongahela on a list of "impaired rivers," and 325,000 residents of the region were at one point told to drink bottled water.

As Ian Urbina reported in the *Times* in February 2011, the water returning from deep underground can carry naturally occurring "radioactivity at levels higher than previously known, and far higher than the level that federal regulators say is safe for...treatment plants to handle." Despite a 2009 EPA study never made public, the federal agency has continued to allow "most sewage treatment plants that accept drilling waste not to test for radioactivity." And most drinking-water intake plants downstream from the sewage treatment plants, with the blessing of regulators, have not tested for radioactivity since 2006, even though the drilling boom began in 2008.

Industry, as usual, is unconcerned, at least in public. "These low levels of radioactivity pose no threat to the public," said the CEO of Triana Energy. They are "more a public perception issue than a real health threat." But as Urbina pointed out, a confidential industry study from 1990, which looked at radium in drilling water dumped into the ocean off the Louisiana coast, found that it posed "potentially significant risks" of cancer for people eating fish from those waters.

The natural gas wells can cause air pollution problems too: Wyoming, for instance, no longer meets federal air quality standards because of fumes seeping from the state's 27,000 wells, vapors that contain benzene and toluene, according to Urbina.

In sparsely populated Sublette County in Wyoming, which has some of the highest concentrations of wells, vapors reacting to sunlight have contributed to levels of ozone higher than those recorded in Houston and Los Angeles. In a county without a single stoplight, regulators this time last year were urging the elderly and children to stay indoors.

There are steps that industry could take to reduce some of the pollution—wastewater, for instance, can be captured in huge on-site tanks and pushed back down so-called "injection wells," precisely the process that apparently set off the Youngstown temblor. Even this process, however, leaves large quantities of salty residue, and the wells can keep oozing out their toxic load for many years after drilling is done. Some enterprising drilling companies have, Urbina wrote, "found ready buyers [for wastewater] in communities that spread it on roads for de-icing in the winter and for dust suppression in the summer. When ice melts or rain falls, the waste can run off roads and end up in the drinking supply."

In any event, overmatched regulators who can't even keep an accurate count of the number of wells are having a hard time coping with waste products—especially since the political power of the industry just keeps growing. Pennsylvania inaugurated a new governor in 2011, Republican Tom Corbett, who had taken more gas industry contributions than all his competitors combined. Not only did he quickly reopen state land to new drilling, he claimed regulation of the industry had been too aggressive. "I will direct the state's Department of Environmental Protection to serve as a partner with Pennsylvania business, communities and local governments," he said.

What is the effect of this surge of gas on national and global efforts to cope with climate change? Though New York and other states make their decisions on drilling largely on the basis of local effects, this may be the most important question of all, since the implications will extend far beyond the borders of particular geologic formations or specific watersheds. Four years ago (2008), when word of the spectacular potential scale of the gas finds began to filter out, many environmentalists were thrilled. Robert F. Kennedy Jr., for instance, who founded the Waterkeeper Alliance and who has been a leader in the fight against mountaintop removal coal mining, wrote an op-ed for the *Financial Times* in the summer of 2009 declaring that "a revolution in natural gas production over the past two years has left

America awash with natural gas and has made it possible to eliminate most of our dependence on deadly, destructive coal practically overnight."

The reason environmentalists prefer gas to coal is simple: when burned, it produces about half as much carbon dioxide per unit of energy. That is, if we could convert our coal-fired power plants to natural gas (which in most cases is not that hard to do), carbon emissions would drop. But it's actually not that simple. Natural gas—CH_4—in its unburned state is a remarkably powerful greenhouse gas itself, molecule for molecule many times stronger than CO_2. So if even a little bit leaks out to the atmosphere in the drilling process, gas, according to some estimates, can cause even more global warming than coal.

The data showing just how much it would do so are scarce. An early study from Robert Howarth at Cornell found that fracked gas might do twenty percent more damage to the climate, at least over the next few crucial decades, than coal; earlier this winter another Cornell team, using different leakage rates, found that it might be only half as bad as coal. More data may eventually clarify the extent of the threat. But fracked gas is not as clear a winner in this fight as many had originally assumed.

There's a deeper question still. If we increased the use of natural gas, it would replace some coal from the planet's power-generating mix. But it would also crowd out truly low-carbon sources of power: abundant and cheap natural gas would make it that much harder to get sun and wind (or, if it's your cup of hot water, nuclear power) up and running on a large scale.

As the International Energy Agency reported last summer, the numbers are significant: their projections for a "Golden Age of Gas" scenario have atmospheric concentrations of CO_2 peaking at 650 parts per million and temperatures rising 3.5 degrees Celsius, far higher than all the experts believe is safe. In September 2011, the National Center for Atmospheric Research tried to combine all the known data—everything from methane leakage in coal mines to the cooling effects of coal-fired sulfur pollution—and concluded, in the words of the scientist Tom Wigley, that the switch to natural gas "would do little to help solve the climate problem."

As a result of such findings, and of all the on-the-ground problems in Pennsylvania and out west, environmental groups are backing away from their earlier support for gas. Robert F. Kennedy Jr., for instance, has grown increasingly critical; and at the grassroots level, tens of thousands of highly organized activists with visible and articulate spokesmen (the actor Mark Ruffalo has been especially notable) are making an impressively strong stand against further drilling. Their efforts come up against the staggeringly deep pockets of the fossil fuel industry, which is used to winning battles. Bowing to that pressure, and trying to ward off the appeal of the GOP's "drill, baby, drill" rhetoric, President Obama praised fracking in his 2012 State of the Union address, promising to "develop this resource without putting the health and safety of our citizens at risk."

The rush to exploit "extreme energy," and to rip the planet apart to get at it, knows no national boundaries. Urbina reported last year that the big energy companies have spread the fracking technology around the planet, finding new shale deposits in more than thirty countries.

One can reasonably expect that if regulators are overwhelmed in Pennsylvania, the same may be the case among the shale deposits in Papua New Guinea. In any event, it should by now be clear that fracked gas is not a "bridge fuel" to some cleaner era, but a rickety pier extending indefinitely out into a hotter future. This is one of those (not rare) cases where abundance may prove a great problem.

Now We're Talking Price

Richard Manning

The simile most often invoked to describe the founding rock of this revolution on the Northern Plains is an Oreo cookie, but while that may serve to capture the Bakken's uniformity and color scheme, it fails miserably to describe the formation's obduracy and scale. The Bakken is a massive bed of rock in three layers, a dark layer on each side and a lighter sandwiched between, ten to fifty feet thick, its pores richly endowed with oil—light, tight crude. The formation is a twenty thousand square mile slab two miles below the surface mostly in the western fourth of North Dakota but extending for a bit into eastern Montana and the south edges of Alberta and Saskatchewan. Were it a state, it would rank near Massachusetts in size, but oilmen are still not sure of limits on its western edge, or if they know, they are not saying. No matter. What is already known about the Bakken tells us this slab of dolomite has sufficient power. Asked to rank American oil-producing states, most of us would begin with Texas, then add Alaska and California, and maybe then North Dakota, the nation's second largest oil-producing state.

The Bakken got its name in the 1950s from the farmer who leased the land for the first producing well, so geologists have known there is oil on the Northern Plains for more than a half century. The technique of hydraulic fracturing to pry oil and gas from rock has been with us even longer, but over the years a growing number of poorly producing but geologically informative wells began to illuminate the gargantuan scope of the Bakken and also suggest refinements in fracking techniques to make it pay. Until almost 2000, geologists thought the oil coming from the region's few wells flowed from isolated pools in separate formations, but Leigh Price, an iconoclastic geochemist with the United States Geologic Survey, concluded the Bakken was one big deposit that held a stunning 413 billion barrels of oil, a giant. (By comparison, current "proven reserves" for the entire United States are about one-fifth of Price's estimate for the Bakken alone.)

Spurred by this prize, oilmen began experimenting with fracking designed to address the simple fact that all of this oil was tied up in a very thin layer of rock, a puny target when viewed from above but plenty big approached horizontally. Decades of directional drilling had finally given oilmen the ability to drill vertically two miles down to the Bakken, then force a ninety degree bend in the hole and send the drill bit another two miles horizontal and centered in the oil-laden white layer of the Oreo. This yielded a two-mile-long hole surrounded by oil but still no oil, the crude still tight in the surrounding rock.

The second phase was fracking, fracturing the surrounding rock. Simple fracking—filling the two miles of vertical and two miles of horizontal with water, sand, and chemicals, then pumping it to pressurize and crack the rocks to force the sand into the cracks to prop them open—was not enough. Bit by bit, the oilmen learned that the rocks yielded best by sending rubber-coated plugs into the hole a given distance, expanding those plugs to block the hole, fracking, then moving the plug down the line and doing it dozens of times. Gang-fracking like this allowed the two-mile reach of a drill's arm with a sharp elbow at the center to reach a rich flow of oil and natural gas.

Legend says one makes an effective monkey trap by finding a hollow in a tree entered by a hole large enough to admit a monkey's open hand, but too small to allow the monkey to withdraw its closed fist. To catch a monkey, simply place an object in the hollow that the monkey wants badly. Thus, these primates are defeated by what lies within their grasp.

The revolutionary fact of the Bakken that threatens to replay in literally scores of oil shale deposits in North America and dozens worldwide is (a) they contain a hell of a lot of oil and (b) it no longer matters where an oilman drills a well; it matters what he does in the hole once it is drilled. The latter fact helps explain why I was nearly wrapped up in two major truck crashes in my first twenty-four hours in the Bakken.

I did not expect the trucks to so dominate this story of money, of the Bakken oil boom and of trouble for all of us, but here they are. In the cafés and on the radio talk shows, that's what you hear about first, the traffic, even before the money and the crime.

The prairie reveals. Any hilltop's field of vision opens to evidence of energy and motion, fresh tracks, today mostly tire tracks of the present but also old tracks through time. The tracks on these hills are legion and include those of mastodons and people who hunt-ed mastodons with stone-tipped spears; of dog-Indians and bison, horse-Indians and bison, horse-cavalry and bloody tracks of massacre; of cattlemen and longhorns in from Texas, shorthorns from Oregon, busted and broke by a bad winter, barbed wire; of settlers on half-section dry-farm homesteads, busted and broke in a few years. Of all of these, I have come to North Dakota especially to single out a particular and peculiar set of tracks, hoof prints really, for what they tell us about our destruction of the natural world. Ultimately, Theodore Roosevelt would become one of the cattlemen who lost his herds in the blue snow winter of 1886-87, but at first he was just a wide-eyed rich kid trying to take it all in, this very stretch of prairie, right here.

Roosevelt first came to the little town of Medora in the center of North Dakota's Badlands in 1883, in his early twenties, then all buckskin, bluster, teeth, and glasses. He came to kill animals and write about it, but as with everything with him, motive was a bit more complicated. He already was an accomplished naturalist and convinced Darwinist who really came to see the raw display of nature then in the Badlands, a stark rockscape of erosion, rock, and red scoria in North Dakota's southwest corner, a bit of geologic chaos that is the counterpoint to gentle prairie all around.

For our present purposes, though, we are more interested in what happened when he returned in 1884 to retreat to the ranch he bought, the Elkhorn, to grieve. On February 14, his mother, Mittie, and his young blue-blood wife, recently a mother, Alice Lee, had both died on the same day in the same house at 6 West 57th Street in Manhattan. Roosevelt never wrote much about what transformed him during that retreat in grief to the Badlands, but it was transforming. He learned a deep engagement with the landscape, certainly a love of the wild, and reinforced an obsession with the strenuous that would take him through life. His character formed. One biographer calls his Elkhorn Ranch the "Cradle of Conservation," arguing what happened here was what propelled Roosevelt to go on the become president and almost single handedly found the American conservation movement.

In any event, there's more in the mix besides his grief. When he bought the Elkhorn, Roosevelt was already making a name for himself as viscerally and implacably opposed to corruption. He was already taking on Tammany Hall in the New York legislature, laying the foundation of what would become a career of trust-busting that closed the Gilded Age and eventually broke up the mega-monopoly of the day, John D. Rockefeller's Standard Oil.

Eventually Roosevelt would write—specifically of Rockefeller and the railroad tycoons of the day—that they were "the most dangerous members of the criminal class—the criminals of great wealth." I think the grit and sand of this excoriation came from the Elkhorn, maybe, but clearly it came from no place today's political leadership has been. Today, the Elkhorn holds at least six active oil wells run by men in John D. Rockefeller's line of work. Cradle, yes, and now cradle to grave.

The popular mythology of oil leans heavily on the term "wildcatter" freighting, as it does, the undeniable rough risk and megabuck rewards that went with pioneering the world's great deposits of petroleum. There are no wildcatters in the Bakken, not now. Every single well drilled in an area the size of Massachusetts has a ninety-nine percent chance of producing oil for about thirty years in predictable and tapering amounts. Every single well enters the black when oil is above sixty-eight dollars a barrel, give or take. Exploiting this is no longer a matter of wildcatting; this is plumbing. The odds of success are literally set in stone.

In 2015, there are 12,500 producing oil wells in western North Dakota. This total, however, forms but a rough sketch of future density and layout, a haphazard pattern so far determined by a caprice of the market. What one sees is not so much production as flags and stakes claiming the future. Almost all of this landscape is privately held as ranches and farms, meaning what happens here is largely a matter of what transacts between willing sellers and willing buyers. The technical breakthroughs of 2005 yielded a rush of leasing rights to explore for oil, and generally three-year leases. To secure the lease beyond three years, drillers must complete a producing well. Then the driller can go back and drill as many wells as necessary to get all the oil.

This rush to perfect leases begins explaining why the star show that was once the prairie's night sky is gone, and it explains a corollary fact: a particular satellite photo. The latter is a recent image, a view as if from a windshield headed due east over the Rockies, taking in a sweep of night-time plains from Montana to Minnesota. It shows only two big sprays of night lights on the ground below: the urban light pool of Minneapolis and Saint Paul sprawl and closer a blob, larger still, around Williston, North Dakota. The latter is formed from gas flares from the Bakken visible from space.

Every Bakken well produces both crude oil and natural gas. There is, however, no infrastructure—pipelines and processing plants—to handle the rush of gas, no time to wait for pipelines and processing plants to build, given the demands of perfecting leases, and the current low price of natural gas undermines incentive to build infrastructure. Thus, about thirty-five percent of the natural gas now flowing from the Bakken, about 100 million cubic feet a day, enough to heat half a million homes for a day, is simply set alight at the well-head, to produce a landscape of perpetual flames in robust competition with the stars. The flares are everywhere but best viewed where a coal-fired power plant is in the frame of view, which is possible in both Montana and North Dakota. Coal is a hateful fuel, far dirtier than natural gas in all regards.

The future, meantime, promises to be even brighter, and this is a simple matter of geometry, determining the optimum spacing for wells, which is something like one every two or three miles, north and south, east and west. The oil does not move or vary in the stone slab below, so grab a map and start sticking pins. Make a grid that roughly replicates the rectilinear cadastral survey first imposed on this landscape with white settlement. People have done the math; fully developed, plumbed and producing, the Bakken will support at least thirty thousand, maybe fifty thousand profitable oil wells, three or more times the current number of 12,500.

Given this, simple multiplication can write the rest of this story. For instance, because of the multiple fracks and because every well is a trick of contortion executed with precision two miles deep in rock, every single well is labor intensive and material intensive. During the first year of a well's life—the hustling year of drilling and fracking—it will require twelve hundred truck trips. The play adds thousands of new wells each year, meaning the couple of beat-up two-lanes and the red scoria section-line roads that thread between them suffer at least a couple of million trips by behemoth trucks. Farmers and ranchers who live on these back roads no longer open windows in summer for the dust. Even the trivial effects seem not so trivial in multiplication. For instance, in cleaning up roadside litter, people couldn't help but notice the general range of debris has become dependably punctuated with what have been named "trucker bombs." These are spent plastic soda bottles refilled with urine and flung from trucks, rest stops on the prairie being few and far.

Each truck has a driver, roads need road builders, fleets need mechanics, men need houses that need builders, rigs need workers, and the three hundred fifty companies in the oil business in the Bakken need accountants, flacks, legislators, surveyors, negotiators, paymasters and all of these need Walmarts, Holiday Inn Expresses, ATV dealers, gun shops, titty bars, greasy spoons, and internet cafés.

What sifts to the outside world about this is its bottom line, that North Dakota has the lowest unemployment rate in the nation, simply because of the Bakken. The Walmart in Williston flies in temporary staff from Minneapolis. The city sanitation department in Dickinson, a town of 21,000 expected to increase to 35,000 in a few years, cannot keep help because its employees are licensed truck drivers, and oil companies recruit them literally right out of the cabs of their government-wage-paying garbage trucks. Skilled workers of any level easily make six figures.

As with any runaway development, there are limiting factors, but in the Bakken, it is not lack of capital or investors, or pipelines. The limiting factor is lack of workers and rigs; the oil companies simply cannot recruit and deploy workers and drilling rigs fast enough to get the job done.

Even more than the wells themselves, the burgeoning labor force is the evidence that lays on the land. Williston, a town of just fewer than fifteen thousand people in the 2000 census, built a grand total of five houses a year as recently as 2006. Five years later, the city needed at least four thousand a year to meet demand. Watford City, an hour southeast of Williston, was just a wide-spot-in-the road-village of twelve hundred people in 2005. No one knows the population today, but the best guess is ten thousand and growing. All of the towns are ringed by man camps, the local term of art for barracks-like installations of trailers and modular homes, blocks set in ranks and rows. Think FEMA trailers. Companies add them in chunks to hold upwards to a thousand workers, the fortunate workers, the established and secure. Oil companies, in fact, take some effort to provide the best barracks, because desirable quarters serve as recruiting tools.

Newcomers lacking status for company housing live in camper trailers and RVs set in clutches in parking lots at the ragged edge of towns or on a couple of acres leased out by a farmer at prices far above the prevailing cash yield of wheat. Many live in cars. In 2011, the Williston Walmart reversed its long-standing nationwide policy of allowing campers to squat in its parking lot, cleared out campers, and began enforcing a ban. This, by the way, is the same Walmart where Lester Waters and Michael Spell, two outsiders come to the Bakken to look for work and alleged to have killed the schoolteacher from Sidney, Montana, bought a shovel to bury Sherry Arnold's body, then returned with the shovel and receipt three days later for a refund.

After traffic, people here talk about the crush of population growth, by which they mean outsiders, and the capstone of this discussion is the Arnold murder. Nor do they simply talk; in the months after the murder, many newspapers in the region said sellers of handguns and pepper sprays all report land office business in this place where less than a decade ago no one locked doors. Local offices in charge of sex offender registries reported a doubling of the rolls. Pharmacies in Williston have been robbed of prescription painkillers, OxyContin or "hillbilly heroin" being a favorite. An RV full of Korean whores opened for business in 2010 just outside of Bainville, Montana, a prairie hamlet once dominated by the white steeple of a clapboard sided church, now by an oil derrick.

Surprise in response to all of this is unjustified given the historical record. These towns are, after all, boomtowns, specifically oil boomtowns, and it has always been thus. The whole industry began in western Pennsylvania in the aptly named town of Pithole Creek just before the Civil War. Reported one visitor there and then, "The whole place ... smells like a corps of soldiers when they have the diarrhoea." Reported *The Nation*, "It is safe to assert that there is more vile liquor drunk in this town than in any of its size in the world." Always thus.

Pulling into Watford City from the south is like driving onto the set of post-apocalyptic movie. To the north, there is an older nucleus of what was once a prairie farm town, but it has been swallowed in a highway sprawl of mancamps, truck yards, pipe yards, fuel stations, machine shops, grit, dust, and gravel. Gene Veeder is the county's director of economic development, which means he's supposed to boost this town, but he freely admits it more resembles "chaos" than town. (An oil industry spokeswoman in Bismarck admitted much the same the day before but added I should report the people around Watford City were living in a "progress zone.")

Veeder, however, is not a glad-handing booster of commerce, but a thoughtful, genial guy in jeans with a guitar case propped in the corner of his office. He took the job of economic development director of Watford City in 1993, and then it was much like being the economic development director in any Great Plains town between the Rockies and the 100th meridian, an entire region of the nation that has been inexorably losing population and economy since 1909.

"Now I meet more people in a week here than I met in twenty years of economic development," he says. Before, the job of effecting economic development in Watford City was simply impossible; now it is something like being charged with ensuring that the wind blows.

He's open enough about the downsides of all of this: "It did bring the world outside into the community, and that was an eye opener," he says. "People are just overwhelmed with the drugs and prostitution and fights and all the things that come with oil fields."

Bottom feeders accumulate in any boomtown, but there's more to be said about this. Veeder tries to get to know some of the men and even families arriving in the unbroken string of pickup trucks, and finds they bear news from rust-belt towns of the Midwest, logging towns of the Rockies and Northwest, upside-down towns of the south. He hears again and again from men getting their first jobs in years: truck drivers, electricians, carpenters, equipment operators, men who were raised to think that if they worked they would get paid, and for a long time and in a lot of places in this country that was not true and now is true in Watford. Difficult to imagine the politician who will now stand between these people and their oilfield paychecks.

Veeder was born and raised nearby on a 2,500 acre ranch, his father's, and now he owns it and owns with it the knowledge that no one can make a 2,500-acre ranch on western North Dakota pencil. He moved away as a young man to take a real job, and migration is indeed the universal story among plains people now for generations, that a farm people raised to value place and stability and family could not keep their kids at home.

Veeder did not get rich in the oil boom. His ranch is typical in that it was cobbled together bit by bit from smaller farms of homesteaders busted in the Dust Bowl. Many of those people had already sold off mineral rights to their places, so today decisions whether to lease are often not made by those who own and occupy the land, instead made by shirt-tail relatives and descendants who never saw the farms. Veeder himself maintains mineral rights on about 10 percent of the acreage of his ranch, a proportion he says is typical. Somebody else is getting rich off the wells on his land.

"I'm looking at oil wells right now from my house and if I had 'em, well my god," he says. Nonetheless, his daughters, who had moved away to begin lives elsewhere, have moved back.

"I've got one son-in-law at Marathon, the other at Halliburton, senior level people. They are building new houses right now," he says. "That's something nobody talks about, but one is living on the ranch, and she could not live on the ranch without oil.

"For me personally, having the ranch out there, I wish it [the oil boom] would have never been here. Okay. But I do remember when my last child left home, and she was never coming back," he says. "Now I get to live the rest of my life the way I want to."

This is not to say out-migration has ceased; it has simply shifted its demographic. Old people are leaving, sick of the clutter, noise, and crime and pushed by the fact that free-and-clear houses are worth five, six, seven times what they were a few years ago.

Dan Kalil, a county commissioner from Williston, testified to a state legislative committee: "The area is short on patience, jail space, groceries, and fuel; and long on sewage, garbage, anger, and frustration. Our quality of life is gone. It is absolutely gone. My community is gone, and I'm heartbroken. I never wanted to live anyplace but

Williston, North Dakota, and now I don't know what I'm going to do."

There's been a change of heart in a place that once viewed the boom as a lasting marriage with big oil. There is a venerable joke about an aging Texas oilman who approaches a beautiful young woman and asks if she would marry him for a piece of his multi-billion dollar fortune. She allows as to how she might consider such a proposal, so the oilman asks if she would spend a night with him for one thousand dollars. The outraged young woman replies, "What do you think I am: a whore?"

"We have already established that," says the oilman. "Now we are talking price."

Aldo Leopold said, "One of the penalties of an ecological education is that one lives alone in a world of wounds," thereby envisioning a world in which vision is a curse. The concept needs no explanation for the handful of biologists and conservationists who have long labored against destruction of the biota of the Northern Plains. These days, these people tend to be forlorn and shell-shocked.

Mike McEnroe is a wildlife biologist retired after a career with the US Fish and Wildlife Service. McEnroe remains active in the North Dakota Wildlife Society, a national group that traces its roots directly to Leopold and then to the circle of New York patricians and scientists a young Theodore Roosevelt recruited to act as the nation's nascent conservation movement. In the winter of 2011, the chapter gathered for its annual meeting, usually a social event, but talk turned to the Bakken, beginning, as these things do, with some problems on wetlands with an obscure little bird, the piping plover.

"To a person, everyone said you can't believe how much everything has changed," says McEnroe.

So the chapter put together a delegation to go have a look, which McEnroe says he envisioned as throwing the golf clubs and beer cooler in the trunk and spending a few fine spring days alternating between golf courses and wetlands tours in prairie country. The visit, however, coincided with the spring melt following epic snowfalls of the winter of 2010 and 2011. The Little Missouri and Missouri rivers were in full flood.

The national opposition to the Keystone XL pipeline rallied around a political flare-up in red-state Nebraska over the possibility of a spill of crude in the Sand Hills. *Possibility* of a spill. There were, in fact, eleven hundred spills in North Dakota's stretch of the Bakken during 2011, a number we only know because oil drillers are required to self-report spills to the state and the state runs a total. Not much more. We don't know much about the nature of each of these, but McEnroe's group saw something of the scope of problem in touring a few dozen of the Bakken's thousands of wells.

At one site, the group counted nine active oil wells, all of them flooded with Missouri Basin water. At the same site, the oil company had to pump its oil storage tanks full of water to prevent them from floating away. Each active drilling site has a swimming-pool-sized hole adjacent to the drilling rig that catches what drillers call "cuttings"—the dust of rock chewed up by drilling—but also salt water and frac water and chemicals pumped back out of the hole along with the first few barrels of crude. State regulators do not keep track of this mix but one farmer did, sending a sample of reserve pit water to a lab. It contained benzene, toluene, and xylene (all carcinogens) along with simple diesel fuel.

The reserve pits were not simply leaking, but flooded, not seeping to the water course, but fully merged with it. The group saw one operator bulldozing a berm designed to isolate a well from the floodplain in order to drain floodwater from the well pad to the river. Another operator took an even more direct route, pumping floodwater and reserve pit water straight into the river. The biologists documented fish kills, streams with layers of belly-up fish floating at the surface. They saw drained pathways of previous spills marked by a sort of scorched earth: dead vegetation killed on contact by effluent. They shot photographs of all of this, wrote a report, and sent it off to the state in December of 2011. McEnroe says they haven't heard much back since.

Yet seizing on spills as a smoking gun misses the larger overlay of consequences from thirty thousand oil wells and, in fact, sucks us straight into a game of reductionism: arguing about a bit of nesting habitat for a few piping plovers, fawning grounds for mule deer, a single sharp-tailed grouse lek, or an isolated nesting site for a pair of golden eagles.

Anne Marguerite Coyle is an eagle biologist, and in the early days of the boom set about the sort of data gathering exercise typical of these matters. She tagged eighteen juvenile golden eagles to monitor the overall effects of oil drilling on their well-being. All are now dead or gone, and her data are inconclusive as to oil's role in this. She thought she had a smoking gun in one case where a drilling rig landed close to one of the eagles nesting site, so when that bird disappeared, she asked people nearby what had happened. "Oh somebody shot that one." Gunplay, the roads, the rigs, the noise, the trucks, the off-duty oil workers on ATVs, the general disregard for anything living that is the consequence of industrializing a once-wild landscape—these are the sponsors of the death by a thousand cuts that is extinction.

Biologists, meantime hold their inconclusive data sets, precise little pictures so focused and refined in scale as to be meaningless. Two years of study? No we'll need more data, maybe another ten. Measure again and assess after another ten thousand wells.

Coyle reminds me of a concept in biology called allelopathy, a devious and successful survival tactic of a number of species of plants that secrete some sort of chemical that alters the environment and make it impossible for competing species to inhabit the same place, maybe not killing them, more subtle, a noxious chemical that makes everything else go away.

The totem animal of the Great Plains is the bison, of course long since extinguished from the landscape in any practical sense. Roosevelt, in fact, came here first not so much to settle grief but to shoot a bison before they were all gone. But he learned something in the process by engaging the landscape. He returned to Manhattan to assemble a collection of his patrician friends to found the American Bison Society, and much of the work of preservation of this animal traces to that single meeting.

Theodore Roosevelt National Park in the Badlands, of course reflects this legacy and maintains a vestigial bison herd. Almost twenty-five years ago, I was in the park then investigating the real possibility the herd could expand into adjacent federal grasslands and even private ranches to create a buffalo commons in the northern Plains. I pitched a tent one night in the park and awoke the next morning to find an enormous bull pawing the grass just outside my tent, I believe challenging me to some sort of *mano a bos*. This animal is the symbol about everything big, bold, vibrant, and wild about the American plains, and the park holds just enough of them to ensure they will remain just that, a symbol. Any hope of restoration of the wild landscape in real terms rests on bison restoration, and oil development that surrounds the park takes that possibility off the table.

The bison is what biologists call a keystone species, so critical is its role in a functioning landscape. The biologists are right about this, but I have finally decided another mammal serves as a better totem, if only because of its deep history. I disagree slightly with Roosevelt in his assessment of the pronghorn antelope. "The curious pronged horns, great bulging eyes, and strange bridle-like marks and bands on the face and throat are more striking, but less handsome, than the delicate head and branching antlers of a deer; and it entirely lacks the latter animal's grace of movement."

Modern biologists, in fact, use the word "gracile" to describe the pronghorn, relevant in our context here. The antelope is the sole survivor of a complement of North American megafauna that disappeared during the Pleistocene extinctions. Pronghorns once shared this landscape with wooly mammoths and saber tooth tigers, but when humans first arrived here at the end of the last Ice Age, maybe thirteen thousand years ago, all of those large mammals disappeared, went extinct, and human hunting likely had a major role in this. Modern megafauna like elk, bison, and mule deer are all immigrants from Eurasia, like the hunters themselves. Pronghorns are not; they are ancient and enduring, even enduring at least thirteen thousand years of man here.

Biologists believe the pronghorn survived because they were indeed "gracile," that and fast, the fastest sprinting mammal on the continent, and so eluded hunters. Many times I have watched the great herds of them—they are nothing if not social, almost always in herds—by crawling on my belly through sage and prickly pear cactus to a bit of bump in the landscape that will conceal my movement, because they can detect motion and threat for miles. When something alarms one of the sentinels, the mass will begin to fold and roil just as a flock of birds does in a winter sky, a mass of motion that seems to take on a unitary intelligence, the grace and intelligence that granted them survival.

Just a couple of years ago, there were as many as fifteen thousand pronghorn remaining in western Dakota mostly in open grasslands around the Badlands. Roosevelt himself noted this was their preference, that they avoided his ranch amid the Badland's buttes and valleys most of the year but would come in near his ranch in winter to use the lee of the Badland's vertical features to escape the worst of winter's winds.

The winter of 2010-11 produced those epic snows that caused the spring floods tracked by the biologists, an abnormally harsh winter, but understand that all winters are abnormal on the Plains. Still there is an overarching irony here, in that the severity of this particular season traced directly to an oscillation in currents in the Pacific Ocean, a La Niña current, a natural and longstanding phenomenon. Nonetheless, some scientists are willing to bet the oscillation is becoming more pronounced and extreme as a result of global warming, of trapping the carbon of burning hydrocarbons.

Oil production cannot wait for snows to recede and so dozers and plows cut through the drifts to the highways and section lines roads, and the trucks continued to run all that winter in the Bakken. Pronghorn too require motion, and a plowed highway is every bit as good for this as a windswept ridge. A pronghorn's gracile body is about the size and shape of a great Dane's, and in most of the cases, a driver of a multi-tonned tanker truck would not even register the bump and crush. The biologists think all of the state's antelope either left the region or died on highways that winter. All fifteen thousand.

To date, what we talk about when we talk about oil in the United States is, in round numbers, about 36.5 billion barrels of proven reserves. Yet the real significance of the Bakken is not so much what we have seen but in what we have learned there about fracking in general. Driller's talk about the "recipe," the particular combinations of technique and chemicals that makes a particular bed of rock yield its payload, and the Bakken and all that came with it came from getting that right. Once that came, there were no decisions to be made, save the hundreds and thousands of piecemeal decisions made over kitchen tables when someone signs a lease. And you might hate the idea of oil rigs on the family ranch, but if you don't sell someone else will, and it's all going to hell anyway so might as well sign. We do not decide whether to drill oil. Price decides. Price and how much is in the ground. This is what is meant by the "tragedy of the commons."

Getting the recipe right in the Bakken placed an estimated four billion barrels of oil within reach of the monkey's arm. Even this number, though, is less than one percent of some estimates as to how much oil is actually in that Oreo rock and is based on current technologies' ability to extract what is there. Meantime, drillers in North Dakota report recovering three to ten percent, small variations that yield wildly different results when multiplied across the vast scale, with existing technology, which for all intents and purposes has existed about ten years, and is now being tinkered with on 12,500 wells. The more interesting question, though, is how all this newfound ability and knowledge lays out across continent and globe.

The US Energy Information Administration estimates there are eight hundred billion barrels of shale oil reserves in the United States. That is, the recipe moves us from twenty-two billion—everything that has driven everything in domestic production to date—to eight hundred billion barrels, a factor of twenty.

The Marcellus formation in the Northeast is indeed energy from shale but natural gas, not oil like the Bakken. And development there has met some resistance, largely because gas is harder to contain than liquid oil and largely because that major force of environmentalism—"not in my backyard"—is in full rage in a place that, unlike North Dakota ranch country, actually has backyards, not to mention major media markets. Nonetheless, the Bakken, now the largest oil play in the United States, has developed as it has without so much as creasing the nation's political discussion.

If not the Bakken, then how about Wolfcamp in Texas, a shale deposit oilmen are now touting as bigger than the Bakken, part of the much larger Permian Basin in Texas? How about the Eagle Ford in South Texas and the Barnett in North Texas? Colorado and Wyoming's Niobara, Arkansas's Fayetteville, Michigan's Antrim, and the Monterey Formation in California? There are at least twenty active shale plays in the United States. Worldwide? There are known and major shale deposits in Canada, Brazil (big in Brazil), Argentina, Chile, South Africa, North Africa, Europe, China, India, and Australia.

Amid a devastating national recession, North Dakota boasted about its three percent unemployment rate and about attracting its kids back home from the Twin Cities with high paying jobs. Amid catastrophic cutbacks in state government nationwide, North Dakota socked away a budget surplus of 1.7 billion dollars, one of two states with a surplus, and oil-and-coal-rich Montana was the other. (In fairness, Montanans do not do balance the books with oil alone; we also do it by selling filthy coal to the Chinese and Koreans.) North Dakota led the nation in 2010 in personal income growth with a rate of 8.1 percent. Why would one expect politicians of any stripe to take any single step that would jeopardize or appear to jeopardize such numbers in the Bakken or anywhere else? Beyond, the boom is pushing the United States toward energy independence, a development that did not happen overnight either technically or politically.

Just before the Civil War, with development of the first "rock oil" in Pennsylvania, marketers began touting the virtues of kerosene. "Those that have not seen it burn, may rest assured its light is no moonshine; but something nearer the clear strong, brilliant light of day. To which darkness is not party," praised one handbook of the day. "Rock oil emits a dainty light; the brightest and yet the cheapest in the world; a light fit for Kings and Royalists; and not unsuitable for Republicans and Democrats."

This is not ad copy; it is political science, and there have been no advances in the field since.

And so we come to the point where the congregation rises and the preacher intones the usual analogy of oil and addiction, but the truth is, this makes a better ritual than it does a sermon. Oil is no more addiction than food is. Both stand on a lower and more fundamental rung on the ladder of Maslow's hierarchy of needs. Food and energy are necessities in all species, and oil is how we handle energy in this life as we know it. Oil is not just something we do; it is who we are, and now that we have decided who we are, it only remains to talk with the oilmen about price. Places like the Bakken ensure that humanity will have a sufficient supply to cook the planet in catastrophic global warming. Cook it we will.

Jan Swenson is distinctly North Dakotan, graying, slight, late middle-aged, and thoughtful. She gives all this away by threading our discussion of Badlands wilderness preservation with references to Art Link and to legacy. Link is a former Democratic (it's the Democratic Non-Partisan League Party in North Dakota, the NPL, the name a vestige of prairie socialism) governor during the fight over coal development in the 1980s, the preface for oil development today. Link was a farmer from Alexander, a sleepy wheat town then, now dead center in the oil boom. Then, Link and his allies in the coal battle invoked a fight-phrase deeply resonant in North Dakota, labeling energy development a "one-time harvest." Nothing could be more offensive to old-school North Dakota, which had an obsession with legacy and land, the idea being it is one's ultimate duty to live in a way that allows the next generation to inherit a landscape whole and undamaged.

Swenson persists in fighting for Badlands wilderness, even in the face, especially in the face, of a crush of development she could not have imagined only five years ago. Her battle is the extension of a family commitment, an attachment she built for the landscape visiting it when she was a child living in Bismarck an hour east, a common enough story but with a North Dakota subtext. Her father grew up in the Red River Valley farther east but left for a career in higher education in Bismarck. Swenson and her father watched from the sidelines as the old family homestead passed from uncles to cousins, as is the way of farm people. When her own father died, there was indeed a legacy, but it was only money, not a farm, and Swenson decided to follow a sort of instinct of the place and convert the legacy to land. She bought a half-section, three hundred twenty acres of land, near Grassy Butte before it was surrounded by oil rigs.

The decision was part of her battle as a conservationist. Only a few years ago, the lines of this fight were drawn between ranchers and environmentalists on the issue of cattle grazing on public lands. Opposition notwithstanding, Swenson had long understood the ranchers' tenure on the landscape gave them an understanding of conditions of life there she did not grasp and would need to begin to understand to be effective in conservation. She bought the half-section with the idea of living on it and fully engaging the natural and human community.

"I was always of the mind I was going to be a crazy old woman living out at Grassy Butte when I was eighty, and I haven't given up on that, but I have to wait and see," she says.

A couple of things happened to change her plan, and oil was one. But the second was personal: her son, Webb, died. With the loss came a parallel loss of her foundation, the ability to engage the landscape of the Badlands—both her own land at Grassy Butte but also the larger region, even the protected public lands.

"The entire Badlands were like a strange landscape that I did not recognize [after Webb's death]," she says. "It was almost like being lost. Like not knowing the roads anymore or the landmarks."

But over time, she recovered. She reattached, and the wild places eased her grief. Except for her own land at Grassy Butte. It has changed. It is different. All around it has been drilled for oil and so lost the power she needed from it. She's still not sure if she can ever live on it as she had once planned.

Theodore Roosevelt was nothing if not self-conscious and something of a huckster at that. He detailed every hunting trip and sold multiple articles on each, some cut-and-paste jobs of earlier versions. He hustled freelance assignments, books and speeches on every set of deer antlers, buffalo mount, elk hide and on every lark and thrush spotted in between. But commerce aside, sometimes he wrote well and philosophically, especially about this odd notion of his, that wilderness itself was of value, an irreplaceable force in shaping American character, a quaint notion, today forgotten and antique as his condemnations of John D. Rockefeller.

He did not, however, write about what he experienced, learned, and felt in this place that allowed him to deal with the death of his mother and young wife in the course of a single day. Too bad, because we're down to grief now, and what he learned about it here is what we need to know.

I've had enough of these winter two-lane highways, and so find my way to an unpaved scoria road, Magpie Road, headed due west from the roar of the highway into the relative quiet of the Badlands. I have a spot in mind just northeast of what was Roosevelt's Elkhorn Ranch. There's a trailhead where I can leave my Jeep. A fine single-track running trail wraps around buttes and coulees, leading on for miles, eventually on to the Elkhorn Ranch itself. Somewhere Roosevelt's tracks are no doubt set in mid-layers of this very trail, just above the deeper layer of moccasin tracks, so I run, because I am a runner, trying now to build the chuff of my breathing loud enough to overmatch the whir and creak of pump jacks every few miles.

It's late February and still plenty cold, despite the sun, but I have a decent pair of cleated running shoes built in China and delivered to me by diesel fuel. I have fleece and polyester miracle fabrics with various trademark names that disguise their common origin in petroleum, so I am warm. My Jeep Liberty burned through six and a half tanks of gas in reporting this story. Roosevelt's ranch is within my running range, but I stop short. I decide I have no right to enter this place now. None of us does.

Insanity

Derrick Jensen

The dominant culture is insane. It has a death urge, an urge to destroy life. Unless it is stopped, it will kill everything on the planet.

Why do I say this? Look around. Take your pick of what evidence you want to talk about. We can talk about this culture intentionally fabricating quadrillions (yes, with a q) of lethal doses of plutonium-239. We can talk about it bathing the world in endocrine disruptors. We can talk about it bathing the world in neurotoxins (Who's the genius who came up with the idea of putting poisons on our own food?). We can talk about it suffocating the oceans in plastic, till there is six to ten times as much plastic as phytoplankton in the oceans. We can talk about it vacuuming the oceans, till the total weight of fish in the oceans is only one-tenth of what it was just one hundred forty years ago. We can talk about ocean acidification. We can talk about stolid scientists saying the oceans could be devoid of fish within forty years. We can talk about how every stream in the United States is contaminated with carcinogens. We can talk about how there has been an average of one large dam built every day in the United States since its inception, which means at this point if we only took out one large dam per day it would take two hundred years to remove them all, and we can talk about how salmon don't have that time, and sturgeon don't have that time. We can talk about how around the world large dams have been built even more frequently than this. We can talk about how, because of this, twenty-five percent of the world's rivers no longer reach the oceans. This includes such once-huge rivers as the Colorado, the Indus, the Amu Darya, the Syr Darya, the Rio Grande, the Yellow, the Teesta, the Murray, and so many others. We can talk about how governments routinely allocate *more than one hundred percent of the water in a river* to be removed. More than one hundred percent. And they are building more pipelines, installing more pumps.

We can talk about how this culture believes you can have infinite growth on a finite planet. We can talk about how it commits land theft and genocide against every Indigenous culture it encounters. We can talk about how this has been going on for thousands of years, and it continues to this day, as Indigenous human languages are being driven extinct at an even faster relative rate than nonhuman species.

We can talk about how, prior to this culture, Iraq was a cedar forest so thick that sunlight never touched the ground. The Arabian Peninsula was oak savanna, with enough trees they were commercially exported out of the region and to the center of empire. We can talk about how the Levant was once forested. North Africa was forested. Greece. Italy. All those forests were cut. We can talk about how there were so many cod in the North Atlantic that their bodies slowed the passage of ships. Whales were so common they were a hazard to shipping. We can talk about the flocks of passenger pigeons so large they darkened the sky for days at a time, and the flocks of Eskimo curlews almost as large. We can talk about the single prairie dog community that spanned twenty-five thousand square miles. We can talk about this culture wiping out all of these. We can talk about this culture causing the greatest mass extinction in the history of the planet.

We can talk about this culture changing the climate. And we can talk about how most Americans, and certainly most Americans in power, don't give a shit. We can talk about the response by members of this culture to the icecaps melting, which is nothing more nor less than lust after the "resources" that will now be available to them. We can talk about luxury cruises through the remains of that biome. We can talk about how emissions from Arctic shipping are estimated to increase up to six hundred percent in the next ten years.

We can talk about how, even faced with all of this evidence, the response by those in power is to continue to promote infinite growth on a finite planet, and the response by mainstream environmentalists is not to try to protect the planet that is our only home, but rather to protect this omnicidal system: what do all of the solutions to global warming presented by mainstream environmentalists have in common? They all take colonialism and industrial civilization as givens, and nature—i.e., the real world—as that which must conform to this culture. A lot of mainstream environmentalists take this culture and not the planet as what must be protected and saved at all costs. This is all literally insane, in terms of being out of touch with physical reality. Without a planet you can't have any social system whatsoever. The planet must be primary.

But within this culture it is not. Even when the planet itself is being murdered, most people cannot question the culture that is murdering it.

Other writers in this anthology have done a magnificent job of describing what fracking is, and some of the problems with it. I wanted to put fracking in its proper cultural context. Fracking is not one lone mistake. It's not one lone act of greed. It's part of a larger pattern. It's one symptom of the disease—the insanity—that is this culture.

In this context, I want to mention three news articles. The first is headlined: "Fracking or Drinking Water? That May Become the Choice." It begins: "Fracking for oil and natural gas—or having enough water to drink. That's the possible dilemma facing a number of countries including the United States, according to a new report released by the World Resources Institute last week—though experts disagree on the real implications of the report and what should be done about it." Yes, it is considered perfectly sane to consider the choice between having water to drink and oil and gas from fracking a dilemma, and it is considered perfectly reasonable for "experts" to disagree as to what should be done about this.

That is, it's considered perfectly sane and reasonable, if fueling this culture is more important than having water to drink, water that we require in order to, you know, not die. It's considered perfectly sane and reasonable if fueling this culture is more important than life, in-cluding human life. More important to the frackers, more important to the political leaders who allow it, more important to those who call it a "dilemma," more important to the experts who disagree as to what should be done about it.

I'm not conflicted as to what should be done about it: fracking should be stopped, and frackers should be stopped, just as one hopes we would stop anyone else who was going to poison water supplies for money (or any other reason). For example, if some psychopath were going to put cyanide into drinking water supplies, I'd hope we'd use any means necessary to stop that person. We should do the same here.

I'm sorry: I lied. When psychopaths *already* put cyanide and other poisons into water supplies, we don't stop them. In fact, governments—from the local to the national to the international through trade agreements—encourage them, pay them, protect them. To provide one example among a near infinitude, large gold mining corporations routinely use "cyanide heap-leaching" to remove gold from ore. Some of this cyanide of course makes its way into rivers, groundwater, and other water bodies. Nothing much happens to those who do it. Except they get rich. Likewise, when BP trashed the Gulf of Mexico, no one went to prison, no one was executed. The corporation only paid in fines less than a fifth of what it set aside for legal fees to *fight* the potential fines. And the CEO? His "punishment" was a severance package worth more than thirty-five million dollars. Also, likewise, pulp mills routinely pump dioxins into waterways, and their routine fines are simply counted as routine costs, which are far less than their routine profits. And of course all that plastic in the oceans has to come from somewhere, right? And we all know how hard this culture is trying to stop that, and how harshly those responsible for it are being punished, right?

Here's how interested this culture is in stopping the rich and powerful from harming the public: it has created fictions called "limited liability corporations," which have as one of their primary functions "limiting liability"—that is, allowing the rich and powerful who run the corporations to not take responsibility for the harm they cause to the public, to communities as a whole, and to the natural world.

It's a great scam for those at the top. Like fracking, like cyanide heap-leaching, like murdering the Gulf of Mexico, like all of the destruction this culture causes, it's a win-win situation, except for those who lose, which is almost everybody.

So I guess it would be more accurate to say that this culture only stops those psychopaths who poison groundwater when that poisoning doesn't serve economic production. Economic production is the (literal) get out of jail free card.

The second article is headlined: "Dead babies near oil drilling sites raise questions for researchers." Yes, you read that correctly. Babies are dying near oil drilling sites, and the response by this culture is not to stop the murderers from continuing their killing spree, but merely to ask some questions.

And what's worse is that even those whose children are being murdered aren't really interested in the answers. As the article states, "Just raising that possibility [of a connection between pollution caused by the oil and gas industry and the deaths of their infant children] raises the ire of many who live in and around Vernal. Drilling has been an economic driver and part of the fabric of life here since the 1940s. And if all that energy development means the Uintah Basin has a particularly nasty problem with pollution, so be it, many residents say. Don't blame drilling for baby deaths that obituaries indicate were six times higher than the national average last year."

Listen to the voice of a mother who had two infant sons die since 2011, "'People like to blame stuff on that all the time, but I don't feel like it has anything to do with oil and gas. I just feel like it's a trial I was given."

Let's be clear about how strong this woman's loyalty is to oil and gas: she lost two of her own infant children, and still refuses to question the economic system—or even the specific industrial sector—that killed them.

Let's be even more clear about what just happened. This culture has supplanted and destroyed what is perhaps the most powerful instinctual interpersonal bond, between mother and child.

And for what are these people sacrificing their children? The article answers that as well, "In Vernal, all that [oil and gas exploitation] is translating into mushrooming amenities. Finishing touches are being put on a sprawling new mall. An energy-funded conference center with swooping modernistic glass walls is taking shape not far from an eye-popping community center. A new library is a daytime magnet for mothers and kids. [At least the ones still alive.] And there are new babies to celebrate. Ben and Caren Moon, who previously lost a pre-term baby, just gave birth to a healthy new baby. They are feeling blessed even as they still grieve their earlier loss. 'Oil-field drilling has been here forever [sic],' Ben Moon said. 'I don't believe it all had anything to do with that.'"

This is how deep the allegiance to this omnicidal system runs: even when it is not killing "just" the oceans, "just" the salmon, "just" the prairie dogs, but when it is poisoning our own drinking water, when it is killing our own children, *still* our loyalty is to the system, not to life, not even to our own babies.

But maybe I'm being too harsh on them. Is a baker's dozen of dead infants really such a bad trade for "mushrooming amenities"? I guess it depends on how cool the stores are in the mall, and how eye-popping the new community center is, and how much the modernistic glass walls swoop. And if there are enough books in the library, then for sure the trade-off is worth it.

In the 1830s a pro-slavery philosopher wrote, "Without it [the coercion of slavery], there can be no accumulation of property, no providence for the future, no taste for comforts or elegancies, which are the characteristics and essentials of civilization."

Let's just change "it" from meaning "the coercion of slavery" to "infants (and the land) sacrificed to oil and gas" and we still have a match.

What is happening with fracking is happening across the globe in all industries. It is the trade off on which this omnicidal culture is based, the trade off which enriches this culture while destroying everyone and everything else. We are trading the lives of all of the human and nonhuman children on the planet so that we can have eye-popping amenities. Fracking is only one of the ways. Comforts or elegancies—or mushrooming amenities—is the price for which we are selling the lives of not only everyone *else* on the planet, and not only everyone else's children, but our own children as well.

This culture is insane.

But perhaps I'm still being unfair. Perhaps when people are simply given the information they make the right choices. Or perhaps not. Let's look at what has been the public response to those who have tried to stop the poisoning of the children. The third headline: "Utah oil town turns against midwife who asked about infant deaths."

The midwife, Donna Young, has helped deliver hundreds of healthy young babies. When one mother's baby was stillborn, Young grieved with the parents and went to the funeral. She noticed new grave markers for too many other infants. She started asking why these infants are dying.

In terms of popularity, that was a terrible mistake on her part: "The questions Young posed have unleashed angry and bitter feelings in this desert town of 35,000, where half the annual budget comes from oil and natural gas exploration. Even mothers of the deceased babies publicly insisted oil drilling wasn't to blame. The midwife became a pariah. She got phone calls warning her to 'shut up' or leave town. One caller said a few dead babies wasn't worth putting any heat on the oil companies. She was dismissed as a meddling midwife and pilloried on local talk radio and in internet chat rooms. Recently, she found rat poison in the cattle feed at her ranch forty miles outside town, although none of her animals got sick."

The town's mayor supported the attacks (of course), saying, "People get very protective of what we have here," by which the mayor meant the oil and gas industry, not the people's own children, and certainly not the natural world. "If you challenge our livelihood, it's considered personal."

Evidently, if you point out that oil and gas exploitation are toxic processes, and that toxic processes can lead to the deaths of infants, people in this culture take your statements personally, far more personally than they do the deaths of their own children. Of course. Because people in this culture identify more with the economic system than they do their own children.

Young contacted the head of the area TriCounty Health Department, who called a public meeting. A few dozen people attended, many of whom, including a number of physicians, were there to show their support of the oil and gas industry. After the meeting the attacks on Young intensified. She was told by one person that the local elite were "coming after you politically; they're going to destroy you." And as the article puts it, "The local Ashley Regional Medical Center wasn't pleased either. 'The physicians were very upset about her stirring this up,' said hospital spokeswoman Debbie Spafford."

Remember, the first rule of medicine is, Do no harm. To the oil and gas industry, that is.

The head of the TriCounty Health Department had to step down. He noted, "Air quality is a touchy issue here." As opposed, of course, to dead babies, which are evidently to be swept under the rug with the other detritus.

Young has been called "despicable" and a "fraud." People have publicly been asking for her address. Young states, "I keep searchlights on and turn the guard dogs loose after dark. And I keep a pit bull on the inside."

The article concludes with a description of one of the local oil and gas supporters:

> George Burnett owns a Main Street smoothie and juice bar called 'I Love Drilling,' which serves organic drinks named after US oil wells, like 'Slick,' 'Dirty Devil #22' and 'Hogback #1.' He believes oil and healthy living can coexist. 'Drilling,' Burnett said, 'brings the earth's energy to life [sic].' He called Young's questions 'alarmist thinking that has gotten ahead of good science.' On one recent afternoon, he stood outside the shop, by a roadside sign reading 'Honk If You Love Drilling.' The horns didn't stop blaring.

This culture loves drilling—loves this culture's destructive activities—far more than it loves life on earth. It loves destroying the planet far more than it loves the planet.

This is the context in which we need to understand fracking. It is merely one way among too many this culture has found to manifest its hatred of the real world, its hatred of life.

My purpose here is not to convince you of this. If what is happening in the real world—and what has been happening for several thousand years now, as this culture steals land from sustainable, land-based Indigenous cultures and destroys the land (As the Shawnee

Chiksika said, "The white man seeks to conquer nature, to bend it to his will and to use it wastefully until it is all gone and then he simply moves on, leaving the waste behind him and looking for new places to take. The whole white race is a monster who is always hungry and what he eats is land.")—doesn't convince you, then a few words and a few stories aren't going to do it. My purpose here is to articulate as clearly as I can the problems I am trying to see as clearly as I can. If you don't perceive or don't believe that fracking is one symptom of this larger, insane, omnicidal culture, then by all means fight fracking because it is evil, immoral, destructive, and wrong. If, on the other hand, you do see the larger pattern—with or without help from my articulation—then by all means fight fracking for all of the reasons above, but do so also because it is one symptom of a very sick, very depraved, insane culture that, unless stopped, will kill everything on the planet.

Homeland Security

Alison Hawthorne Deming

What is a day to the astronaut
floating two-hundred miles
above Earth the space station
whirling fifteen times a day
around the globe's circumference
while he drifts weightless as if
unmoving sipping meals from
a plastic pouch. Is that how it works
keeping everything contained
against the drift? His twin is
down there donating biometrics
to the database. What is a year
to them, to their bones and hearts
and brains? That's what the instruments
want to know or what we've taught
them to want. Did I mention that
the space twin too is donating
his stats. He'll pay the higher price

for his unearthly habitation. Bodies
need gravity or some system
that simulates the magnetic pull
of mantle and core. He can see home
from a small window in space
the planet from out there sublime
a blue and white ball so tender it
might be made of glass just forming
at the tip of the glassblower's rod.

The Earth twin watched his brother
lift off from the cosmodrome.
Zero to seventeen thousand
in twelve minutes. "It feels like
the hand of God has come down
and grabbed you by the collar
and ripped you off the planet.
You're either going to float
in space or you're going to be dead."
What is Earth to the astronaut?
It is the exception to emptiness.
Sure other planets lie further out
in the black concealment of space.
Best perhaps that we do not know
their voraciousness and need.
Ours we know is troubled by
privileged greed yet still
in the heyday of its

experiment with life.
What is an atmosphere
and how did Earth get one?
Thanks cyanobacteria
for your evolutionary gift
the Great Oxygenation Event
that made us possible.

I'm writing this to find my way
into the fray over fracking—
wild card as it seems now that
I've gone so far out into space.
But no one wants to hear again
about flaming water faucets
exploited towns and farms
heartland riddled with quakes
water poisoned and stuck back
in the ground to find its way home.
Space might be the only way
to see what kind of sky we need
and how the Great Carbonation
Event might be flipping the way
Earth does or doesn't do life.
We say "blue marble" we say
"Mother Earth" we say "home."
The astronaut says "Beautiful."
Earth from space says "Keep me."
Homeland Security means

leave it in the ground. Lock it up
with soldiers standing guard
cover it with grassland and trees.

NOTES:

"A Miniature Handbook for New Women Activists," Amy Weldon

Rachel McCarthy, "This Land Is My Land," *The Story*, June 2013. See http://www.thestory.org/stories/2013-06/land-my-land.

Florence Williams, *Breasts: A Natural and Unnatural History*, New York: W. W. Norton, 2012.

Sarah Horner, "Spring Lake Park: Suspect arrested in Internet dating abduction," *Pioneer Press*, 2011. See http://www.twincities.com/crime/ci_19597242.

"Austria incest suspect charged with murder," CNN, 2008. See http://edition.cnn.com/2008/WORLD/europe/11/13/austria.fritzl/index.html.

Trip Gabriel et al., "Cleveland Man Charged With Rape and Kidnapping," *New York Times*, May 2013. See http://www.nytimes.com/2013/05/09/us/cleveland-kidnapping.html?pagewanted=all.

Camille Hahn, "Virgin Territory," *Ms. Magazine*, Fall 2004. See http://www.msmagazine.com/fall2004/virginterritory.asp.

Alex Dominguez, "Elizabeth Smart speaks about abstinence education," *The Salt Lake Tribune*, May 2013. See http://www.sltrib.com/sltrib/news/56248622-78/abstinence-smart-elizabeth-trafficking.html.csp.

Katie McDonough, "Texas company uses image of kidnapped woman to advertise truck decals," *Salon*, September 2013. See http://www.salon.com/2013/09/09/texas_company_uses_image_of_kidnapped_woman_to_advertise_truck_decals/.

Naomi Oreskes and Erik M. Conway, *Merchants of Doubt: How a Handful of Scientists Obscured the Truth on Issues from Tobacco Smoke to Global Warming*, New York: Bloomsbury Press, 2010.

Rebecca Solnit, "Men who explain things," *LA Times*, 2008. See http://articles.latimes.com/2008/apr/13/opinion/op-solnit13.

"The View from 31,000 Feet: A Philosopher Looks at Fracking," Kathleen Dean Moore

The Blue River Declaration: An Ethic of the Earth. See http://liberalarts.oregonstate.edu/sites/default/files/blueriverdeclaraton.2012.pdf.

"Frackenstein's Monster: A History of Unconventional Oil and Gas Technology," Tyler Priest

U.S. Energy Information Administration, http://www.eia.gov/naturalgas/.

F. Kate Sinding quoted in Darrick Evensen, Jeffrey B. Jacquet, Christopher E. Clarke, and Richard C. Stedman, "What's the 'Fracking' Problem? One Word Can't Say It All," *The Extractive Industries and Society* 1, 2014.

Russell Gold, *The Boom: How Fracking Ignited the American Energy Revolution and Changed the World,* New York: Simon & Schuster, 2014.

Bruno Latour, "Love Your Monsters: Why We Must Care for Our Technologies As We Do Our Children," *Breakthrough Journal*, Winter 2012. See http://thebreakthrough.org/index.php/journal/past-issues/issue-2/love-your-monsters/.

"Lower 48 States Shale Plays," Energy Information Administration (EIA), 2015. See http://www.eia.gov/oil_gas/rpd/shale_gas.pdf.

George E. King, "Hydraulic Fracturing 101: What Every Representative, Environmentalist, Regulator, Reporter, Investor, University Researcher, Neighbor and Engineer Should Know About Estimating Frac Risk and Improving Frac Performance in Unconventional Gas and Oil Wells," SPE 152596, Paper Presented to the Society of Petroleum Engineers Hydraulic Fracturing Technology Conference, The Woodlands Texas, February 6-8, 2012, 3; Gold, *The Boom*.

Richard J. Davies, Sam Almong, Robert S. Ward, Robert B. Jackson, Charlotte Adams, Fred Worrall, Liam G. Herringshaw, Jon G. Gluyas, Mark A. Whitehead, "Oil and Gas Wells and Their Integrity: Implications for Shale and Unconventional Resource Exploitation," *Marine and Petroleum Geology* 56, September 2014.

Susan Borowski, "Idea for 'Fracking' Came from Civil War Battlefield," *Scientia*, November 12, 2012.

Carl T. Montgomery and Michael B. Smith, "Hydraulic Fracturing: History of An Enduring Technology," *Journal of Petroleum Technology*, December 2010.

National Energy Technology Laboratory, Strategic Center for Natural Gas and Oil, U.S. Department of Energy, "DOE's Unconventional Gas Research Programs, 1976-1995, An Archive of Important Results," January 1, 2007.

Mary Shelley, *Frankenstein*, New York: Penguin Classics, 2003.

Energy Information Administration, Office of Oil and Gas, U.S. Department of Energy, "Drilling Sideways—A Review of Horizontal Well Technology and Its Domestic Application" DOE/EIA-TR-0565, April 1993.

Ralph F. Spinnler, Frederick A. Stone, and C. Ray Williams, "Mud Pulse Logging While Drilling Telemetry System—Design, Development, and Demonstrations," Technical Information Center, United States Department of Energy, BERC/TPR-78/4, July 1978.

Jonny Haugen, "Rotary Steerable System Replaces Slide Mode for Directional Drilling Applications," *Oil & Gas Journal*, March 2, 1998.

Jeff Reed, "Top Drives: From Rig Jewelry to Essential Equipment," July 2014. See http://oilpro.com/post/4992/top-drives--from-rig-jewelry-to-essential-equipment.

Ed Crooks, "The U.S. Shale Revolution," *Financial Times*, April 24, 2015.

Dan Murtaugh, Lynn Doan, and Bradley Olson, "Refracing Fever Sweeps Across Shale Industry After Oil Collapse," *World Oil*, July 7, 2015.

Donald I. Siegel, Nicholas A. Azzolina, Bert J. Smith, A. Elizabeth Perry, and Rikka L. Bothun, "Methane Concentrations in Water Wells Unrelated to Proximity to Existing Oil and Gas Wells in Northeastern Pennsylvania," *Environmental Science & Technology* 49, 2015.

Stephen G. Osborn, Avner Vengosh, Nathaniel R. Warner, and Robert B. Jackson, "Methane Contamination of Drinking Water Accompanying Gas-Well Drilling and Hydraulic Fracturing," *Proceedings of the National Academy of Sciences* 108, no. 20, May 17, 2011.

Robert B. Jackson, Avner Vengosh, Thomas H. Darrah, Nathaniel R. Warner, Adrian Down, Robert J. Poreda, Stephen G. Osborn, Kaiguang Zhao, and Jonathan D. Karr, "Increased Stray Gas Abundance in a Subset of Drinking Water Wells Near Marcellus Shale Gas Extraction," *Proceedings of the National Academy of Sciences* 110, no. 28, July 9, 2013.

Fred J. Baldassare, Mark A. McCaffrey, and John A. Harper, "A Geochemical Context for Stray Gas Investigations in the Northern Appalachian Basin: Implications of Analyses of Natural Gases from Neogene-through Devonian-Age Strata," *AAPG Bulletin*, DOI:1.1306/06111312178, February 2014.

Robert W. Howarth, Renee Santoro, and Anthony Ingraffea, "Methane and the Greenhouse-Gas Footprint of Natural Gas from Shale Formations," *Climate Change*, Letter, DOI 10.1007/s10584-011-0061-5, March 13, 2011.

Mohan Jiang, W. Michael Griffen, Chris Hendrickson, Paulina Jaramillo, Jeanne VanBriesen, and Aranya Venkatesh, "Life Cycle Greenhouse Gas Emissions of Marcellus Shale Gas," *Environmental Research Letters* 6, July-September 2011, 034014.

Timothy J. Skone, "Life Cycle Greenhouse Gas Inventory of Natural Gas Extraction, Delivery and Electricity Production," DOE/NETL-2011/1522, Final Report, October 24, 2011.

Mark Fulton and Nils Mellquist, "Comparing Life-Cycle Greenhouse Gas Emissions from Natural Gas and Coal," Worldwatch Institute, August 25, 2011.

Francis O'Sullivan and Sergey Patlsev, "Shale Gas Production: Potential Versus Actual GHG Emissions," MIT Joint Program on the Science and Policy of Global Change, Report No. 234, November 2012.

David T. Allen, Vincent M. Torres, James Thomas, David W. Sullivan, Matthew Harrison, Al Hendler, Scott C. Herndon, Charles E. Kolb, Matthew P. Fraser, A. Daniel Hill, Brian K. Lamb, Jennifer Miskimins, Robert F. Sawyer, and John H. Seinfeld, "Measurements of Methane Emissions at Natural Gas Production Sites in the United States," *Proceedings of the National Academy of Sciences* 110, no. 44, October 29, 2013.

T. Bruckner, I.A. Bashmakov, Y. Mulugetta, H. Chum, A. de la Vega Navarro, J. Edmonds, A. Faaij, B. Fungtammasan, A. Garg, E. Hertwich, D. Honnery, D. Infield, M. Kainuma, S. Khennas, S. Kim, H.B. Nimir, K. Riahj, N. Strachan, R. Wiser, and X. Zhang: *Energy Systems. In: Climate Change 2014: Mitigation of Climate Change, Contribution of Working Group III to the Fifth Assessment Report of the Intergovernmental Panel on Climate Change*, Edenhofer, O., R. Pichs-Madruga, Y.Sokona, E. Farahani, S. Kadner, K. Seyboth, A. Adler, I. Baum, S. Brunner, P. Eickmeier, B. Kriemann, J. Savolainen, S. Schlömer, C. von Stechow, T. Zwickel and J.C. Minx, eds., Cambridge: Cambridge University Press, 2014.

J.A. De Gouw, D.D. Parrish, G.J. Frost, and M. Trainer, "Reduced Emissions of CO_2, NOx, and SO_2 from U.S. Power Plants Owing to Switch from Coal to Natural Gas with Combined Cycle Technology," *Earth's Future* 2, February 2014.

"U.S. Greenhouse Gas Emissions," United States Environmental Protection Agency. See http://www.epa.gov/climatechange/science/indicators/ghg/us-ghg-emissions.html.

The Future of Natural Gas: An Interdisciplinary MIT Study, MIT, 2010. See http://mitei.mit.edu/system/files/NaturalGas_Report.pdf.

"One Well: Drilling the Bears Ears," Stephen Trimble

Research for this essay was made possible due to help from the following people: Steve Bloch and Ray Bloxham, Southern Utah Wilderness Alliance; Josh Ewing, Friends of Cedar Mesa; Gavin Noyes, Utah Diné Bikeyah; Tim Peterson, Grand Canyon Trust; and Kevin Jones of Ancient Places Consulting.

Quotations from Mary Johnson and Willie Grayeyes from http://utahdinebikeyah.org.

"Oil Town Palimpsest, or a Brief Material History of Frackland," Stephanie LeMenager

Shell Refinery Exhibit text, California Oil Museum, Santa Paula, California, December 20, 2012.

Francis W. Hertel, interviewed by Allen Stauch, September 1, 1979, "Petroleum Industry in Ventura County, Especially the Ventura Avenue Field," Ventura County Museum Library.

A neat summary of complaints about the refinery through the 1970s and early 1980s can be found in Constance Sommer, "Homes Proposed at Site of Old Refinery: Ventura: The Council Will Consider USA Petroleum's Bid for a Zoning Change. Environmentalists Voice Opposition," *Los Angeles Times*, January 7, 1995. From *Los Angeles Times* archive (1985–present), accessed January 3, 2013, at http://articles.latimes.com// through the University of California at Santa Barbara online articles database. For a vintage spill photograph, see "Crews Mop Up Oil Spill at River Mouth," *Ventura County Star Free Press*, section A-1, October 23, 1970.

Citizens to Preserve the Ojai v. County of Ventura et al., Defendants and Respondents; USA Petrochem Corporation, Real Party in Interest and Respondent. 176 Ca. App. 3d 421; 222 Cal. Rptr. 247, Dec. 1985.

Cheri Carlson, "EPA Investigates Reports of Possible Toxic Waste at Old Refinery Near West Ventura," *Ventura County Star* online, November 29, 2012. See http://www.vcstar.com/news/epa-investigates-reports-of-possible-toxic-waste.

Karen Jurist, Environmental Protection Agency contact for USA Petrochem site, personal communication by telephone, December 21, 2012.

The information-gathering techniques about forty-nine sites are described in the Executive Summary of Appendix 4.7, "Hazards and Hazardous Materials Study," *Preliminary Environmental Site Assessment and Identification of Areas of Potential Concern Westside Community Planning Project*, Ventura, California. Ref. No. 0161-39P. Available at the City of Ventura online: http://www.cityofventura.net/page/community-plan-amp-development-code.

Susanne Antonetta, *Body Toxic: An Environmental Memoir*, Washington, D.C.: Counterpoint Press, 2001.

The salutary news of local clean-up—as of 2009, appears in Kit Stolz, "Tar on Your Foot: The Down and Dirty about Ventura County's Oil Legacy," *Ventura County Reporter*, April 16, 2009. See www.vcreporter.com. Surfrider's Paul Jenkins also credits the city with responding to community members' concerns about hazardous waste. Jenkins, personal communication.

606 Studio (Yarnie Chen, Matt Deines, Henry Fleischmann, Sonya Reed, Isby Swick), *Transforming Urban Environments for a Post-Peak Oil Future*, Pomona: Department of Landscape Architecture, California State Polytechnic University, 2007. Available at the City of Ventura online, "Green Ventura": http://www.cityofventura.net/greenventura.

"Very good examples of industrial buildings from this era [post World War II] include 2220 North Ventura Avenue and 4777 Crooked Palm Road [the USA Petrochem refinery]." City of Ventura, *Westside Historic*

Context and Survey Report, prepared by Galvin Preservation Associates, Inc., January 2011.

"Ventura Oil Refinery," *Atlas Obscura*. See http://www.atlasobscura.com/places/ventura-oil-refinery.

"Ventura Oil Refinery, Abandoned—Part 1," *Avoiding Regret*, July 13, 2012. See http://www.avoidingregret.com/2012/07/photo-essay-ventura-oil-refinery.html.

"Ventura Bike—Part 5: Abandoned Oil Refinery," YouTube, April 21, 2011. See http://www.youtube.com/watch?v=puDwHD7m2Xk.

Susan Chistopherson, "The False Promise of Fracking and Local Jobs," *The Conversation* Jan. 27, 2015.

Natalie Cherot, "Hooked on Frack? Where Oil Companies Could Be Fracking in Santa Barbara County," *Santa Barbara Independent*, November 15, 2012. See www.independent.com.

Exemptions and loopholes that protect fracking from federal laws are neatly laid out by Santa Barbara's environmental defense center. See http://www.edcnet.org/learn/current_cases/fracking/federal_law_loopholes.html.

Matthew Hornbach, "Why is oil and gas activity causing earthquakes?" *The Conversation* May 11, 2015.

"What We Take for Granted," Scott Slovic

"Fracking Across the United States," Earthjustice. See http://earthjustice.org/features/campaigns/fracking-across-the-united-states#.

"Fracking and Its Two-Pronged Problem," Frederick L. Kirschenmann

Dale Allen Pfeiffer, *Eating Fossil Fuels*, British Columbia: New Society Publishers, 2006.

Brian Walker and David Salt, *Resilience Thinking; Sustaining Ecosystems and People in a Changing World*, Washington: Island Press, 2006.

Western Organization of Resource Councils, "Gone for Good; Fracking and Water Loss in the West," 2013.

"North Dakota Oil Spill Cleanup of Farmland Enters Second Year," *Associated Press*, 2013. See http://www.agweb.com/article/north-dakota-oil-spill-cleanup-of-farmland-enters-second-year-associated-press/.

Herman Daly, *Beyond Growth: The Economics of Sustainable Development*, Boston: Beacon Press, 1996.

"Weather Underground," *The New Yorker*, 2015. See http://www.newyorker.com/magazine/2015/04/13/weather-underground.

IPCC Report, 2014. See http://www.globalchange.gov.

Tim Kasser, *The High Price of Materialism*, Cambridge: MIT Press, 2002.

Marjorie Kelly and David Korten, *Owning Our Future: The Emerging Ownership Revolution*, San Francisco: Berrett-Koehler Publishers, 2012.

"Epic Fail," Robert Jensen

Wendell Berry, *Given: New Poems*, Washington, DC: Shoemaker Hoard, 2005.

Fredric Jameson, "Future City," *New Left Review*, May-June 2003. See http://newleftreview.org/II/21/fredric-jameson-future-city.

Wendell Berry, *The Unsettling of America: Culture and Agriculture*. San Francisco: Sierra Club Books, 1996.

Robert Jensen, *Plain Radical: Living, Loving, and Learning to Leave the Planet Gracefully*, Berkeley, CA: Counterpoint/Soft Skull, 2015.

Fyodor Dostoyevsky, *The Brothers Karamazov*, edited and with a revised translation by Susan McReynolds Oddo. New York: W.W. Norton, 2011.

"The Tree of Life Holds the Scales of Justice," Carolyn Raffensperger

A Declaration of the Rights of All Waters, Second Gathering of the Women's Congress for Future Generations Minneapolis, Minnesota, November 2014.

"Why Not Frack," Bill McKibben

Seamus McGraw, *The End of Country*, Random House, 2012.

Tom Wilber, *Under the Surface: Fracking, Fortunes, and the Fate of the Marcellus Shale*, Cornell University Press, 2012.

"Insanity," Derrick Jensen

Mark Koba, "Fracking or Drinking Water? That May Become the Choice," *NBC News*, September 14, 2014. See http://www.nbcnews.com/business/business-news/fracking-or-drinking-water-may-become-choice-n202231.

Nancy Lofholm, "Dead babies near oil drilling sites raise questions for researchers," *The Denver Post*, October 26, 2014. See http://www.denverpost.com/news/ci_26800380/dead-babies-near-oil-drilling-sites-raise-questions.

John M. Glionna, "Utah oil town turns against midwife who asked about infant deaths," *LA Times*, January 10, 2015. See http://www.latimes.com/nation/la-na-utah-baby-deaths-20150111-story.html.

CREDITS:

Barbara Hurd's "Fracking: A Fable," appeared in *Brevity*, Issue 42, March 2013.

Debra Marquart's "Small Buried Things" is excerpted from *Small Buried Things*, New Rivers Press, 2015.

An earlier version of Kathleen Dean Moore's "The View From 31,000 Feet: A Philosopher Looks at Fracking" appeared in *High Country News* on May 11, 2015.

An expanded version of Jan Bindas-Tenney's "The Story of Staying," appeared in *Gulf Coast Online*, Fall 2015.

An earlier version of Jacqueline Robb's "Double Run" appeared in *Vox Populi*, July 2014.

An earlier version of David Gessner's "The Town That ♥s Drilling" appeared as "How Vernal, Utah Learned to Love Big Oil" in *OnEarth Magazine* in March 11, 2013. The current version is adapted from "Oil and Water" from Gessner's book *All the Wild That Remains: Edward Abbey, Wallace Stegner and the American West*, Knopf, 2015.

Pieces of Andrea Peacock's "Three Rivers Quartet" appeared in print through the Alicia Patterson Foundation.

Linda Hogan's poem "Greed" appeared in her collection *Dark. Sweet. New and Selected Poems*, Coffeehouse Press, 2014.

Bill McKibben's "Why Not Frack" is adapted from an earlier version in the *New York Review of Books*, March 8, 2012.

An earlier version of Richard Manning's "Now We're Talking Price" appeared as "Letter from Elkhorn Ranch" in the March 2013 edition of *Harper's*.

About the Editors

Taylor Brorby is an award-winning essayist and poet. A fellow at the Black Earth Institute, his work focuses on the Bakken oil boom and fracking. He received his MA in Liberal Studies from Hamline University and is currently pursuing his MFA in Creative Writing and Environment at Iowa State University. Taylor's work has appeared in *High Country News, Canary, Written River, Rock, Paper, Scissors, The Englewood Review of Books, the Northern Plains Ethics Journal*, among others.

Taylor has been awarded grants from Hamline University, St. Olaf College, Iowa State University, and the North Dakota Humanities Council. He has held residencies at Blue Mountain Center, Holden Village, St. Olaf College, and St. John's University. He has been interviewed about his work as a writer and environmentalist on North Dakota Public Radio and National Public Radio.

Taylor is currently writing *A Vespers for Climate Change*. His chapbook of poetry, *Ruin: Elegies from the Bakken*, is through Red Bird Chapbooks. He is a blogger for *The Huffington Post*, where he writes on education and environmentalism, a contributing editor at *Assay: Journal of Nonfiction Studies*, a reviewer of books for *The Englewood Review*, of journals for *The Review Review*, and Reviews Editor at *Orion Magazine*. He is working on a collection of poetry as well as an essay collection, both focused on western North Dakota.

Stefanie Brook Trout is a Midwestern writer whose nonfiction, fiction, poetry, and drama explore the dynamic interactions between people and their surroundings—including social and built environments as well as the ecosphere. Her work has appeared or is forthcoming in *The Writing Disorder, Cardinal Sins, Festival Writer, ELM, Safe to Chew: An Anthology*, and other literary, place-based, and environmental publications.

In 2014, Stefanie edited *Prairie Gold: An Anthology of the American Heartland* (Ice Cube Press) with Lance M. Sacknoff and Xavier Cavazos. She formerly edited nonfiction for *Flyway: Journal of Writing and Environment* and was the Iowa Lakeside Laboratory's 2013 Environmental Writing Fellow.

Stefanie holds a Master of Fine Arts in Creative Writing and Environment from Iowa State University as well a Master of Arts in Teaching from Marian University in Indianapolis and a Bachelor of Arts from the University of Michigan in Ann Arbor. She has spoken at numerous conferences on pedagogy, publishing, and environmental writing. She also reviews literary magazines for *The Review Review*.

A native Michigander, Stefanie recently returned home to marvel at the splendor of the Great Lakes while finishing her first novel, *Call It Eden*, and working on a number of other writing projects. Find her online at www.stefaniebrooktrout.com.

About the Contributors

Rick Bass is an environmental activist and author of more than thirty books, including, most recently, *For a Little While: New and Selected Stories*. He lives in northwest Montana, where he is a board member of the Yaak Valley Forest Council (www.yaakvalley.org).

Jan Bindas-Tenney is a candidate in the nonfiction MFA Creative Writing Program at the University of Arizona. She is at work on a book-length collection of essays exploring enclave (gated, secluded, and intentional) communities and their relationships to a continually dissatisfying and unattainable desire for the good life. Her essays have appeared or are forthcoming in *Arts & Letters, Gulf Coast Online, Guernica,* and *CutBank Online,* among other places.

Louise A. Blum is a novelist, short story writer, essayist, and kayaker living in Corning, New York. She is the author of the memoir *You're Not From Around Here, Are You? A Lesbian in Small-Town America* and is currently working on a YA novel called *FRACKED,* about the effects of fracking on a small town in rural Pennsylvania. She was finally arrested for blockading Crestwood Midstream almost immediately after writing this essay and is currently awaiting trial.

Paul Bogard is author of *The End of Night: Searching for Natural Darkness in an Age of Artificial Light* (Little, Brown, 2013) and editor of *Let There Be Night: Testimony on Behalf of the Dark* (U of Nevada Press, 2008). A native Minnesotan, Paul has lived and taught in Minneapolis, Albuquerque, Reno, northern Wisconsin, and Winston-Salem. A graduate of Carleton College, the University of New

Mexico, and the University of Nevada-Reno (PhD in Literature and Environment), Paul is now an assistant professor at James Madison University in Harrisonburg, Virginia, where he teaches creative writing and environmental literature. Find him at paul-bogard.com.

Angie Carter is a sociologist, writer, activist, and the seventh generation of her family to call Iowa home. Her work focuses on social justice and change in agricultural and environmental systems. She and others founded the Bakken Pipeline Resistance Coalition in 2014 in response to the expansion of Bakken oil pipelines across Iowa and the Midwest.

Alison Hawthorne Deming's most recent book is *Zoologies: On Animals and the Human Spirit* (Milkweed Editions, 2014). Her new book of poems *Stairway to Heaven* will be out from Penguin in 2016. She teaches at the University of Arizona where she is Agnese Nelms Haury Chair of Environment and Social Justice. She received the Guggenheim Fellowship Award in 2015.

Michelle Donahue has work published in *CutBank, Word Riot, Beloit Fiction Journal*, and others. She was the managing editor of *Flyway* and is a prose editor for *Adroit Journal*. She has an MFA from Iowa State University and is pursuing a PhD in Creative Writing at the University of Utah.

Sarah Lyn Eaton is a freelance writer, penning the weekly online blog *Walking with Ancestors*. Living in the Southern Tier, the fight against fracking has been close to her environmental heart. She has previously published "Hold the Door" in Northlore Series, Volume

One: *Folklore*, "The White Sisters" in *What Follows*, and "Of Roots and Rings" in *Elf Love*.

Antonia Felix is the author of *Fatal Remedy*, a novel (Calumet Editions, 2014); *La Divina*, a play; and sixteen nonfiction books including several political biographies, most recently *Sonia Sotomayor: The True American Dream* (Berkley/Penguin USA). While earning her MFA in Creative Writing-Fiction at Wichita State University, she wrote an award-winning environmental/sustainability column for the historic *Emporia Gazette*. She is an adjunct faculty member at Hamline University and lives in rural Dakota County, Minnesota.

David Gessner is the author of nine books, including *All the Wild That Remains: Edward Abbey, Wallace Stegner and the American West, Return of the Osprey, Sick of Nature, My Green Manifesto,* and *The Tarball Chronicles*, which won the 2012 Reed Award for Best Book on the Southern Environment and the Association for Study of Literature and the Environment's award for best book of creative writing in 2011 and 2012. He has published essays in many magazines, including *Outside* magazine and the *New York Times Magazine*, and has won the John Burroughs Award for Best Nature Essay, a Pushcart Prize, and inclusion in *Best American Nonrequired Reading*. Gessner taught Environmental Writing as a Briggs-Copeland Lecturer at Harvard and is currently a Professor at the University of North Carolina at Wilmington, where he founded the award-winning literary journal of place, *Ecotone*. He also puts a lot of energy into blogging for *Bill and Dave's Cocktail Hour*, a website he created with the writer Bill Roorbach.

Linda Hogan (Chickasaw) is former Writer in Residence for The Chickasaw Nation, Professor Emerita at the University of Colorado, and an internationally recognized public speaker and writer of poetry, fiction, and essays. She has received a National Endowment for the Arts Fellowship, a Guggenheim Fellowship, and has received the Lifetime Achievement Award from the Native Writers Circle of the Americas, The Wordcraft Circle, and The Mountains and Plains Booksellers Association.

Barbara Hurd is the author of *Listening to the Savage / River Notes and Half-Heard Melodies* (forthcoming from University of Georgia Press, 2016), *Tidal Rhythms* (with photographer Stephen Strom, forthcoming from George F. Thompson Publishing, 2016), and six other collections of essays and poetry. The recipient of an NEA Fellowship for Creative Nonfiction, winner of the Sierra Club's National Nature Writing Award, five Pushcart Prizes, five Maryland State Arts Council Awards, and a 2015 Guggenheim Fellowship, she teaches in the MFA in Writing Program at the Vermont College of Fine Arts.

Derrick Jensen is a long-term grassroots environmental activist. He is the author of more than twenty books, including *Endgame*, and *A Language Older Than Words*.

Jon Jensen directs the Center for Sustainable Communities and teaches Environmental Studies at Luther College in Decorah, Iowa. He has a PhD in philosophy and is the co-author of *Questions That Matter: An Invitation to Philosophy* as well as numerous essays in environmental philosophy and sustainability. Jensen lives on a small acreage near the Upper Iowa River with his wife and two daughters.

Robert Jensen is a professor in the School of Journalism at the University of Texas at Austin and board member of the Third Coast Activist Resource Center in Austin. He is the author of *Plain Radical: Living, Loving, and Learning to Leave the Planet Gracefully* (Counterpoint/Soft Skull). Jensen's other books include *Arguing for Our Lives: A User's Guide to Constructive Dialogue* (City Lights, 2013); *All My Bones Shake: Seeking a Progressive Path to the Prophetic Voice* (Soft Skull Press, 2009); *Getting Off: Pornography and the End of Masculinity* (South End Press, 2007); *The Heart of Whiteness: Confronting Race, Racism and White Privilege* (City Lights, 2005); *Citizens of the Empire: The Struggle to Claim Our Humanity* (City Lights, 2004); and *Writing Dissent: Taking Radical Ideas from the Margins to the Mainstream* (Peter Lang, 2002). Jensen can be reached atrjensen@austin.utexas.edu and his articles can be found online at www.robertwjensen.org.

Michele Johnson's narrative nonfiction has appeared in *Puerto del Sol* and won an AWP Introduction to Journals Project award. Her fiction has been published or is forthcoming in *Necessary Fiction, The Conium Review*, and *The Newer York Press*. Michele lives in Tucson, Arizona, where she works as an environmental engineer and strategy consultant.

John Kenyon is an Iowa City writer and editor who has published extensively in the crime fiction world. He is the author of the story collection *The First Cut* and the novella *Get Hit, Hit Back*, and edits the crime fiction journal *Grift*. He is director of the Iowa City UNESCO City of Literature organization.

Frederick L. Kirschenmann is the Distinguished Fellow for the Leopold Center and President of Stone Barns Center for Food and Agriculture in Pocantico Hills, New York. He has held numerous appointments, including the USDA's National Organic Standards Board and the National Commission on Industrial Farm Animal Production operated by the Johns Hopkins School of Public Health and funded by Pew Charitable Trusts. Kirschenmann converted his family's farm in North Dakota to a certified organic operation in 1976 and developed a diverse crop rotation that has enabled him to farm productively without synthetic inputs (fertilizers or pesticides) while simultaneously improving the health of the soil.

Claire Krüesel grew up collecting wild blackberries, Lake Superior agates, and monarch caterpillars from the dusty leaves of ditch milkweed—and she still anchors her perception of beauty to the Midwest. She earned an MFA in Creative Writing and Environment from Iowa State University, where she served as Poetry Editor for *Flyway: Journal of Writing and Environment*. She loves singing with her sister, second chances for historical buildings, and maple syrup anything.

Ahna Kruzic is an activist, sociologist, and Iowan who is passionate about justice through food and environment. A community organizer at heart, Ahna has played the role of researcher, digital strategist, web developer, and more. She has worked with others to build the Bakken Pipeline Resistance Coalition, a growing coalition working to stop the expansion of Bakken oil pipelines while envisioning a more socially, environmentally, and economically just future.

Stephanie LeMenager is Barbara and Carlisle Moore Professor of English and Professor of Environmental Studies at the University of

Oregon. Her latest book, *Living Oil*, will be out in paperback in early 2016. She is co-editor of the forthcoming collection *Teaching Climate Change in the Humanities*.

Maryann Lesert is a playwright, novelist, and journalist who teaches writing based on the environment at Grand Rapids Community College. Her first novel, *Base Ten*, was published by the Feminist Press (2009). *Threshold*, her current novel in progress, grew from two years of "boots on well sites" research on fracking in Michigan's state forests.

The Faculty Director and Chair of the Board of the Center of the American West at the University of Colorado, **Patricia Nelson Limerick** is a Western American historian, best known for her book, *The Legacy of Conquest: The Unbroken Past of the American West*. She has participated in many forums on energy issues and hosted a lecture series called FrackingSENSE. In recent years, she has become intrigued and even enchanted by the subjects of infrastructure and bureaucracy, two subjects that many people, who ought to know better, consider boring.

Beth Loffreda is the author of *Losing Matt Shepard: Life and Politics in the Aftermath of Anti-Gay Murder* (Columbia University Press) and co-editor of *The Racial Imaginary* (Fence Books). She grew up in Audubon, Pennsylvania, and attended the University of Virginia and Rutgers University. She lives in Laramie, Wyoming, where she teaches American Studies and creative writing at the University of Wyoming.

Mort Malkin has formally studied poetry composition in different college courses under different poets, the last twenty-five years in the José Garcia Villa workshop under the direction of the master himself. He has had many poems published in a variety of journals and has three books of poetry to his credit—*Data-Matter-O, Over the Banks,* and the *Upper Delaware River In Verse and Image.* He is also a founding member of the Milanville Poets, Unlimited.

Richard Manning, a journalist, has been writing about environmental issues since 1975. He is the author of ten books and numerous magazine articles and has lived in Montana for thirty years.

Debra Marquart directs the MFA Program in Creative Writing and Environment at Iowa State University and teaches in the Stonecoast Low-Residency MFA Program. Marquart's books include *The Hunger Bone: Rock & Roll Stories; The Horizontal World: Growing Up Wild in the Middle of Nowhere;* and three poetry collections, including *Small Buried Things: Poems.*

Bill McKibben is the Schumann Distinguished Scholar in environmental studies at Middlebury College and the author of *The End of Nature,* the first book for a general audience about climate change. The founder of the global climate campaign 350.org, he was the 2014 recipient of the Right Livelihood Award, sometimes called the "alternative Nobel."

Wayne Mennecke is a high school science teacher from Islip, New York. His summers are spent either in the badlands of the Dakotas and Montana hunting for dinosaur fossils with the Marmarth Research Foundation, or fishing and swimming along the beaches of

Long Island. He lives with his wife and their high-spirited seven year-old daughter.

Karla Linn Merrifield has had over 500 poems appear in dozens of publications with twelve books to her credit, the newest of which, from FootHills Publishing, is *Bunchberries, More Poems of Canada*, a sequel to her award-winning *Godwit: Poems of Canada* (FootHills). She is assistant editor/poetry book reviewer for *The Centrifugal Eye*. Visit her blog, *Vagabond Poet*, at www.karlalinn.blogspot.com.

Jeremy Miller writes from his home in Richmond, California. His recent writing on science, energy, and the environment has appeared in numerous publications including *Harper's*, *Orion*, and *Earth Island Journal*.

Stephanie Mills is the author of *Epicurean Simplicity*, *In Service of the Wild*, and four other books. Over the past forty-plus years, her writing has appeared in *Orion*, *Resurgence*, and numerous bygone periodicals, notably *CoEvolution Quarterly*. A longtime devotee of bioregionalism and a Fellow of the Post Carbon Institute, she has lived in Northwest Lower Michigan since 1984.

Kathryn Miles is the author of three books including *Superstorm: Nine Days Inside Hurricane Sandy*. Her work has appeared in publications including *Best American Essays*, *The Boston Globe Sunday Magazine*, *The New York Times*, *Outside*, *Popular Mechanics*, and *Time*. She currently serves as writer-in-residence at Green Mountain College, where she teaches in their Environmental Studies graduate program.

Kathleen Dean Moore is a writer, philosopher, and environmental advocate whose most recent books are *Moral Ground: Ethical Action for a Planet in Peril* and *Great Tide Rising*. Distinguished Professor of Philosophy Emerita at Oregon State University, Moore speaks and publishes widely about the moral urgency of climate action.

Rachel Morgan is a graduate of the Iowa Writers' Workshop, and currently she teaches at the University of Northern Iowa and is the Poetry Editor for the *North American Review*. Her recent work appears or is forthcoming in *Crazyhorse, Fence, Denver Quarterly, Appalachian Heritage, Bellevue Literary Review, Mid-American Review, DIAGRAM, Barrow Street,* and *Hunger Mountain.*

Mary Heather Noble is an environmental scientist, writer, and mother. Her writing has been honored with the 2014 Siskiyou Prize for New Environmental Literature, and has appeared in *Creative Non-fiction, Literal Latté,* and *Utne Reader,* among others. She is a 2015 Oregon Arts Commission Fellowship recipient and a graduate of the Stonecoast MFA in Creative Writing Program with the University of Southern Maine.

Andrea Peacock is a former editor of the *Missoula Independent* and author of *Wasting Libby: The True Story of How the WR Grace Corporation Left a Montana Town to Die (and Got Away With It).* She co-authored *The Essential Grizzly: The Mingled Fates of Men and Bears* with her husband Doug Peacock and was awarded an Alicia Patterson Fellowship for her work on oil and gas in the West. She is the co-owner of Elk River Books in Livingston, Montana.

Tyler Priest is Associate Professor of History and Geography at the University of Iowa. He is the author of the prize-winning book, *The Offshore Imperative: Shell Oil's Search for Petroleum in Postwar America* (College Station: Texas A&M Press, 2007), and coeditor of a 2012 special issue of the *Journal of American History* on "Oil in American History." In 2010, he served as a senior policy analyst for the President's National Commission on the BP Deepwater Horizon Oil Spill and Offshore Drilling. His current book project is *Deepwater Horizons: The Epic Struggle over Offshore Oil in the United States.*

Carolyn Raffensperger is an archaeologist and lawyer. She is the executive director of the Science and Environmental Health Network and co-founder of the Women's Congress for Future Generations. Sometimes she thinks that she was sent back from the future to guarantee that there would be a beautiful and habitable Earth for generations to come.

When **Jacqueline Robb** tried to describe the rural area where she grew up, her friends didn't "get it" until she added "with just one traffic light for the whole county." The natural beauty of this area in the mountains of Pennsylvania has stayed with her, prompting her concerns about fracking. She is currently working on a collection of essays with a water theme, one of which is this piece.

Bill Roorbach is the author of numerous books of fiction and nonfiction, including *The Remedy for Love*, which was a finalist for the 2014 Kirkus Fiction Prize. His novel *Life Among Giants* is in development for a drama series at HBO. His memoir in nature, *Temple Stream: A Rural Odyssey,* has just been re-issued by Down East Books. His short work has appeared in *The Atlantic, The New York Times, Harper's, Playboy*, and many other magazines and journals. He lives in Western Maine.

Stephanie Schultz's poems and essays have appeared in *Vermillion Literary Project, Midway Journal, Wild Quarterly*, and *Prairie Gold: An Anthology of the American Heartland*, and are forthcoming in *South Dakota Magazine*. She received her MFA in creative writing from Hamline University and lives in St. Paul, Minnesota, where she is perpetually training for her next marathon.

Scott Slovic is professor of literature and environment and chair of the English Department at the University of Idaho. He was the founding president of the Association for the Study of Literature and Environment, and he has edited *ISLE: Interdisciplinary Studies in Literature and Environment* since 1995. His recent co-edited books include *Currents of the Universal Being: Explorations in the Literature of Energy, Ecocriticism of the Global South,* and *Numbers and Nerves: Information, Emotion, and Meaning in a World of Data.*

Mark Trechock is an inner-city Minneapolis native who has lived more than twenty-five years in North Dakota, where he served as a Lutheran pastor in the 1970's, and from 1993 to 2012 worked to organize North Dakota residents seeking reforms in oil, coal, waste, and agriculture policy as Director of Dakota Resource Council. Mark holds degrees from Augsburg College, Princeton Theological Seminary, and the Iliff School of Theology. He has published more than fifty poems in various journals and is currently at work on two collections of poetry, *West of Town* and *Eating in the Presence of Coyotes.*

As writer, editor, and photographer, **Stephen Trimble** has published more than twenty award-winning books. Steve spent ten years collecting stories and photographing in Southwest Indian Country. He helped defeat an anti-wilderness bill in Congress with the essay collection *Testimony*. He lives in Salt Lake City and in the redrock country of Torrey, Utah. His website is www.stephentrimble.net.

In 1997, **Susan Truxell Sauter** left a journalism career to farm organically, dedicating herself to this pursuit for seven years while also starting a statewide farmer's market association and local foods campaign in West Virginia. She continues to raise and preserve food for her family but considers herself a recovering farmer as well as a recovering activist. She monitors West Virginia streams for environmental effects and writes about the impact of horizontal gas well drilling.

Vivian Wagner's essays have appeared in *The Kenyon Review, McSweeney's, Silk Road Review, Zone 3*, and other publications, and she's the author of *Fiddle: One Woman, Four Strings, and 8,000 Miles of Music*. She's an associate professor of English at Muskingum University in New Concord, Ohio.

A native Alabamian, **Amy Weldon** is associate professor of English at Luther College. Her fiction and nonfiction have appeared in many places, including *Best Travel Writing 2012* (Solas Press), *Cornbread Nation 2: The Best of Southern Food Writing* (UNC Press), *Los Angeles Review of Books, The Millions, Bloom, Shenandoah, Fiction Southeast,* and *The Carolina Quarterly*. She blogs on sustainability, spirit, and self-reliance at *The Cheapskate Intellectual*, www.cheapskateintellectual. wordpress.com.

1. Fables are a didactic genre—they illustrate a moral lesson. What is Barbara Hurd's lesson in "Fracking: A Fable"? How does the compressed form follow that lesson?

2. *Fracture* concludes with Alison Hawthorne Deming's poem "Homeland Security," in which the speaker views Earth through the eyes of an astronaut in space. Some of the contributors in this collection have chosen to illustrate the ugly aftermath of fracking (i.e., "flaming water faucets / exploited towns and farms / heartland riddled with quakes / water poisoned and stuck back / in the ground to find its way home.") while others have focused more on showing a planet worth protecting in the first place ("We say 'blue marble' we say / 'Mother Earth' we say 'home.' / The astronaut says 'Beautiful.' / Earth from space says 'Keep me.'"). Which approach was more moving to you or do they work together?

3. A number of authors in this collection focus on their home regions—but fracking is a national phenomenon. How does fracking affect certain regions of the US differently? What effects impact us all?

4. In several of the pieces in this anthology, the authors acknowledge their own complicity in supporting unsustainable practices, often by invoking a "we" or "us" (see Truxell Sauter, Schultz, Trout, and Manning—among others). What is the effect of that "we"/"us" on you, the reader? How does this make you feel about your own complicity?

5. In "Small Buried Things," Debra Marquart speaks directly to North Dakota, while in "The Tree of Life Holds the Scales of Justice," Carolyn Raffensperger speaks as "the voice of water." What is the significance of including Earth in the conversation about fracking?

6. Multiple pieces in this collection directly discuss faith and "the sacred" (see Moore, Blum, and Kenyon—among others). How does religion or spirituality intersect with a scientific, economic, and political issue like fracking?

7. In both Taylor Brorby's "White Butte" and Jacqueline Robb's "Double Run," the authors return to the landscapes of their childhood and experience them in a new way. To what extent is this a reflection of the changes in the land; to what extent is it a reflection of changes in the authors? Relate an experience when you returned to a place to find it transformed from the way you remembered it. How did you feel about the changes?

8. The prose pieces in this collection are predominantly nonfiction. What is the effect of including short stories (see Roorbach, Kenyon, Eaton, Felix, and Lesert) as well? How does fiction deepen our understanding of fracking beyond what we would get from essays alone?

9. *Fracture*'s poetry ranges greatly in form and style, from Karla Linn Merrifield's twenty-one-word "Tercet for Kitty" to Claire Krüesel's four-part "Surfacing." What were some of your favorite poems in this collection? What about them did you find so compelling?

Fracture partners:

◄350.org ORION
MAGAZINE

The number 350 means climate safety: to preserve a livable planet, scientists tell us we must reduce the amount of CO_2 in the atmosphere from its current level of 400 parts per million to below 350 ppm.

350.org is building a global climate movement. Our online campaigns, grassroots organizing, and mass public actions are coordinated by a global network active in over 188 countries.

We believe that a global grassroots movement can hold our leaders accountable to the realities of science and the principles of justice. That movement is rising from the bottom up all over the world, and is uniting to create the solutions that will ensure a better future for all.

Follow on Facebook, Twitter, or online at 350.org

Orion Magazine challenges and inspires its readers through deeply thoughtful articles, distinctive and compelling visuals, and an overall editorial sensibility that approaches nature and environmental concerns as a context, rather than a niche interest. The magazine hosts a conversation about the environment that is not happening anywhere else—a conversation that includes sustainability, politics, economics, science, spirituality, and philosophy, but transcends the distinctions between them to examine, with depth, breadth, and emotion, the relationship between human culture and the natural world.

Follow *Orion* on Facebook, Twitter, Instagram, or online at orionmagazine.org

The Ice Cube Press began publishing in 1993 to focus on how to live with the natural world. We've since become devoted to using the literary arts to better understand how people can best live together in the communities they share, inhabit, and experience here in the Heartland of the USA. We have been recognized by a number of well-known writers including: Gary Snyder, Gene Logsdon, Wes Jackson, Patricia Hampl, Greg Brown, Jim Harrison, Annie Dillard, Ken Burns, Roz Chast, Jane Hamilton, Daniel Menaker, Kathleen Norris, Janisse Ray, Craig Lesley, Alison Deming, Frank Deford, Paul Hawken, Harriet Lerner, Richard Rhodes, Michael Pollan, David Abram, David Orr, Boria Sax, and Barry Lopez. We've published a number of well-known authors including: Governor Robert Ray, Congressman James Leach, Mary Swander, Jim Heynen, Mary Pipher, Bill Holm, Connie Mutel, John T. Price, Carol Bly, Marvin Bell, Debra Marquart, Ted Kooser, Stephanie Mills, Bill McKibben, Craig Lesley, Elizabeth McCracken, Dean Bakopoulos, Dan Gable, Rick Bass, Pam Houston, and Paul Gruchow. Check out Ice Cube Press books on our web site, join our facebook group, follow us on twitter, visit booksellers, museum shops, or any place you can find good books and discover why we continue striving to, "hear the other side."

Ice Cube Press, LLC (Est. 1993)
North Liberty, Iowa 52317-9302
steve@icecubepress.com
twitter: @icecubepress
www.facebook.com/IceCubePress
www.icecubepress.com

to Laura Lee & Fenna Marie
clean energetic
alternatives
of the safest kind

ENVIRONMENTAL BENEFITS STATEMENT

Ice Cube Press saved the following resources by printing the pages of this book on chlorine free paper made with 100% post-consumer waste.

TREES	WATER	ENERGY	SOLID WASTE	GREENHOUSE GASES
30	14,192	13	950	2,617
FULLY GROWN	GALLONS	MILLION BTUs	POUNDS	POUNDS

Environmental impact estimates were made using the Environmental Paper Network Paper Calculator 3.2. For more information visit www.papercalculator.org.

MIX
Paper from
responsible sources
FSC® C016245

FSC
www.fsc.org